PRAISE FO
OF A CHRISTIAN UNIVERSITY

This is an extremely illuminating book that will be of great help to our universities and to the LCMS as a whole. At a time when synodical universities are struggling with "Lutheran Identity," this book serves as a template for faculty, administrators, boards, and students for how that can be achieved and for how that identity can help colleges to be truly excellent at every level.

—Gene Edward Veith, PhD
Professor of Literature
Patrick Henry College

Clearly articulating the Lutheran interaction model for relating faith and learning, this volume is a gift to everyone interested in understanding the Lutheran difference in Christian higher education. Ranging from background theological and historical essays to reflections from scholarly disciplines and administrative and student life perspectives, this text is an up-to-date compendium of the important and distinct dimensions found in Lutheran higher education. Persons interested in understanding the role of the liberal arts in a Christian education for vocation will also find this text particularly helpful. I heartily recommend this anthology to anyone seeking to understand the Lutheran heritage and promise in higher education.

—The Rev. Ernest L. Simmons, PhD
Professor of Religion
Director, The Dovre Center for Faith and Learning
Concordia College, Moorhead, MN
Author of *Lutheran Higher Education: An Introduction*
(Augsburg Fortress, 2001)

Impressively comprehensive and theologically articulate, this book turns a spotlight on church-related academic pursuits within the Lutheran (Missouri Synod) tradition. Its thoughtful analysis of Lutheran perspectives and values will enrich the national conversation concerning the place and role of religion in university education.

—Douglas Jacobsen, PhD, and Rhonda Hustedt Jacobsen, EdD
Authors of *No Longer Invisible: Religion in University Education*
(Oxford University Press, 2012)

The essays assembled in this volume provide valuable glimpses into the splendor of Lutheran higher education properly delivered. The reader is invited to immerse himself in the beauty of Lutheran higher education through discussions that engage the interaction of core Lutheran fundamentals and the heart of higher education. This work offers a refreshing explication of the richness that is the Lutheran approach to Christian higher education. *The Idea and Practice of a Christian University: A Lutheran Approach* is an essential text for anyone involved or interested in Lutheran higher education.

—The Rev. Dr. Paul A. Philp
Director of Institutional Research and Integrity
The Concordia University System

The effort to transfer Lutheranism's European Protestant heritage into American culture has not always been easy. This unusually helpful collection of essays explains what Lutheran higher education tries to do, has done, and would like to do—both in maintaining the best of the heritage and serving the needs of the present. The book's many contributors offer much to ponder for anyone who values the heritage of the Reformation, the cause of Christ in the United States, and the application of specifically Lutheran insights to the practices of higher education.

—Mark A. Noll
Francis A. McAnaney Professor of History
University of Notre Dame
Author of *Jesus Christ and the Life of the Mind* (Eerdmans, 2011)

Scott Ashmon and his colleagues are to be commended for their effort. Collectively, they draw upon the Lutheran tradition as an insightful and much needed means of making sense of today's confusing higher education landscape. Individuals serving in Lutheran contexts should be amongst the first to read, ponder, and act upon what this work offers. However, the model they unfold in their own ways is also of considerable value to individuals serving in contexts nurtured by a wide variety of Christian traditions.

—Todd C. Ream, PhD
Professor of Higher Education
Taylor University

The diverse contributors to this volume succeed in achieving a difficult aim—speaking from a particular tradition in winsome ways that will resonate with and engage the wider academy. Indeed, this book illuminates how and why certain Lutheran-shaped concepts and skills such as vocation, the two kingdoms, and "faith seeking understanding for service" should continue to interact with and influence Christian and even secular higher education. Moreover, I found that the creative insights from authors spanning multiple disciplines, and even the co-curricular arena, added fresh and engaging new ideas regarding how Lutheranism can nourish the university.

—Perry L. Glanzer, PhD
Professor of Educational Foundations
Resident Scholar, Baylor Institute for Studies of Religion
Baylor University

THE IDEA AND PRACTICE
OF A CHRISTIAN UNIVERSITY

A LUTHERAN APPROACH

Peer Reviewed

EDITED BY SCOTT A. ASHMON

CONCORDIA PUBLISHING HOUSE · SAINT LOUIS

Peer Reviewed

Similar to the peer review or "refereed" process used to publish professional and academic journals, the Peer Review process is designed to enable authors to publish book manuscripts through Concordia Publishing House. The Peer Review process is well-suited for smaller projects and textbook publications. For more information, visit: www.cph.org/PeerReview.

Published by Concordia Publishing House
3558 S. Jefferson Ave., St. Louis, MO 63118–3968
1-800-325-3040 • www.cph.org

Manufactured in the United States of America

Library of Congress Cataloging-in-Publication Data

The idea and practice of a Christian university : a Lutheran approach / edited by Scott A. Ashmon.

    pages cm

  ISBN 978-0-7586-5040-5

  1. Lutheran Church—Education—Philosophy. 2. Lutheran universities and colleges—United States. 3. Church and college—United States. I. Ashmon, Scott A., editor.

  LC574.I38 2015

  371.071--dc23   2015002262

1 2 3 4 5 6 7 8 9 10   24 23 22 21 20 19 18 17 16 15

CONTENTS

CONTENTS

FOREWORD

The reader of the essays in this volume will benefit from and enjoy a rich tapestry of clear and substantive perspectives on the Christian university in its Lutheran expression. In the tradition of Cardinal Newman's *The Idea of a University* (Oxford, 1873) and Jaroslav Pelikan's *The Idea of a University: A Reexamination* (Yale, 1992), the authors engage this topic with freshness and transparent expertise. In a culture that increasingly renders higher education value-neutral and reduces its aims to utilitarian goals, this work casts a bright beam on how faith and reason complement and enrich human knowledge. The great *solas* of the Reformation—*sola gratia, sola fide, sola scriptura*—inform the collective analysis that ultimately orders all knowledge rightly in relation to God's definitive disclosure of himself and reality in Jesus Christ, who holds all things together (Col 1:17).

Within this framework, there are distinctive accents that enrich the multifaceted aspects of the Christian, and in this instance, the *Lutheran* rendering of university education. Two such foci are: (1) the Lutheran two-kingdom lens of God's power and grace that emphasizes the interaction of faith and learning; and (2) the insightful emphasis on the doctrine of vocation as a guide to placing mind and soul in service to God and neighbor. This paradigm is decidedly different from the Reformed (neo-Calvinist) model—seen in books such as Arthur Holmes' *The Idea of a Christian College* (Eerdmans, 1987)—that uncritically merges God's two kingdoms through the "integration of faith and learning." The emphasis on vocation also helpfully places learning in service to the neighbor, whether in God's right-hand kingdom of grace or in his left-hand kingdom of power.

One can only rejoice that this volume raises the question of the Christian university with fresh energy and mind-heart-soul engagement. Since James Burtchaell's *The Dying of the Light: The Disengagement of Christian Colleges and Universities from Their Christian Churches* (Eerdmans, 1998), the loss of Christian identity in many colleges and universities has become indisputable. The result is a virtual wasteland in many universities on questions of ethics and philosophy. How ironic that just as human learning advances with dazzling technology, the very meaning of human existence has been removed as a legitimate, even crucial, question for what is truly significant in higher education. May this volume challenge modern university culture, and, as the authors propose, provide a richer and more beautiful, and above all else, a more truthful reading of the human condition.

Dean O. Wenthe
President of the Concordia University System

PART ONE

FOUNDATION FOR LUTHERAN HIGHER EDUCATION

1

The Purpose of a Christian University: A Lutheran Vision

Scott A. Ashmon[1]

Welcome to AnyU

Rebekah Nathan, a cultural anthropologist, had spent most of her professional life doing ethnographic studies in a remote overseas village. Over her years of university teaching in the United States, though, she realized that the culture of her students had become increasingly foreign to her. So she decided to spend a whole year incognito as an older, returning freshman at her university—taking classes and living in the dorms—to write an ethnography about her fellow freshmen. In learning about these new university "villagers," Nathan also saw what her university, which she anonymously calls AnyU, proclaimed to be the purpose of a university.

The defining moment came not at the middle or end of the academic year, but at the very beginning during the Welcome Week, when freshmen were introduced to their living and learning community, and the Freshman Colloquium, when they were initiated into academic life. Nathan describes this initial experience as "replete with competing messages." The Welcome Week revved students up with messages of fun, independence, and careerist pragmatism. The colloquium then tried to instill in students the idea that university life is preparation for citizenship through liberal arts learning and the development of virtues. These conflicting messages, palpable during Nathan's entire year at AnyU, left her wondering, "How are these to be reconciled? Is one message preferable to the other? Can we really have both? Do they put limits on each other?"[2]

---

[1] Scott Ashmon, PhD (Hebrew Union College), is Professor of Old Testament and Hebrew and Director of Core Curriculum at Concordia University Irvine (CUI).

[2] Rebekah Nathan, *My Freshman Year: What a Professor Learned by Becoming a Student* (New York: Penguin, 2006), 155–56. Rebekah Nathan is a pseudonym. For a

Where can the answer to these questions be found? It is the contention of this essay that a historically-rooted and biblically-based Lutheran vision for education answers these questions with its goal of educating students in wisdom and vocation for freedom and service to society, nature, and the church. Growing out of the fruitful interaction of historical educational theory and practice, Scripture, and the Lutheran doctrines of Christian freedom, vocation, and the two kingdoms, this vision offers "a supple, serviceable, and sophisticated" framework for supporting and coordinating both educational ends and guiding the practices of university life.[3] To demonstrate this contention, this essay will examine the purpose of a Christian university from this view. It will then describe how this educational vision impacts one key practice at Christian universities: connecting faith and learning.

WISDOM AND VOCATION FOR FREEDOM AND SERVICE

Conflict between a Liberal and Useful Education

Conflict over the purpose—and value—of higher education is neither unique to AnyU nor new to the public forum. Clashes between occupationalism, which sees the purpose of higher education as job training, and liberal education, which sees it as developing individual intellect and character for citizenship, are still evident today. Some institutions focus exclusively on vocational training. On the opposite spectrum, some institutions shun (pre-)professional programs and majors for a purely liberal arts education. Clashes within universities that have liberal arts requirements and (pre-)professional programs are also palpable as students—and parents and government officials—tend to think that the majors provide relevant education for "the real world" while the liberal arts set up annoying, useless hurdles in the race to a degree and job.

---

similar observation of conflict and question of reconciliation between liberal and vocational education, see Derek Bok, *Our Underachieving Colleges: A Candid Look at How Much Students Learn and Why They Should be Learning More* (Princeton: Princeton University Press, 2006), 78–79.

[3] See Mueller's chapter for a summary of the Lutheran doctrine of vocation and two-kingdom theology. The quoted phrase comes from David W. Lotz, "Education for Citizenship in the Two Kingdoms: Reflections on the Theological Foundations of Lutheran Higher Education," in *Institutional Mission and Identity in Lutheran Higher Education: Papers and Proceedings of the 65th Annual Convention, Lutheran Educational Conference of North America* (Washington DC: Lutheran Educational Conference of North America, 1979), 18–19.

Such conflict existed in the Reformation era too. Martin Luther's letter to the councilmen of Germany in 1524 responded to this question: "What is the use of teaching Latin, Greek, Hebrew, and the other liberal arts?"[4] In a sermon six years later, Luther railed against parents who—as avaricious, idolatrous, servants of Mammon—would say, "Ha, if my son can read and write German and do arithmetic, that is enough. I am going to make a businessman of him."[5] Philip Melanchthon, Luther's colleague at the University of Wittenberg, also had to address this clash. In 1531 he penned an oration reminding students that while the "higher disciplines"—the professional programs in theology, law, and medicine—were obviously useful personally and to society, they were not to "neglect or scorn the remaining disciplines [i.e., the liberal arts] as though useless for life" in their rush toward "ambition" or "gain." While the liberal arts may have "little outward appeal for the crowds," they are useful as the foundation for studying the higher disciplines. The two, in his analogy, work together like vowels and consonants. Without both working in harmony, speech—or rather an education for life—is impossible.[6]

The roots of the conflict over education's purpose are diverse with the common need for a job, desire for wealth, and social mobility being a few. Another root is the educational thought of John Locke and subsequent utilitarians. In 1692 Locke proposed that the "welfare and prosperity of a nation so much depends on [education]" that youth should receive the "easiest, shortest, and likeliest [education] to produce virtuous, useful, and able men in their distinct callings" in society.[7]

Other roots that "enthroned the practical" in America are the rise of specialized research disciplines and the advancement of science and technology in universities after the Civil War coupled with major funding from business and industry moguls and government land-grant acts for training professionals in business, science, agriculture and mechanical arts; for amassing profit; and for societal progress. The same root is seen after World War II when the government, businesses, and industries funded universities

---

4 Martin Luther, "To the Councilmen of All Cities in Germany that They Establish and Maintain Christian Schools," in AE 45:357.

5 Luther, "A Sermon on Keeping Children in School," in AE 46:215, 244, 251–52.

6 Philip Melanchthon, "On the Order of Learning," in *Orations on Philosophy and Education*, ed. Sachiko Kusukawa, trans. Christine F. Salazar (Cambridge: Cambridge University Press, 1999), 3–5.

7 John Locke, *Some Thoughts Concerning Education* (Cambridge: Cambridge University Press, 1895), lxiii.

to train scientists, engineers, technicians, and businessmen for the same ends.[8]

Each of these roots nourishes the tree of higher education to bear fruit that is useful, hirable, and lucrative. The tartest parts of this fruit hold the view "that all of life is a preparation for business—or, perhaps, more bluntly, that life *is* business."[9] This fruit is ripe in modern America. For-profit universities with a mission for mammon market themselves to students looking solely for technical and professional training. Non-profit universities, looking to keep themselves solvent, also offer condensed, or abridged, occupational programs for career-minded students. Even the U.S. Department of Education's College Scorecard quantifies every university's "value" by financial and occupational metrics: cost, graduation rate, loan default rate, median borrowing, and employment upon graduation.[10]

Yet another root of this conflict goes back to Aristotle in the fourth century BC. In Book VIII of *Politics*, Aristotle discusses public education and draws a deep divide between liberal education suited to freemen and mechanical education for professionals. With the premises that "the first principle of all action is leisure," that "leisure is better than occupation and its end" since leisure "gives pleasure and happiness and enjoyment in life," and that "learning and education" is best done "with a view to the leisure spent in intellectual activity," Aristotle concludes that the rational soul's leisurely contemplation of truth is happiness and the highest end of educa-tion. Aristotle describes the dichotomy between the liberal ("free" from work/service) and servile activities this way:

> The object also which a man sets before him makes a great difference; if he does anything for his own sake or for the sake of his friends, or with a view to excellence, the action will not appear illiberal; but if done for the sake of others, the very same action will be thought menial and servile.

For Aristotle only knowledge pursued for its own sake and the pursuer's happiness is liberal and noble; knowledge pursued for professional

---

[8] For an analysis of the influence of the Germanic research ideal and government, business, and industry funding on the utilitarian end of higher education and the commodification and corporatization of universities, see Christopher J. Lucas, *American Higher Education: A History*, 2nd ed. (New York: Palgrave Macmillan, 2006).

[9] Benjamin R. Barber, *An Aristocracy of Everyone: the Politics of Education and the Future of America* (New York: Ballantine, 1992), 205.

[10] U.S. Department of Education, accessed September 19, 2014, http://www.whitehouse .gov/issues/education/higher-education/college-score-card.

purposes is servile and suited for the "vulgar crowd" whose "minds are perverted from the natural state."[11]

Aristotle's dichotomy between liberal and servile education is reflected in *The Idea of a University* (1852) by Cardinal John Henry Newman, a scholar whom Jacques Barzun hails as "the greatest theorists of university life" and a book that Jaroslav Pelikan lauds as "the most important treatise on the idea of the university ever written in any language."[12] Newman, who draws heavily on Aristotle as "the oracle of nature and truth" in delineating the purpose of higher education, similarly contrasts liberal and commercial education and holds that the highest end of education—being "a direct need of our nature" and, quoting Cicero, "a condition of our happiness"—is liberal knowledge and a cultivated mind:

> [T]hat alone is liberal knowledge, which stands on its own pretensions, which is independent of sequel, expects no complement, refuses to be *informed* . . . by any end, or absorbed into any art, in order duly to present itself to our contemplation. The most ordinary pursuits have this specific character, if they are self-sufficient and complete, the highest lose it, when they minister to something beyond them.
>
> Liberal education . . . is simply the cultivation of the intellect . . . its object is nothing more nor less than intellectual excellence. . . . To open the mind, to correct it, to refine it, to enable it to grow, and to digest, master, rule, . . . to give it power over its own faculties, application, flexibility, method, critical exactness, sagacity, resource, address, eloquent expression.[13]

Pursuing knowledge for vocational or societal ends is a lower, servile form of education, even if it is beneficial. This root, of which Aristotle and Newman are exemplars, nourishes the tree of higher education to bear fruit that is intrinsically aluable for knowledge and the joy of the noetic self.[14]

---

[11] Aristotle, "Politics" in *The Complete Works of Aristotle*, ed. Jonathan Barnes (Princeton: Princeton University Press, 1984), 2:1337b18–1338a12, 1341b9–16, 1342a17–23. Reprinted by permission of Princeton University Press, Copyright © 1984 by the Jowett Copyright Trustees.

[12] Jaroslav Pelikan, *The Idea of a University: A Reexamination* (New Haven: Yale University Press, 1992), 6, 9.

[13] John Henry Newman, *The Idea of a University* (Notre Dame: University of Notre Dame Press, 1982), 78–79, 81–83, 92.

[14] For a recent example see Mark William Roche's award-winning book, *Why Choose the Liberal Arts?* (Notre Dame: University of Notre Dame Press, 2010). Roche says, on pages 15 and 26, that a liberal arts education is its own end and that through it humanity achieves its highest end: the leisurely joy of contemplating the eternal.

Neither Aristotle nor Newman, however, denies that liberal education can be very useful. Aristotle avers that there "can be no doubt that children should be taught those useful things which are really necessary, but not all useful things." For this lower goal of utility, a liberal education is "useful" for "moneymaking," "the management of a household," and "political life." Still, youth should only be taught "such kinds of knowledge as will be useful to them without making mechanics of them" since the personal happiness of contemplating the truth free from service is the highest end of education and life.[15] Newman grants that, "If then a practical end must be assigned to a University [education], I say that it is that of training good members of society" whose cultivated intellects prepare them to "fill any post with credit," "master any subject with facility," and bring "a power and a grace to every work and occupation" enabling them "to be more useful, and to a greater number" than those educated for a "temporal calling, or some mechanical art."[16] In this vision, utility is a felicitous byproduct and lower end of liberal education.

In response to the rise of professional and technical studies at universities in the nineteenth and twentieth centuries, some liberal educators intensified the dichotomy between liberal and servile education to the point where "only a 'useless' education can be called 'liberal' " thus making its fruit void of nourishment.[17] This dichotomy is evident even in the twenty-first century, most notably with Stanley Fish's declaration that the humanities, or liberal arts, do nothing useful for society whatsoever; they are purely their own good and only meant to give pleasure to those who enjoy studying them.[18] But such a division between liberal and useful education, whether from staunchly intrinsic or utilitarian quarters, does not, however, represent the theory and practice of the bulk of Western higher educational history. A few salient examples will suffice to illustrate this point.

Liberal Education and Vocation
in the History of Western Higher Education

In ancient Egyptian scribal schools, students read classic wisdom texts like *The Instruction of Amenemope*, written around 1200 BC by a successful

---

[15] Aristotle, "Politics," 2:1337b3–9, 1338a15–17.

[16] Newman, *The Idea of a University*, 126, 134–35.

[17] Bruce A. Kimball, *Orators and Philosophers: A History of the Idea of Liberal Education*, exp. ed. (New York: The College Board, 1995), 231.

[18] Stanley Fish, "Will the Humanities Save Us?" *The New York Times*, January 6, 2008, accessed September 19, 2014, http://opinionator.blogs.nytimes.com/2008/01/06/will-the-humanities-save-us/?_r=0.

and well-respected scribe to his son on how to think, speak, and act temperately, piously, and virtuously in his future scribal office and life. Students also learned writing, arithmetic, geometry, foreign languages, geography, astronomy, and the names of flora, fauna, and minerals. Later in their education students specialized in theology, medicine, administration and other subjects so that they could work for the palace or temple as a scribe, physician, priest, judge, or administrator of agriculture or commerce.[19] In ancient Egypt what would later be called liberal and professional education, or wisdom and vocation, went hand in hand with the former serving as the foundation for the latter and life.

The connection between liberal education and vocations also appears in ancient Greece and Rome. Book VII of Plato's *Republic* (ca. 370 BC) outlines an ideal education for future warriors and philosophers who will protect and rule society. This education "mustn't be useless," declares Plato. Studies in arithmetic, geometry, astronomy, music, and logical inquiry will enable students to perceive what is true, good, and beautiful. Besides achieving education's great goal of knowing "the eternally real and not what comes into being and then passes away," this knowledge will be invaluable for performing the vocations of defender and leader.[20] Likewise the Roman rhetorician Cicero, advancing the dominant educational program of the Greek orator Isocrates (fourth century BC), argues in *On the Orator* (ca. 55 BC) that students should be well versed in the liberal arts, all knowledge, so that they can assume any position in public life and wisely, virtuously, and eloquently address any matter. While, as Bruce Kimball remarks, the Roman oratorical curriculum "eschews specialization," it is does not eschew usefulness. Its first goal is broadly vocational: "training the good citizen to lead society."[21]

Medieval universities also connected liberal and vocational education. The curriculum was grounded in the seven liberal arts developed in ancient Greece and Rome: grammar (Latin, literature, and history), rhetoric, and logic (together called the *trivium* or "three [language] ways [of knowing]") and arithmetic, geometry, music, and astronomy (the *quadrivium* or "four [mathematical] ways [of knowing]"). These seven arts led, under Thomas Aquinas' curricular expansion in the thirteenth century, to the study of

---

[19] Patrizia Piacentini, "Scribes," in *The Oxford Encyclopedia of Ancient Egypt*, ed. Donald B. Redford (Oxford: Oxford University Press, 2001), 3:187–92.

[20] Plato, *Republic: Books 6–10*, trans. Chris Emlyn-Jones and William Preddy (Loeb Classical Library; Cambridge, MA: Harvard University Press, 2013), 521d, 527b.

[21] Kimball, *Orators and Philosophers*, 36–37.

three philosophies: natural, moral, and metaphysical.[22] The crowning study was theology, the contemplation of God. These disciplines also prepared students for professional graduate studies in theology, law, and medicine. These contemplative and useful ends of education were mirrored, in Aquinas' view, by the ends of teaching. Question eleven of *Disputed Questions on Truth* (ca. 1256) asks, "Is teaching an act of the active or contemplative life?" Aquinas gives two answers. When the object of teaching is the subject matter itself, the end is "the contemplative life . . . the seeing of truth." When the object is the student, the end is "the active life . . . , which is aimed at for its usefulness to neighbours."[23]

At the University of Wittenberg, following Renaissance humanism's revival of the oratorical tradition, Melanchthon reformed the liberal arts curriculum to emphasize classical and biblical languages, literature, history, rhetoric, and logic. "Dare to know . . . it is your task to seek the truth," Melanchthon charged his students.[24] This truth was to be found in studying human wisdom in classical texts, natural wisdom in creation, and divine wisdom in Scripture in their original languages. A major thrust of this education, then, was for students to pursue wisdom by reading and interpreting texts and, ultimately, eloquently proclaiming God's revealed Word, especially the Gospel. Another thrust of this education, which included the higher disciplines of theology, law, and medicine, was to cultivate wise, virtuous citizens for life itself and for their vocations in service to the church and state. "[A]ll disciplines that are taught in the schools are necessary for life," Melanchthon exhorts his students, so "keep in view the purpose of your studies, and decide that they are provided for giving of advice for the state, for teaching in the churches and for upholding the doctrine of religion."[25]

A final example comes from colonial America. Harvard College, established in 1636, created its curriculum to mirror the humanist education of Oxford and Cambridge. Freshmen studied Latin, Greek, Hebrew, rhetoric, logic, history, geography, and theology; sophomores added the study of physics; juniors added ethics and metaphysics; and seniors added arithme-

---

[22] Kimball, *Orators and Philosophers*, 66–67.

[23] Aquinas, "Disputed Question on Truth," in *Thomas Aquinas: Selected Writings*, ed. Ralph McInerny (London: Penguin, 1998), 214–15.

[24] Philip Melanchthon, "On Correcting the Studies of Youth (1518)," in *A Melanchthon Reader*, trans. Ralph Keen (New York: Peter Lang, 1988), 50, 56. Reprinted by permission of Peter Lang Publishing.

[25] Melanchthon, "On the Order of Learning," 5–6. For more on the University of Wittenberg, see the chapter by Dawn and Mallinson.

tic, geometry, and astronomy. This non-specialized curriculum was meant to mold learned, pious, and civil graduates who could go serve as clergy and statesmen. This model, which saw liberal education as vocational education for the church and state, served as the paradigm for every American college prior to the American Revolution.[26]

These examples show that while there have been shifts in the curricular balance between liberal and vocational education, one constant theme remains: liberal education served as the foundation for vocations. Whether as a base for further education in a specific vocation, for directly entering into vocations in church or state, or as a broad preparation for life's various vocations, a liberal education was clearly connected and useful to vocation.

A Biblical Paradigm of Education

The educational vision that wisdom and vocation, learning and usefulness, go together is not only apparent from history, but also, and significantly for the Christian university, from Scripture. Tradition holds that Plato's Academy had this sign above its entrance: "Let no one who is ignorant of geometry enter." If this was the placard above the gate to education in Athens, what would the placard be in Jerusalem? It would be Ps 1.

Psalm 1, which contrasts the wise righteous person with the foolish wicked person, stands at the beginning of the Psalter to invite those desiring wisdom to enter the Psalms and drink in more wisdom. It also invites readers to pursue wisdom in the wisdom texts that follow it in the canons: Proverbs, Ecclesiastes, and Job.[27] Based on Ps 1 and related biblical passages (e.g., Isa 55:1–3; John 4:13–14, 7:37; Rev 22:17), the invitation on the placard above Jerusalem's gate would read, "Let everyone who thirsts after wisdom freely enter."

---

[26] Kimball, *Orators and Philosophers*, 103–13 and Lucas, *American Higher Education*, 103–5. Even after this period, American higher education continued to uphold both liberal and vocational education for the next two centuries, although the content and mixture of these two aspects of education changed in various ways (Christopher Jencks and David Riesman, *The Academic Revolution* [New York: Doubleday, 1968], 199).

[27] The Jewish division of the Hebrew Bible, which extends back at least to the early second century BC (see the prologue to Ecclesiasticus/Sirach), falls into three parts: Torah, Prophets, and Writings (cf. Luke 24:4). Psalms heads the Writings section with Job, Proverbs, and Ecclesiastes after it. Bishop Mileto in the late second century AD offers the earliest Christian list of Old Testament books. It is arranged in four parts: Pentateuch, Historical, Wisdom/Poetic, and Prophetic Books. Psalms heads the Wisdom/Poetic section with Proverbs, Ecclesiastes, and Job after it. The same order is seen in the earliest, most complete Christian Bibles in the fourth century.

But what sort of wisdom? Wisdom to what end? Certainly there is practical human wisdom and natural wisdom in the biblical wisdom texts. Observations or admonitions about the good and bad effects of effort and idleness as seen in nature (Prov 6:6–11) or wealth and poverty (Prov 10:15, 23:4–5) are part of Scripture's wisdom. But the principal focus is on divine wisdom: "The beginning of wisdom is the fear/reverence of the LORD" (Prov 9:10).[28] This is the golden thread that runs through the wisdom texts (Ps 34:11; Job 28:28; Eccl 12:13) and culminates in the incarnation of God's wisdom in Christ the Savior (1 Cor 1:18–24; Col 2:2–3). It is divine wisdom that heads the Psalter and invites the reader to enter and receive it.

The invitation of Ps 1 portrays the wise person as one "whose delight is in the teaching (i.e., Law and Gospel) of the LORD" and who "meditates day and night on his teaching" (v. 2).[29] This person "will be like a tree transplanted beside canals of water so that it will produce its fruit in its season and its leaves will not wither, and all that it will do will succeed" (v. 3).[30] To understand the message of these verses, their parallelism and extended simile need to be unpacked. This tree (wise person) is transplanted (implicitly by the grace of God from an arid land of self-reliance [see Jer 17:5–8]) next to an intentionally-dug waterway (God's revelation) that continuously brings life-sustaining and nourishing water (God's teaching) to the tree. The tree drinks by continually meditating on God's revealed Word. Such learning is personally delightful and beneficial because it contains God's good Law and saving grace.[31] It also has the planned outcome of causing the wise person to produce timely fruit, constant foliage, and success.

---

[28] Translations of the Hebrew Bible are my own.

[29] "Teaching" is used instead of the normal translation "law" for the Hebrew word *tôrāh* because *tôrāh* generally means "instruction, teaching." Sometimes it refers to God's Law (Exod 18:16, 20); other times to God's grace (Exod 13:9 and the Torah of Genesis to Deuteronomy in the Jewish canon). "Teaching" best fits this context because after Ps 1 the reader encounters psalms devoted to God's Law and grace (e.g., Ps 119 and 136).

[30] This verse ubiquitously reads "which/that yields" in English translations. The Hebrew word behind the relative pronoun "which, that" is *'ăšer*. Translating *'ăšer* this way here is legitimate, but it misses the nuance that the tree has been transplanted by God from an arid place, where it was fruitless and withered, to a well-watered orchard in order that it naturally fulfill its good functions as a tree. Given this, it is best to translate *'ăšer* as a purpose clause. For other relevant examples of this use of *'ăšer*, see Deut 4:10, 40 where God gave Israel his words "so that" they would learn to fear/revere God, "so that" it would go well for them in the Promised Land, and "so that" (here the Hebrew is *lĕma'an*, a clear purpose clause) their lives would be long.

[31] James L. Mays, *Psalms* (Louisville: John Knox, 1994), 42.

One way of reading this psalm is to see it as speaking to the personal prosperity of the wise. This is a legitimate reading. It resonates with wisdom texts that connect God's Word, wisdom, and righteousness to the divine blessings of health, wealth, peace, offspring, and honor (Prov 3:1–8, 13–18; 22:4; Job 1:1–3). A tree that is constantly watered will naturally flourish. The water supply ensures that the tree's roots drink in water to keep its leaves verdant (Jer 17:8) and produce abundant fruit at just the right time. Its leafy shade reciprocally protects its roots from the harsh, desiccating rays of the sun. Its fruit can fall to the ground to fertilize the soil and nourish the tree more. All of this causes the tree to prosper in its own stature, strength, and life.

To leave the psalm at this level, though, misses the thrust of the tree imagery. The primary purpose of a fruit tree for any human reader— regardless of whether the reader looks at Ps 1 through a first person (the tree is me) or third person (the tree is her) lens—is that it benefits others. This is commonly understood by fruit farmers and everyone who eats fruit. It is also seen in Gen 1:11, 29 and 2:8–9, 15 when God creates fruit trees. The trees are to be self-reproducing and aesthetically pleasing. But their ultimate purpose is to nourish and sustain human life. This end is also achieved by providing never-ending shade to protect people from the fatal heat that beats down on them (cf. Judg 9:15; Ezek 17:23; Jonah 4:6–8). And where there are trees there is water—especially in an orchard with an intentionally-dug waterway as in Ps 1. The fruit and shade that trees offer to those who come near also direct them to the same free water that nourishes the trees. The success of a fruit tree is vitally important for itself, but ultimately it is for the provision and protection of others.

This reading is strengthened by the contrast with the wicked fools whose ways are opposed to God's and likened to "chaff" (vv. 1, 4). Chaff, the husk that surrounds harvested grain, was thrown into the air in ancient Israel so that the wind would blow it to the side while the heavier grain would fall to the ground to be collected for food. Chaff was insubstantial compared to grain and nutritionally useless to people. The point of this imagery is clear: while wicked fools (chaff) are found with wise righteous people (grain), they lack the wisdom (nourishment) that is useful to others so they are cast aside.

So why pursue an education in wisdom? There is personal pleasure and benefit to be found in divine, human, and natural wisdom. This is a good end, but it is not the ultimate end. The great end of an education in wisdom is to be useful to others, to be life-sustaining people in the place(s) you have been planted.

This purpose, manifest in Ps 1, is reflected in other biblical passages. The second great command of Scripture is "Love your neighbor as yourself"

(Lev 19:18; Matt 22:39). It is presumed here that a person will love himself. That is a good end, but the ultimate end is loving the neighbor. Even the greatest command—"Love the LORD your with the all of your mind and with all of your soul and with all of your strength" (Deut 6:4; Matt 22:37)—is fulfilled, Jesus says, in loving the neighbor (Matt 25:31–40). The example of God's prophets and apostles shows that they did not keep their education in the wisdom of God's Law and Gospel to themselves. As per God's calling—and warning—they proclaimed God's wisdom for the salvation of others (Ezek 3:1–21, 33:1–8; Gal 1:11–24). Moses stood before God's presence on Mount Sinai receiving God's revealed Word, but did not stay there. He, too, as per his calling, came down to proclaim God's Law to Israel (Exod 19–24). Jesus' divinity and glory shone forth on a mountain in a moment of comfort, but he did not remain there despite Peter's temptation (Luke 9:28–35). He too descended the mountain setting aside his heavenly glory to complete his calling by revealing the mysterious wisdom of God's Gospel through his teaching, healing, death, and resurrection. All of these texts support the educational paradigm of Ps 1 that a person learns wisdom ultimately to serve others through her God-given callings.

Applying this biblical paradigm to higher education—which at a Christian university includes the study of divine, human, and natural wisdom—a clear analogy emerges. Education should be personally pleasurable and beneficial. That is a good end. It is not, however, the highest end. An education in wisdom is ultimately for watering trees—whether students, faculty, staff, administrators, or constituents—so that they can produce nutritious fruit and protective shade for the lives of others in their vocations in life.

Lutheran Theology and Education

Lutheran theologians, whose *sola Scriptura* ("Scripture alone") exegesis directly influences their faith and practice, likewise uphold the value of pursuing the truth. Melanchthon dares his students to know the truth. Luther rhetorically asks, "How dare you not know what can be known?"[32] O. P. Kretzmann, a past president of Valparaiso University, asserts that a Christian university is dedicated to a two-fold task: "the search for Truth and the transmission of Truth."[33]

---

[32] Quoted in Robert Benne, "A Lutheran Vision/Version of Christian Humanism," *Lutheran Forum* 31, no. 3 (1997): 42.

[33] O. P. Kretzmann, "The Destiny of a Christian University in the Modern World (1940)," in *The Lutheran Reader*, ed. Paul J. Contino and David Morgan (Valparaiso,

Lutheran theologians recognize the personal joy and benefit that come with education. Luther himself speaks of God creating humans so that they can understand God's creation and "take delight in that knowledge as part of [their] nature."[34] He talks of how the "pure pleasure a man gets from having studied" also leads to "great wealth and honor" through the vocations that the educated attain.[35] In the same vein, Kretzmann declares that the first two premises of a Christian education are that "God created man a moral being, with body and soul, endowed with reason, emotion, and will . . . for man's good and enjoyment" and that "God created heaven and earth and all that is therein for man's use and enjoyment." Education is meant to develop these joyous gifts within God's will.[36]

To be within God's will, though, the good ends of pursuing truth and personal joy and benefit must not become the highest ends of education. When they do, education falls to two temptations: idolatry and self-centeredness. On the one hand, the pursuit and contemplation of truth as the highest end of education leads to what can be called "idealatry," where ideal truth becomes the sole, sufficient end of erudition and is thus effectively worshiped as god by its ivory tower devotees.[37] On the other hand, making personal pleasure and profit the greatest goal of education leads to the sinful self-centeredness that Luther lambasts when he laments that, "our nature has been so deeply curved in upon itself because of the viciousness of original sin that it . . . turns the finest gifts of God in upon itself and enjoys them . . . for its own sake."[38] None of these good gifts of God—truth, pleasure, or profit—should be misplaced in the order of good ends lest they

---

IN: Valparaiso University, 1999), 110. Reprinted by permission of Valparaiso University.

[34] Luther, *Lectures on Genesis: Chapters 1–5*, AE 1:46.

[35] Luther, "A Sermon on Keeping Children in School," in AE 46:243–44.

[36] O. P. Kretzmann, "Christian Higher Education," in *New Frontiers in Christian Education* (River Forest, IL: Lutheran Education Association, 1944), 84.

[37] C. F. W. Walther makes a similar point in his 1849 speech at the laying of the cornerstone for the German Evangelical-Lutheran College and Seminary in St. Louis, Missouri. In this speech Walther encourages the Lutheran Church to remain "a faithful and upstanding promoter of art and scholarship," but warns that "art and scholarship [should] never become the idol to whom one builds altars, but only the means by which the church . . . promotes the true enlightenment and well-being of the world" (C. F. W. Walther, "Rede bei Gelegenheit der feierlichen Legung des Grundsteins zu dem deutschen evang.-luther. Collegium- und Seminar-Gebäude zu St. Louis, Mo.," *Der Lutheraner* 6, no. 21 [1850]: 161–63. The English translation of this speech was kindly provided by David Loy).

[38] Martin Luther, *Lectures on Romans*, AE 25:291.

lose their God-given goodness and become temptations to put ideas and the self above the two highest ends: God and neighbor.

The best gift that a liberal education can give an individual is freedom. One definition of this freedom is the intellectual and moral liberty that a "liberating" education gives. That is, a liberal education is liberating because it frees the individual from ignorance, vice, and falsehood for critical thought, virtue, and truth. This definition of "liberal" education arose after the Civil War and has been picked up by liberal educators of all stripes, including Lutherans.[39]

As helpful as this definition of freedom through liberal education is, Lutheran theologians are not content to rest there. For Lutherans the foremost freedom that a Christian liberal education can offer people is the freedom from sin, death, and the devil received by faith through grace in Jesus Christ (Rom 3:21–25, 6:23, 8:2; Eph 2:8–9). It is the truth of the Gospel that truly sets people free (John 8:32). The Law, even in the form of liberally learned virtues that guard and guide civic life, ultimately only shows people their sins (Rom 3:20). Neither the Law nor education frees people from sin and makes them righteous before God; only the Gospel does. It is in this light that Kretzmann contends that a Christian university should,

> Above all . . . [be] deeply committed to the recovery of the one great fact which our wayward world has forgotten: The reality of God and the individual's responsibility to Him, a responsibility which can only be met by the fact of the Atonement and the re-establishment of an intimate relationship with the Ruler of the Universe through Him who once entered the stream of time in order to tell men that they could know the truth and that it would make them free.[40]

As the doctrine of justification in Christ is central to all theology, Lutherans hold, so the Gospel must be central to any Christian university. Since a Christian university seeks the truth and confesses the Truth to be Christ, so the message of the Gospel must be a part of the university's fabric and communicated to students, faculty, staff, administrators, and constituents in multiple relevant and appropriate ways.

The origin and import of this Gospel freedom is wonderfully expressed by Luther in his 1520 treatise on "The Freedom of a Christian." Summarizing the whole of Christian life, Luther states that "A Christian is a perfectly free lord of all, subject to none. A Christian is a perfectly dutiful servant of

---

[39] Kimball, *Orators and Philosophers*, 158.

[40] Kretzmann, "The Destiny of a Christian University," 112–13.

all, subject to all."[41] This apparent paradox comes from biblical passages like 1 Cor 9:19 ("For though I am free from all, I have made myself a servant to all"), Rom 13:8 ("Owe no one anything, except to love one another"), and Phil 2:6–7 where Jesus is described as both Lord and servant.

Based on these and other passages, Luther argues that through God's gracious Gospel a Christian is both free from sin, death, and the devil and obligated to serve one's neighbor in response to the Gospel. Being free from the condemnation of the Law and freely receiving eternal life instead, the Christian is free to be unconcerned for the self and solely, cheerfully, and lovingly concerned with others instead. Such freedom does not lead to avoiding good works or doing evil; Christian liberty does not lead to license. Rather, as Rom 6:18 and 1 Pet 2:16, 24 say, being freed from sin by God's Gospel means that a Christian is now enslaved to serve God by righteously loving others. Christians are, in Luther's words, both the "freest of kings" in that "all things are made subject to him and are compelled [by the gospel] to serve him in obtaining salvation" and the freest of servants whose "faith is truly active through love" as little "Christs" to the world.[42]

This is the freedom that a Christian university in a Lutheran vision offers first and foremost. Liberation of the mind should occur in liberal education. To be a truly liberating education, though, the proclamation of the Gospel must also be present since it is the Gospel that liberates the whole person from sin and death for eternal life and motivates for loving others here and now. This freedom ought to affect a Christian education and harness the liberation of the mind not just for the good ends of pursuing truth, personal joy, and benefit, but ultimately for the highest end of serving the neighbor in the name of Christ.[43]

This end must also include serving nature as this is a key—albeit often overlooked—component of creation and salvation. In creation God makes humans "in the image of God" and calls them to "rule" over the earth (Gen 1:26–27) and "serve" and "preserve" the garden (Gen 2:5).[44] These verbs are later used for kings, who are to shield and support people as God's shepherds (1 Kgs 4:24; 2 Sam 5:2; Ezek 34:1–6), and of Levitical priests, who are

---

[41] Martin Luther, "The Freedom of a Christian," in AE 31:344.

[42] Luther, "The Freedom of a Christian," in AE 31:354–55, 365, 368.

[43] William H. K. Narum, "The Role of the Liberal Arts," in *Christian Faith and the Liberal Arts*, eds. Harold H. Ditmanson, Howard V. Hong, and Warren A. Quanbeck (Minneapolis: Augsburg, 1960), 20 and Gene Edward Veith, "Classical Education as Vocational Education: Luther on the Liberal Arts," *LOGIA* 21, no. 2 (2012): 25–26.

[44] The verbs in Hebrew are *rādāh* ("rule, have dominion"), *ʿābad* ("serve, work, cultivate"), and *šāmar* ("preserve, guard, keep").

to minister to and protect God's sanctuary (Num 3:7–8, 18:7). These verbs in Genesis, then, coupled with the context of God's "very good" acts of creation, indicate that humans are God's royal and sacred stewards who are to take very good care of creation (cf. 1 Pet 2:9). This vocation is also implied in salvation where God conforms sinful humans in the image of Christ, who sacrificed himself unto death to redeem nature too and one day make it "very good" again (Rom 8:19–21, 29; Rev 21). Thus in creation and salvation God calls people to be his exalted agents who serve, protect, and even sacrifice themselves for nature.

In this light, a Christian education should funnel to Christ and flow out to all. It should direct people to their vocations in Christ's creation and salvation (Col 1:15–20), offer them freedom in Christ's Gospel, and prepare them for service as Christs to their neighbors and nature in response to the Gospel.

In line with Ps 1 and other biblical passages, Lutheran theologians are adamant that the greatest good of education is enabling people to serve. Fundamental to this task is a Christian liberal and professional education that cultivates "wise, honorable, and well-educated citizens."[45] This education not only serves as a "handmaiden" to understanding, teaching, and proclaiming God's revealed Word, especially the Gospel, but enables people adeptly to assume various vocations in God's two kingdoms—church and society, and adroitly address the issues that arise in them. This education promotes peace and justice on earth while serving the eternal welfare of humanity with God's Gospel. A couple of key passages from C. F. W. Walther, a nineteenth century Lutheran theologian, and Luther illustrate this two-kingdom vision for education:

> We are keenly aware of the incomparable importance . . . of learning, not only for the temporal welfare of mankind but also for the eternal welfare of the world. . . . We know full well not only that all branches of knowledge can enter and be drawn into the service of sacred theology, but also that without many of them, particularly without thorough acquaintance with the original languages of Holy Scripture, without knowledge of secular and sacred history . . . a thorough and relatively comprehensive understanding of Scripture and thus the development and preservation of pure Biblical teaching is impossible. . . . As long as and wherever the Christian church flourished, it always and everywhere proved itself to be a friend and cultivator of all good arts and sciences, gave its future servants a scholarly preparatory

---

[45] Luther, "To the Councilmen of All Cities in Germany," in AE 45:356.

training, and did not disdain to permit its gifted youth at its schools of higher learning to be trained by the standard products of even pagan art and science.[46]

Now if . . . there were no souls, and there were indeed no need at all of schools and [biblical and classical] languages for the sake of the Scriptures and of God, this one consideration alone would be sufficient to justify the establishment everywhere of the very best schools . . . , namely, that in order to maintain the temporal estate outwardly the world must have good and capable men and women. . . . [who are able] to converse intelligently on any subject, or to assist and counsel anyone. . . . [If they learned] the languages, the other [liberal] arts, and history, they would then hear of the doings and sayings of the entire world, and how things went with various cities, kingdoms, princes, men, and women. Thus, they could in a short time set before themselves as in a mirror the character, life, counsels, and purposes— successful and unsuccessful—of the whole world from the beginning; and on the basis of which they could then draw proper inferences and in the fear of God take their own place in the stream of human events.[47]

Because of the value that Lutherans place on *sola Scriptura* and the doctrine that every Christian is part of "the priesthood of all believers" (1 Pet 2:9), who are to teach others God's Word, Lutherans since Luther's day have consistently held that all Christians should receive a liberal education so that they can read, interpret, and proclaim God's Word. Furthermore, since Lutherans hold that God's holy vocations are not limited to churchly offices (like bishop, priest, and nun), but include all honorable vocations in God's two kingdoms, people should receive an education that prepares them to fulfill those vocations excellently and faithfully. Education should prepare them to think independently, critically, and wisely; communicate clearly and persuasively; and act virtuously and faithfully in their various vocations in life.

Education for vocations in the church and society are both godly ends and mutually supportive in Lutheran theology. The church and its vocations not only proclaim the Gospel, but support and sustain the temporal life and its worldly vocations as part of God's originally good creation and

---

[46] C. F. W. Walther, "Foreword to the 1875 Volume: Are We Guilty of Despising Scholarship," in *Selected Writings of C. F. W. Walther: Editorials from "Lehre und Wehre,"* trans. August R. Suelflow (St. Louis: Concordia, 1981), 124–25.

[47] Luther, "To the Councilmen of All Cities in Germany," in AE 45:368–69.

the "masks" through which God hiddenly works to love and preserve his creation. The churchly vocations, Luther explains, inform and instruct people "on how to conduct themselves outwardly in their several [worldly] offices and estates, so that they may do what is right in the sight of God."[48] Likewise, education gives Christians knowledge of Scripture and theology so that they can thoughtfully and faithfully apply its divine and human wisdom to their unique vocations. Thomas Korcok, a historian of Lutheran education, expresses this need for thoughtful and faithful application well:

> As Christians live their lives under the tensions of vocation, each responds uniquely. There is no template of Christian living that can be traced. . . . The doctrine of vocation . . . demand[s] that education teach people to think independently, not to be imitators. The unique circumstances in which God places each individual require unique applications of the theological principles of the Evangelical faith to the myriad choices a person encounters on a daily basis.[49]

As for worldly vocations, these too are all honorable and praiseworthy gifts of God for they preserve and promote peace, justice, and life for all. In doing so, they also serve the church so that God's Word—and especially the Gospel, which is of ultimate importance—has free course. Moreover, the worldly liberal arts serve the church by educating Christians so that they can accurately and insightfully read God's Word and cogently and persuasively proclaim and defend it.[50]

For Luther and other Lutheran theologians, a Christian liberal and professional education is the means by which God would have young men and women learn about human, natural, and divine wisdom; reason and revelation; Law and Gospel; freedom and service, the liberal arts and professional studies so that they can serve their neighbors and nature, be excellent and faithful leaders in the church and society, and promote temporal peace and life while proclaiming eternal peace and life in Christ. The importance placed on this education for God's two kingdoms is perhaps nowhere better seen than in Luther's exposition of the Fourth Commandment in his Large Catechism (1529). In explaining the command to "Honor your father and

---

[48] Luther, "A Sermon on Keeping Children in School," in AE 46:226, 246.

[49] Thomas Korcok, *Lutheran Education: From Wittenberg to the Future* (St. Louis: Concordia, 2011), 51, 55.

[50] Luther, "A Sermon on Keeping Children in School," in AE 46:231, 237 and Philip Melanchthon, "On the Role of the Schools," in *Orations on Philosophy and Education*, ed. Sachiko Kusukawa, trans. Christine F. Salazar (Cambridge: Cambridge University Press, 1999), 10–12, 16–19.

mother," Luther turns the table and charges parents "at the risk of losing divine favor" to instruct youth "in the fear and knowledge of God" and "in formal study [i.e., liberal education] . . . so that they may be of service wherever they are needed."[51]

THE INTERACTION OF FAITH AND LEARNING

With the educational interaction of wisdom and vocation for freedom and service to society, nature, and the church in view, this leads to an examination of a key related practice of Christian universities: the relationship between faith and learning. Much has been written on this topic in recent years with the typical theme being "the integration of faith and learning" and the typical question being "How does the Christian faith impact learning?"

The thrust of this theme and unidirectionality of this question already reflect, however, a particular theological stance that is dominant in modern American discussion: a neo-Calvinist worldview. This view, which has roots in the sixteenth century reformer John Calvin and the Dutch theologian Abraham Kuyper (1837–1920), holds that Christians have a "cultural mandate" from God (Gen 1:28; Matt 28:18–20) to transform society so that it conforms to God's sovereign will.[52] Since fallen humans are totally depraved, their reason and knowledge of God's Law and will are also totally depraved. Truth can be found among non-Christians because God's "common grace" extends to all. This truth is useful to Christians since "all truth is God's truth, wherever it be found."[53] However, non-Christians cannot perceive truth fully, unite it, or act upon it properly in accord with

---

[51] Martin Luther, "Large Catechism," in *The Book of Concord: The Confessions of the Evangelical Lutheran Church*, eds. Robert Kolb and Timothy J. Wengert (Minneapolis: Fortress, 2000), 410 (part I:174). For "liberal education," see the Latin translation in *Concordia Triglotta* (St. Louis: Concordia, 1921), 630–31.

[52] This summary draws on Arthur F. Holmes, *The Idea of a Christian College*, rev. ed. (Grand Rapids: Eerdmans, 1987); James D. Bratt, "What Can the Reformed Tradition Contribute to Christian Higher Education?," in *Models for Christian Higher Education: Strategies for Success in the Twenty-First Century*, eds. Richard T. Hughes and William B. Adrian (Grand Rapids: Eerdmans, 1997), 125–40; Richard T. Hughes, "Christian Faith and the Life of the Mind," in *Faithful Learning and the Christian Scholarly Vocation*, eds. Douglas V. Henry and Bob R. Agee (Grand Rapids: Eerdmans, 2003), 5–8; and Nicholas Wolterstorff, "The Point of Connection between Faith and Learning," in *Educating for Shalom: Essays on Christian Higher Education*, eds. Clarence W. Joldersma and Gloria Goris Stronks (Grand Rapids: Eerdmans, 2004), 64–86.

[53] This quote comes from Holmes, *The Idea of a Christian College*, 17.

God's will. Only the regenerate minds of Christians educated in an all-encompassing Christian worldview can transform all aspects of society—including universities—to bring them into conformity with God's will and unite them in truth. Thus, there are two types of people and two types of learning: Christian and non-Christian. The task of Christian learning is to integrate faith and learning so that the Christian faith fully affects and unites all learning in God's truth and transforms society to bring it in line with God's Law and will.

A passage that illustrates well this integration approach to faith and learning comes from James D. Bratt of Calvin College:

> The restoration of order in nature the Reformed have deemed to be largely God's business. . . . The redemption of society is a different matter: it depends more directly on human agency and is all the more urgent because society shows less of the steadying regularity of divine constraints than does nature. If sin from the outset radiated out of human perversity, so must restoration begin from human regeneration. If God's elect are called out of themselves into the society of the church, then the church is called as agent of renewal for all humanity. If God spoke especially to the Old Testament Israel in a law for their nation and bequeathed that example as special revelation to this New Testament people, then those people are mandated to institute its principles of justice and charity among themselves and among their neighbors so as to restore as much as possible God's will for earthly life. Calvinists, in short, feel called to be social and cultural leaders and therefore turn to education to teach that knowledge and wisdom, social and historical, theological and political, that are required to make leadership obedient to heaven and effective on earth. For Calvinists this constitutes the supreme religious service, the true worship of God. To return to our beginning, God would have due honor and proven glory; He would have them by "reclaiming all of his creation: the cosmos, human nature, and society"; and He would have his elect lead the way in this project.[54]

This integration approach to faith and learning has greatly influenced the theory and practice of Christian higher education in modern America. Its influence can be seen in the challenge that Duane Litfin—the past president of the evangelical flagship, Wheaton College—gives Christian colleges to integrate faith and learning in every academic discipline in order to discov-

---

[54] Bratt, "What Can the Reformed Tradition Contribute to Christian Higher Education?," 131–32.

er and unite all truth in Jesus Christ the Lord, to "take every thought captive to obey Christ" (2 Cor 10:5), and to glorify God.[55] Its influence can also be seen in Christian colleges with classes in Christian Mathematics or Christian Psychology and residential halls that mandate Christian morals and lifestyles. It is an approach that many find appealing and marketable because it integrates faith and learning in a distinct and all-encompassing manner.[56]

There are, however, other ways to approach the relationship between faith and learning. Another prevalent path is what can be called the "two books, two truths" or separation approach. In this vision faith and learning, or revelation and reason, each have their own dignity and sphere of knowledge, so are autonomous. This approach looks to Luther for its roots since he argued that God's left-hand kingdom (society) is ruled by reason, experience, and law, while God's right-hand kingdom (church) is ruled by revelation, grace, and faith. As each of these kingdoms is God's with its own way of operating, each has its own dignity. "Every occupation has its own honor before God," Luther states, "as well as its own requirements and duties."[57] "No science [i.e., discipline] should stand in the way of another science," Luther cautions, "but each should continue to have its own mode of procedure in its own terms. . . . Every science should make use of its own terminology, and one should not for this reason condemn the other or ridicule it."[58] The separation approach also has roots in the scientist Francis Bacon and the Enlightenment project that separated reason from faith, science from revelation. In *The Advancement of Learning* (1623) Bacon argues that while no one can be "too well studied in the book of God's word, or in the book of God's works," Scripture and nature are to be studied separately so as not to "unwisely mingle or confound these learnings together."[59]

A good example of the separation approach comes from Mark Edwards Jr., the past president of St. Olaf College. Responding to criticisms by James Burtchaell and George Marsden that the light of Christian universities and scholarship has died out due to secularization, Edwards counters that "we

---

[55] Duane Litfin, *Conceiving the Christian College* (Grand Rapids: Eerdmans, 2004), 128, 138, 143, 145–47, 164, 173.

[56] Ernest L. Simmons, *Lutheran Education: An Introduction* (Minneapolis: Augsburg Fortress, 1998), 32.

[57] Luther, "A Sermon on Keeping Children in School," in AE 46:246.

[58] Luther, *Lectures on Genesis: Chapters 1–5*, AE 1:47–48.

[59] Francis Bacon, "The Advancement of Learning," in *Francis Bacon: The Major Works*, ed. Brian Vickers (Oxford: Oxford University Press, 2008), 126. Reprinted by permission of Oxford University Press.

are only seeing a different refraction of the light as the prism of society changes." Defending liberal Christian universities and "culture Protestantism," Edwards appeals to H. Richard Niebuhrs' description of Luther's two-kingdom theology as "Christ and culture in paradox." In this view, Edward says, "Christian revelation and secular knowledge" are in "significant—perhaps humanly unresolvable—tension with each other." Furthermore, Christian universities, because they are situated in the left-hand kingdom of God, are "called to employ reason to pursue truth" with the result that "in most cases [there will be] no substantive difference between scholarship by Christians and non-Christians." The "Christian substance" of Christian universities should only appear "in the Christian calling of faculty, staff and students and in the Christian context surrounding the academic enterprise—only rarely in the results of scholarly inquiry itself."[60] In other words, revelation and reason, or faith and learning, should not mix because they are deeply at odds. They should be separated at a Christian university so that Christianity simply provides the space and staff for the rational pursuit of truth, not any substance for interacting with, critiquing, or informing the pursuit of truth.

The problem with this approach is that it plays up a purported paradox to the point of conflict. First, it fails to pay attention to the final part of Luther's quote about the integrity of each science/discipline. After saying that each discipline should have freedom to pursue its own procedures with its own terms without being ridiculed, Luther concludes that "[each] one should . . . be of use to the other, and they should put their achievements at one another's disposal." This is a much different tone than a paradox of conflict that results in separation. Luther's approach is about integrity, mutuality, and interaction. It is consonant with his own, Melanchthon's, and other Lutheran theologians' statements that the liberal arts have their own integrity and value for society, but also serve the church by helping Christians understand and proclaim God's Word; that the temporal vocations have their own dignity and purpose, but also serve the church by keeping the peace so that Gospel can have free course; and that the church has its own integrity and value eternally, but is connected and useful to supporting and guiding temporal vocations "as their conscience" of what is just, beautiful, and true.[61] This separation model also suffers from a misreading of Niebuhr's understanding of Luther:

---

[60] Mark U. Edwards Jr., "Christian Colleges: A Dying Light or a New Refraction?," *Christian Century*, April 21–28, 1999, 459–63.

[61] Narum, "The Role of the Liberal Arts," 27.

[Luther's] antimonies and paradoxes have often led to the suggestion that Luther divided life into compartments, or taught that the Christian right hand should not know what a man's worldly left hand was doing . . . Luther does not, however, divide what he distinguishes. The life in Christ and the life in culture, in the kingdom of God and the kingdom of the world, are closely related. . . . It is a great error to confuse the parallelistic dualism of separated spiritual and temporal life with the interactionism of Luther's gospel of faith in Christ working by love in the world of culture.[62]

Finally, it is problematic even to use the term *paradox* when referring to Luther's two-kingdom view of Christian life. As the Luther scholar Robert Kolb comments, "In Luther's view the basic structure of God's design of human life in the two dimensions" is "not paradoxical." The relationship of God's two kingdoms and all that go with them are "complementary," "two inseparable dimensions of human life" that Christians live in "simultaneously."[63]

So what best defines a Lutheran approach to faith and learning? Like the integration approach, Lutheran theologians hold that all truth is one and that a *university*—being a place where all branches of knowledge are "turned into one (whole)"—should seek unity of truth. Lutherans ecumenically confess that all truth coheres in Christ because Christ is the Creator and Savior of all (Col 1:15–20). Lutherans believe that truth expressed by non-Christians is still truth and to be used by Christians. "There is only one truth," Melanchthon declares; Christians can use the Law of God and the philosophy of non-Christians because Christians know "that philosophy is the law of God."[64]

But Lutherans do not make unity of truth the primary goal of education. Confessing that humans are not and were never created to be omniscient, that sin has adversely affected human reason, and that Christians are *simul iustus et peccator* ("simultaneously justified and sinful"),

---

[62] H. Richard Niebuhr, *Christ and Culture* (New York: Harper and Row, 1951), 173–74, 179. Copyright © 1951 by Harper & Row Brothers. Reprinted by permission of HarperCollins Publishers.

[63] Robert Kolb, "Niebuhr's 'Christ and Culture in Paradox' Revisited: The Christian Life, Simultaneous in Both Dimensions," in *Christ and Culture in Dialogue: Constructive Themes and Practical Applications*, ed. Angus J. L. Menuge (St. Louis: Concordia, 1999), 113–15.

[64] Philip Melanchthon, "On the Distinction between the Gospel and Philosophy," in *Orations on Philosophy and Education*, ed. Sachiko Kusukawa, trans. Christine F. Salazar (Cambridge: Cambridge University Press, 1999), 24.

Lutherans know that humans are incapable of conceiving of all truth together, are prone to error, and therefore must pursue truth with humility.[65] Lutherans take God's rebuke of Job—who presumed to know all things about his suffering—seriously when God tells him, in so many words, "Put on your big boy pants and riddle me this" (Job 38:1–3). Upholding the unity of truth in Christ as Creator and Savior, Lutherans see the Christo-centric unity of truth as a reality accomplished by Christ, revealed in God's Word, and received by faith; it is not a perspective that Christian universities can make society espouse through the integration of faith and learning. As the Lutheran scholar Martin Marty says, the unity of truth in Christ "must be ascertained, striven for, and then accepted as gospel gift."[66] Basing the highest end of education on the interaction of wisdom and vocation, Lutherans prefer what can be called a "faith seeking understanding for service" approach to the unity of truth in Christ.[67] The more Christians know about truth in Christ's creation and salvation and how it coheres, the better they will be able to think, speak, and act in loving service to their neighbors and nature.

If the great goal of education for Lutherans is not the unity of truth, neither is it the transformation of society. Faith and learning are to connect with each other, but not in a way that makes society conform to God's Law and will. There are several reasons for this. First, Lutheran theology holds that society is already God's kingdom; it does not need to be claimed for Christ by Christians since Christ already accomplished this in creation and salvation, and will do so again in recreation when he comes again on the last day to recreate the "very good" utopia (Rev 21). In the meantime, Christians are called to preserve and promote peace in this temporal life, care for creation, and share the saving message of eternal peace in Christ. Second, it is the Gospel of salvation by grace through faith that brings people to know, trust, and follow God (Eph 2:8–10). Legalism cannot do this for society (Rom 7:7–11); it can only be accomplished by the Holy Spirit working faith in individuals. Third, God has made reason, experience, and law to rule over society, and these gifts are commonly available to all

---

[65] Richard W. Solberg, "What Can the Lutheran Tradition Contribute to Higher Education?," in *Models for Christian Higher Education: Strategies for Success in the Twenty-First Century*, eds. Richard T. Hughes and William B. Adrian (Grand Rapids: Eerdmans, 1997), 74–75.

[66] Martin E. Marty, "The Church and Christian Higher Education in the New Millennium," in *Faithful Learning and the Christian Scholarly Vocation*, eds. Douglas V. Henry and Bob R. Agee (Grand Rapids; Eerdmans, 2003), 59.

[67] This is an adaptation of the motto of Anselm of Canterbury (ca. 1100): "faith seeking understanding" (*fides quaerens intellectum*).

people including non-Christians. God has also given people great freedom in creation to create their own cultures within the bounds and designs of God's structure.[68] God did not give humanity a comprehensive law to construct a monolithic Christian worldview and culture. Additionally, God has made the church to be ruled by revelation, grace, and faith, which are gifts freely received from God. To integrate faith and learning in the transformation model risks confusing God's two kingdoms with the result that God's church improperly triumphs over God's society and revelation inappropriately trumps reason, which distorts the good purpose and relationship of both.[69]

Given the Lutheran two-kingdom approach to church and society, revelation and reason, Christ and culture, the best approach to the relationship of faith and learning for a Christian university in a Lutheran vision is one that maintains their God-given integrity and inseparable complementarity of being useful to each other and working together to serve society, nature, and the church with Christ's love. The best term for this approach to faith and learning is interaction. Thus, the Lutheran answer to the question of how the Christian faith impacts learning is neither integration for transformation nor avoidance via separation, but the mutual, responsible, and fruitful interaction of faith and learning for service.

How does this interaction occur? Much of this answer has already been illustrated above by how the Lutheran two-kingdom theology describes the integrity and mutuality of the church and society, revelation and reason, biblically-based theology and historical liberal education. Interaction occurs by each discipline having the integrity to pursue the truth in its areas with its own methods and terms. This includes the integrity of Christian theology, which, grounded in God's revealed Word and built up over two millennia, addresses the crux issue of mankind's justification before God by grace through faith in Christ and aims to offer a "comprehensive and coherent vision of life."[70] Coupled with integrity is an inseparable comple-

---

[68] An example of this is the imagination and freedom people have in God's left-hand kingdom to construct political systems that best serve the neighbor. While God instituted government for the sake of preserving and promoting peace, justice, and life for all (Rom 13), "Christians recognize how many options God has given for achieving His horizontal, temporal will within the structures of humanity as He designed it" (Kolb, "Niebuhr's 'Christ and Culture in Paradox' Revisited," 117).

[69] The caution of triumphalism and distortion is raised by Hughes, "Christian Faith and the Life of the Mind," 8.

[70] Benne, "A Lutheran Vision/Version of Christian Humanism," 43 and Robert Benne, *Quality with Soul: How Six Premiere Colleges and Universities Keep Faith with Their Religious Traditions* (Grand Rapids: Eerdmans, 2001), 197–99. This comprehensive,

mentarity where Christian theology and each discipline are connected and useful to the other. This occurs by Christian theology and each discipline confidently and humbly dialoguing, questioning, critiquing, and informing each other as is appropriate to their spheres of knowledge so that they mutually benefit each other. This occurs by collegially probing life's problems and pursuing God's truth for the purpose of more wisely serving the whole of God's creation with Christ's love.

How does the Christian faith affect learning? In the Lutheran interaction approach this question needs to be broadened and asked positively and negatively. For instance, how should the Christian faith impact the presuppositions that a Christian professor brings to bear on her particular discipline? Will that impact vary depending on whether the discipline is in the sciences, technology, engineering, mathematics, the humanities, or professional studies?[71] How ought the Christian faith critique a discipline whose reigning paradigms or practices conflict with truth or goodness revealed in God's Word? How should the Christian faith affect the professor's choice of subjects to study, the theories and methodologies to use, or the study's aims and applications? How ought the Christian faith influence the relationships that professors have with each other, students, and their supervisors? How should it inform the vocations of regents, administration, staff, faculty, and students? How should the Christian faith enlighten the purpose and practices of campus life? How ought it color and shape the purpose, constitution, and character of a university? Also, are there some aspects of university life that revelation, faith, or grace ought *not* influence because doing so would inappropriately trump the rightful sway of reason, experience, and law appropriately exercised?

Another crucial question that needs to be asked in the interaction approach is, "How does learning aid the church?" As was common in Christianity for centuries starting in the early Church, the main direction of

---

coherent vision should not be taken as an all-compassing worldview where Scripture or theology have an answer to every question or a law for every situation, but a body of revealed and confessed truth on many crucial matters of life—especially God, human nature, sin, and salvation—and a corpus of divine and human wisdom for approaching the whole of life.

[71] C. Stephen Evans argues for a "relevance continuum" where the Christian faith impacts philosophy and theology the most and mathematics the least, with other liberal arts and sciences falling in between (C. Stephen Evans, "The Calling of the Christian Scholar-Teacher," in *Faithful Learning and the Christian Scholarly Vocation*, eds. Douglas V. Henry and Bob R. Agee [Grand Rapids: Eerdmans, 2003], 40). This scheme is a helpful starting point, but it should expand to include every discipline in universities, including professional studies.

connection between faith and learning was that the liberal arts served as a handmaid to theology. So Luther, for example, calls the liberal arts a John the Baptist, a forerunner, to the flourishing of God's Word because they show the fallen condition of the world and enable people to read Scripture, which prepares them for the Gospel revealed in God's Word.[72] This is but another manifestation of the two-kingdom notion that God uses the vocations of the left-hand kingdom to serve the eternal ends of his right-hand kingdom. In this light, every discipline should ask how it can help the church understand itself biblically, historically, artistically, socially, economically, etc. Each discipline should ask itself what good gifts it can bring to Christ's church for the left-hand operation of congregations or the right-hand work of the Gospel. The church needs the questions and insights of human wisdom for it to flourish.

Each of these questions, and many more like them, need to be addressed honestly, carefully, and regularly by the whole community of a Christian university. While no simple answers can be provided here, several examples of the interaction approach will be given in subsequent chapters in this book. They will address many fundamental aspects of university life by inquiring into the interaction of Lutheran theology with academic disciplines, university vocations, and campus life.

For the integrity and inseparable complementarity of this interaction approach to work well, each academic discipline needs to have the freedom to ask questions and pursue the truth. Luther needed such freedom to rediscover the Gospel; Christian universities need this freedom now too. Christian academic liberty is not to be equated with license, though, but with freedom to pursue the truth in accord with the epistemology appropriate to each discipline and freedom to be faithful to the truth.[73] This liberty includes the freedom—individually and institutionally—to confess the truth confidently based on revelation, or reason, as Luther did when he declared at the Diet of Worms in 1521: "Unless I am convinced by Scripture and plain reason. . . . I cannot and will not recant anything [I have written about Scripture]."[74] Implicit in Luther's assertion is the humble allowance that he could be wrong and would change his views if convinced otherwise.

---

[72] See Luther, "To Eobanus Hessus, March 29, 1523," in AE 49:34.

[73] Cf. Holmes who talks about academic freedom at Christian colleges as "responsible freedom" where faith and learning work together "to see all things from a confessional perspective . . . to unite loyalty with liberty" (Holmes, *The Idea of a Christian College*, 61, 67).

[74] Translated and quoted in Roland H. Bainton, *Here I Stand: A Life of Martin Luther* (Peabody, MA: Hendrickson, 2010), 180.

Thus, Luther's statement indicates that academic freedom is also open to making mistakes (that is, after all, a key ingredient in the scientific method) and being corrected toward the truth by reason or revelation, whichever holds sway in a given area.

The apostle Paul is instructive here as well. Paul encourages Christians in Phi 4:8 to pursue what is true, good, and beautiful: "Finally, brothers, whatever it true, whatever is honorable, whatever is just, whatever is pure, whatever is lovely, whatever is commendable, if there is any excellence, if there is anything worthy of praise, think on these things." In 1 Cor 10:23–24, Paul tempers the liberty that Christians have in the Gospel with love for others: "All things are lawful, but not all things are helpful. All things are lawful, but not all things build up. Let no one seek his own good, but the good of his neighbor." In sum, Paul tells Christians that they are free to pursue all truth and every good thing, but this liberty is not ultimately to be used for the self; rather, it is for the good of others. Luther echoes Paul when talking about Christian freedom. In a Christian academic setting, this freedom means that all questions are possible to pursue for Christians, that truth and every good thing is freely to be pursued, and that academic freedom should ultimately be an instrument for loving and serving others.[75]

"WHAT IS BEAUTIFUL MAY BE DIFFICULT"

In his inaugural lecture to colleagues and students at the University of Wittenberg, Melanchthon unfolded a vision for education that was rooted in the Christian liberal arts tradition of educating students in human, natural, and divine wisdom so that they could assume vocations that were

---

[75] Non-Christians also have freedom to pursue the truth and every good thing, but this freedom rests solely in creation—not salvation—and is limited by (using Luther's language) their "bondage of the will" to sin and opposition to God and his will. They are free, like the Greeks, to pursue truth, goodness, and beauty for the sake of creating a good society, but this liberty is limited since they do not have freedom from selfish sin and rebellion against God or freedom from the demands and eternal consequences of the Law as Christians do in Christ. They do not have faith that holds to the Truth, who is Christ the Creator and Savior. Consequently they do not have the Gospel-generated "freedom of a Christian" to put aside sin and rebellion and, instead, pursue all of God's truth, goodness, and beauty to serve others in love as little Christs for their temporal well-being and eternal salvation. Because of this non-Christians lack full academic freedom. (For rebuttals that Christian universities are less free academically than secular institutions because of their theological commitments, see Litfin's response that every university has orthodoxies that qualify academic freedom and that Christian universities have true freedom because religious questions are not ruled out [Litfin, *Conceiving the Christian College*, 214–22].)

useful as they excelled "in sacred things" and "the marketplace." Concerning this education, Melanchthon conceded that "what is beautiful may be difficult," but counseled that "industry conquers difficulty."[76]

Indeed, the historically-rooted, biblically-based, Lutheran educational vision of wisdom and vocation for freedom and service to society, nature, and church is beautiful. It answers the conflicting messages that students at AnyU experience between fun, independence, and career, on one hand, and a liberal education in wisdom and virtue for citizenship, on the other. A Christian university in a Lutheran vision resolves this conflict and directs the whole higher educational enterprise to the highest end of faith active in love by bringing both aspects of education into a fruitful relationship where students encounter the freedom and joy of learning human, natural, and divine wisdom; develop the ability to think, speak, and act on their own so that they can intelligently and faithfully fulfill their vocations; and become wise, honorable, and cultivated citizens of God's church and society who love their neighbors and nature as little Christs because of Christ.

This vision is beautiful and difficult to achieve. Indeed, as the Lutheran historian Richard Solberg assesses, "The most serious critique one could level at Lutheran higher education in America is that it has failed to fulfill the educational challenges implicit in its own theology."[77] This failure may be due to several factors: Lutheran universities may have forgotten the treasures of their own theology and history; they may be chasing too much after the ways of secular universities; or they may not have (set aside) the time, talent, and treasure needed to bring this vision to reality. Whatever the reason may be, this vibrant vision must be preserved, promoted, and implemented across the whole of university life. This vision is aesthetically pleasing and harmonious. Moreover, it is scripturally sound and produces fruit, shade, and success for the temporal and eternal peace of the whole of God's creation.

QUESTIONS

1. If a cultural anthropologist spent a year as a student on your campus, what would she discover about your university? What would she see as the purpose of your university?

2. What foundations—biblical, theological, historical, philosophical, economic, etc.—most inform the vision of your university?

---

[76] Melanchthon, "On Correcting the Studies of Youth," 54, 56.
[77] Solberg, "What Can the Lutheran Tradition Contribute to Higher Education?," 80.

3. How do you see Christianity (Scripture, theology, or the Christian church) interact with your discipline or vocation in the university? Are these appropriate or inappropriate interactions?

4. How can your discipline or area of the university serve as a handmaiden to the church?

5. What would a university look like—from academics to university vocations to collegiate life—if it fully implemented the educational vision of pursuing wisdom and vocation for freedom and service to society, nature, and church?

2

A GENEALOGY OF LUTHERAN HIGHER EDUCATION

Russell Dawn[1] and Jeff Mallinson[2]

INTRODUCTION

Cultivating *good* students is at the heart of any university's mission. This seems simple enough. But unless one understands an academic institution's genealogy—that is, its history and "genetic" characteristics—faculty, staff, administration, regents, and constituents may unintentionally work at cross purposes, failing to recognize what a good student outcome means to that particular university. Such an unfortunate circumstance occurs when colleagues use the same words about education—like "vocation"—but understand them in different ways. The most deceptively difficult objective to define, however, is the nature of a *good* graduating student. To elucidate the ways Lutheran universities have defined the nature of a good graduating student over the centuries, this chapter will highlight key contours of Lutheran higher educational history from the Reformation to Protestant scholasticism, pietism, liberalism in Europe, and immigrant and recent Lutheran higher education in the United States.

THE REFORMATION

Before he engaged the indulgence controversy and sparked the Protestant Reformation, Martin Luther was a university reformer: he cared not only about cultivating good Christians but also good students. He was dissatisfied with both the content and methods of the scholastic theology that predominated at the University of Wittenberg and elsewhere. His "Disputation against Scholastic Theology" (1517) set forth theses against

---

[1] Russell Dawn, DPhil (Oxford) is Associate Professor of History at CUI.
[2] Jeff Mallinson, DPhil (Oxford) is Associate Professor of Theology at CUI.

not only the theological positions of scholastic theologians (such as the freedom of the will), but also against their methodological tendencies, such as emphasizing syllogistic reasoning over faith, and dependence on Aristotle as opposed to God's grace.[3] The theses were defended by a student in fulfillment of his degree in September of 1517,[4] indicating that Luther's reform of the university's approach to theology into a more biblical, exegetical model was well under way by that time.

The Wittenberg arts curriculum, however, still needed a substantial overhaul. That work began in earnest under a new professor of Greek hired in 1518, one Philip Melanchthon. Over the years, with key moments of reform in 1518, 1523, and 1536, Luther and Melanchthon transformed their university into a model, if an imperfect one, of Lutheran higher education. The Wittenberg approach involved a quest for truth and intellectual formation through the liberal arts (the humanist element) in furtherance of, and in conjunction with, fidelity to Scripture rightly understood according to Reformation principles (the evangelical or Gospel element), all for the purpose or *telos* of preparing students for service to their neighbors (the vocational goal), whether in the church or in the civic realm—the *polis*.[5]

When Melanchthon arrived in Wittenberg at the age of 21, the university's arts curriculum fit squarely within medieval tradition. Coursework centered on Aristotle, as received through the channels of different interpretive schools (inspired, respectively, by Thomas Aquinas, John Duns Scotus, and Gregory of Rimini) and through corrupted Latin translations of Greek texts.[6] Hiring Melanchthon, who had studied at Heidelberg and Tübingen and earned the respect of the great humanist Erasmus, was an important move as part of a wider humanist reconstitution of the curriculum approved by Elector Frederick the Wise.[7] Humanism, in its fifteenth- and sixteenth-century context, was an intellectual and artistic movement that rejected late medieval trends in favor of what the humanists saw as cultural riches from the ancient world. Scholasticism, the then-current philosophical and pedagogical method, so emphasized a pursuit of dialectical logic and its theological and philosophical outcomes that language, the

---

[3] Martin Luther, "Disputation against Scholastic Theology," in AE 31:9–16.

[4] Luther, "Disputation against Scholastic Theology," 6.

[5] For a discussion of the doctrine of vocation and the related teachings of Law and Gospel and two-kingdom theology, see Mueller's chapter.

[6] Jon Steffen Bruss, "Philipp Melanchthon and the 'Poor Roof' of Wittenberg Humanism," *LOGIA* 21, no. 2 (2012): 36.

[7] Marilyn J. Harran, *Martin Luther: Learning for Life* (St. Louis: Concordia, 1997), 144–45.

arts, rhetoric, and the knowledge to be drawn from human experience had, according to the humanists, suffered severe degradation. The humanists viewed their project as the replacement of pedantic scholasticism with the eloquence of classical antiquity. They exchanged layers of commentary on ancient medieval texts, which the scholastics favored as tools of intellectual precision, for the ancient texts themselves. *Ad fontes*, the humanists declared, calling educators back to the original sources. The humanists also replaced poor Latin translations of Greek texts with Greek originals. They replaced theological obscurantism (or, as the scholastics might argue, precision) with poetry, history, and the wisdom of the ancients and of experience.[8]

Less than a week after his arrival, Melanchthon gave his inaugural oration to the university, "On Correcting the Studies of Youth." The tone and emphasis of the speech were undeniably humanistic. He stated, for instance, that "it is your industry, planning and work that are bringing literature out of decay and squalor, in the hope that it may be received everywhere in its natural splendor." He related the history of classical learning in the West, including its loss with the fall of Rome, its preservation by some in Scotland and Ireland, its revival under Charlemagne, and its decline into emphases on commenting, philosophizing, and a "mutilated and mangled" Aristotle to the exclusion of the other ancients. He dwelt on criticisms of the scholastics before enumerating the good aspects of the curriculum at Wittenberg: the "natural and sincere" Aristotle, Quintilian, Pliny, mathematics, poetics, and oratory. Throughout, the focus was on the goodness and importance of humanist learning.[9]

As Lewis Spitz has argued persuasively, Luther himself had a relation to humanism that was both deep and broad. "Not only did Luther have an impressive knowledge of the classics and a keen interest in history," notes Spitz, "but he also savored the use of words."[10] Luther lamented the lack of the proper use of grammar, dialectic, and rhetoric before the reforms began,

---

[8] See Charles G. Nauert Jr., "Humanist Infiltration in the Academic World: Some Studies of Northern Universities," *Renaissance Quarterly* 43, no. 4 (1990): 800, 804–8; Lewis W. Spitz, "Luther and Humanism," in *Luther and Learning: The Wittenberg University Luther Symposium*, ed. Marilyn J. Harran (Selinsgrove, PA: Susquehanna University Press, 1985), 71; and James M. Kittelson, "Luther the Educational Reformer," in *Luther and Learning: The Wittenberg University Luther Symposium*, ed. Marilyn J. Harran (Selinsgrove, PA: Susquehanna University Press, 1985), 97.

[9] Philip Melanchthon, "On Correcting the Studies of Youth," in *A Melanchthon Reader*, ed. Ralph Keen (New York: Peter Lang, 1988), 47–53.

[10] Spitz, "Luther and Humanism," 74, 81. Reprinted by permission of Associated University Presses.

and exclaimed that the "pagans of old, especially the Romans and the Greeks" put the Germans of his age to shame in preparing men for service in civic government.[11]

The humanist leanings of Luther and Melanchthon, the strongly humanistic flavor of the curricular changes being made at the Wittenberg in 1518, and the content of Melanchthon's opening oration have led Timothy Wengert to conclude that Wittenberg's reforms in 1518 were purely humanistic, not evangelical or Gospel-related.[12] Wengert states: "As Heinz Scheible has shown, the reform of the University of Wittenberg in 1518 was simply one more accomplishment of this humanistically-minded young scholar and his coworkers."[13] It was not until 1521–23, says Wengert, that evangelical reform came to the university.

Viewing the curricular changes alone, Wengert is undoubtedly correct. The university added professorships in Hebrew and Greek, and around this time Luther boasted that they had lectures on Pliny and Quintilian and cut back on the time spent on Aristotle, Petrus Hispanus, and the commentators on Peter Lombard's *Sentences*. Moreover, the clearly evangelical nature of later reforms accentuates just how humanistic these earliest reforms were.[14] Granting all this, Wengert's conclusion all but ignores the evangelical impetus visible behind the humanistic changes. In his inaugural speech, Melanchthon waxed:

> In what truly pertains to the sacred, consider particularly how it refers to the spirit. For if, as a class of studies, the sacred things are the most powerful for the mind, work and care are necessary. For the odor of the ointments of the Lord is far sweeter than the aromas of the human disciplines: with the spirit as leader, and the cult of our arts as ally, we may approach the holy. Just as Synesius writes to Herculianus: when it

---

[11] Luther, "Ecclesiastes, Song of Solomon, and Last Words of David, 2 Samuel 23:1–7," in AE 15:202 and Luther, "To the Councilmen of All Cities in Germany that They Establish and Maintain Christian Schools," in AE 45:367.

[12] The term *evangelical* in its Reformation context referred to the teachings of Scripture, and specifically those regarding the Gospel and its relationship to the Law, as understood by Luther and those of like mind. Today's sub-category of Protestantism known as "Evangelicalism" is historically and theologically connected to the original evangelicalism, but only tenuously.

[13] Timothy J. Wengert, "Higher Education and Vocation: The University of Wittenberg (1517–1533) between Renaissance and Reform," in *The Lutheran Doctrine of Vocation*, ed. John A. Maxfield (St. Louis: Concordia Historical Institute, 2008), 3. Reprinted by permission of Concordia Historical Institute.

[14] Wengert, "Higher Education and Vocation," 3–10.

is healthy, in good spirits, and well practiced, philosophy is admirably used in pursuit of the divine.[15]

Melanchthon here acknowledged that the liberal arts ultimately serve the Gospel. As Walter Rüegg asserts, Melanchthon's main idea in this address was "to seek out in the ancient authors the sources of the *artes*, and to seek out in the Bible and in the writings of the church fathers the sources of theology."[16] Although certainly humanistic, this idea was not purely pedagogical. Humanism was the tool, the Gospel was the *telos*.

The centrality of the Gospel in university reforms was even clearer in Luther. His "Disputation against Scholastic Theology" of 1517 contained clear and repeated pronouncements of the Gospel, indeed far more so than the famous Ninety-five Theses, and blasphemy was among the things he hoped he would see decline in the university.[17] By 1520, the relationships among humanism, the Gospel, and vocation began to take shape in Luther's writings, and by 1524 they were fully formed. In his letter "To the Christian Nobility of the German Nation Concerning the Reform of the Christian Estate" (1520) he stated: "The universities, too, need a good, thorough reformation. I must say that, no matter whom it annoys. Everything the papacy has instituted and ordered serves only to increase sin and error." He viewed university reform as of crucial importance: "Actually a great deal depends on it, for it is here in the universities that the Christian youth and our nobility, with whom the future of Christendom lies, will be educated and trained." The reforms of which he spoke were both humanistic and evangelical, and the reasons they were so critical had to do with "training young people to speak and to preach properly" for the good of both state and church. Still, for Luther the Scriptures were at the center of education at all levels: "I would advise no one to send his child where the Holy Scriptures are not supreme. Every institution that does not unceasingly pursue the study of God's word becomes corrupt."[18] Drawing together the strands of these quotations from 1520, one can see that Luther advocated the liberal arts for young nobles and Christians for the sake of better speaking (a civic need) and preaching (an ecclesiastical need). He also advocated evangelical teaching in order to avoid corruption of the orthodox faith. Thus, a good

---

[15] Melanchthon, "On Correcting the Studies of Youth," 54–55.

[16] Walter Rüegg, "Themes," in *Universities in Early Modern Europe (1500–1800)*, vol. 2 of *A History of the University in Europe*, ed. Walter Rüegg (Cambridge: Cambridge University Press, 1996), 38.

[17] See Wengert, "Higher Education and Vocation," 5.

[18] Martin Luther, "To the Christian Nobility of the German Nation Concerning the Reform of the Christian Estate," in AE 44:200–202, 205–7.

student was able to engage the world effectively, share the Gospel appropriately, and avoid theological error discerningly.

Then, four years later, Luther wrote with clarity and concision regarding the connections among the liberal arts, the Gospel, and civic or ecclesiastical vocations. He taught that the study of languages and the arts "are greater ornament, profit, glory, and benefit, both for the understanding of Holy Scripture and the conduct of temporal government." Elaborating specifically on the study of languages, he continued: "Although the gospel came and still comes to us through the Holy Spirit alone, we cannot deny that it came through the medium of languages, spread abroad by that means, and must be preserved by the same means. . . . Hence, it is inevitable that unless the languages remain, the gospel must finally perish."[19] In short, Luther saw humanistic learning as needed for the Gospel, and both the liberal arts and the Gospel as required in a university education so that good students go on to meet the vocational needs of society.

From the beginning Luther held to both humanistic and evangelical ideals, and it appears that, as Luther clarified in his own writing the connections between them and the goal of preparing people to serve their neighbors through various vocations, so he also came to privilege the evangelical ideal over the humanistic in university education.[20] Thus, Spitz aptly describes Luther's humanistic evangelicalism: "Just as he considered the Renaissance to be a John the Baptist pointing to the coming evangelical revival, so he himself used the new tools of humanist learning in behalf of the gospel."[21]

Although throughout his life Melanchthon remained more favorable toward humanism than Luther was, Melanchthon also increasingly emphasized biblical teaching and the Gospel as he matured. Thus, writing in 1543, Melanchthon noted that for understanding and expounding Scripture, defending the faith, explicating the major controversies throughout the history of the church, and understanding and explaining Christian prayer and what distinguishes it from non-Christian prayer, one needs erudition, including knowledge of the "good arts." In sum, Melanchthon said, "God wants the Scriptures and the good arts to be always fostered in the Church," and "the preservation and spreading of learning is the highest of all human achievements." In his perspective, the good arts included "the sacred books,

---

[19] Luther, "To the Councilmen of All Cities in Germany," in AE 45:358–60.

[20] See discussions in Kittelson, "Luther the Educational Reformer," 99–100; Wengert, "Higher Education and Vocation," 6; and Thomas Korcok, *Lutheran Education: From Wittenberg to the Future* (St. Louis: Concordia 2011), 52–54.

[21] Spitz, "Luther and Humanism," 88.

but also the art of disputation, fluent speech and a knowledge of history, antiquity and judgments of the past."[22] Jon Bruss goes so far as to assert that the heart of Melanchthon's humanist program is found in the distinction between Law and Gospel. Bruss explains Melanchthon's distinction thus:

> In God's world, if I want to read the Greek New Testament, I have to learn Greek, and speaking persuasively requires me to know the precepts of rhetoric. Through all of these things, God brings blessings. Through the gospel, God grants eternal blessing, the forgiveness of sins, salvation, and eternal life. Through the law, his ordinances, and philosophy, he brings about the realization of human intellectual potential, good for one's neighbor, and good for one through one's neighbor; and he grants a certain depth of understanding of his workings in this realm, of goods, and of means and ends.[23]

In this way, Luther's doctrine of vocation and the distinction between Law and Gospel are related. God uses the liberal arts in furtherance of both the Gospel—the forgiveness of sins—and the Law—the carrying out of human vocations in service to others.

Melanchthon and Luther continued reforming the University of Wittenberg over the years. For instance, when, during Luther's exile at the Wartburg after the Diet of Worms, Karlstadt fueled an anti-intellectual fervor that threatened the university's very existence, Luther risked his life to return to Wittenberg in 1522 and guide the city back onto course in liberal learning and in faith in God's Word. Luther also showed both his commitment to the truth and authority of Scripture and his intellectual humility by allowing Copernican astronomy to be part of Wittenberg's academic conversation, even though he distrusted it. Melanchthon, meanwhile, became one of the most influential individuals in all of German education, more influential even than Luther. Among other achievements, he oversaw the founding of the University of Marburg in 1529 and influenced reforms there and at older universities such as Tübingen, Heidelberg, and Strasbourg. He also wrote widely-used textbooks and created a school curriculum that was utilized all over Germany.[24] In Clyde Manschreck's

---

[22] Philip Melanchthon, "On the Role of the Schools," in *Orations on Philosophy and Education*, ed. Sachiko Kusukawa, trans. Christine F. Salazar (Cambridge: Cambridge University Press, 1999), 16–19.

[23] Bruss, "Philipp Melanchthon and the 'Poor Roof' of Wittenberg Humanism," 33–34.

[24] Harran, *Martin Luther*, 252; Günter R. Schmidt, "Foundations of Melanchthon's Views on Education," in *Luther and Melanchthon in the Educational Thought of Central and Eastern Europe*, eds. Reinhard Golz and Wolfgang Mayrhofer (Münster: Lit, 1998), 16; and Olaf Pedersen, "Tradition and Innovation," in *Universities in Early*

words, when Melanchthon died in 1560, "there was hardly a city in Germany which did not have a teacher who had been trained by him. The influence thus exerted by Melanchthon on secondary and higher education in Germany is beyond estimate."[25] It is little wonder he became known as *Praeceptor Germaniae*, "Teacher of Germany." In addition, reform spread indirectly from Wittenberg's influence, not just directly through Melanchthon's efforts. Moreover, all men seeking evangelical ordination had to pass an examination at Wittenberg, making the university enormously influential over the churches in Lutheran Germany.[26] As Paul Grendler remarks, "Wittenberg was the most important university of the Protestant Reformation by a wide margin."[27] In sum, Luther's and Melanchthon's emphases on humanism for the sake of the Gospel, and on humanism and the Gospel together for the sake of preparing good graduating students to be humble but courageous servants in civic and ecclesiastical vocations, spread from Wittenberg to the rest of Lutheran Germany.

PROTESTANT SCHOLASTICISM

Popular narratives about the intellectual shift from the era of Reformation humanism to the era of Protestant scholasticism often overstate the incongruities between the core theologies of each era. Simplistic divisions here are not helpful, and many recent, serious scholars argue that there is more continuity between the sixteenth and seventeenth centuries than was previously assumed.[28] Scholasticism is a method, not a commitment to a particular philosopher or conception of the core of theology. It is essentially a rigorous method of executing the task of higher education. Nonetheless, methods matter and affect any academic ethos. Thus, several important pedagogical shifts indeed took place as confessionally-rooted academies defined the unique educational and

---

Modern Europe (1500–1800), vol. 2 of *A History of the University in Europe*, ed. Walter Rüegg (Cambridge: Cambridge University Press, 1996), 462. See also discussion of Melanchthon's influence on the University of Tübingen in Susan Mobley, "Making a University Lutheran: Philipp Melanchthon and the Reform of the University of Tübingen in the 1530s," *LOGIA* 21, no. 2 (2012): 41–45.

25 Clyde Manschreck, "The Bible in Melanchthon's Philosophy of Education," *Journal of Bible and Religion* 23, no. 3 (1955): 203.

26 Harran, *Martin Luther*, 250 and Kittelson, "Luther the Educational Reformer," 98.

27 Paul F. Grendler, "The Universities of the Renaissance and Reformation," *Renaissance Quarterly* 57, no. 1 (2004): 20. Reprinted by permission of the University of Chicago Press.

28 See Carl R. Trueman and R. Scott Clark, eds., *Protestant Scholasticism: Essays in Reassessment* (Carlisle, Cumbria: Paternoster, 1999).

theological structures of Lutheran and Reformed thought. All of this mirrored an increased interest in reason and science throughout European universities, with a corresponding decreased emphasis on rhetoric, common to other disciplines within European universities. Likewise, increasingly scholastic methods within theology faculties were part of a larger phenomenon in European universities: specialization. Whatever the downsides of this turn of events, this trend toward specialization arguably "made the German universities the greatest in the world" and later became an important aspect of the American university, which melded the British collegiate and German university approaches to higher education.[29]

The academic progeny of Luther and Melanchthon became increasingly scholastic in their writing and teaching style in the century after the Reformation. Nevertheless, it is important to note that, despite Luther's vitriolic statements against the late medieval scholastics of his own educational experience, he turned to scholastic distinctions when the situation required them. As D. V. N. Bagchi observes:

> It is evident that Luther saw no conflict between good theology and good logic: rather, scholastic theology was poor because it was based on poor logic. Again, we can say that Luther's use of the scholastic method as an antidote to scholastic theology was meant seriously, not ironically. We may conclude that while *theologia scholastica* [scholastic theology] was always to be opposed to the *theologia crucis* [theology of the cross], the *modus loquendi scholasticus* [the scholastic way of speaking] was not always for Luther contrary to the *modus loquendi theologicus* [theological way of speaking]. Far more important than method was content, context, and motive.[30]

The structure of Luther's thought was influenced early on by certain aspects of William of Ockham's (ca. 1287–1347) philosophy.[31] In particular, one

---

[29] Donald Matthew Mackenzie and Manning Mason Pattillo, *Church-sponsored Higher Education in the United States: Report of Danforth Commission* (Washington DC: American Council on Education, 1966), 9–10.

[30] D. V. N. Bagchi, "Sic et Non: Luther and Scholasticism," in *Protestant Scholasticism: Essays in Reassessment*, eds. Carl R. Trueman and R. Scott Clark (Carlisle, Cumbria: Paternoster, 1999), 14.

[31] Luther's tolerance of Copernican thought mentioned above and Melanchthon's penchant for astrology are both examples of how Luther's Ockhamism played out in the life of the academy. Ockham's approach to knowledge, unlike that of the medieval Thomists, did not emphasize the importance of systematizing knowledge. Thus, there was a greater tolerance for anomalous data (like they were getting from the

sees this when Luther calls reason the "Devil's Whore;" this was not a call for anti-intellectualism, but a rejection of rationalism in favor of attention to the empirical world, and a rejection of speculation about divine mysteries and ways of obtaining salvation in favor of attention to knowledge at the foot of the cross.[32] These observations, coupled with his willingness to teach on Aristotle's *Nicomachean Ethics* and comfort with Aristotelian logic within the classroom suggests that many of his key concerns were with a particular Aristotelian addiction that led to speculative doctrines within late medieval theology, such as the doctrine of transubstantiation.

With this in mind, Luther's successors demonstrated little hesitation in consolidating and defining earlier teachings in the arts and theology in increasingly scholastic ways. During this period of scholasticism, polymaths might still exist within faculties, but an academic career increasingly required rigorous precision within one's primary field. The shift to scholasticism involved an ethos in which eloquence—so prized by the humanists—gave way to polemic needs. Thus, good Lutheran students were those who learned how to distinguish their position from, and defend it against, Catholic Reformation and Reformed opposition. The seventeenth century, therefore, was not considered an appropriate time for innovation, according to scholastic minds. It was a time for detailed consolidation. While this was different from the universal aspirations of the early medieval centers, which worked for the good of the whole Christian community, and the Renaissance humanists, who worked for the good of the whole intellectual community, scholasticism's emphasis on specialization and a local confessional identity mirrors late medieval shifts.

On the eve of the Reformation, higher learning had already begun to focus on the interests of local ecclesial or magisterial authorities. Likewise, in the century after the Reformation, universities responded to the needs of the local civil community and its particular confessional identity by defining good students as those who could serve their sponsoring community.[33] In practical terms, this meant that secular and church authorities wanted university faculty in their region to spend less time thinking freely and cre-

---

astronomers) and a corresponding tolerance for fringe ideas (like astrology) because empirical research promised to weed out and defeat sloppy thinking.

[32] David Andersen, *Martin Luther, the Problem of Faith and Reason: A Re-examination in Light of the Epistemological and Christological Issues* (Eugene, OR: Wipf and Stock, 2012).

[33] For more insight on the importance of authority structures and the nature of European universities, see Notker Hammerstein, "Relations with Authority," in *Universities in Early Modern Europe (1500–1800)*, vol. 2 of *A History of the University in Europe*, ed. Walter Rüegg (Cambridge: Cambridge University Press, 1996), 113–53.

atively about various ideas, and more time focusing on solidifying and articulating the ideas of their national and religious traditions. Notker Hammerstein explains this phenomenon well:

> As political and religious matters were not conceived of separately in the sixteenth and seventeenth centuries, but rather as "corresponding forms of social existence," it was inevitable that opposing attempts to influence or to determine different answers to leading questions might not complement one another or exist concurrently. The answers might become confused or they might lead to conflict. Even in places where universities and schools were regarded as an affair of the state—as for example in the Lutheran or Anglican Churches—there was never any guarantee that the ecclesiastical authorities would abstain from intervention or avoid competition with secular governments.[34]

In other words, the Protestant shift in emphasis to orthodoxy and scholastic formulations had a distinctly practical reason for being. Protestant scholasticism was not simply a shift in temperament amongst scholars themselves, and it was not a betrayal of the original, invigorating message of the Reformers. It was arguably a response to the contextual demands for a clear identity.

Another important external factor that led to Protestant scholasticism was the rising importance of the Society of Jesus, or Jesuits. During the Renaissance and Reformation, emerging middle class families might look to humanist tutors for their children. Many of these tutors joined the evangelical cause and influenced their students with evangelical teaching. In response, the Catholic Reformation relied on Jesuit scholars, who followed Ignatius of Loyola (1491–1556) in thinking of their vocation as intellectual soldiers. Their strong tradition of scholarly training provided an alternative to the Protestant humanists' scholarship. Their polemic against the new evangelical thinkers required evangelical universities to bone up on logic, debate, and theological precision.[35]

---

[34] Hammerstein, "Relations with Authority," 119.

[35] Thus, a chief exemplar of Lutheran scholasticism, Martin Chemnitz (1522–86), wrote his famous criticism of Catholic Reformation ideas, *Examen Concilii Tridentini* (1565–73), in response to obvious contemporary ideological conflict, not as the perfect articulation of Christian theology for all time. Another key representative of this scholastic trajectory was Johann Gerhard (1582–1637), who followed the structure of Melanchthon's *Loci Communes*, but sought to provide more technical sophistication to the elaboration and defense of these ideas for his polemical age. This bolstered theology was necessary in the face of Catholic Reformation challenges.

North of the Reformation's "ground zero" in Germany, Scandinavian Lutheran institutions were not as homogenous as those nearer to Wittenberg, and scholastic methodology was unevenly adopted in their universities. Nonetheless, some places, like Swedish schools overseen by monarch, orthodox Lutheran, and military genius Gustavus Adolphus (1594–1632), encouraged service to the state and Lutheran cause through education that reflected the methodologies of orthodox centers in Germany. Even so, the subsequent burst of Scandinavian pietism reversed some of these emphases, eventually leading to key differences between Scandinavian and German immigrant higher education in nineteenth- and twentieth-century Lutheran schools in the United States.

Eventually, the Enlightenment challenged the pedagogy of Protestant scholasticism. Institutions like the University of Halle—founded in the early 1690s as an alternative to the orthodox scholastic Lutheran centers—shifted their mission from consolidating core theological positions to rational and scientific thought.[36] Nevertheless, universities that operated in both the scholastic and Enlightenment modes shared a common social purpose: to bring unity to a local community in the midst of intellectual and cultural disunity. For the scholastics, this meant doctrinal unity that settled confessional conflicts through clearly articulated orthodox dogmatics. For Enlightenment scholars, this meant cultural unity that settled inter-religious conflicts through an appeal to universal reason. In both cases, scholars responded to the needs and desires of sponsoring authorities—whether church or state—to bring settlement and firm articulation of divi-sive matters. In both cases, a good student was one who could specialize, articulate, distinguish, and defend a true position from falsehood. Both highly prized logic and the intellect. The difference was that the scholastics thought that supernatural revelation ought to be included in the range of subjects a scholar could investigate, whereas Enlightenment rationalists increasingly took methodological atheism to be essential to good scholar-ship.

RESPONSES TO THE ENLIGHTENMENT:
PIETISM AND LIBERALISM

Pietism, as a movement, initially involved a turning away from what the Pietists saw as a dead orthodoxy that was coupled with disciplinary hairsplitting within scholastic theological education. Leading Pietists called

---

[36] Halle also became an important center for Pietist thought that would influence early Lutheran immigrant intellectual traditions in America.

on the church and its schools to cultivate lives of devotion, prayer, personal biblical study, and individual morality. Meanwhile, they were skeptical about Enlightenment confidence in unaided reason. They were also ambivalent about academic and church hierarchies, and, in many cases, were anticlerical.

While there were many representatives and varieties of this Pietist spirit, Philipp Jakob Spener (1635–1705) provides the best example of how this affected Lutheran education. In his *Pia Desideria* (1675), Spener provided clear instructions regarding the kind of good student professors should encourage. He argued that Christian teachers should publicly discourage students who were studious but lacked piety, and that they should praise students who, even when lacking in academic aptitude, demonstrated spiritual and moral uprightness. Spener writes:

> It would be especially helpful if professors would pay attention to the life as well as the studies of the students entrusted to them and would from time to time speak to those who need to be spoken to. The professors should act in such a way toward those students who, although they distinguish themselves in studying, also distinguish themselves in riotous living, tippling, bragging, and boasting of academic and other pre-eminence . . . that they must perceive that because of their behavior they are looked down upon by their teachers, that their splendid talents and good academic record do not help by themselves, and that they are regarded as persons who will do harm in proportion to the gifts they receive. On the other hand, the professors should openly and expressly show those who lead a godly life, even if they are behind the others in their studies, how dear they are to their teachers and how very much they are to be preferred to the others. In fact, these ought to be the first, or the only students to be promoted. The others ought to be excluded from all hope of promotion until they change their manner of life completely.[37]

While leaders in all Lutheran universities might agree with certain aspects of these sentiments, Spener's ideas here arguably led to the unintended consequence of an ethos of anti-intellectualism coupled with an emphasis on moral correctness and party-line approaches to devotion, at least in the theological disciplines.

If it is uncharitable to assert that the Pietists were anti-intellectual, it is perhaps easier to defend the thesis that they moved toward a greater em-

---

[37] Philipp Jakob Spener, *Pia Desideria* (Philadelphia: Fortress, 1964), 107–8.

phasis on practical issues. Thomas Korcok rightly connects this emphasis on the practical to the Pietist theological approach to work in general:

> Work, in the sense of one's occupation, was more often understood as a duty or spiritual obligation that was owed to God by the redeemed sinner. It was the means by which prosperity came to God's kingdom. In classical Pietist thinking, idleness was sinful and diligence was holy. With this theological elevation of work as a godly duty, the Pietists structured their educational model with the goal of building a strong work ethic in the lives of their pupils.[38]

This thinking brought into Lutheran higher education two competing emphases related to the good student: one group wanted to focus on inculcating personal values while the other wanted to focus on cognitive apprehension and sophistication in each subject matter. These divergent impulses affect the very conception of an educator's vocation, especially when it comes to assessing students.[39]

Few American Lutheran trajectories rejected all Pietist emphases. Even Missouri Synod institutions maintained an interest in a life of worship, prayer, and personal biblical study, especially when compared to contemporary institutions in the old country. Moreover, many Lutherans resonated with the philosophical criticism of the Enlightenment found in the Christian existentialism of Dane Søren Kierkegaard (1813–55) and Radical Pietists such as Johann Georg Hamann (1730–88) and Friedrich Heinrich Jacobi (1743–1819), who recognized the importance of subjectivity in language and epistemology and believed Enlightenment thought was perilously reductionistic and nihilistic.[40] For instance, despite the clearly confessional stance of the German-American dogmaticians Francis Pieper (1852–1931) and J. T. Mueller (1885–1967), they demonstrate deep suspicions regarding modern thought and share a kind of fideism, or resistance to the idea that the Christian faith could be demonstrated through evidential apologetics. For Mueller, "Christian apologetics has therefore only one function: it is to show the unreasonableness of unbelief. Never can it

---

[38] Korcok, *Lutheran Education*, 106.

[39] For example, see Taylor's chapter for ways in which confusing the two kingdoms hinders a professor's appropriate vocation, especially when grading student papers or being called to enforce tough academic standards on sweet, but underperforming, students.

[40] See John Milbank, "Knowledge: The Theological Critique of Philosophy in Hamann and Jacobi," in *Radical Orthodoxy: A New Theology*, eds. John Milbank, Catherine Pickstock, and Graham Ward (London: Routledge, 1999), 21–37.

demonstrate the truth with 'enticing words of man's wisdom.' "[41] Theology was about learning to preach the Gospel properly; it was not about demonstrating Christianity's truth, which was something the Holy Spirit validated as Scripture was preached. This sentiment, while certainly concerned with cognitive content, put study of the faith into the curriculum in a way that was intentionally practical for future preachers and lay leaders (something the Pietists wanted), not intensely academic and never speculative.

A typical orthodox Lutheran response to the Enlightenment—when nominal Lutherans themselves were not leading the Enlightenment charge—was not to emphasize the importance of a rational mind, but to allow the secular sciences to run their course as Lutheran educators cultivated a religion of the heart and hands. In other words, Lutherans often responded to intellectual challenges by removing themselves from the conversation. This response did not involve a rejection of the advances of reason and natural philosophy so much as it set a separate course for theology, allowing faculty members in non-theological disciplines to go about their business, relatively unconcerned with the problems created by modernism.

Thus, while they certainly had their ideological differences, Pietist and liberal Lutherans in the eighteenth and nineteenth centuries shared an interest in experience and emotion. More precisely, one might think of the spectrum in the era's Lutheran educators as Pietists of the right (low-church, somewhat anti-intellectual types) and Pietists of the left (usually more academically sophisticated scholars who granted the legitimacy of Enlightenment science and biblical criticism, but turned toward more emotive ways of expressing theology). An exemplar of the latter approach is Friedrich Schleiermacher (1768–1834), son of a Reformed Chaplain, higher critic of the Bible, and founder of a kind of romantic liberalism that emphasized a feeling of dependence upon God, rather than cognitive propositions about theology. It is more than a coincidence that Schleiermacher emerged from the University of Halle, a former center of Pietist theology. For Pietists and liberals, ethics and personal behavior were the most important Christian aspects of student formation. For Pietists of the right, this meant a disciplined life of prayer, moral behavior, and devotional biblical study. For Pietists of the left, this meant attention to the aesthetic and experiential qualities of religious life, coupled with an emphasis on ethical principles taught by Jesus, but accessible to all reasonable people.

What is important for the present investigation is that, in both cases, cognitive and dogmatic education became de-emphasized. James Burtchaell

---

[41] John T. Mueller, *Christian Dogmatics: A Handbook of Doctrinal Theology for Pastors, Teachers, and Laymen* (St. Louis: Concordia, 1955), 71.

rightly notes the similarities between the Pietists and liberals when he explains that "[the] direct disciples of the Piestists were the liberals, whose reductive pieties were a midway stage between Pietism and Rationalism."[42] Korcok helps relate and differentiate Pietist, liberal, and orthodox models for Lutheran education by the dawn of the twentieth century:

> Both Pietism and rationalism [liberalism] emphasized works done in service to mankind. For the Pietists this emphasis, which was rooted in the inner spiritual renewal of the individual, found its fullest expression in the establishment of hospitals, orphanages and schools. For the rationalists, this emphasis which was rooted in the desire to achieve a more practical form of Christianity, sought to improve the physical well-being of the individual through communal reform. However, according to the Confessional [orthodox] Lutherans, both theologies resulted in a theology based on works, and both allowed for the participation of the individual in coming to faith.[43]

Whatever a group's response to the Enlightenment, Lutheran education that emphasized faithful doctrinal teaching—within a strong liberal arts tradition—lost ground within the mainstream intellectual conversation during the centuries that followed.

Some Roman Catholic scholars have argued that this *de facto* secularization of Lutheran higher education was the natural result of the Lutheran doctrines of the two kingdoms and vocation. They suggest that by separating sacred from secular thought, the non-theological disciplines ran off on their own trajectory without reference to theological reflection, while theology itself became divorced from the proven methodologies of the academic disciplines.[44] If this is a Roman Catholic misreading of the Lutheran understanding of the relationship between God's two kingdoms and vocation (and we think it is), it seems to have been a misunderstanding shared by the Pietists and liberals too. If nothing else, it became the ostensible way to carve out space for Christian thought in an increasingly secular academic landscape. In more nefarious ways, it seems to have been a tool for duplicitous undermining of Lutheran identity in the name of vocation and two kingdoms theology. The eventual result in many American Lutheran uni-

---

[42] James T. Burtchaell, *The Dying of the Light: The Disengagement of Colleges and Universities from Their Christian Churches* (Grand Rapids: Eerdmans, 1998), 463.

[43] Korcok, *Lutheran Education*, 101.

[44] See John C. Haughey, ed., *Revisiting the Idea of Vocation: Theological Explorations* (Washington DC: Catholic University of America Press, 2004).

versities was a drift either toward unfettered academic freedom and secularity, or a culturally disengaged and anti-intellectual ethos.

IMMIGRANT HIGHER EDUCATION IN THE UNITED STATES

Early American religion's major players had English DNA. Anglicans, Presbyterians, Congregationalists, Baptists, and eventually Wesleyans dominated the scene and established most of the first universities. Like these early Anglophone institutions, later nineteenth-century institutions, founded by Scandinavian, Dutch, and German immigrants, arose from necessity. It was also natural to create church-related universities on American soil, especially after 1819 when the Supreme Court ruled that private institutions should not have any interference from the states.[45] What immigrants needed were institutions that could train teachers and pastors. Thus, many immigrant churches, having cut loose from the old world's hierarchies, universities, and seminaries, asserted an obligation to support schools and higher education in their founding documents. The Lutheran concept of two interrelated but distinct kingdoms seemed to be a natural fit for private, religious higher education within the United States. Immigrant Lutherans also used this opportunity to cultivate a thriving but cohesive presence in America. Even though the original impetus for investment in education was to prepare qualified teachers and clergy, the Lutheran perspective on education, coupled with the secularizing trajectory of state-sponsored universities, soon led to an emphasis on liberal arts education for various young adults in emerging communities. Knute Lee describes the rationale for this move well:

> From early times a liberal arts education was considered a prerequisite for more specialized theological seminary training. Given the priesthood-of-all-believers principle, the same general higher education in the liberal arts was seen as valid for both clergy and laity. So some of the schools founded as seminaries to educate pastors either branched into two institutions, or simply became liberal arts colleges.[46]

To understand the history of American Lutheran education, it is important to trace both Scandinavian and German immigrant institutions, noting their distinct trajectories along the way.

---

[45] Mackenzie and Pattillo, *Church-sponsored Higher Education in the United States*, 5.

[46] Knute Lee, "Establishing Lutheran Colleges in the United States," *Concordia Historical Institute Quarterly* 46, no. 1 (1973): 21. Reprinted by permission of Concordia Historical Institute.

The first major development of an American Lutheran presence came from the work of Henry Melchior Muhlenberg (1711–87), who was influenced by pietism through theologian August Hermann Franke (1663–1727) and his intellectual circles at the University of Halle. The brand of American Lutheranism he helped establish eventually led to the founding of Gettysburg Seminary (1826) and College (1832), under the leadership of Samuel S. Schmucker (1799–1873). Subsequently, two additional, competing impulses manifested. As Ernest Simmons observes, some who thought Gettysburg was too formal and confessional founded Susquehanna University (1858); those who thought it was not confessional enough, including Henry Melchior's great-grandson Frederick A. Muhlenberg, founded Muhlenberg College (1848).[47] These competing trajectories became even more apparent with the emergence of schools founded by the Missouri Synod Lutherans.

One complicating factor in the immigrant Lutheran educational experience is the deep but underappreciated influence of Nicolaj Frederik Severin Grundtvig (1783–1872) on Danish Lutheran education. His *Folkehøjskole* or folk-school movement stood out as representing, in Denmark, the "happy Lutherans" as opposed to the stern ethos of the Pietists. But it was no stale rationalist religion. Grundtvig opposed Enlightenment hubris, but did not resort to anti-intellectualism. During and after his theological studies at the University of Copenhagen, he encountered a personal crisis of faith in the face of liberal biblical criticism, and returned to a form of historical Christianity. Like the Pietists, he downplayed dogmatics, but insisted on the importance of the Bible, audible confession of the creed within the schools (since the spoken word was a living word and the spoken creedal pronouncements concerning Christ defined the Christian community), and an approach to history that tells a coherent, biblically-informed story from creation to the present. Grundtvig's vision for education served rural students and included programming for older adults, thus making him a forerunner of non-traditional higher education in Europe. He was interested in a kind of great-books curriculum, but one that downplayed the Roman elements of the Western canon in favor of Nordic mythology, Scandinavian languages, and Greek (but not Latin). It also downplayed the importance of books themselves. He emphasized oral presentations, discouraging the traditional emphasis on note taking and essay examinations. Perhaps due to the rise of common accreditation standards in America, non-traditional Grundtvigian education did not sur-

---

[47] Ernest L. Simmons, *Lutheran Higher Education: An Introduction* (Minneapolis: Augsburg Fortress, 1998), 18.

vive in its original form. But its emphases are worth noting since they had vestigial effects on Danish approaches to liberal arts education. Richard Solberg describes this as follows:

> Contrary to the rising emphasis upon the practical and vocational in both secondary and higher education [the Grundtvigians] sought instead to introduce students to great ideas and personalities in history and literature and thereby to awaken both mind and spirit. Rather than books and recitations they made extensive use of the lecture as a means of instruction. They set no examinations, established no grades, awarded no diplomas.[48]

For Grundtvig, the value of the liberal arts rested in its ability to infuse practical life with what he called *spirit*, which sought to cultivate a sense of wonder and help students break free from a mechanical and reductionistic understanding common to secular education. A good student outcome was one that enlivened students to live richly and virtuously; it endeavored to produce students who were neither rigid like the Pietists nor full of facts like the scholastics. Grundtvigians believed so strongly in the enriching aspects of a liberal arts experience that the tangible outcomes of education, in terms of status and a certificate, seemed irrelevant enough to ignore altogether. Many Danish Lutheran elementary schools in the Midwest reflected Grundtvig's pedagogy and differed somewhat from the Norwegian Pietist schools. His influence on collegiate-level education was felt in Danish Lutheran colleges and in some aspects of the Lutheran Bible Institute's curricula and structure.[49]

A shorthand approach to understanding the history of American Lutheran universities might cause one to think in terms of a Pietist Scandinavian track (leading to pietism and liberalism) and a German confessional track (contributing more doctrinally-focused and conservative approaches to theology). Grundtvig disrupts this neat categorization. Moreover, confessional Scandinavians founded colleges too. As Simmons notes, "among the Norwegian Lutherans there were those who emphasized confessional and liturgical matters." Despite political complexities within Norwegian

---

[48] Richard W. Solberg, *Lutheran Higher Education in North America* (Minneapolis: Augsburg, 1985), 253.

[49] On Grundtvig, see Charles A. Hawley, "Grundtvig and Danish Theological Education in the Middle West," *Church History* 9, no. 4 (1940): 299–304; Jindra Kulich, "The Danish Folk High School: Can It Be Transplanted: The Success and Failure of the Danish Folk High School at Home and Abroad," *International Review of Education* 10, no. 4 (1964): 417–30; and Ernest D. Nielsen, *N. F. S. Grundtvig: An American Study* (Rock Island, IL: Augustana, 1955).

Lutheranism and its merging of moderate and Pietistic, low-church groups, their colleges typically sought "to preserve the values of church and ethnic family while preparing students for effective leadership in a new land."[50] Therefore, simplistic characterizations of the nature of Lutheran education in the United States fail to account for the historical evidence. Likewise, while the Missouri Synod universities are the most noticeable specimens of the German approach, even their histories involved encounters with pietism. Perhaps, then, it is best to distinguish schools that became part of the Evangelical Lutheran Church in America (ELCA) university family from those who ended up in the Lutheran Church—Missouri Synod (LCMS) fold (with the two independent Lutheran institutions, Valparaiso University and Trinity Lutheran College, standing out as pan-Lutheran exceptions to the rule). The ELCA universities tend to end up on some point within the Pietist-liberal spectrum, while the LCMS universities tend to emphasize the confessional, doctrinal aspects of Lutheranism.

Despite the shifting allegiances and relationships to the Lutheran Confessions throughout American Lutheran history, the easiest way to understand the differing trajectories is to ask about the kind of *good* students universities sought to cultivate. It is not immediately clear whether maintaining piety or confessional identity is an easier task for an American private institution. Indeed, American university life by the end of the 1960s became virtually synonymous with both hedonism (as opposed to piety) and free thought (as opposed to confessional orthodoxy). Nonetheless, it seems that for institutions that became affiliated with the ELCA, moral standards were easier to apply than doctrinal purity, especially given their diverse intellectual lineages. These identifying standards could be prohibitions on dancing and alcohol (which continued into the second half of the twentieth century at places like Pacific Lutheran University, alongside liberal theology and modern biblical criticism), or—more recently—emphases on social justice, vocation, and ecology. Either way, emphasis was placed on ethical citizenship in God's kingdom of the left rather than on protecting confessional standards. Institutions associated with the LCMS, on the other hand, did not neglect student character, but were far more concerned with confessional identity.

The history of the LCMS universities helps explain why German Lutheran institutions tended to emphasize confessional and doctrinal identity over pietism. In 1817, Prussian King Frederick William III, inspired by nationalist fervor, honored the three hundredth anniversary of the start of the Reformation by announcing a new national church that would be a

---

[50] Simmons, *Lutheran Higher Education*, 19–20.

union of the Lutheran and Reformed churches in Prussia. Confessional Lutherans—those for whom fidelity to the Scriptures as expounded by the unaltered, sixteenth-century Augsburg Confession and Formula of Concord was a *sine qua non* of the faith—resisted. Many faithful pastors suffered arrest rather than use the approved Union liturgy in the divine service. In the neighboring German state of Saxony, confessional Lutherans, already deeply concerned about Rationalism's profound weakening of the German church, feared similar enforced union in their churches. They were also deeply concerned about the rationalist education their children were receiving. Moreover, there was a perception within the group, fueled by the 1837 arrest and suspension of Pastor Martin Stephan, that they were being persecuted by the civil and religious authorities. Tapping into a trend of emigration that would see an exodus of some fifty million Europeans to points around the world by the time of World War I, Stephan organized a group of around seven hundred Lutherans who sought to emigrate to the United States or Australia to form a faithful, German-speaking community. The group pooled their finances and settled on Missouri as their destination. They eventually purchased land in Perry County, south of St. Louis, and began to settle there in the spring of 1839. Before summer had arrived, though, Stephan's leadership came to an ignominious end amid accusations of sexual misconduct, financial mismanagement, and teaching of false doctrine. The community was thrown into an existential crisis as many members questioned the legitimacy of the venture and their identity as a church with the authority to call a new pastor. Added to this were financial difficulties, the physical challenges of establishing a new community in a wilderness, and the energy-sapping heat and humidity of a Missouri summer, leading many settlers to wish they had never left Saxony.[51]

In the midst of these trials, four clergymen in the group announced plans to open a gymnasium or college (that is, a preparatory school) offering all the liberal arts, and did so in a small log cabin in December of 1839. This striking dedication to the educational enterprise is not surprising given that the colony included many educated, middle-class members, and at least fifteen clergymen and candidates educated in theology at German universities.[52] The founding, as Solberg describes, "exemplified the com-

---

[51] Solberg, *Lutheran Higher Education in North America*, 113–18; Korcok, *Lutheran Education*, 140–44; and C. F. W. Walther, *Law and Gospel: How to Read and Apply the Bible*, trans. Christian C. Tiews (St. Louis: Concordia, 2010), xxi–xxiii.

[52] A. C. Stellhorn, "The Period of Organization, 1838–1847," in *One Hundred Years of Christian Education*, ed. Arthur C. Repp (River Forest, IL: Lutheran Education Association, 1947), 17–20 and Solberg, *Lutheran Higher Education in North America*, 118–19, 139–40.

mitment to higher education which was transmitted by Luther and Melanchthon to succeeding generations of Lutheran pastors and scholars and carried to North America by missionary pastors from a variety of European universities."[53] It exemplified also the founders' commitment to passing on confessional Lutheran beliefs to the next generation.[54]

In 1843, Perry County College, as the log college was called, started receiving financial support ($12 a month) from the congregation of Trinity Church in St. Louis, accompanied by a request that the college's emphasis be placed on training future Lutheran teachers and pastors (with a particular emphasis on languages) rather than preparing students for university entrance. In 1849 the school was moved to St. Louis, placed under the direct oversight of the Missouri Synod, and renamed Concordia College. The Missouri Synod's first president, C. F. W. Walther, also served as the school's first professor of theology.[55]

Its association with the St. Louis congregation had effectively developed Concordia into a combination gymnasium and theological seminary. The gymnasium comprised a six-year program of study that was roughly equivalent to that obtainable in a secondary school plus a two-year college. Although Concordia emphasized preparing church workers, the intentions of many intimately involved in it were to maintain classical learning at the gymnasium for the sake of preparing students both for church work and secular vocations. G. H. Loeber, a pastor and teacher at the school so stated in 1845, as did Walther shortly after the move to St. Louis. These and most of the other early pastors among the Saxons in Missouri were products of the neo-humanist movement of the eighteenth and nineteenth centuries, and regarded a classical education as an excellent foundation for both pastoral and civic leaders.[56] Clearly, "from the outset a plan for general education was in the mind of Synod."[57]

By 1859, however, Walther was advising parents whose children were not seeking the pastorate to send the children instead to the English Academy established by Immanuel Lutheran Church in St. Louis in 1857. The curriculum at the gymnasium leaned heavily toward the study of classical languages, which was not suited to non-ministerial students. As

---

[53] Solberg, *Lutheran Higher Education in North America*, 141.

[54] Korcok, *Lutheran Education*, 173–74.

[55] Stellhorn, "The Period of Organization, 1838–1847," 21–23 and Solberg, *Lutheran Higher Education in North America*, 142–43.

[56] Solberg, *Lutheran Higher Education in North America*, 144 and Korcok, *Lutheran Education*, 204–5.

[57] Repp, "The Period of Planting, 1847–1864," 52.

Korcok explains, "Pastors and teachers required a classical education to be faithful in their calling. The laity did not."[58] The emphasis here must be placed on the word *required*, for Walther and other founders had initially envisioned a classical education for the needs of the church and of the state. This departure may be explained in part by the LCMS's growth during the massive German migrations of the 1850s, as well as the spread of revivalism throughout America. Providing the church with enough pastors and ensuring that those pastors were theologically sound became matters of central concern for the gymnasium as well as the seminary. As L. G. Bickel describes, "It was in the nature and the spirit of the founders and fathers of the Church to put first things first. The preparation of an adequate supply of pastors and teachers was of primary concern to them."[59] Walther believed that a classically- and confessionally-educated pastorate was needed for the growing LCMS. Indeed, given the historical context of mid-nineteenth century America, Missouri Synod pastors were remarkably well educated in the liberal arts, ancient and modern languages, and theology.[60] Luther's and Melanchthon's emphases upon humanism and the Gospel found continuity in LCMS higher education; only the breadth of their vocational goals were not yet matched, and that probably due more to historical exigencies than to philosophical differences.[61]

The gymnasium, which was moved to Fort Wayne, Indiana in 1861, established one of the main templates for what would soon become the LCMS's system of colleges. A gymnasium under the name of Concordia College was established in Milwaukee, Wisconsin in 1891, and other gymnasia followed in St. Paul, Minnesota; New York (later Bronxville), New York; and Portland, Oregon.[62]

The other main template for institutions of the Concordia system, the teachers college, was established in Addison, Illinois in 1864. Similar to the gymnasium format, the college in Addison featured a five-year curriculum (six-year by 1908) that overlapped secondary school and early higher edu-

---

[58] Korcok, *Lutheran Education*, 177.

[59] L. G. Bickel, "The Period of Integration, 1914–1947," in *One Hundred Years of Lutheran Education*, ed. Arthur C. Repp (River Forest, IL: Lutheran Education Association, 1947), 209.

[60] Korcok, *Lutheran Education*, 187.

[61] Solberg, *Lutheran Higher Education in North America*, 145–47, 149, 295–96 and Repp, "The Period of Planting, 1847–1864," 50–55, 61–62.

[62] Repp, "The Period of Planting, 1847–1864," 59–61; Walter F. Wolbrecht, "The Period of Expansion, 1864–1894," in *One Hundred Years of Lutheran Education*, ed. Arthur C. Repp (River Forest, IL: Lutheran Education Association, 1947), 112 and Solberg, *Lutheran Higher Education in North America*, 148–49, 153–56.

cation. The curriculum differed from the gymnasium for future pastors, however, in that the former focused less on the classical and more on the pedagogical. The LCMS's teachers were still, however, quite well educated compared to their peers. In 1911, the college was removed to River Forest, Illinois and named Concordia Teachers College. A teachers college also opened in Seward, Nebraska in 1894 and gained full five-year college status in 1905.[63]

The period between the end of World War I and America's entry into World War II brought important changes to the Concordia system of colleges. From their beginnings, the gymnasia and the teachers colleges had treated education at the secondary and early-higher levels as a unitary whole. This approach was modeled on the German gymnasium, and the German language had retained primacy. Beyond the perception that the defense of doctrinal orthodoxy rested in part upon retaining the German language, there was a strong component of German nationalism behind this commitment to German cultural heritage. World War I, however, brought widespread cultural and institutional changes to America. These included American nationalism, xenophobia, and attacks on Germans and their institutions. The period after the war was marked, additionally, by growing governmental centralization of power and by a trend of severing education's ties with religion and replacing them with ties to government. All of these things had inevitable effects on the LCMS and its institutions, including a reduction in institutional commitment to German heritage and a concomitant increase in openness to American culture. Thus, the 1920s saw the Concordia system replace the gymnasium format with an American-style format of high schools and junior colleges, and also adopt more widely the use of the English language (not merely teaching the language, but teaching in it). By the late 1930s, the language curriculum was restructured to focus less on Latin and move Greek to the junior college level. Furthermore, schools in the Concordia system began to adhere to state accreditation requirements, bolster education in the social and natural sciences, and, especially in the face of declining enrollments during the Great Depression, accept female students and students who did not seek church

---

[63] John F. Stach, "The Period of Assimilation, 1894–1914," in *One Hundred Years of Lutheran Education*, ed. Arthur C. Repp (River Forest, IL: Lutheran Education Association, 1947), 149–50, 156; Korcok, *Lutheran Education*, 190–91; and Solberg, *Lutheran Higher Education in North America*, 150–53, 155–56.

vocations. The teachers colleges in River Forest and Seward also became four-year colleges in 1939.[64]

The LCMS Concordia system and its colleges continued to evolve after World War II. In the 1950s, the LCMS opened Concordia Senior College in Fort Wayne so that pre-ministry students could earn a B.A. degree before entering the St. Louis seminary. In the 1960s Concordia St. Paul became the LCMS's third teachers college and began awarding four-year bachelor's degrees. In the 1970s, the Senior College at Fort Wayne was closed and its program transferred to Concordia College in Ann Arbor, Michigan in 1977, transforming the Ann Arbor junior college into a four-year institution.[65] This decade also saw Christ College (now Concordia University Irvine) open as a bachelor's degree granting institution in Irvine, California. Currently, the Concordia University System comprises ten colleges and universities—including campuses in Selma, Alabama; Austin, Texas; and Mequon, Wisconsin—with all granting four-year degrees and some offering graduate-level studies. As a whole, the Concordias still prize their calling to prepare church workers, but they also now award vast numbers of degrees to students seeking vocations in society.

In light of Reformation Wittenberg's emphasis on higher education for the needs of the state as well as of the church, and in light of the Missouri Synod founders' similar aspirations, the course of historical development of this academic breadth in synod institutions is curious. Historical exigencies of the mid-nineteenth century kept the LCMS from providing lay higher education, and likewise historical exigencies of the 1930s effectively pushed the Concordias into providing the same—and this only at the junior college level. Further, although the teachers colleges had become four-year colleges by the end of that decade, a full college education for non-church workers would not reach the Concordias until decades later. Even then such breadth resulted more from responses to external forces than from the intention to embrace the vocational roots of Lutheran higher education. As Burtchaell describes with specific reference to the college in River Forest, but with broader applicability across many of the Concordias, market forces compelled the broader scope for the sake of institutional survival. As synodical high schools declined and closed,[66] and as the synod's seminaries began

---

[64] Bickel, "The Period of Integration, 1914–1947," 173–77, 192, 196–98 and Solberg, *Lutheran Higher Education in North America*, 141, 278, 285–86, 292–94. Concordia Seward began accepting female students as early as 1919.

[65] Solberg, *Lutheran Higher Education in North America*, 313–14, 320, 344.

[66] This refers to schools operated by the LCMS, not schools operated by congregations that are members of the synod.

accepting students from colleges with no connection to the LCMS, the Concordias' traditional supply line of students dried up. Beginning in the 1950s and accelerating through the succeeding decades, Concordia colleges increasingly recruited students who sought vocations outside the church and its schools. Burtchaell further shows that the Lutheran ethos or identity of the Concordias has been severely compromised as the study of theology has become a "muted" discipline, the percentages of Lutheran faculty and students have declined significantly, and the conservation of Lutheran institutional character appears to have declined in importance.[67] Moreover, there is substantial reason to question the extent to which humanist pedagogy is the driving force in educating students for secular vocations across the Concordia system.[68]

This is not to say that influential members of the LCMS are, or have historically been, insensitive to these gaps. Three generations before the current efforts to establish the centrality of the liberal arts at Concordia University Irvine,[69] a group of LCMS pastors and laymen saw opportunity in the form of a dilapidated and nearly bankrupt college in northern Indiana, Valparaiso University. The group incorporated the Lutheran University Association as the purchasing body, through which they then borrowed funds, raised more funds, and purchased the university in 1925. Over the next twenty years, the university struggled to survive amidst rehabilitation

---

[67] Burtchaell, *Dying of the Light*, 518–35. Although certain of Burtchaell's assertions may be questioned, in particular regarding a lack of robust biblical scholarship in the LCMS, his argument that the Concordias are largely divorced from synodical control is compelling, and his assertion about declining Lutheran ethos in the colleges is very persuasive. This decline is evident in diminishing percentages of Lutheran faculty on campus. At one Concordia, for instance, 80 percent are now non-Lutheran.

[68] Although the best definition of a humanist education may be more qualitative than quantitative, it is notable that at one Concordia the liberal arts general education requirement has recently been reduced to thirty credit hours while at least one major requires over eighty credit hours of major courses. Eric Childers describes three main influences or "status drivers" that challenge church-related colleges: secularization, financial viability, and faculty professionalization. See Eric Childers, *College Identity Sagas: Investigating Organizational Identity Preservation and Diminishment at Lutheran Colleges and Universities* (Eugene, OR: Pickwick, 2012). Although not based on Childers' taxonomy, the present account suggests that these drivers have moved many of the Concordias toward approaches that align more with modern secular education than with either their own original approaches or Wittenberg's evangelical humanism for church and state.

[69] See http://www.cui.edu/aboutcui/heritage/index.aspx?id=24746 and http://www.cui.edu/core.

of the property, the Great Depression, and World War II.[70] It was during the last of these, in October of 1940, that a new president outlined ambitious goals for the university—goals that were substantially in line with those of Luther and Melanchthon four hundred years before.[71] In his inaugural address, President O. P. Kretzmann stated that a university is to be dedicated to a two-fold task: the search for, and the transmission of, Truth. Moral, philosophical, and scientific Truth, he said, is universal, albeit not universally ascertained. "Above all," he proclaimed,

> we are deeply committed to the recovery of the one great fact which our wayward world has forgotten: The reality of God and the individual's personal responsibility to Him, a responsibility which can be met only by the fact of the Atonement and the re-establishment of an intimate relationship with the Ruler of the Universe through Him who once entered the stream of time in order to tell men that they could know the Truth and that it would make them free.

Luther's evangelical emphasis found a resounding echo in Kretzmann's address. The latter continued:

> There can be no doubt that the world of tomorrow will be the scene of two battles. One will be fought with bombs and guns on land, on the sea, and in the air; the other, and, I suspect, the far more important, will be fought in quiet classrooms, in libraries, in laboratories, and in the hidden meetings of men of thought and good will. . . . It will revolve about the great questions which must be answered in our time—our view of god, of the Church, of the State, of man, of the human mind and spirit, its origin, nature, function, and destiny, of the nature of Truth, and many other related issues.[72]

In short, it will revolve around the questions that Christian theology and the liberal arts seek to answer. Kretzmann sought to revive Christian humanism at the tiny, struggling college in northern Indiana.

For decades, Kretzmann's influence on the university was decisive. Robert Benne describes Valparaiso's postwar development in glowing terms: "Never having the resources of a Baylor or a Notre Dame to become

---

[70] Bickel, "The Period of Integration, 1914–1947," 209–10 and Solberg, *Lutheran Higher Education in North America*, 294–96.

[71] O. P. Kretzmann, "The Destiny of a Christian University in the Modern World," in *The Lutheran Reader*, ed. Paul J. Contino and David Morgan (Valparaiso, IN: Valparaiso University, 1999), 109–16.

[72] Kretzmann, "The Destiny of a Christian University in the Modern World," 112–13.

a research university, Kretzmann and his successors nevertheless have built the school into an excellent liberal arts college with a law school and several master's programs. . . . Valparaiso, reflecting the beloved and charismatic Kretzmann, became an unusual combination of the parochial and the cosmopolitan."[73] True to Kretzmann's Christian humanist vision, Valparaiso formed a college within the university, Christ College, which remains distinctive for its selectivity and focus upon the liberal arts.[74] At Valparaiso, the echoes of Luther and Melanchthon were clear. Valparaiso was the first LCMS-associated institution to embrace all aspects of the Wittenberg project in higher education: classical, Christian higher education to meet the needs of both the church and the state.[75]

LUTHERAN UNIVERSITIES TODAY:
TYPES, CHALLENGES, AND BENEFITS

In 1966, the Danforth Foundation sponsored a study of church-related institutions. In the process, they identified four types of church-related colleges and universities that have emerged during the history of Christian higher education in America:

1. *Defender of the Faith.* This type offers liberal arts education for future lay and church leaders. Faculty are almost all members of the sponsoring denomination or movement. Students are usually required to subscribe to the institution's faith. Worship and religious activities are central. Theology and biblical courses are required for all majors.

2. *Non-affirming.* This type may have historic ties to a church body, but theology and religious affiliation do not factor into selection of faculty or students, though there is usually church representation on the board of directors or trustees. Chapel is offered, but poorly attended.

3. *Free Christian.* This type of institution maintains a Christian commitment. Faculty consider religious matters important to the mission and life of the college. Chapel attendance may not be

---

[73] Robert Benne, *Quality with Soul: How Six Premiere Colleges and Universities Keep Faith with Their Religious Traditions* (Grand Rapids: Eerdmans, 2001), 94

[74] Solberg, *Lutheran Higher Education in North America*, 322.

[75] Unfortunately, it appears that for at least a generation the draw of secularism has gradually been pulling the university off its Christian moorings. Despite Benne's high praise for Valparaiso in 2001 as having kept its soul, even his own account betrays a troubling movement toward the secular. See Benne, *Quality with Soul,* 137–40.

required, but it is a vibrant part of the community. Students are not required to believe in Christianity, but they must engage theological and biblical themes within the curriculum.

4. *Church-related University.* While supported or founded by a church body, it serves a regional rather than sectarian purpose. While it may have a department of theology, its offerings are diverse and its student body is large. The relationship between such institutions and their associated denomination is "tenuous."[76]

Benne's more recent categorization may be more helpful in identifying the various ways that institutions relate to their church affiliation in the twenty-first century. They are as follows:

1. *Orthodox.* These universities emphasize commitment to a confessional identity.

2. *Critical-Mass.* These universities emphasize having sincere Christians serve as the heart and motivation for the institution, with several outsiders included in the conversation.

3. *Intentionally Pluralist.* These universities embrace and foster religious diversity.

4. *Accidentally Pluralist.* These universities respond to the demographic realities of their environment and thus cannot maintain faculty or student bodies consistent with their denominational tradition.[77]

These taxonomies are important to the history of Lutheran universities for three reasons. First, they show significant differences among institutions that share the label "Lutheran." Second, while most LCMS institutions have operated within the Orthodox and Defenders of the Faith categories, regional and national demographic shifts, the rise of evangelical non-denominationalism, new waves of Roman Catholic immigration, institutional desires for numeric growth, and the recent trend of young people to be theistic, but non-churchgoing, all conspire to make it increasingly challenging for these institutions to maintain a confessionally-unified faculty. Third, schools that have tried to embrace pluralism, while often creating vibrant liberal arts centers, have inevitably drifted from their unique theological identities toward either Church-related and Accidentally Pluralist models or Free Christian models. In short, the landscape is challenging for

---

[76] Mackenzie and Pattillo, *Church-sponsored Higher Education in the United States*, 196.

[77] Benne, *Quality with Soul*, 49.

all Lutheran institutions that seek to remain Lutheran in some manner. It is important for all members of an institution to have some sense of their institution's history and the ways that their governing body and mission statements endorse one kind of church relatedness or another.

Challenges to Lutheran universities are not just institutional, though. They reflect the *problem of identity and relevance* that Christians have faced since the first century. To the extent that a Christian institution is biblical and creedal, it will care about being relevant to neighbors and contemporary thought. Excessive concern for relevance, however, tempts Christian institutions to lose their identity in an attempt to correlate their work to the trends of the larger culture. To the extent that a Christian institution maintains its identity, it will care about theological purity. Intense concern for identity, however, tempts Christian institutions to withdraw from the public square and become culturally irrelevant. Jürgen Moltmann describes this problem throughout Christian history as a *crisis* of relevance and involvement:

> The more theology and the church attempt to become relevant to the problems of the present day, the more deeply they are drawn into the crisis of their own Christian identity. The more they attempt to assert their identity in traditional dogmas, rights and moral notion, the more irrelevant and unbelievable they become. This double crisis can be more accurately described as the *identity-involvement dilemma*.[78]

This is no simple curiosity of history or question for theologians to examine. The strategy for any university to remain Lutheran in any meaningful sense must include attention to this dilemma. Most would agree that a Lutheran university seeks to influence students holistically. They ought to be taught to be both honorable members of the civic community and rooted in the riches of Lutheran theology. If a *good* graduating student is to reflect both of these, universities will have to model for them ways of maintaining both identity and relevance for each new day. But this is not easy. Part of a Lutheran university's *identity* is to be a vibrant, relevant member of God's left-hand kingdom and to fulfill the Great Commission of God's right-hand kingdom, to be out and about conversing with the world. In other words, the history of Lutheran universities suggests that an institution can cling so tightly to its identity that it paradoxically loses its identity as salt and light in the world. It is hard to make new disciples without non-believers in the student body or without faculty conversant with the larger intellectual

---

[78] Jürgen Moltmann, *The Crucified God: The Cross of Christ as the Foundation and Criticism of Christian Theology* (San Francisco: Harper Collins, 1991), 7.

landscape. Conversely, this same history suggests that an institution can so desperately seek to be relevant in contemporary culture that its parody of secular universities renders it irrelevant as a distinctly Lutheran alternative to the reductionistic curricula of public and secularized private higher education.

The interplay between faith and learning seen in the original model of Luther and Melanchthon can help overcome the challenge of Christian higher education to maintain faithfulness to theological identity while providing relevant engagement with the life of the mind in all disciplines. The bleak history of failure in this regard among many Protestant institutions has been well documented. The practical factors Burtchaell and others observe include the need for strong confessional identity in senior leadership, presidents who know how to guide the interaction between faith and learning, the sponsoring church body's voice within university governance, a critical mass of confessional faculty members, faculty involvement in church alongside loyalty to their academic guilds, required biblical and theological coursework for students, and chapel attendance for faculty and staff. [79] As these elements erode, the ethos of a Christian university inevitably drifts from its founding mission.

Part of this unfortunate mission drift among Lutheran universities has also involved a failure to understand the rich nature of a proper Lutheran relationship between faith and learning and a duplicitous use of Lutheran doctrine of the two kingdoms or the doctrine of vocation to justify secularization. Some Lutheran universities have sadly secularized under the banners of vocation or two-kingdom theology.[80] Such a move is usually made by administrators who want to justify new institutional directions for the purposes of academic prestige and financial viability or by faculty members who, seeking to conform to the secular standards of and advance within their academic guilds, want autonomy from obligations to their sponsoring church bodies. But proper two-kingdom theology involves Christians excellently serving their neighbors through their vocations in society and the church, as *larvae Dei* or "masks of God." It has nothing to do with erecting an artificial barrier between theological and non-theological disciplines. Nevertheless, the failure of some Lutheran universities to understand the theological depth behind the doctrine of vocation and God's two-fold reign does not excuse them from modeling this important, but arduous, way of grappling with the world. The work of cultivating *good* students for our

---

[79] Burtchaell, *Dying of the Light*, 819–51.
[80] Robert Benne, "The Hazards of Lutheran Distinctives," *Lutheran Forum* 43, no. 4 (2009): 45–48.

complex times is admittedly hard work, but it is the work to which we are called; and when it is done well, it produces ennobling results.

We are at a juncture in history when Lutheran intellectual contributions may be particularly beneficial in helping Christian universities graduate *good* students. If other Christians consider Lutheran contributions, they may find them enriching and practically viable, even if they do not join our confession.[81] The most critical contribution to consider is the *interaction* between faith and learning; such a model is based on Luther's and Melanchthon's theology of two kingdoms and vocation.[82] This model fosters biblical and theological reflection on data in the natural world (including everything from business to art). This allows, for example, the biologist to explain when a fetus is capable of experiencing pain; Christian students (as well as professors) can then ask theological and ethical questions about what we should do with this scientific information. Students using this Lutheran model need not attempt to derive theological or ethical imperatives from the examination of natural data, as the Roman Catholics sometimes do, nor need they shoehorn the biological data into a Christian worldview, as some Reformed approaches encourage. Two-kingdom thinking, coupled with the doctrine of vocation, allows students to treat their work in the natural world with responsibility and respect, while identifying appropriate and helpful connections to Scripture and theology. It encourages students to work excellently in their vocations as a means to serve God by serving their neighbors, and do so ethically, with healthy biblical and theological insights to aid in interpretive understanding.

Lutheran universities can also help students resist the academic trend toward the myth of radical secularism, which leads to a tragically meager view of the world. Through this process, students learn to develop a pro-

---

[81] In recent years, Protestants have begun to look for an approach to faith and learning besides the Reformed integration model. See, for instance, Douglas Jacobsen and Rhonda Hustedt Jacobsen, *Scholarship and Christian Faith: Enlarging the Conversation* (Oxford: Oxford University Press, 2004) and Todd C. Ream, Jerry Pattengale, and David L. Riggs, eds., *Beyond Integration?: Inter/Disciplinary Possibilities for the Future of Christian Higher Education* (Abilene, TX: Abilene Christian University Press, 2012). Unfortunately neither of these works gives much play to a Lutheran approach as the former devotes less than a page to "The Lutheran Tradition" and the latter has nary a reference at all. Cf. Darryl G. Hart who advocates for a Lutheran approach instead of the Reformed model in "Christian Scholars, Secular Universities, and the Problem with the Antithesis," *Christian Scholar's Review* 30, no. 4 (2001): 383–402.

[82] For further discussion of a Lutheran interaction approach to faith and learning compared to an integration or separation model, see Ashmon's chapter.

phetic voice and proclaim that, when we take all things into account, our universe and we ourselves are more than the sum of our parts. They can engage in education in a manner that, informed by the cross of Christ, is humble and loving in its intellectual endeavors and critical of arrogant power plays that override the honest research of others. They can find courage to stand for goodness, truth, and beauty, fortified by their trust in God's Word. They can develop mature faith in a Christian explanation of the world, and develop confidence that this perspective is a thoughtful and intellectually responsible alternative to the nihilistic reductionism of the materialists. By truly understanding culture, including educated culture, they can become intellectual missionaries, who speak effectively to unbelievers within their disciplines. Ideally, they will be well received by their non-Christian peers because they do not play fast and loose with evidence or disciplinary methods. Rather, they can articulate nuanced perspectives that are informed by sound biblical and theological reflection about the world around them.

CONCLUSION

What defines *good* graduating students? For the Reformers, *good* graduating students were liberally trained and polished members of the community who used the tools of the liberal arts to fulfill their civic vocations with eloquence, and understand Scripture and proclaim the Gospel of Christ in the churches. For the Protestant scholastics, a good graduating student was able to define the fine points of theology and defend them well in the public square. For the Pietists, it was a student who had a passionate faith and acted morally. For Grundtvig, it was a student who caught a teacher's passion for a thoughtful and engaged life of the mind. For the liberals, it involved a student's ability to balance a private, emotionally-centered faith with open-minded secular knowledge. For the first hundred years of most second-wave German immigrant schools in the United States, it was a student versed in the liberal arts, languages, and theology for the sake of seminary study or teaching in Lutheran primary schools. Since then, for many Lutheran universities, it has also included students well-prepared for secular vocations.

As one explores the history of each Lutheran academic tradition, it will help to note the ways these historical trajectories have affected institutional identity, relevance, curricula, and priorities. It is the responsibility of twenty-first century faculties, staff, administrators, regents, and constituents to explore the ways that their institutions can be faithful to their vocations and Lutheran heritage. They must define and model how to cultivate *good* students in each facet of academic life for civic and ecclesiastical vocations of service.

QUESTIONS

1. What is your definition of a good graduating student? How does your definition fit with the implied or explicit definition of your institution?

2. Reviewing the types of Christian universities, what is your institution's historical model? What is its current model? Where would you like to see it be in twenty-five years?

3. How do you think a university can best balance the goals of identity and relevance in practical, structural ways? What is the role of chapel, required Bible and theology courses, and hiring practices in the preservation of the Christian mission at your institution?

4. In what ways ought religious curricula include or exclude elements of Reformation-era, scholastic, Pietistic, Grundtvigian, and confessional goals for student growth?

5. How can extra-curricular, administrative and residential life elements support your ideal for Lutheran higher education?

3

DISTINCTIVES OF LUTHERAN THEOLOGY FOR HIGHER EDUCATION

Steven P. Mueller[1]

WHAT IS A LUTHERAN?

What is a Lutheran? What is Lutheranism? At first glance, these are simple questions but, at least in popular parlance, or in reflection, they yield a wide range of answers. If we are to have any significant reflection on the interaction of Lutheranism and higher education, it is important to clear about what is meant when we use the word *Lutheran*. This chapter aims to explore theological distinctives of Lutheran Christianity. What do the theological teachings of Lutheranism have to do with higher education? To aid focus on this specific topic, it is helpful to note that, at times, the word *Lutheran* is used with different connotations.

Some invoking the title Lutheran are referring to a historical origin. This makes a valid point. Lutheranism arose and was transmitted in specific times and places. Lutherans founded a variety of institutions and made a lasting impact on their societies. This history is part of who Lutherans are. At times, however, the link may be merely historical and not necessarily connected to belief or confession. An individual might say that they grew up in a Lutheran church or attended a Lutheran school. Their link may be through parents or grandparents who are, or were, Lutheran. Such a person might return to a Lutheran congregation in time of need such as a wedding or funeral—perhaps to their childhood congregation. They may recall a particular minister who once served there and be unaware of the changes that passing time has brought. Lutheranism is, in some way, a religion of origin for them, though they may have no current connection. Such historical connections may undergird institutions that were founded by Luther-

---

[1] Steven P. Mueller, PhD (Durham), is Professor of Theology and Dean of Christ College at CUI.

ans. They may have been constituted, built, and funded by a church or group of churches, but, over the years, this historical origin has faded and may have lost any real significance. When a university is the institution in view, it may be like many of the institutions described in James Burtchaell's *The Dying of the Light*: founded for religious ends and, perhaps, paying tribute to that heritage in small ways in a particular department, but otherwise having no meaningful connection. Such colleges may, in fact, be Lutheran in name only. They may invoke their Lutheran origins when appealing to donors, but those donors grow increasingly suspicious that they are being sold a bill of goods—an "identity" that does not hold true in reality. Since our subject is Lutheranism, we are using this as our example, though one can easily find similar stories in various denominational traditions. While Lutheranism may well be a historical origin, we are concerned with a much broader sense than this alone.

A second use of the Lutheran moniker describes cultural markers. In this sense Lutheranism may be referenced with fondness and nostalgia, or it may be viewed with derision and embarrassment. Descriptions may vary with the national origin of the Lutheranism in view and may be tied up with cultural stereotypes both of other nations and of regions of one's own nation.[2] One who considers Lutheranism through culinary memes (e.g., bratwurst, lutefisk, or beer), nationality (e.g., German or Scandinavian countries), or geographic region (e.g., the Midwestern United States) may be employing this imprecise meaning of Lutheran. Garrison Keillor's stories of Lake Wobegon Lutherans fall into this category, though they are far more indicative of stereotyped Midwestern life than they are of Lutheranism. Now, certainly, religions express themselves in cultural ways and are themselves part of cultures. Cultural expressions and reflections are necessary and inevitable. Yet such expressions are not identical to theological Lutheranism that is intertwined with many different cultures and has different cultural expressions. Viewing only cultural aspects (many of which are not related to the beliefs of Lutheranism but arise from different sources) may lead to very misleading assumptions about what it means to be Lutheran and may, in fact, make it harder to recognize the theological concord that can help connect various cultures.

Colleges and universities may be attracted to cultural expressions that they identify as Lutheran in an effort to shore up their Lutheran heritage or

---

[2] Since Lutheranism began in Germany, this often references German culture or perhaps other European origins such as Norway or Sweden. Those who reference European origins are often surprised to learn of the thriving global presence of Lutheranism, particularly in the global south.

identity. This is particularly true if they are confused or conflicted regarding theological identity. They may, for example, sponsor a concert featuring Bach cantatas or hymns by Martin Luther or Paul Gerhard and identify these as evidence of their Lutheranism. They may hold broader cultural events (e.g., German Days) hoping to appeal to Lutherans. Certainly some of these events have interesting possibilities and may be worthy of consideration. They may be an important part of the heritage of a specific community. However, while some of these details may flow from a Lutheran ethos, many have little or nothing to do with Lutheranism per se, but rather are expressions of a broader cultural identity. Moreover, confusing cultural markers with the essence of Lutheranism tends to imply the dangerous conclusion that Lutheranism is a religion from a particular culture and for that culture alone. It easily increases the chance that many will feel like outsiders and it risks marginalizing other cultures and, in particular, Lutherans in other cultures.[3]

LUTHERANISM IS A THEOLOGICAL DESIGNATION

There is, as we have noted, a point in recognizing and celebrating heritage and culture. These and other cultural expressions may be important parts of a university community and may help unite constituents in meaningful ways. Whether recognized or not, such cultural expressions are always with us. Yet such things are not, of themselves, the essence of Lutheranism. Properly speaking, Lutheranism is a living confession of the Christian faith. Lutheran Christians carefully articulated their shared identity by corporately adopting a common confession of their faith in the sixteenth century. Lutheranism emerged in a time of crisis in the Christian church—a crisis that affected all Christian groups. At a time when the Christian forebears of all Western churches had drifted from clear biblical teaching, Martin Luther and others sought to reform the Catholic Church and restore biblical teachings. When this was met with resistance, Luther and his colleagues drafted various documents showing the biblical basis for their teaching and demonstrating that theirs was not a new teaching but rather the faith that had been confessed by Christians of all ages. Those Confessions were eventually collected in the Book of Concord. That book does not presume to be on the level of Scripture, nor is it an inspired text. It

---

[3] While we are speaking of Lutheranism in this book, we should note that other religious traditions have similar challenges. Christians within each tradition are prone to think that they are the only ones who struggle with identity issues such as these. Disrespectful Christians sometimes try to present other groups as facing such challenges while ignoring their own. Such hypocrisy should be resisted.

is, rather, a summary statement. Lutherans believe that these Confessions accurately summarize what Scripture teaches about specific theological topics.[4] The Confessions never replace the Bible, which is always the theological authority. However, once a group of people has studied the Scriptures, it is legitimate and arguably necessary for them to draft statements of agreement that demonstrate precisely what they think the Scriptures teach and specifically mean by those teachings.[5] Confessional Lutheran churches and institutions specifically agree to these Confessions as do ministers in those churches.[6]

Thus at its core, Lutheranism is a confession of faith; it is a theological movement. To claim the name Lutheran is, properly, to affirm a theological grounding that guides and shapes doctrine, faith, life, practice, mission, and direction. An institution may have Lutheran origins but without a theological commitment to a living expression of that commitment, it is not truly a Lutheran institution. Lutheranism, like all other human institutions, expresses itself in cultural forms. Yet Lutheranism is not primarily a culture and cannot be limited to cultural elements nor to any particular culture.

---

[4] This is the historical position of Lutheranism. There have been, and are, some Lutheran bodies that do not affirm all of the documents in the Book of Concord and some, today, who make little to no use of these Confessions. In this chapter we are considering these Confessions in the historical sense, that is, as a whole. Confessional Lutherans subscribe to these Confessions because these Confessions agree with Scripture.

[5] Some Christian groups insist that they have no confessions. One church famously proclaims that they have "No creed but Christ." It does not take much investigation to realize the inaccuracy of such claims. While they may not follow *historic* creeds and confessions that are shared with others, most groups do provide statements of what they believe. A quick look at a church's website often reveals their creed as a summary of beliefs. In fact, even the statement "No creed but Christ" is, in effect, a creed!

[6] Those who have been appropriately trained and equipped for specific offices of ministry, who confess that the Bible is the inspired Word of God and subscribe to the Book of Concord as a faithful witness to the teachings of Scripture, and whose ministry is connected to the ministry of Word and Sacrament (in the case of some ministerial offices, connected to the Gospel without sacramental authority) may be formally recognized by confessional Lutheran churches as called ministers. The difference between a "called" and "contracted" person is not academic or professional qualifications or dedication, but a full commitment to the Confession of the Lutheran Church and willingness to take appropriate responsibility for their part in that confession and ministry both locally and throughout the whole church. This is a key point: those who are formally called to their positions as ministers of the Gospel are ministers not just in one place but of the whole church. Their ministry is explicitly connected with the Gospel and is conducted accordingly.

Lutherans, at the core, believe that Scripture is the Word of God, the source of all doctrine, and the only infallible source of faith and practice. Lutherans believe that Christians can reach reliable conclusions about what the Bible teaches and that we can confess those truths together as we carry out our callings. Lutheranism is not a mere denominational moniker but a living, guiding confession that is normed by Scripture and seeks to be faithful to God and his Word.

So if Lutheranism is, properly, a living confession, what does it mean to be a Lutheran university? This book engages the interaction of the Lutheran faith with various aspects of higher education. But if this is to be done in any meaningful way, we can have no watered-down, least-common-denominationalism (or non-denominationalism). Lutheranism is part of the one holy Christian/catholic church. This naturally means that much of Lutheran teaching is shared with other biblical Christians. In fact, the first three documents in the Book of Concord are the Apostles' Creed, the Nicene Creed, and the Athanasian Creed. These ecumenical confessions are shared with all Christians. The majority of Christians even confess these creeds in worship today, just as our Christian ancestors have done for over 1,500 years.[7] But if we are to identify and embody a distinctively Lutheran ethos, we must do more than merely articulate the common ecumenical teachings. We must be honest about both our commonalities and our distinctions.

DISTINCTIVES OF LUTHERAN THEOLOGY
FOR HIGHER EDUCATION

A single chapter cannot present all topics of Lutheran Christian doctrine, nor can a single book. Many other books are written which help map out that territory, albeit incompletely.[8] Instead, this is an attempt to examine a few theological themes that have a particularly formative effect on Lutheran higher education.

It is important to remember that Lutheranism considers itself to be a faithful confession of Christian theology that is based on Scripture alone. While recognizing that there is disagreement among various Christian traditions on important doctrinal topics, Lutheranism believes (as do many, though not all, denominations) that its presentation of these topics is an

---

[7]   See Steven P. Mueller, ed., *Called to Believe, Teach, and Confess: An Introduction to Doctrinal Theology* (Eugene, OR: Wipf and Stock, 2005), 485–505 for an introduction to the creeds and to other Confessions.

[8]   In addition to The Book of Concord, readers may find other doctrinal expositions useful. *Called to Believe, Teach, and Confess* is one example.

expression of biblical teaching. Thus we will not be surprised that some of these doctrines are shared by other Christians. Indeed, this is to be expected and celebrated. There are, of course, doctrines that are debated among Christian groups. Many of these are matters of considerable importance and included among them are some significant Lutheran distinctives. The fact that this chapter does not address all such topics should not imply that these are unimportant. Rather, here we are focusing on topics with a particular importance for the enterprise of higher education.

As we identify key topics they come together to form a holistic ethos. These are not isolated teachings; each is connected to the others. Lutherans prefer to speak of doctrine in the singular (a body of doctrine), rather than a collection of doctrines. Recognizing this interconnectedness frees us to consider teachings in various orders often starting not at the center but at an epistemological point of entry: the nature of the Word of God.

Sola Scriptura

One of the great principles of the Reformation is commonly summarized by the Latin phrase *sola Scriptura*, which is translated, "Scripture alone."[9] This theological principle highlights the Lutheran belief that the Word of God is to be the sole source and norm of genuine Christian doctrine. Christian teaching must accord with Scripture. While many (though certainly not all) Christians consider this an obvious point, there are competing sources in other traditions and Lutherans recognize that other influences may exist. The most common alternative sources are reason, human authority, tradition, and experience.[10] Holding that doctrine comes from Scripture alone does not mean that there is no place for other things, but rather that Scripture must guide and govern them. Reason, for example, is used in service to the teachings of Scripture as we read, interpret, and apply God's Word. Yet reason is not able to sit in judgment over clear teachings of Scripture and cannot do so if it is fallen and corrupted by sin as Scripture demonstrates. Scripture is the inspired Word of God (2 Tim 3:15–17) and truth (John 17:17).

Holding to this biblical principle does not, however, eliminate human intellectual pursuits. Scripture is not the sole source of all knowledge; it is

---

[9]   *Sola Scriptura* is commonly linked with *sola gratia* ("grace alone"—by which we are saved) and *sola fide* ("faith alone"—through which we receive grace. This counters notions of salvation by works). A fourth "alone" permeates the rest: *solus Christus* ("Christ alone").

[10] For a more detailed look at these epistemological sources, see Mueller, *Called to Believe, Teach, and Confess*, 8–13.

the only *inspired* and *infallible* source of doctrine. Scripture is able to make us wise for salvation (2 Tim 3:15) and is perfect in its teachings, but its teachings are not utterly comprehensive of all knowledge and every topic. The Bible is not the textbook for all academic disciplines and, indeed, it would be insufficient for such a purpose. Note how this is clearly reflected in the pledges of those who hold called ministerial offices in the Lutheran Church—Missouri Synod. They pledge that they believe that Scripture is the inspired Word of God and the only infallible guide of faith and life; Scripture is not the only guide in life, but it is the only infallible one.[11] Other gifts of God through human wisdom may be quite helpful, though not infallible.

Thus the claims of Scripture are doctrinal. Where the Word of God speaks, it is authoritative. This may have implications for all academic disciplines, but it does not replace academic work.

Law and Gospel

The inspired Word of God needs to be read and understood. We approach it with our reasonable capabilities subject to its authority, but use our intellectual capacities in faith to understand, interpret, and apply God's Word. As Lutherans approach the Word of God, they recognize that two overarching doctrines permeate this book: God's Law and God's Gospel. While both are essential and God's will, they are different in important ways. Recognizing this helps us understand the message of Scripture more accurately.[12]

The Law is God's word of command. It is given for our good and decrees what God desires. He reveals his will for us perfectly in Scripture but also, to a degree, through natural knowledge. We are rightly concerned with the Law's teaching, but we misread God's Law if we see it as the path to salvation or self-justification. When we take the Law's teachings seriously, we see that we are incapable of fulfilling it ourselves. The Law demands perfect obedience ("Be holy" [Lev 19:2]) and promises blessings to those who fully keep the Law, if that were possible (e.g., "do this, and you will live" [Luke 10:28]). If we are ignorant of the Law's perfection, we might draw inaccurate conclusions about our ability to fulfill it, or assume that

---

[11] These pledges are made by those who teach theology and by all who are called to teach, regardless of discipline.

[12] For further discussions of Law and Gospel, see C. F. W. Walther, *Law and Gospel: How to Read and Apply the Bible*, trans. Christian C. Tiews (St. Louis, Concordia, 2010); Mueller, *Called to Believe, Teach, and Confess*, 55–74; and Smalcald Articles III:2 and Formula of Concord, Solid Declaration V, VI in the Book of Concord.

God simply wants us to do our best. We might attempt to point to our efforts to keep parts of it while overlooking our failures and inadequacies. But when the Law is considered in its fullness, the depth of the human condition becomes crushingly clear. Paul writes, "For by works of the law no human being will be justified in his sight, since through the law comes knowledge of sin" (Rom 3:20). The Law is the Word of God, but when we consider ourselves against its perfection, it perfectly reflects the truth to us: by ourselves we are hopeless sinners. That is a devastating word. The Law is God's check-mate. Through it we see the will of God and we see our failure. We learn that God justly might condemn and reject us. The Law thus reflects the reality of our true condition to us and shows our need for the Gospel.

The Law crushes, destroys, and kills, but it is not God's final word. He does not show us our inability to lead us to despair, but so that we might receive his solution. The Gospel is likewise his Word and it is the message of life and grace. While the Law tells us what we must do and have failed to do, the Gospel reveals what God has done on our behalf. The Gospel shows us our perfect Savior, his atoning death on our behalf, and the forgiveness we have in him. God's will is that we have life through the work of Jesus (John 3:16–17) and that life is ours through his free gift. While we are the subject of the Law (*you* shall), Christ is the subject of the Gospel (*he* died); we are the object of his work (he died *for you*). This Gospel will be considered in more detail in the next section on justification.

The distinction between Law and Gospel is a vital one for understanding the message of Scripture and God's will for us. It teaches, for example, how to understand the applicability of various biblical commands to modern Christians without allowing ourselves to become the supreme authority (e.g., there are biblical reasons why some of the Old Testament's commands are no longer in effect.) This provides a Lutheran distinction compared to various Christian groups who present Christianity primarily as a moral or behavioral code, or who cannot provide a biblical reason why certain biblical commands (fulfilled by Christ) are not binding on believers. The difference is freedom. Christ has freed us from the Law's demands by fulfilling them for us. We are not saved by our works, not even by the works that follow our conversion; we are saved by faith alone in Christ Jesus alone. Above all, the distinction between Law and Gospel demonstrates that Christ is the center of Scripture.

Justification by Grace through Faith

One cannot rightly talk about Lutheran theological distinctives without considering the topic of justification by grace through faith. This description of how we are saved is the heart of Lutheran theology. Paul writes in

Eph 2:8–10, "For by grace you have been saved through faith. And this is not your own doing; it is the gift of God, not a result of works, so that no one may boast. For we are his workmanship, created in Christ Jesus for good works, which God prepared beforehand, that we should walk in them."

Lutherans see this as the central Christian teaching. It is the article on which the church stands and falls. Luther wrote, "On this article rests all that we teach and practice against the pope, the devil, and the world. Therefore we must be quite certain and have no doubts about it. Otherwise all is lost."[13] Justification is what Christianity is all about. God has declared us righteous for the sake of Christ and his work and not on the basis of anything we have done. This is a free gift of his grace apart from our merit or worthiness. This doctrine acknowledges that God doesn't demand our best attempt; he demands that we be holy (Lev 19:2). But truth admits that even our best efforts—our righteous acts—are like filthy rags (Isa 64:6). Our only hope is for God's gracious gift of righteousness earned by Christ. This is not a development in us or a reward for our efforts, but a gracious gift. God does not change us so that we are worthy of salvation; he declares us righteous for Christ's sake while we are sinners. Christ puts us in a right relationship with the Father once more not for the sake of what we have done, but because of what he has done for us.

Faith is not the work that earns this but is the vehicle through which God gives the gift. Galatians 3:6 says, "Abraham believed God, and it was counted to him as righteousness." This was not a reward but a free gift and blessing. It was not earned; God credited it to him by grace. This is what Paul had earlier said in Gal 2:16: "[W]e know that a person is not justified by works of the law but through faith in Jesus Christ, so we also have believed in Christ Jesus, in order to be justified by faith in Christ and not by works of the law, because by works of the law no one will be justified."

We are declared righteous for the sake of Christ. Because of that, Lutherans acknowledge that when we look at ourselves we see that we are sinners but, in grace, God sees us as just. Both of these things are true; they are a matter of perspective. We see ourselves and our sinful state; God sees us as holy through Christ. This dual reality, which is the subject of Rom 7, is sometimes summarized by the Latin phrase, *simul iustus et peccator* ("simultaneously justified and sinful"). This recognition in no way minimizes sinfulness nor does it remove the importance of the response of

---

[13] Martin Luther, "Smalcald Articles," in *The Book of Concord: The Confessions of the Evangelical Lutheran Church*, eds. Robert Kolb and Timothy J. Wengert (Minneapolis: Fortress, 2000), 301 (part II:1).

faith as we strive to live as God's children. Rather, it humbly acknowledges that everything in our Christian life is dependent on the grace of God. We do not cease to be sinners when we are converted. Rather, even as we strive to live lives that are pleasing to God, we remember that we are always dependent on his grace and that we always stand before God in the forgiveness that Christ has won for us.

Many Christians of other traditions note the importance of this doctrine, though their articulation may reveal differences of belief by including elements of human contribution to this through preparation or transformed lives. Lutherans are clear to articulate the biblical truth that this work is completely gracious—the work of God alone apart from human contribution. Our response to justification, while important, is not the gift in itself and needs to be distinguished from it lest we diminish the work of our Savior and place it in our own fallen, fallible hands.

Other Christians, while believing in the salvation of Christ, may put other doctrines at the center. One influential alternative makes the doctrine of the sovereignty of God the central doctrine. Lutherans naturally affirm God's sovereignty, but believe that Scripture places God's gracious character expressed in justification at the center. We see God's character most clearly not in his sovereignty, but in the gracious way he acts.

Still others may make other teachings the center of their theology, including themes such as Christian living, justice, enacting the example of Jesus, contemplating God, or any number of other human activities. Lutherans resist giving Christ's central place to human beings in this way.

Justification is the central doctrine of Christianity and it needs to be the central doctrine at a Lutheran university. A theology of higher education that is centered on things other than Christ misses the point (the Truth it pursues [John 14:6; 2 Tim 3:7]) and, in the end, has little to distinguish itself from any other university or institution.

What does this mean for academic work? It certainly does not mean that each class is an evangelistic appeal, that the right answer to academic questions is "Jesus," or that all instructors are theologians. Yet, in the university's holistic calling, the work of Christ is proclaimed and glorified. We want the members of our community to encounter Jesus—the Jesus who justifies.

It also means that we recognize the members of our community for who they really are: sinners for whom Christ died. Some of them know and believe this gracious truth; some do not yet believe and may not have previously heard the Gospel. All should encounter this message and all should be treated with respect, care, and love. Their dignity and value comes from God and we share that together. Nor is this just for our students. Colleagues and constituents need to be seen in this way. We all need to be seen in this way.

The centrality of justification is manifest in the ordering of a campus community. One who truly believes in justification will gladly recognize the Scriptural truth of Christian freedom. God's gracious forgiveness applies to all. A Christian who recognizes that they themselves are saved by grace and not by their works cannot then act and speak as if others must be saved by works. This does not mean that there will not be rules and consequences. Such things are necessary for society in this fallen world. But they will not equate obedience and submission to faith nor can they identify transgressions with unbelief. Instead, they will boldly confess the Gospel that applies to all. The Christian community while striving to live in accord with God's Word will allow the Gospel to predominate. Those who have been forgiven can, empowered by the Spirit, forgive one another.

Finally, the centrality of justification fuels the mission of the church to make disciples of all nations (Matt 28:18–20). This good news is to be shared with others. That happens when graduates are sent out to the world and when we share the Gospel on campus and in our communities.[14]

Incarnational and Sacramental Theology

God's forensic declaration of justification is for the sake of Christ Jesus, his perfectly holy life, his innocent suffering and death for the sins of the whole world, and his victorious resurrection from the dead. To accomplish these things, the eternal Son of God became a genuine human being and lived among us (John 1:14). He fully shared our human experience without succumbing to temptation and sin (Heb 4:15). God became man in Christ, taking humanity into God. The divine creator became part of creation to redeem it. This wondrous mystery affirms creation. God made this world, and he created us. He became part of his creation to redeem it.

So it is no surprise that the God who came in human flesh comes also in ways that affirm the physical world. The Word of God comes to us in human words, written on a page and spoken by human beings. God joins his Word to physical elements and promises blessings through them. Water joined to God's Word of promise becomes the saving gift of Baptism's new birth (Matt 28:19–20; 1 Pet 3:21). With his Word, Christ's body and blood are given and received in bread and wine for the forgiveness of sins (Matt 26:26–29). Words of Absolution, spoken by a forgiven sinner, are spoken

---

[14] For more detailed examination of Justification, see Mueller, *Called to Believe, Teach, and Confess,* 231–44 and Augsburg Confession IV, Apology of the Augsburg Confession IV, and Formula of Concord, Solid Declaration III in the Book of Concord.

with God's own binding authority (John 20:21–23). God affirms the physical and uses it to accomplish his will.[15]

Seeing the incarnational way that God consistently works helps Christians resist the temptation to divorce faith from everyday life. It guards us from making the faith a private, internal experience. It keeps us from overly "spiritualizing" our belief or looking down on the physical existence that God gave to us. Indeed, we believe in the resurrection of the body (1 Cor 15:12–22). An incarnational and sacramental theology recognizes that God can and does use physical means to accomplish his will. God chooses physical elements and physical people to be holy means and agents through which he accomplishes his will.

Christ's Kingdoms

Another significant teaching for Lutheran education is a doctrine commonly known as the two kingdoms or two reigns of Christ. This Lutheran teaching considers how Christ exercises his authority as king. Citizens of the United States may quickly identify this with the separation of church and state, but this theological distinction is much richer, and far older, than that political principle.

In essence, this doctrine works to understand the biblical teaching about how Christ exercises his divine authority over all things (e.g., Col 1:15–20). Considered in its wholeness, this is an important teaching that helps us consider how God works. Unfortunately, it is a doctrine that is often misunderstood and misapplied which results in much confusion. One Lutheran professor considers part of this challenge, saying,

> In the 20th century, much of what was written and said about God's two kingdoms (including our catechetical and doctrinal instruction) was simplistic and misleading. Often this profound biblical teaching was reduced to views about the separation of church and state, the so-called "real world" and our hope of heaven, science and religion, or public policy versus private belief. But these oversimplifications wrongly divorced God's two kingdoms as though each has nothing to do with the other and that God himself is somehow divided in his own interests and aims.[16]

---

[15] For more detailed examination of the Sacraments, see Mueller, *Called to Believe, Teach, and Confess*, 311–69.

[16] Russ Moulds, "One Kingdom Teaches the Other: The Two Strategies of Lutheran Education" in *Learning at the Foot of the Cross: A Lutheran Vision for Education*, eds.

Though it has sometimes been misapplied, the doctrine of Christ's reign is an extremely useful one when its true meaning is grasped. To understand this better, it might be helpful to note that in its full articulation, this doctrine speaks of Christ's three kingdoms. The third is the kingdom of glory. In heaven Christ reigns openly and visibly and is honored and worshiped by his redeemed for all eternity. While we are not yet directly experiencing this kingdom, it is a present reality that we celebrate. We are comforted by the communion of saints and the fact that the faithful departed now rest in Jesus' presence. As we gather at the Lord's Supper, we remember the ancient words of the *Sanctus*: that we join in worship with "angels and archangels and all the company of heaven"—a picture that we also see in the book of Revelation. Jesus reigns in glory!

Christ's Kingdom of Power

The reign of Christ is not restricted to heaven. The doctrine of the two kingdoms addresses how that power is exercised here on earth. When we consider Scripture, we see that Christ's authority and power is manifest in two very different ways. These are typically called the kingdom of power and the kingdom of grace.

The kingdom of power includes all things and creatures in the universe.[17] Jesus claims all authority in heaven and earth (Matt 28:18) and Eph 1:22 says, "[God] put all things under [Jesus'] feet and gave him as head over all things to the church." This aspect of his reign demonstrates that all-encompassing reign. All creatures and all persons are under the reign of Christ. But how does he reign over every*one*, including those who do not know or acknowledge him? How does he reign over every*thing*? He reigns through his divine power and might. As the one through whom all things were made (John 1:3; Col 1:16), he works through the means of his creation. So-called natural laws operate in the universe. Reason, though affected by sin, still functions. Parents act, albeit imperfectly, with delegated divine authority, as do governments that God also established to provide for peoples and to keep order through law and its enforcement (Rom 13). In his reign Christ provides for all, causing, for example, the rain to fall on the righteous and unrighteous alike (Matt 5:45) and watching over even the sparrows (Matt 10:29).

Joel D. Heck and Angus J. L. Menuge (Austin, TX: Concordia University Press, 2011), 80.

[17] The kingdom of power is sometimes referred to as the left-hand kingdom, and the kingdom of grace as the right-hand kingdom. These descriptions utilize the biblical image of the right hand of God being the source of blessings.

In this kingdom God provides for the needs of others through means including the vocations of believers and unbelievers alike (e.g., farmers provide food whether they recognize the true God or are atheists; healthcare providers care for others; firefighters and police officers protect). While not always noticed, God is at work in all of these things and, with some reflection, certain things can be clearly learned of God and his attributes in this reign (Rom 1:20).

As an expression of power, Christ's reign in this kingdom is expressed in Law. We do not learn the Gospel here. We may experience God's goodness, but we do not encounter his grace and salvation through it. Saying this does not diminish the good things that are found here, but it does recognize their incompleteness.

Christ's Kingdom of Grace

The kingdom of power expresses biblical ideas, but it is not the complete picture. Christ also reigns over those who know him. The kingdom of grace includes those who believe in Christ. In this kingdom Christ rules through the Gospel and faith. For that to be true, we must have God's self-revelation in non-natural ways. We need Christ and his Word to learn of this kingdom and be ruled by him. Here we see the character of God that cannot be discerned merely from external events and actions. Here we see his holiness and goodness as well as his graciousness and true mercy. The Gospel cannot be discerned by natural man. It must be revealed.

Just as God works through means in the kingdom of power, so he also works through means here. The reason is similar in both kingdoms. God can work directly, but his unmediated presence would overwhelm and terrify. Here in the kingdom of grace, God brings his Gospel through means that he has promised to use. He comes gently and mercifully through Scripture where he has promised to speak. He comes with grace in Baptism (Acts 2:38) and the Eucharist (1 Cor 10:16) where he combines physical elements with the Gospel to give his promised grace. He comes in the word of Absolution (John 20:31) that he commands his church and pastors to speak over the believing penitent. In each of these cases, he locates his grace in concrete places and thus gives confidence and assurance. In this kingdom he acts with gracious invitation and not with coercive or punishing force. He gently invites rather than forcefully compels.

People frequently equate this kingdom with the church. This is understandable, since the tools of the kingdom of grace are all part of the church's ministry, but we need to be careful. Not everything the church does is the ministry of the Gospel. Furthermore, as specific churches are human organizations (even if constituted around God's call), there are left-hand (kingdom of power) issues that are part of their common life. Churches are entrusted with the Gospel and Sacraments, but they also may own property, maintain a payroll, or be engaged in any number of other activities that are not directly connected to the Gospel. Many of these things may, in fact, be elements of the kingdom of power that are taking place within a church. Churches thus need to be aware of what they are doing and not assume that everything they do is a matter of the Gospel.

Two Kingdoms and Universities

This is doubly true of church-related institutions. A university is not a church even if it is a Christian university. It does not exist solely in the kingdom of grace nor, if it is faithful to its Christian mission, is it solely in the kingdom of power. The work of a Christian university exists partially in both of these kingdoms. It is, in short, in the same situation as an individual Christian. This teaching helps us see some of the challenges faced by Christian universities and provides helpful guidance. Other chapters in this book will address particular dimensions of this, but for now, consider at least a few implications.

Seen in such a context, matters of conduct may be seen with a more helpful complexity. A student who repents of plagiarism or some other misconduct may be brought to the cross and be absolved of their sins. That is a right-hand, kingdom of grace concern. Yet in the kingdom of power a violation of rules or laws may have temporal consequences. Thus they may be forgiven and assured of grace yet still fail a class or lose campus housing. A fornicating couple may be absolved, but forgiveness does not cause a baby to disappear. Grace may be proclaimed to a sinning colleague even while their actions may damage their career. These are challenging situations, but both dimensions are necessary.

Another application of the two kingdoms may be seen in understanding the methods and subjects of various academic disciplines. Though we follow the principle of *sola Scriptura*, we do not expect that the Bible is the textbook for every class. God's left-hand rule includes human inquiry, reason, observation, experimentation, and the like. Exploration of various academic subjects thus is primarily—sometimes exclusively—an activity in the kingdom of power. This does not diminish these subjects in any way— as they are a part of God's creation; rather, this notes the nature of these disciplines. Even the selection of disciplines and topics within a discipline to be covered are part of the kingdom of power. This is true whether such a decision is made on religious grounds ("That would be an inappropriate topic") as much as when it is made of secular grounds ("We do not have the resources" or "That is not one of our foci"). Even when the topic of a class or course is a sacred one (e.g., a class on Baptism), the class itself is primarily an activity in the kingdom of power. Grades are never an application of grace; neither is the salary received by the teacher. A student may fail a test on the Gospel without his or her faith being graded. Yet in a Lutheran university, our life together may have broader dimensions. While an academic course is a function of the kingdom of power, Christian professors, regardless of academic discipline, are empowered to be in gracious, right-hand relationships with Christian students and colleagues. They are likewise empowered to pray for and share the Gospel, in appropriate and non-coercive ways, with those who do not believe. University staff members are likewise able to serve students in both left- and right-hand ways.

While much of our academic work takes place in the kingdom of power, it is helpful to remember that this may result in some academic differences from our colleagues at secular universities. All universities place some restrictions on their faculties. Some topics and disciplines are welcomed or resisted more at one university than another. Areas of study may be less appropriate or even discouraged in some places. This is as true of Christian universities as it is at secular ones. Those who serve Christian universities do well to remember that while they may encounter some limits not faced by their counterparts at secular schools, the reverse is also true. When this is considered, some have noted that professors at Christian liberal arts institutions may, in fact, have more freedom to discuss a range of topics than do those at other schools since we do not have to avoid religious topics.[18]

Vocation

Another Lutheran theological distinctive that impacts higher education is vocation. Many Lutheran institutions have latched onto this topic as a marker of their educational work—with good cause. At times, however, this significant theological teaching has been underestimated or trivialized. Most universities are concerned with vocation in the generic sense of the word. When vocation is reduced to the concept of a career, most human beings have an interest in the topic. But that general sense of vocation is just a small portion of what the doctrine of vocation entails. Vocation comes from the Latin word *vocatio*, which means "calling." Our vocations come from outside of ourselves; God calls us to serve our neighbor through them. A biblical understanding of vocation demonstrates ways in which God works in the world.

God works in two ways: mediately and immediately. God may, and sometimes does, work immediately or directly in this world. He may

---

[18] For a more detailed examination of the twofold rule of Christ, see Mueller, *Called to Believe, Teach, and Confess*, 216–21.

respond to a situation by manifesting his presence visibly or by performing a miracle. God may see a hungry nation and daily deliver manna or cause a spring of water to miraculously appear. God may respond to a terminal illness with supernatural healing. More often, however, at least from our limited human perspective, it seems that God chooses to work through means as we have discussed in the kingdom of power. Manna provides for human hunger, but so does the food produced by farmers, delivered by truckers, sold by merchants, and cooked by chefs. Supernatural healing may end a disease, but so can the skilled application of medicine that was developed by researchers and administered by doctors and nurses. God may speak with a booming voice from heaven but he more frequently speaks through the inspired Word written down by prophets and apostles and proclaimed by Christians today. God works not only through things (grain or medicine), but through people (farmers or nurses). The doctrine of vocation acknowledges this reality. God calls people to be the agents of his work in this world. Martin Luther described vocations as the "masks of God." They are ways in which God is acting in the world, though hidden.

God can act immediately, although his ordinary way of acting is through ordinary means. The failure to recognize this is at the root of much modern Christian misunderstanding. We assume that God did not answer a prayer for healing because health came through a doctor's visit and not in an instantaneous miracle. We act as if our daily bread is a reward for our hard work and fail to see that God provided that bread through the vocations of others and through our own vocations.

Martin Luther articulated this doctrine in contrast to the limited medieval notion of vocation. That idea considered vocation as something that was exercised only by a few. The medieval church only spoke of the vocations of monks, nuns, and clergy. Luther recognized that God worked in many other ways. As 1 Pet 2:9–10 says,

> You are a chosen race, a royal priesthood, a holy nation, a people for his own possession, that you may proclaim the excellencies of him who called you out of darkness into his marvelous light. Once you were not a people, but now you are God's people; once you had not received mercy, but now you have received mercy.

God calls Christians as his people and he calls them to various vocations through which they serve their neighbor.

All Christians have multiple vocations. We misuse this doctrine when we turn that into a singular. You do not have *a* vocation; you have multiple vocations. The university is not promoting this teaching if it claims to prepare students for their vocation. Students are to be equipped for their various vocations in life and to recognize them as divine callings. Luther considered vocation in light of four estates: the family, the church, the state, and the common order (where all of these areas and vocations interact). In any of these estates we may have multiple vocations. For example, a person may have a vocation as a child to their parents, a spouse, and a parent to their children. The object of these vocations is always the neighbor. God calls us to serve others—specific others—in specific ways. Here we may see a distinction from other Christians. The chief object of our vocations is not to find ways to serve God directly (after all, God does not really need our money or work or service or praise). Nor are we doing works for others in a self-serving manner—that is, doing them so that we can show God what we have done. Our purpose is to serve our neighbor because he is in need. This is what God has called us to do. Our neighbors need our service. Amazingly, God considers those acts as if they were done for him (Matt 25).

While it impossible for a chapter to outline the details of every vocation, we will make some general observations. Many vocations are addressed in Scripture. For example, it gives direction to parents and children, to citizens and to masters (where we find guidance for employees and employers). Luther brought together some of these biblical teachings in the Table of Duties found in his Small Catechism.[19] We should note that these teachings may be the content of vocation, but not its motivation. That is found in Christ.

Vocations may authorize and even obligate a person to do certain things. Professors are authorized to teach, assess, and grade students and to carry out many other duties including research, serve on committees, and the like. They are also obligated to do these things if they want to remain employed. In marriage a person is authorized to share all aspects of life with his/her spouse and obligated to be faithful to that spouse. Even these examples have more authorizations and obligations associated with them, but this gives the general idea. The specificity of calling may also limit a person. Marriage authorizes and sanctifies a sexual relationship with a spouse while simultaneously excluding others from a sexual relationship with the individuals in that marriage.

There are things that are part of one person's vocation that do not belong to another. What is permissible for one vocation may not be permissible for another. My brother is a physician and can legitimately prescribe drugs for other people. Though I, too, am a doctor, my vocation does not allow me to procure drugs. His vocation does not authorize him to preach or conduct a wedding. Our vocations authorize and limit. Our egalitarian society sometimes resists this notion of different callings but

---

[19] The Small Catechism can be found in the Book of Concord.

there is a wonderful freedom that comes from this notion. I am authorized and obligated to do certain things. But I am not responsible for another person's vocations. In vocation, I am empowered to recognize their calling and to let them do it rather than thinking that it is my responsibility as well.[20]

Vocation and Education

The doctrine of vocation is significantly connected to education and, particularly, to a liberal arts education. The Lutheran reformers' influential work in establishing and supporting education was grounded in this doctrine. It was precisely because of their belief that all Christians were called by God to various vocations that they saw the need for well-educated laypersons. All Christians needed to be equipped to know their vocations and to be able to fulfill them. They needed knowledge of their faith and knowledge of the liberal arts—the tools of both kingdoms—to fulfill God's various callings in their lives. The reformers wanted to equip students for better service through their various vocations. Gene Veith writes,

> For the Reformers, a liberal arts education was more than a broad, general exposure to many subjects; nor was it simply the pursuit of knowledge that is good in itself, the Aristotelian emphasis that Cardinal Newman would make definitive three centuries later. Rather, the Reformers saw liberal education as a means of cultivating human gifts and forming free human beings. Thus Melanchthon's curriculum was intrinsically connected to Luther's doctrine of vocation, according to which God works through human beings in their diverse callings as they live out their faith in love and service to their neighbors.[21]

While the reformers rightly criticized the medieval distortion of vocation to include only clerical or monastic orders, this does not change the fact that God calls some people to specific vocations of ministry within the church and that these offices contain their own authorizations and obligations from God. As Paul says, "He gave the apostles, the prophets, the evangelists, the shepherds and teachers, to equip the saints" (Eph 4:11–12). Church-related universities, then, may also be called to serve the church

---

[20] It may help to remember, though, that some vocations obligate a person to supervise another person in a particular vocation. As a dean, I have responsibilities to supervise some even as I am supervised by a provost.

[21] Gene Edward Veith, "Vocation in Education: Preparing our Callings in the Three Estates," in *Learning at the Foot of the Cross*, eds. Joel D. Heck and Angus J. L. Menuge (Austin, TX: Concordia University Press, 2011), 98.

faithfully by preparing students for ministerial vocations in full-time church work. This preparation not only includes specialized training in theology and practice, and spiritual and ministerial formation, but an even broader liberal-arts education to equip these students for service both in the ecclesiastical vocation and in the other vocations in which they will serve.

Seen as a response to God's calling and motivated by the grace we have received in Christ, our various academic disciplines can all be masks of God through which he blesses the world as our neighbors are served. God works through our various offices to serve and form our students. Our graduates are sent forth to serve in their vocations. This blessing is not limited to churchly offices (though it certainly occurs there); it is manifest across the university. Among our various vocations, we are together called to serve our students in various ways. In so doing, we are among the means that God uses to accomplish his purposes in the world. The university community joins in this work together. While our specific callings and roles are different, all are called to serve our students in this vocation of higher education. Those vocations happen in classrooms and offices, in residence halls and in co-curricular venues. They are enacted in formal and informal ways. Each person may have different vocations, but all are called to serve their neighbor in specific ways according to God's purposes.[22]

CONCLUSION

These are but a few doctrines with significance for higher education. A single chapter is pressed to do justice to even these few themes. As members of a university reflect further on theological themes that impact their callings, they might fruitfully pursue a deeper reflection on these topics along with many other theological themes. Indeed, one of the blessings of serving in a university that strives to uphold her theological heritage in a liberal arts and multi-disciplinary context is the range of voices and perspectives that can be brought to theological discourse.

Ongoing theological reflection, which is part of the calling of all Christians, is a particularly strong need in a university context. Without ongoing study, dialogue, and the expression of a shared faith through doxology, a confession can easily transform into a historical religion of origin or a mere cultural characterization. Without a common confession we might work for an organization, but we can never have *concordia*: true unity of the heart

---

[22] For more detailed presentations of the doctrine of vocation, see Mueller, *Called to Believe, Teach and Confess*, 431–35; Gene Edward Veith Jr., *God at Work: Your Christian Vocation in All of Life* (Wheaton, IL: Crossway, 2002); and Gustaf Wingren, *Luther on Vocation*, trans. Carl C. Rasmussen (Eugene, OR: Wipf and Stock, 2004).

that results in vibrant action. Bound together in common confession, we may be united in our diverse vocations and accomplish more than we can individually.

QUESTIONS

1. Justification by grace through faith in Christ is the central teaching of Lutheran Christianity. What are the implications of this for your relationships with faculty, staff, students, and other constituents?

2. How do Law and Gospel function in your work with the university? What are the challenging areas? Where do you need to be clearer about this distinction? How can the Gospel predominate?

3. Vocations in a university have many dimensions. For example, a faculty member's vocation includes teaching, research, service, mentoring, and many other things. What are some of the dimensions of your vocation? How does the freedom we have in Christ empower us for these various dimensions?

4. How do you see the doctrine of Christ's two kingdoms played out in your position in the university?

PART TWO

UNIVERSITY VOCATIONS

4

THE VOCATION OF A STUDENT

Korey D. Maas[1]

INTRODUCTION

The subject of the present essay must undoubtedly strike some readers as, if not oxymoronic, odd. Perhaps most immediately prompting such a judgment is the confusion inevitably attending references to vocation. The term has become all but anathema in contemporary discussions of the nature and ends of university education, not least that purporting to be liberal education, or education as a good end in itself. The popular understanding of vocation as synonymous with occupation will, for those who have been liberally educated, call to mind Aristotle's distinction between learning that might be called liberal and that deemed servile.[2] Those whose conception of the university is especially indebted to the influential John Henry Newman (himself, of course, in debt to Aristotle) will further insist that a university deserving of the name *just does* provide a liberal education, existing to serve no subsequent and extrinsic end, and certainly not one so narrow as a particular occupation.[3] Thus, a university education has come to be understood—even by those not conscious disciples of Newman or Aristotle—as an education to be clearly distinguished from that often dismissed as merely vocational, of the sort one might receive at a beauty school or as an electrician's apprentice.

We need not dwell on the evidence indicating that this understanding of the university is quite at odds with reality, that, as has been observed with only some small hyperbole, "All academic disciplines in the late-modern research university have become servile arts," and that the university itself

---

[1] Korey Maas, DPhil (Oxford), is Assistant Professor of History at Hillsdale College.

[2] See, e.g., Aristotle, "Politics," in *The Basic Works of Aristotle*, ed. Richard McKeon, trans. W. D. Ross (New York: Random House, 1941), 8.2.

[3] See, e.g., John Henry Cardinal Newman, *The Idea of a University* (Garden City, NY: Image, 1959), esp. Discourse V, "Knowledge Its Own End," 127–47.

has become merely "a contingent conglomeration of means that serve changing extrinsic ends."[4] Instead, it is simply noted that any consideration of vocation in the context of university education—if such education is indeed to be distinguished from occupational training—must break free of the reductive conception of vocation as merely synonymous with employment.

As historical uses of the term reveal more than one alternative to the currently popular understanding, the first part of this essay provides a brief articulation of what might be called the classic Lutheran doctrine of vocation, comparing and contrasting this with other notable expressions. It will be argued, first, that certain strands of the distinctively Lutheran understanding might, better than alternatives, allow for conceiving of the university student as having a vocation *as a student*. At the same time, however, a potential difficulty for acknowledging the vocation of student, arising from a central tenet of the Lutheran doctrine, will be noted. In light of this potential difficulty, the second part of this essay examines in more detail the manner in which being a student might be and has been understood in vocational terms. Where competing conceptions of vocation might allow for speaking meaningfully of a student's vocation, comparisons and contrasts will further elucidate the essential characteristics of any distinctively Lutheran understanding of the vocation of a student. Finally, in view of the conclusions reached in these sections, the third offers a more concrete and practical examination of some specific relationships and obligations inhering in the vocation of a student.

CONCEPTIONS OF CALLING: THREE ALTERNATIVES

The necessity of some brief examination of the doctrine of vocation, and especially its distinctively Lutheran expression, is highlighted by Gene Veith's lament that, even within the church, it "has become all but forgotten in our time."[5] Veith is right to lament, for as the German theologian Jürgen Moltmann has suggested, after its theology of Word and Sacrament, the doctrine of vocation was "the third great insight of the Lutheran Reformation."[6] As with his theology of Word and Sacrament, however, Luther himself hardly understood his insight respecting vocation to be his

---

4   Reinhard Hütter, "Polytechnic Utiliversity," *First Things* 236 (November 2013), 47, 48.

5   Gene Edward Veith Jr., *God at Work: Your Christian Vocation in All of Life* (Wheaton, IL: Crossway, 2002), 16.

6   Jürgen Moltmann, "Reformation and Revolution," in *Martin Luther and the Modern Mind*, ed. Manfred Hoffmann (Lewiston, NY: Edwin Mellen, 1985), 186.

own novel invention. Rather, he viewed his teaching as being nothing other than that of Scripture, and its being brought to light again as part of the broader reformation of those biblical teachings that had, over time, been obscured or distorted.

With respect to vocation specifically, the western medieval church had employed the Latin term *vocatio* with exclusive reference to the spiritual estate. A priest or a nun, for example, had a vocation, a calling; a cobbler or a mother did not. Countering the popular perception that such a distinction degraded the good and necessary work carried out in the secular or non-ecclesiastical sphere, Luther would insist (even in a treatise on education) that "[e]very occupation has its own honor before God."[7] Indeed, in light of the biblical *locus classicus* concerning vocation, where, between his discussion of wives and husbands and masters and slaves, Paul exhorts readers to "let each person lead the life that the Lord has assigned to him, and to which God has called [*vocavit* in Latin] him" (1 Cor 7:17), Luther consistently maintains that all legitimate stations in life, even the unremunerated, comprised honorable callings or vocations. So he asks, for example, "How is it possible that you are not called? You have always been in some state or station; you have always been a husband or wife, or boy or girl, or servant."[8] It is this "justification of worldly activity" that sociologist Max Weber, more famously than Moltmann, called "one of the most important results of the Reformation, especially of Luther's part in it."[9]

This broader conception of vocation as including worldly activity was, however, very soon narrowed again, this time typically to denote only legitimate, paid secular endeavors. Though this transition is evident even in post-Reformation Lutheranism, it has become primarily associated with the Reformed wing of Protestantism, not least on account of the influence of Weber, whose work on *The Protestant Ethic and the Spirit of Capitalism* focused primarily on the heirs of the Genevan reformer John Calvin. On either side of Luther, then, one sees what Os Guinness has named the "Catholic" and "Protestant" distortions of vocation,[10] though less polemically they might simply be called the medieval and modern understandings. Whatever merits these two views of vocation might have,

---

[7] Martin Luther, "A Sermon on Keeping Children in School," in AE 46:246.

[8] Martin Luther, "Sermon on the Day of St. John the Evangelist," in *Sermons of Martin Luther*, ed. John Nicholas Lenker (Grand Rapids: Baker, 1983), 1:242.

[9] Max Weber, *The Protestant Ethic and the Spirit of Capitalism*, trans. Talcott Parsons (New York: Charles Scribner's Sons, 1958), 81.

[10] See Os Guinness, *The Call: Finding and Fulfilling the Central Purpose of Your Life* (Nashville: Thomas Nelson, 2003), 31–42.

however, it is exceedingly difficult to see how either might facilitate the notion of the student having a vocation *as a student*. Rather than being paid to attend university, for example, most students (or their parents) are paying to be students. Nor, even in the church-related university, is the student's life typically understood to be in any way analogous to that of the clergy. On its face, then, it would appear that any desire to speak of a student's vocation would, by default, require using the term in its "Lutheran" understanding.

Forestalling this conclusion, however, is an essential—perhaps *the* essential—component of the Lutheran doctrine. Central to the Lutheran understanding, and further distinguishing it from both Catholic and Protestant counterparts, is not only the nature and scope of vocation, but its object or end. Inherent in the medieval, spiritual concept of vocation is its having God himself as the object. Thus, the *raison d'etre* of the priestly vocation is that of sacrifice, of making offering to God. Similarly, the monastic vocation, with its conscious withdrawal from worldly affairs, is directed first and foremost to the service of God. The divine direction of monastic vocation is not only acknowledged, for instance, in the Benedictine motto, *ora et labora* ("prayer and work"), but is even more specifically highlighted in its popular development into the phrase *laborare est orare* ("to work *is* to pray"). Thus, even mundane monastic activities, such as farming or brewing, became understood as spiritual, as offered to God.

By way of contrast, it is easy to view the secularized modern understanding of vocation as having the self as its object, since the remuneration associated with one's occupation most obviously and immediately benefits oneself. This simple dichotomy between medieval and modern understandings is, though, a bit too simple, as there exists considerable overlap between them. As even Dom Jean Leclercq noted in his classic study of monastic culture, the monk's service of God did not preclude the recognition that in performing such service the monk was also serving himself; the monastic life's "reason for existing is to further the salvation of the monk."[11] Conversely, many Protestants (though not only Protestants), uncomfortable with modernity's reductively self-serving concept of vocation, have increasingly emphasized the manner in which one might also be serving God through "secular" occupations.[12] In this respect, at least some

---

[11] Jean Leclercq, *The Love of Learning and the Desire for God* (New York: Mentor Omega, 1961), 28.

[12] To note only a few of the many recent books in the "faith and work" genre, see, e.g., Tom Nelson, *Work Matters: Connecting Sunday Worship to Monday Work* (Wheaton, IL: Crossway, 2011), Ben Witherington III, *Work: A Kingdom Perspective*

contemporary Protestant theologies of vocation merge—even if unwittingly—with the medieval confession of work as a form of prayer.

Any self-serving end must similarly be rejected in a distinctly Lutheran understanding of vocation. As early as his seminal 1520 treatise on Christian liberty, for instance, Luther was insisting that the Christian "should be guided in all his works by this thought and contemplate this one thing alone, that he may serve and benefit others in all that he does, considering nothing except the need and the advantage of his neighbor."[13] Indeed, operating as something like a definition of legitimate vocations is Luther's understanding that "[a]ll stations are so oriented that they serve others."[14] In his classic analysis of Luther's theology of vocation, Gustaf Wingren summarizes this view by writing that "vocation is ordained by God to benefit, not him who fulfils the vocation, but the neighbor."[15] But this emphasis on serving one's neighbor not only precludes an understanding of vocation as self-directed; it also stands at odds with that understanding of vocation—whether Catholic or Protestant—in which the one being served is God. As Wingren again observes, "God does not need our good works, but our neighbor does."[16] This being the case, Luther confesses in his Large Catechism that only faith "serves God, while our works serve people."[17] Perhaps most forcefully contrasting his view with the medieval and modern, Luther asserts already in 1520 that "[i]f you find yourself in a work by which you accomplish something good for God . . . or yourself, but not for your neighbor alone, then you should know that the work is not a good work."[18]

Absolutely essential to the Lutheran doctrine, then, is the understanding that "[a] vocation is a 'station' that is by nature helpful to others if followed."[19] It is this central premise, though, that poses potential difficulties for any Lutheran understanding of the student having a vocation *as a*

---

on Labor (Grand Rapids: Eerdmans, 2011), and Timothy Keller and Katherine Leary Alsdorf, *Every Good Endeavor: Connecting Your Work to God's Work* (New York: Dutton, 2012).

[13] Martin Luther, "The Freedom of a Christian," in AE 31:365.

[14] Martin Luther, "Sermon on 1 John 3:13ff.," in *D. Martin Luthers Werke, Kritische Gesamtausgabe, Schriften*, (Weimar: Böhlau, 1883–1986) [hereinafter WA], 15:625.

[15] Gustaf Wingren, *Luther on Vocation*, trans. Carl C. Rasmussen (Evansville, IN: Ballast, 1994), 29.

[16] Wingren, *Luther on Vocation*, 10.

[17] Martin Luther, "Large Catechism," in *The Book of Concord*, eds. Robert Kolb and Timothy J. Wengert (Minneapolis: Fortress, 2000), 406 (part I:147).

[18] Martin Luther, "Sermon on Matthew 21:1–9," in WA 10/1.2:41.

[19] Wingren, *Luther on Vocation*, 4.

student. It is to this question of the student's vocation—if there be such a thing—that we now turn.

VOCATION AND EDUCATION: LUTHERAN DISTINCTIONS

Given the apparent difficulty in articulating a coherent concept of vocation as it might apply in academia, there exists an understandable temptation simply to abandon the concept, or at least to shift the emphasis from the student as student.[20] Such a move, though, often results in acquiescing to the modern reduction of vocation to occupation. To be sure, this need not entirely remove talk of vocation from the university context. So, for example, one might still refer to the "Professorship as a Legitimate Calling."[21] The university itself might be said to exist "to educate students so they will be prepared for the vocations to which God has called them."[22] Faculty might even be understood to act, as Michael Cartwright has suggested, as "vocation exploration guides."[23]

Certainly none will want to deny that the professorship is a legitimate calling, that a university education plays some role in equipping students for future vocations, or that faculty are integrally involved in helping students discern the vocations to which they are being called. Speaking of education's importance for preparing graduates to serve in temporal offices, for example, Luther himself asserts that "this one consideration alone would be sufficient to justify the establishment everywhere of the very best schools."[24] His university colleague and *Praeceptor Germaniae* ("Teacher of Germany") Philip Melanchthon is even more pointed in urging his audience to "execrate" as "the most loathsome pests" those refusing to

---

[20] Michael G. Cartwright, "Moving Beyond Muddled Missions and Misleading Metaphors: Formation and Vocation of Students within an Ecclesially Based University," in *Conflicting Allegiances: The Church-Based University in a Liberal Democratic Society*, ed. Michael L. Budde and John Wright (Grand Rapids: Brazos, 2004), 202.

[21] Nicholas Wolterstorff, "Professorship as a Legitimate Calling," *The Crucible* 2, no. 3 (Spring 1992): 19–22.

[22] David S. Dockery, "The Great Commandment as a Paradigm for Christian Higher Education," in *The Future of Christian Higher Education*, ed. David S. Dockery and David P. Gushee (Nashville: Broadman and Holman, 1999), 9.

[23] Cartwright, "Moving Beyond Muddled Missions and Misleading Metaphors," 198.

[24] Martin Luther, "To the Councilmen of All Cities in Germany that They Establish and Maintain Christian Schools," in AE 45:369.

recognize the utility of a liberal education for future service to church and state.[25]

Nevertheless, any distinctly Lutheran reflection upon the matter cannot ignore the fact that the reformers also identified students as exercising vocations *as students*. Luther speaks this way when he says, "whether you are a preacher, a magistrate, a husband, a teacher, a pupil, . . . [y]ou must listen to the Law and follow your vocation."[26] Melanchthon speaks similarly when countering the accusation that the studious life is one of "slothful leisure." "[T]hat error has to be censured," he remarks, "so that we may understand better the kind of life to which we are called by divine agency."[27] Nor are Lutherans alone in speaking about vocation with regard to students. The contemporary Methodist-cum-Episcopalian (with Anabaptist leanings) Stanley Hauerwas is even more direct: "The Christian fact is very straightforward: To be a student is a calling."[28]

Hauerwas is hardly naïve, however, in his understanding of the hurdles to be cleared if this "Christian fact" is to be sufficiently recognized and appreciated. One of the greatest of these is the self-perception of students themselves, described in what he imagines would be a typical response to the above assertion:

> What is *he* thinking? I'm just beginning my freshman year. I'm not being called to be a student. . . . I'm going to college so I can get a better job and l.ave a better life than I'd have if I didn't go to college. It's not a *calling*.[29]

One source of this proclivity of students to dismiss their status as comprising a vocation, especially in the sense of its being a station or office

---

[25] Philip Melanchthon, "On Philosophy," in *Orations on Philosophy and Education*, ed. Sachiko Kusukawa, trans. Christine F. Salazar (Cambridge: Cambridge University Press, 1999), 127.

[26] Martin Luther, *Lectures on Galatians* (1535), AE 26:117.

[27] Philip Melanchthon, "On the Role of Schools," in *Orations on Philosophy and Education*, ed. Sachiko Kusukawa, trans. Christine F. Salazar (Cambridge: Cambridge University Press, 1999), 9.

[28] Stanley Hauerwas, "Go with God," *First Things* 207 (November 2010): 50.

[29] Hauerwas, "Go with God," 50 (emphases in original). Happily, such a response is not universal. See, for example, a recent short essay in which a college student addresses his peers: "You all have a vocation. Not just a future calling for future fulfillment. You have a vocation now. . . . The vocation to be a student may be a 'vocation of the moment,' but it is as real in this moment as any career or call to follow." Micah Meadowcroft, "The Obligation of Perfection," *The Hillsdale Forum* (December 2013), 8.

oriented toward the service of others, is bluntly identified in Allan Bloom's provocative diagnosis of American higher education: "Students these days are pleasant, friendly and, if not great-souled, at least not particularly mean-spirited. Their primary preoccupation is themselves, understood in the narrowest sense."[30] More than a century before Bloom, however, an even more fundamental source of this attitude was identified by the insightful French commentator on American life, Alexis de Tocqueville. Tocqueville viewed the self-regard noticed by Bloom as characteristic not only of young adults, but as inhering in a democratic mentality. "In democratic communities," he wryly noted, "each citizen is habitually engaged in the contemplation of a very puny object: namely, himself."[31]

Nor was Tocqueville the first to offer such an interpretation; it is evident in some of the earliest reflections upon the potentially problematic aspects of democracy. The "democratic man" as Plato had come to know him in Athens, for example, spent his days

> indulging the pleasure of the moment, now intoxicated with wine and music, and then taking to a spare diet and drinking nothing but water; one day in hard training, the next doing nothing at all, the third apparently immersed in study. Every now and then he takes part in politics, leaping to his feet to say or do whatever comes into his head. ... His life is subject to no order or restraint, and he has no wish to change an existence which he calls pleasant, free, and happy.[32]

Though there is thus no reason to ascribe an undisciplined self-regard exclusively to university students, Plato's own description, *mutatis mutandis*, does sound strikingly like much student life in the late-modern university. Indeed, it sounds not entirely unlike that being observed in the early-modern university, whose students Melanchthon bemoaned as "wander[ing] at random and without order or reason from one discipline to the other."[33]

---

[30] Allan Bloom, *The Closing of the American Mind: How Higher Education has Failed Democracy and Impoverished the Souls of Today's Students* (New York: Simon and Schuster, 1987), 83.

[31] Alexis de Tocqueville, *Democracy in America*, trans. Henry Reeve (New York: J. & H. G. Langly, 1899), 2.1.18.

[32] Plato, *The Republic*, trans. Francis MacDonald Cornford (Oxford: Clarendon, 1941), 8.561. Reprinted by permission of Oxford University Press.

[33] Philip Melanchthon, "Preface to *Cicero's On Duties*," in *Orations on Philosophy and Education*, ed. Sachiko Kusukawa, trans. Christine F. Salazar (Cambridge: Cambridge University Press, 1999), 79.

It was precisely for this reason that, when addressing his own students, Melanchthon consistently insisted that "not only private benefit is sought" from their studies.[34] To be sure, standing firmly in the liberal arts tradition, both Melanchthon and Luther could sometimes speak of education as an end in itself, something pursued for its own sake and its own pleasure. Recognizing the arts to be "fine and noble gifts of God," Luther could encourage their study even "if there were no other benefit."[35] Similarly, recognizing the desire for knowledge as itself a divine gift, Melanchthon defended the study of natural philosophy "even if no use followed."[36] Yet even liberal education purists acknowledge that further benefits and uses of knowledge do follow. Thus, when speaking to his own students, even Cardinal Newman echoes Melanchthon on the subject of "private benefit." With respect to the education they were receiving at the university he had founded, he confessed: "I do not desire this benefit to you, simply for your own sakes. For your own sakes certainly I wish it, but not on your account only. Man is not born for himself alone."[37] Hauerwas sounds this theme even more bluntly: "[Y]our job as a student is to serve and not to be served. College isn't for you; it's for your Christian calling as an intellectual."[38]

If man "is not born for himself alone," though, and if even students are "to serve and not to be served," immediate questions arise. For whom else is one born and whom is one to be serving? More specifically, if the student's vocation is not to be understood merely as a future office or occupation, but a present calling, whom is he or she to be serving *now*, as a student? As previously noted, certain attempts to avoid a self-regarding and "secularized" occupational understanding of vocation have answered such questions with reference to God. That is, man is born for God and so is to conceive of his stations, offices, and occupations as venues for serving God.

The logic of such an understanding often begins with a premise such as that famously articulated by Aristotle that "all men by nature desire to know."[39] This natural desire, being acknowledged even by later Christians,

---

[34] Melanchthon, "On Philosophy," 127.

[35] Luther, "To the Councilmen of All Cities in Germany," in AE 45:358. Cf. similarly "A Sermon on Keeping Children in School," in AE 46:243, where Luther comments on "the pure pleasure a man gets from having studied, even though he never holds an office of any kind."

[36] Quoted in Sachiko Kusukawa, *The Transformation of Natural Philosophy: The Case of Philip Melanchthon* (Cambridge: Cambridge University Press, 1995), 150.

[37] Newman, *The Idea of a University*, 434.

[38] Hauerwas, "Go with God," 52.

[39] Aristotle, "Metaphysics," in *The Basic Works of Aristotle*, ed. Richard McKeon, trans. W. D. Ross (New York: Random House, 1941), 1.1.

has then to be accounted for; not surprisingly, Christian theologians have emphasized that God has "implanted in the human mind a certain desire of investigating truth"[40] and "placed in the minds of men the desire of considering things."[41] Further, on the conviction that God does not act superfluously, his creation of man with this innate desire must be understood as having implications for the manner in which man understands his unique nature, and thus also his unique obligations. So, for example, commenting upon the work in which Aristotle's above-noted assertion is found, the medieval theologian Thomas Aquinas concludes that "[t]he proper operation of man as man is to understand, for by reason of this he differs from all other things."[42] In the last century the same conclusion was articulated even more pointedly by Mortimer Adler: "It is man's glory to be the only intellectual animal on earth. That imposes upon human beings the moral obligation to lead intellectual lives."[43] Indeed, even the oft irenic Melanchthon draws graphically hyperbolic implications from this obligation. Because God has given us eyes to aid in the acquisition of knowledge, for example, those refusing to "contemplate the work of nature" deserve "to have their eyes plucked out, since they do not want to use them for the purpose for which they are chiefly made."[44]

Though not a necessary conclusion of this train of thought—from man's innate desire to know, through the divine origins of this desire, to its resultant duties—it is not an illogical conclusion that the duties attending this desire are duties owed its author. That is, since the desire to know is divine in origin, so too are its obligations directed back toward the divine. This, for example, is the implicit understanding of titles such as *Love Your God with All Your Mind*.[45] It sometimes reveals itself even in consciously Lutheran works. Ernest Simmons, for instance, deems the intellectual life

40 John Calvin, *Institutes of the Christian Religion*, trans. Henry Beveridge (Edinburgh: T&T Clark, 1863), 2.2.

41 Philip Melanchthon, quoted in Sachiko Kusukawa, *The Transformation of Natural Philosophy*, 149.

42 Thomas Aquinas, *Commentary on the Metaphysics*, trans. John P. Rowan (Chicago: Henry Regnery, 1961), 1.1.

43 Mortimer J. Adler, *Intellect: Mind over Matter* (New York: Collier Macmillan, 1990), 185.

44 Philip Melanchthon, "Preface to *On the Sphere*," in *Orations on Philosophy and Education*, ed. Sachiko Kusukawa, trans. Christine F. Salazar (Cambridge: Cambridge University Press, 1999), 106.

45 J. P. Moreland, *Love Your God with All Your Mind* (Colorado Springs: NavPress, 1997); cf. also Gene Edward Veith Jr., *Loving God with All Your Mind* (Wheaton: Crossway, 1987).

"an acceptable expression of Christian vocation" because "scholarship itself is a spiritual endeavor."[46]

To be sure, as with the mundane occupational understanding of vocation, this "spiritual" understanding cannot entirely be dismissed. The exhortation to love God with all one's mind is, of course, biblical (see, e.g., Mark 12:30). So, too, on the basis of passages such as 1 Cor 10:31—"whatever you do, do all to the glory of God"—one might understand every endeavor of the Christian to be in some sense spiritual. Thus, even the Wittenberg reformers sometimes speak of schools as "the most sacred temples,"[47] and of the activity carried out therein as "a sacrifice most pleasing to God."[48] At the same time, however, they would insist, counterfactually, that the life of study would be warranted even if "there were no souls, and there were no need at all of schools and languages for the sake of the Scriptures and of God."[49] This was the case precisely because, as Richard Solberg has rightly observed, "Luther's philosophy of education grew directly out of his concept of the two kingdoms. He placed education squarely within the 'orders of creation' or God's 'secular realm.' "[50] That is, education was understood to be situated in the "left-hand" realm of the Law and its ordering of man's relationship with his fellow man, rather than in the "right-hand" realm of the Gospel and its ordering of the relationship between the Christian and God.[51]

Thus, from a Lutheran perspective, even while the divine origins of an innate desire for knowledge might be recognized, the specific obligations attending the pursuit of knowledge are not understood to be carried out in service to God. Indeed, the distinctively Lutheran understanding is that God, rather than being served in vocation, is himself the one serving others in and through legitimate offices and the individuals situated within them. As Wingren summarizes Luther on this point, "In the exercise of his voca-

---

[46] Ernest L. Simmons, *Lutheran Higher Education: An Introduction* (Minneapolis: Augsburg Fortress, 1998), 37.

[47] Philip Melanchthon, "On the Life of Aristotle," in *A Melanchthon Reader*, trans. Ralph Keen (New York: Peter Lang, 1988), 78.

[48] Philip Melanchthon, "On Anatomy," in *Orations on Philosophy and Education*, ed. Sachiko Kusukawa, trans. Christine F. Salazar (Cambridge: Cambridge University Press, 1999), 158.

[49] Luther, "To the Councilmen of All Cities in Germany," in AE 45:369.

[50] Richard W. Solberg, "What Can the Lutheran Tradition Contribute to Christian Higher Education?" in *Models for Christian Higher Education: Strategies for Survival and Success in the Twenty-First Century*, ed. Richard T. Hughes and William B. Adrian (Grand Rapids: Eerdmans, 1997), 76.

[51] For two-kingdoms theology, see Mueller's chapter in this volume.

tion man becomes a mask for God,"[52] the disguise behind which and the instrument through which God acts to serve his creation. Even those vocations that might be called academic or intellectual, therefore, if they are to be understood as vocations in the traditional Lutheran sense, will have the neighbor, rather than God himself, as their object and end.

When Luther himself speaks of callings and the called being "masks" behind which God operates in the world, however, he does not reject the notion of human cooperation and so human responsibility. While confessing that "God gives all good gifts," for example, he yet insists that "you must work and thus give God good cause and a mask."[53] Working in such a way as to be an instrument of God's own work, though, means working within the parameters of the particular stations or offices into which one has been called, each of which, Luther notes, has "its own requirements and duties."[54] This and other emphases in the preceding paragraphs do, though, put Luther's doctrine on a trajectory even more potentially discomfiting to advocates of a "spiritual" understanding of vocation.

The Lutheran doctrine locates vocation in God's left-hand realm, and this realm (including both Christians and non-Christians) is understood to be ruled by means of law and reason—rather than the Gospel or, even more broadly, the special revelation of Scripture. For this reason, not only are the specific duties inhering in vocations not fulfilled for God's sake, they can be understood even without special reference to God's Word. In Luther's own characteristically straightforward manner of expression, "God does not in the Scriptures teach us how to build houses, to make clothing, to marry, to wage war, to sail the seas, and so on."[55] Even more to the point, he rhetorically asks, "Do you want to know what your duty is . . . ?" and immediately replies: "You do not have to ask Christ about your duty."[56]

The potentially ironic conclusion is that, while one might give formulation to a distinctly Lutheran doctrine of vocation, an essential component of this doctrine is the recognition that there will be no obviously distinct Lutheran practice of vocation. Though the motivation to fulfill them may differ, the vocational obligations of the lawyer or the baker—or the student—inhere in the station itself and so do not differ depending upon whether one is a Lutheran (or even a Christian) or not. Wingren expresses

---

[52] Wingren, *Luther on Vocation*, 180.

[53] Martin Luther, "Commentary on Psalm 147," in AE 14:115.

[54] Luther, "A Sermon on Keeping Children in School," in AE 46:246.

[55] Martin Luther, "1522 Epiphany Sermon," in *Sermons of Martin Luther*, ed. J. N. Lenker (Grand Rapids: Baker, 2000), 6:319.

[56] Martin Luther, "The Sermon on the Mount," in AE 21:110.

this point by suggesting that "[f]or him who heeds his vocation, sanctification is hidden in offensively ordinary tasks, with the result that it is hardly noticed that he is a Christian."[57] Later in the same work even this small equivocation disappears: "Where works and external behavior are concerned it is not merely difficult to make a sharp demarcation between Christians and non-Christians; it is erroneous."[58]

What remains, then, is to address the manner in which the Lutheran understanding of vocation might apply to the university student. Most immediately, this will require some explanation of how the student as student might be understood to act in service to others (or, to serve as a "mask" behind which God serves others). As any such service will occur with the fulfillment of those obligations inherent in the particular vocation of student, some explication of these specific duties will also be offered.

COLLEGE AND CALLING:
RECIPROCAL RELATIONSHIPS AND RESPONSIBILITIES

The idea that students might, as such, have specific responsibilities is not in any way novel. The vocabulary of duty and obligation has been ever present in considerations of the studious life. In antiquity, for example, the Greek historian Plutarch says that "our duty is to grapple with every question"[59] and the Roman statesman Cicero's famous treatise, in which he explains to his own son what and how to study, is simply titled *On Duties*. In the medieval and early-modern eras, Aquinas speaks of "study, which is commended as a virtue"[60] and Melanchthon says to his own students, "Gentlemen, I tell you, it is your task to seek the truth."[61] So, too, in our own day students and professors alike can emphasize that "as you are called student, so you are called to study,"[62] and can speak of "the vocation of being a student, which has specific obligations of its own (study!)."[63]

---

57 Wingren, *Luther on Vocation*, 73.

58 Wingren, *Luther on Vocation*, 151.

59 Plutarch, "On the Student at Lectures," in *The Great Tradition: Classic Readings on What It Means to Be an Educated Human Being*, ed. Richard M. Gamble (Wilmington, DE: ISI Books, 2007), 152.

60 Thomas Aquinas, *Summa Theologica*, trans. Fathers of the English Dominican Province (London: Burns Oates and Washbourne, 1920), Second Part of the Second Part, Question 166, Article 1.

61 Philip Melanchthon, "On Correcting the Studies of Youth," in *A Melanchthon Reader*, trans. Ralph Keen (New York: Peter Lang, 1988), 50.

62 Meadowcroft, "The Obligation of Perfection," 9.

63 Veith, *God at Work*, 49.

This is, in a way, all very obvious. Less so, as intimated in previous sections, is the question of to whom these duties or obligations are owed or directed. If, in a Lutheran theology of vocation, the obligations of one's office are to be understood as having neither God nor the self as their primary end, to whom are they then directed? In many vocations, the answer is quite clear. The husband's duties are owed his wife, the mother's responsibilities are to her child, and the employer's obligations are directed toward both employees and customers. As an initial attempt to understand the student's status as vocational, it is proposed that the responsibilities inhering in the student's station be understood as oriented to peers and professors as well as (in most cases) to parents. That students are obligated to their professors, and so might serve and benefit them as students, will perhaps be the most intuitive, though not entirely uncontested claim. That they also have certain duties to their peers will likely be more controversial. We begin, however, with what might appear to be the most counterintuitive claim, that students, even as students, stand in relationship to and so have obligations of service to their parents.

The potentially controversial or counterintuitive nature of this claim results from the modern revolution in educational thought described by D. G. Hart, in which education became "a form of liberation that would free persons from the narrowness and constraints of human limitations. In its Enlightenment iteration, it signified liberation from family, land, and creed."[64] Emblematic of modern education's "liberation from family" is the frank admission of Woodrow Wilson, then U.S. President and formerly president of Princeton University: "I have often said that the use of a university is to make young gentlemen as unlike their fathers as possible."[65] Undoubtedly this "use of a university" is even more prevalent today than when Wilson noted it in 1914, not least because students themselves are willing to allow it. Being, often for the first time, beyond the immediate supervision of parents, and being encouraged to "spread their wings" and "think for themselves," students can quickly forget the debt—and so the duties—they owe to those who have made a university education possible for them, financially and otherwise.

One small but revealing indication of such forgetfulness is the cheering that regularly occurs when classes are cancelled. As one commentator

---

[64] D. G. Hart, "Education and Alienation: What John Henry Newman Could Learn from Wendell Berry," *Touchstone* 18, no. 8 (October 2005), 32.

[65] Woodrow Wilson, "The Power of Christian Young Men" (October 24, 1914), in *Selected Addresses and Papers of Woodrow Wilson* (New York: Boni and Liverlight, 1918), 49.

rightly notes: "This makes no sense. . . . In no business are customers excited to get *less* than they were promised."[66] It perhaps makes more sense when it is remembered that many students are not paying for their own education; they may be getting less than promised, but not necessarily less than they paid for. But someone, very often a parent, is paying, which only underscores the student's obligation to the parent. In keeping with the crudely consumerist language above, the student's obligation is to take possession of what has already been purchased. The student serves his or her parents simply by obediently fulfilling the wish that their child become educated.

To be sure, parental desires might not always run in the direction of an education, much less a liberal education. As the authors of the famous "Yale Report" lamented in the nineteenth century, "We are concerned to find that not only students, but their parents also, seem frequently more solicitous for the *name* of an education than the substance."[67] Nor has the cause for this lament changed greatly over time. Not only did Bloom much more recently express the concern that "fathers and mothers have lost the idea that the highest aspiration they might have for their children is for them to be wise";[68] even in the sixteenth century Luther was berating parents who would say, "If my son learns enough to earn a penny, he is learned enough."[69] The same was heard in antiquity where the learned preacher John Chrysostom, for example, chastises parents for being more concerned to provide their children with wealth than wisdom.[70]

Nevertheless, the primary reason for conceiving of the student as a student standing in a relationship of service and obligation to parents is not simply that parents are often financing their children's studies. A more fundamental reason is that within the left-hand kingdom in which education is situated, the responsibility for education has traditionally been

---

[66] William Voegeli, "The Higher Education Hustle," *Claremont Review of Books* 13, no. 2 (Spring 2013): 15 (emphasis in original).

[67] Jeremiah Day, "Course of Instruction in Yale College," in *The Liberal Arts Tradition: A Documentary History*, ed. Bruce A. Kimball (Lanham, MD: University Press of America, 2010), 273 (emphasis in original).

[68] Bloom, *The Closing of the American Mind*, 58.

[69] Ewald M. Plass, ed., *What Luther Says: A Practical In-Home Anthology for the Active Christian* (St. Louis: Concordia, 1959), §1331. In the same passage Luther refers to those holding such opinions as "the most noxious and harmful folk on earth."

[70] John Chrysostom, "Address on Vainglory and the Right Way for Parents to Bring Up Their Children," in *The Great Tradition: Classic Readings on What It Means to Be an Educated Human Being*, ed. Richard M. Gamble (Wilmington, DE: ISI Books, 2007), 192.

understood as an extension of familial responsibilities. That is, within the "three estates" typically denominated in Lutheran social thought[71]—church, state, and family—the family is the estate from which primary authority regarding education has been understood to derive. This traditional understanding is by no means limited to Lutheran thought;[72] it also stood behind the long-established common law understanding of schools operating *in loco parentis*. The cultural and legal rejection of this principle with respect to universities, especially since the 1960s, is simply one manifestation of modern education's "liberation from family."

Catechized Lutherans will recall, though, that even the explicitly theological instruction of children was a task that Luther located first in the household when he prepared the chief parts of his Small Catechism in "a simple way in which the head of a house is to present them."[73] The reciprocal vocations of teaching and learning could be located first in the family not only because the family is by nature the first and fundamental locus of vocation,[74] but also because, as Luther understood, "all other authority is derived and developed out of the authority of parents."[75] Revealingly, the example he most immediately provides to illustrate this assertion is that of the father engaging an instructor to assist in educating his children. The instructor acts by and under the authority of the father; he represents the father, as it were. Conversely, then, the student honors, serves, and obeys his father even in the person of the teacher.

The student's relationship with and obligations to his or her instructor certainly entail more than is broadly encompassed by analogy with the parent-child relationship, though. More specific duties arise not only from the unique educational endeavor drawing student and professor together in the first place, but also from the unique institution where this endeavor is carried out. "A University," as C. S. Lewis concisely defined it, is "a society

---

[71] Or, sometimes, four estates if the broader category of civil society is distinguished.

[72] See, e.g., Reformed theologian David VanDrunen, who also notes that "Within the common kingdom the family is of first and foremost importance when it comes to education," and that it retains "primary jurisdiction" in spite of the interests both state and corporation might have in an educated populace. David VanDrunen, *Living in God's Two Kingdoms* (Wheaton, IL: Crossway, 2010), 176.

[73] Martin Luther, "Small Catechism," in *The Book of Concord*, eds. Robert Kolb and Timothy J. Wengert (Minneapolis: Fortress, 2000), 351 (part I:1).

[74] Thus, in the Table of Duties, appended to his Small Catechism, Luther could include children as among those in "holy orders and walks of life," and so having an "office and duty" (cf. pp. 365–66).

[75] Luther, "Large Catechism," 405 (part I:141).

for the pursuit of learning."[76] The societal or communal nature of the university also highlights, however, that the learning that there takes place results not only from the interactions between a professor and student. This is emphasized by the terminology long associated with those subdivisions of which the greater university is comprised: colleges. The *collegium*, as the English derivative "collegiality" implies, denotes the cooperative nature of the learning there taking place. As such, it points implicitly toward the relationships and attendant obligations existing not only between students and professors, but also between students. The college, like the broader university, is that place in which is fulfilled, even if temporarily, that good articulated by the Renaissance pedagogue Juan Luis Vives, that "[l]earned men should live in unity with one another."[77] Vives further explains the good of such collegial unity with a rhetorical question: "[W]hat greater or closer union can we find than that of the mind of one man who is helped by another man's mind"?[78]

In view of the collegial nature of university education, and an understanding of the good arising from learned minds helping and being helped by one another, it is perhaps unsurprising that an actual duty to aid in the enlightenment of one's fellow students has occasionally been enshrined in university policy. Harvard in the seventeenth century, for example, exhorted perplexed students to inquire first "of their fellows," and then only "in case of non satisfaction" to inquire "modestly of their Tutors."[79] It is, of course, highly unlikely, perhaps even undesirable, that such a mandate be revived for codification in twenty-first century student handbooks. The "spirit of the law," though, remains a salutary reminder that the collegiate ideal was, until relatively recently, precisely that—collegiate. That is, it invoked an ideal of intellectual cooperation that has too often become foreign to students steeped in an ethos of individualism and an understanding of education marked more by competition—for grades, scholarships, or future employment—than by cooperation in pursuit of the common goal of truth or wisdom. Even more worrisome is the manner in which this spirit of

---

[76] C. S. Lewis, "Learning in War-Time," in *The Weight of Glory and Other Addresses* (New York: Harper Collins, 1980), 47. Reprinted by permission of The C. S. Lewis Company Ltd., Copyright © C. S. Lewis Pte. Ltd. 1949.

[77] Juan Luis Vives, "The Scholar and the World," in *The Great Tradition: Classic Readings on What It Means to Be an Educated Human Being*, ed. Richard M. Gamble (Wilmington, DE: ISI Books, 2007), 402.

[78] Vives, "The Scholar and the World," 403.

[79] Harvard College, "New England's First Fruits," in *The Liberal Arts Tradition: A Documentary History*, ed. Bruce A. Kimball (Lanham, MD: University Press of America, 2010), 199.

competition sometimes manifests itself in the relationship between students and professors. The most egregious examples will, of course, be plagiarism and other forms of academic dishonesty, which evidence a diminishing of the collegial understanding of shared intellectual activity and mutual academic obligations. It was precisely this collegial understanding, though, that could allow Melanchthon, when speaking of the pursuit of knowledge, to say to his students, "I want you to share that common cause with me."[80]

This understanding of education entailing the sharing of a common cause, of thinking together, is more memorably highlighted already in the model of Socrates. As James Schall helpfully explains, the dialogue was Socrates' preferred pedagogical method because he understood that for one to engage in conversation one must actually have the desire to learn. Thus, he condescended to the monologue only in the presence of those he deemed unteachable, men like Gorgias and Callicles, who refused to dialogue because they were unwilling to question their own actions and ideas.[81] This notion of education requiring the give-and-take of conversation is similarly highlighted by Newman. "You do not come merely to hear a lecture, or to read a book," he told his students, "but you come for that catechetical instruction, which consists in a sort of conversation between your lecturer and you."[82]

To conceive of education as in some sense a conversational enterprise is at the same time, at least implicitly, to recognize that the obligations inhering in the enterprise cannot be those of the instructor alone, as even the most mundane dialogue requires the active participation of two parties. Thus, Schall can bluntly state that which necessarily follows: "Students have obligations to teachers."[83] He does so, however, even while acknowledging how strange this must sound in contemporary ears. Indeed it will if recent surveys of college students are to be believed. One, for example, finds that "on a typical school day" more than 90 percent of college students make use of digital devices in class for activities unrelated to class (such as talking, texting, or browsing the internet); some 15 percent admit to doing so *more than thirty times* "on a typical day."[84] It hardly needs be emphasized how

---

[80] Melanchthon, "On Correcting the Studies of Youth," 48.

[81] James V. Schall, *The Life of Mind: On the Joys and Travails of Thinking* (Wilmington, DE: ISI Books, 2006), 25.

[82] Newman, *The Idea of a University*, 440.

[83] James V. Schall, *Another Sort of Learning* (San Francisco: Ignatius, 1988), 30.

[84] Bernard R. McCoy, "Digital Distractions in the Classroom: Student Classroom Use of Digital Devices for Non-Class Related Purposes," *Journal of Media Education* 4, no. 4 (October 2013): 7, accessed September 19, 2014, http://en.calameo.com/read/000091789af53ca4e647f.

such distractions prevent the possibility of any true conversation, and so any true education, taking place in the classroom.

Yet it would be too easy simply to explain these distractions with reference to new technologies. Already in the sixteenth-century, in a delightfully titled oration *On the Miseries of Teachers*, Melanchthon complains that students' minds are ever "outside, as if in another world, in brothels, at dice games, in schools of pernicious associations."[85] He laments that "[n]ever, unless compelled by a teacher, does a boy take a book into his hands," and that "[m]onstrous is the effort to convince them to write even a single letter during the entire semester."[86] Thus, he concludes despairingly that students can be placed in two categories: "the more idle, and the less."[87] To be sure, Melanchthon's causes for complaint cannot rival that of the unofficial patron saint of professors, Cassian of Imola, whose students bound him to a stake and slowly martyred him with their pens.[88] Such examples highlight that Schall's assertion regarding student obligations to teachers might indeed sound strange, but not only to contemporary students.

Nor is Schall's assertion itself only contemporary. In the first century Plutarch addresses his essay "On the Student at Lectures" to his young friend Nicander in order "to teach [him] the right attitude towards [his] philosophic teacher." The necessity of such an address was prompted, he notes, because

> There are some who think that, though the speaker has a duty, the hearer has none. They expect the former to present himself with his thoughts studiously prepared; yet, without a thought or care for their own obligations, they drop casually in and take their seats, for all the world as if they had come to a dinner to enjoy themselves while others are doing the work. Yet even a polite table-companion has his part to play, much more a polite hearer. He is a partner in the speech and a coadjutor of the speaker.

By way of analogy with "ball-play," in which "the catcher has to regulate his movements according to those of the thrower," Plutarch insists that, also, "in the case of a speech, there is a certain consonance of action in which

---

[85] Philip Melanchthon, *De miseriis paedagogorum, in Corpus Reformatorum, Philippi Melanthonis Opera* [hereinafter CR], 28 vols, ed. C. G. Bretschneider (Halle: Schwetschke, 1834–1860), 11:123.

[86] Melanchthon, *De miseriis paedagogorum oratio*, CR 11:123 and 124.

[87] Melanchthon, *De miseriis paedagogorum oratio*, CR 11:126.

[88] See Alban Butler, *The Lives of the Fathers, Martyrs, and Other Principal Saints* (Dublin: James Duffy, 1866), vol. 8, s.v. Saint Cassian, Martyr.

both speaker and listener are concerned, if each is to sustain his proper part."[89]

In emphasizing the "duty," the "obligations," and the "part to play" in the vocation of the student, Plutarch also highlights the manner in which the meeting of such obligations provides a real service to the professor. By fulfilling the duties of "his proper part," the student allows the professor effectively to fulfill his or her own obligations as a teacher. A similar insight regarding education's cooperative nature and mutual obligations is offered by Michael Oakeshott, who remarks that "[t]he activity of the teacher is, then, specified in the first place by the character of his partner."[90] Mortimer Adler presses this point by comparing what takes place in the classroom not with "ball-play," but with the Hippocratic philosophy of medicine. For Hippocrates, the art of healing was a cooperative art in which the physician, at least ideally, only assists the body in its own natural healing. Surgery, for example, was viewed as a measure of last resort, because "it was, strictly speaking, an *operative* rather than a *cooperative* procedure."[91] Adler draws out the educational implications by concluding that "[o]nly when teachers realize that the principal cause of the learning that occurs in a student is the activity of the student's own mind do they assume the role of cooperative artists."[92]

As is noted with some regularity, however, in the modern university this sort of cooperation all too often gives way to that of a more insidiously counterproductive sort. Students and professors enter into a "mutual non-aggression pact,"[93] or a "mutually assured nondestruction pact,"[94] in which they cooperate in what amounts to the avoidance of real teaching and learning. Professors implicitly agree to provide good grades for substandard work, while students in turn provide positive evaluations for subpar teaching. Because this is often the case, the real duties of the student must begin even before entering the classroom. Hauerwas touches on this point in what might be described as an open letter to students: "Although some universities make it quite easy to avoid being well educated, I think you will

---

[89] Plutarch, "On the Student at Lectures," 142, 150.

[90] Michael Oakeshott, "Learning and Teaching," in *The Voice of Liberal Learning*, ed. Timothy Fuller (New Haven: Yale University Press, 1989), 44.

[91] Mortimer J. Adler, "Teaching, Learning, and Their Counterfeits," in *Reforming Education: The Opening of the American Mind*, ed. Mortimer J. Adler (New York: Macmillan, 1988), 171 (emphasis in original).

[92] Adler, "Teaching, Learning, and Their Counterfeits," 171.

[93] Voegeli, "The Higher Education Hustle," 15.

[94] Geoffrey L. Collier, "We Pretend to Teach, They Pretend to Learn," *Wall Street Journal*, December 26, 2013, sect. A13.

find that every university or college has teachers who deserve the titles they've been given. Your task is to find them."[95]

Once this task has been fulfilled, and the properly collegial understanding of university education is grasped, the student's further vocational duties become more or less self-evident. These include not only study itself, which is perhaps the most obvious, or the similarly commonsensical etiquette demanded by Plutarch.[96] They include what Schall calls the "first obligation" of all students, which is simply an attitude of goodwill toward the professor,[97] that is, an acknowledgement that the professor is one from whom the student can learn and one who desires to assist the student in learning. Related to this goodwill is what both Schall and Adler call the virtue of docility.[98] This will perhaps sound strange in an age that often associates docility with meekness, or even mere passivity. Etymologically, though, the term derives from the same Latin root as *docere* ("to teach"), via the adjective *docilis*, denoting both an ability and willingness to be taught. Explicitly recognizing this to be among the duties inhering in the student's vocation, Adler closely associates it with the cardinal virtue of justice, understanding it to consist in "rendering to teachers what is their due" and to be "a kind of piety toward teachers as among the sources of our learning."[99]

Such a piety does not imply that the student uncritically accepts all that is said by a professor. As Augustine pointedly asks, "Who is so stupidly curious as to send his son to schools that he may learn what the teacher thinks?" Understanding, as Melanchthon later expressed it, that the student's most fundamental task is "to seek the truth," Augustine continues: "Those who are pupils consider within themselves whether what has been explained has been said truly."[100] Still, the virtue of docility—and of humility—will not allow the student simply to dismiss ideas deemed disagreeable. As even Friedrich Nietzsche wisely counseled, "Never ignore, never refuse to see what may be thought against your own thought."[101] In

---

[95] Hauerwas, "Go with God," 52.

[96] Plutarch, "On the Student at Lectures," 150.

[97] Schall, *Another Sort of Learning*, 34–35.

[98] Schall, *Another Sort of Learning*, 35; Mortimer J. Adler, "Docility and Authority," in *Reforming Education: The Opening of the American Mind*, ed. Mortimer J. Adler (New York: Macmillan, 1988), 192–93.

[99] Adler, "Docility and Authority," 193.

[100] Quoted in Schall, *Another Sort of Learning*, 30.

[101] Quoted in A. G. Sertillanges, O.P., *The Intellectual Life: Its Spirit, Conditions, Methods* (Washington DC: The Catholic University of America Press, 1998), xxv.

the same vein, Plutarch advised Nicander that "in listening to admonition and reproof, the pupil must be neither insensible nor unmanly."[102] And again, it is not surprising that some version of such commonsense advice has occasionally made its way even into formal university statutes. Those of the University of Paris in the thirteenth century, for example, insist that "if it happens that bachelors are failed . . . they shall not bring contumely or complaints or threats or other evils against the examiners"; instead, "they ought to suppose that the examiners have acted according to their consciences and good faith."[103] This unpleasant reference to the real possibility of failure allows us finally to turn toward some concluding remarks.

CONCLUSION

University students will sometimes fail. Sometimes the cause must be located in their unwillingness to fulfill the obligations inhering in their vocations as students. Sometimes, however, it must be acknowledged that the more fundamental cause of failure may be that particular students do not in fact have such a vocation. As Basil of Caesarea honestly acknowledges in the fourth century, "it is not given to everyone to climb this road, so steep it is, nor, if one essays to climb it, easily to reach the summit."[104] Thus, the previously mentioned Yale Report declares "the call, which is so frequently made upon us, to admit students into the college with *defective preparation*" to be a major problem.[105] This remains no less a problem today, even when admission requirements are nowhere near so demanding as they were, for instance, at Harvard in the seventeenth century, when prerequisites for admission included the *ex tempore* reading and understanding of classical Latin, being able to "make and speak true Latin in verse and prose" and being able to "decline perfectly the paradigms of nouns and verbs in the Greek tongue."[106]

Indeed, the admission of unprepared students is arguably more problematic in our day of consistent, even drastic, tuition increases. Especially

---

[102] Plutarch, "On the Student at Lectures," 151.

[103] University of Paris, "Rules for Determinations in Liberal Arts, 1252: Statutes of the Artists of the English Nation," in *The Liberal Arts Tradition: A Documentary History*, ed. Bruce A. Kimball (Lanham, MD: University Press of America, 2010), 133.

[104] Basil the Great, "To Young Men, on How They Might Derive Profit from Pagan Literature," in *The Great Tradition: Classic Readings on What It Means to Be an Educated Human Being*, ed. Richard M. Gamble (Wilmington, DE: ISI Books, 2007), 185.

[105] Day, "Course of Instruction in Yale College," 273 (emphasis in original).

[106] Harvard College, "New England's First Fruits," 199.

since much of modern higher education is financed by means of borrowing, failure to complete a degree leaves former students in an unenviable double-bind; they have not only incurred great debt, but the lack of a diploma significantly reduces the likelihood that they will be able to pay down such debt. This is one—though not the only—reason for firmly rejecting the conclusion that "[o]ur role is not to tell students what their vocation is."[107] It must especially be rejected by those granting the premise embedded not only in the Lutheran doctrine of vocation, but also in the very terminology of vocation. That is, vocations are not self-chosen; they are stations into which one is *called*, even by God. Further, on the Lutheran premise that God works via means and behind "masks," his calling of individuals into vocations is extended and confirmed by other persons. With reference to the vocation of student, then, Gene Veith rightly says that "[o]ur vocations are, literally, in the hands of others—college admissions boards."[108] That is, it is precisely the university's role to tell applicants whether being a student is indeed their vocation at this point in time. The very act of admitting an individual is by its nature *calling* him or her to be a student.

Even beyond the initial offer of admission, however, it would be naïve to assume that students are not being told "what their vocation is," even implicitly and unwittingly, by means of common policies and practices. Nor or these restricted to the mundane responsibilities outlined in student handbooks or course syllabi. If students enter the university with some intuitive understanding of vocation, particularly that reductive equation of vocation with occupation, they will not illogically conclude that their primary obligations pertain to those endeavors for which they are being "paid." The student recruited for his athletic or musical talents, for example, would somewhat reasonably conclude that his primary vocation is that for which he is being given scholarship money. Thus, it will ever remain among the vocational responsibilities of faculty, staff, and even fellow students, explicitly to "tell students what their vocation is," to explain to them, remind them of, and hold them to the particular obligations incumbent upon them *as students*. Given the mutual obligations arising from the collegial nature of the university and its enterprise, one of the professor's duties must be to articulate the students' duties—to say to them, and to explain for them, what C. S. Lewis famously said to his own students: "The

---

[107] Cartwright, "Moving Beyond Muddled Missions and Misleading Metaphors," 198.
[108] Veith, *God at Work*, 50, 55, 56.

learned life then is, for some, a duty. At the moment it looks as if it were your duty."[109]

QUESTIONS

1. Why might a Lutheran understanding of vocation in the university context be preferable to other alternatives? Does it have any drawbacks? Might alternative conceptions complement or supplement the Lutheran understanding? Why?

2. Given the Lutheran understanding of vocation, what relationships and responsibilities might the student (as student) have in addition to those discussed above?

3. Do you agree or disagree with the claim that it is the role of university faculty and staff "to tell students what their vocation is"? Why?

4. In what practical ways might parents, peers, and professors encourage students to think of themselves as having a calling to be students?

---

[109] Lewis, "Learning in War-Time," 59.

5

The Vocation of a Professor: Tensions and Tightropes between Two Kingdoms

Bret Taylor[1]

Introduction

I can remember the first time I saw the title on an envelope from Concordia University Irvine. There it was, written for all to see: "Professor Bret Taylor." Having taught for ten years already, I was used to seeing titles and the occasional formality from schools I was employed at, but this was different somehow. A few weeks later, Princess Diana was killed in an automobile accident and on the television was an analyst speaking about the significance of her life. While I cannot remember the analyst's name, her title was "Professor." "My," I thought to myself, "that would have been impressive a few weeks ago, but now I feel like they give that title to any knucklehead who teaches at a college."

What is a "professor?" What are we "professing," or "declaring?" What is unique regarding the role of a professor at a distinctively Lutheran university? These questions have been of interest to me since I saw that first envelope, and while I do not claim to have a foothold on all the answers, I do believe that the mission and foundation of such an institution, built upon a Lutheran doctrinal understanding, give me a better understanding of what this might mean and what I am called to do in this place.

In this chapter we will look at the role of professor through the doctrine of vocation as well as another key doctrine of the church: the two kingdoms. We will conclude with a section called "Tensions and Tightropes," dealing with struggles and decisions that need to be carefully thought through in the role of professor, which will help to define the uniqueness of the position in a Lutheran context.

---

[1]   Bret Taylor, PhD (Curtin), is Professor of Mathematics at CUI.

TWO KINGDOMS IN ONE POSITION

The Kingdom of the Left

The Christian has been placed as a citizen of two kingdoms under God's authority and rule: the kingdom of the left where entities such as society, schools, and families are governed by rules, regulations and authority, and the kingdom of the right where we find salvation and grace in the church through faith in Christ Jesus.[2] While many have pointed out that the vocation of a professor is found predominantly in the left-hand kingdom,[3] the fact that it is located within a church-related, faith-based institution also yields right-hand kingdom opportunities. Robert Kolb describes these two dimensions of Christian life as the "vertical realm" of faith in God and his means of grace for us (Scripture, Baptism, and Holy Communion) and the "horizontal realm" where we respond to God's grace by doing works of love for others with whom God has placed us.[4] We will analyze both kingdoms and their impact on the vocation of a professor at a Lutheran university here.

There are many responsibilities of a professor at a Lutheran university that are identical to those found at a state or public university: grading papers, holding office hours, serving on committees, attending faculty meetings, and preparing for instruction, just to name a few. These duties of office can seem of less value to many professors, and at times, are forsaken or ignored on behalf of more noteworthy or beneficial tasks, at least to their thoughts. Gene Veith helps remind us that faith in Christ, and the concept of vocation that comes with it "transfigures the ordinary, everyday life with the presence of God" and that "faith gives inner meaning to that which we would otherwise experience as meaningless."[5] The duties we fulfill as professors enable the university to function fully and operate so that the main educational mission of the university can reach its highest potential. These duties also provide some of the opportunities that can come through God's right-hand kingdom, as we will look at later. Simply because these are ex-

---

[2] See Steven Mueller, ed. Called to Believe, Teach, and Confess: An Introduction to Doctrinal Theology (Eugene, OR: Wipf and Stock, 2005), 244–55.

[3] Darrell Jodock, "The Lutheran Tradition and the Liberal Arts College: How Are They Related?," in Called to Serve: St. Olaf and the Vocation of a Church College, ed. Pamela Schwandt (Northfield, MN: St. Olaf College, 1999), 13–38.

[4] Robert Kolb, "Niebuhr's 'Christ and Culture in Paradox' Revisited: The Christian Life, Simultaneous in Both Dimensions," in Christ and Culture in Dialogue, ed. Angus Menuge (St. Louis: Concordia Academic Press, 1999), 104–25.

[5] Gene Edward Veith Jr., God at Work: Your Christian Vocation in All of Life (Wheaton, IL: Crossway, 2002), 17, 154.

pectations of our job and clearly defined in policy and contracts, we are, as a result of the love Christ has shown us, asked to fulfill these duties to the best of our ability.

The main purpose and role of the professor is as an educator. Here is one place where "professor" gets its title from. We are to "profess" content that we have become experts in and that our students have entered, willingly or not, into our classrooms to learn. The day-to-day sharing of facts, questioning and assessing student understanding, and preparing for our time in the classroom will take up most of our energy and effort in this vocation. But make no mistake, many of these actions still fall within the kingdom of the left. Laws, regulations, syllabi, and discipline are the norm and source for what happens within the daily classroom instruction. Salvation and God's gift of grace are tough things to find within most classroom exams or lectures on topics like calculus or chemistry.

The opportunities for us to demonstrate to our students, as well as many others colleagues outside of our specific institution, God's gifts of intellect, reason, and hard work can be some of the greatest blessings in professorship. C. Stephen Evans refers to this as a "double missionary" role for professors at faith-based institutions.[6] As Christian professors we represent intellectual and thoughtful insight with respect to our content and field of study, but also represent the Christian faith to those in our fields and classrooms who value intellectual learning and discourse but are not a part of God's family by faith. The tension of being faithful to our confession and beliefs, while at the same time excellent in our content and field of study, is a palpable and real issue in our roles and callings.

So how do we best serve as teachers within a faith-based university? I believe that by preparing and crafting our lessons to their very best we are demonstrating to our students that God's gift of intellect and reason are uniquely formed within his human creation and that their use glorifies God, even if the content is not directly "God-related." Angus Menuge shares that Christian witness is most clear when a believer's work is excellent. He says, "A Christian auto mechanic who leaves evangelistic tracts in each car, but fails to repair them well, is not a good Christian witness." Menuge goes on to say, "Our vocations are means of showing love by giving our neighbor

---

[6] C. Stephen Evans, "The Calling of the Christian Scholar-Teacher," in *Faithful Learning and the Christian Scholarly Vocation*, eds. D. V. Henry and B. R. Agee (Grand Rapids: Eerdmans, 2003), 33.

what he really needs. This is accomplished by honest, trustworthy work of high quality, not by shoddy work adorned with superficial piety."[7]

When topics or content are difficult, or even go against Scriptural thought or beliefs, we need to make sure students know that content also to the best of their ability while counter-balancing it with why Christianity has shaped tenets that go against those secular ideas. An example of this might involve the randomness and pointlessness of naturalistic thought. Students should know the impact of these starting points within a logical outflow in certain fields of study. They should be well versed in these concepts and ideas. But, if they do not know that the Triune God desires to be in relationship with each of them and that he has the ability to control even nature itself in order to demonstrate his love to his people, they are missing the qualities of what makes Lutheran education eternal.

The left-hand kingdom of God is also shown clearly in the vocation of professor in the authority roles that are related to this office. Professors find that they are in a unique situation with respect to authority in a university setting. They are both under the authority of a board of regents, president, and others in administration, yet serve as an authority with respect to their students, selected staff, and in some way over the entire university as they consider the policies and planning through faculty governance. We understand from the Fourth Commandment, and most notably Luther's explanation of this commandment as summarized in Veith's book *God at Work*, that "all authority is the Triune God's and that any authority here on earth is given by him."[8]

As we serve in our office as professors, there are those who, by God's guidance and hand, have been placed in authority over us and to whom we are accountable. While our human nature, and some of the traditions of higher education, will move us to refer to "them" or "they" as we hear of decisions made at upper levels of the university, especially if we do not agree with those decisions, we too must remember that we are not called into administration and, as a result of our understanding of God's authority, we are called to submit to these decisions. However, much like American citizens in our democracy, there are other times when plenary faculty are asked to make decisions on policies or cast votes that guide and direct the university as overseers of even the administration itself. This "ruler-servant" duality calls for humbleness and discernment, especially

---

[7] Angus Menuge, "Vocation," in *The Lutheran Difference: An Explanation and Comparison of Christian Beliefs*, ed. Edward Engelbrecht (St. Louis: Concordia, 2010), 472, 481.

[8] Veith, *God at Work*, 72.

within the confines of governance structures within a university. But it also calls us to action and involvement in order for that governance structure to perform as it should.

Professors are also in positions of authority when it comes to our classes, student workers, and others we may serve with in the university (in our roles as program directors, chairs, lead instructors, etc.). Veith reminds us that "bosses" are under God's authority as well and accountable to him for their actions.[9] This gives us great responsibility that must be taken seriously as we consider our vocational actions. The ability to represent how those in authority can model God's qualities, albeit imperfectly, is an important opportunity within our office as professor.

This modeling of authority can be started via some fairly basic steps. The requiring of proper titles or names within the academic setting can be a good start. "Professor," "Doctor," or even "Sir" or "Madam" gives a sense that authority is present and teaches a level of respect that is representative of the respect God deserves. I tell my students once they graduate and become alumni that I can and should be called "Bret" by them as they have "paid their dues" and I no longer have authority over them. But until that time, there is a sense of "boss-employee" relationship they need to understand and become comfortable with, and the university setting is a place to learn this. This is not about me personally or anything I have accomplished, but that God has called me into this office and the associated title reflects the office that I hold, just as "Pastor" can do the same within a congregation or "Mr. President" can in American society.

But probably the most demonstrable moments of representing God's authority and his divine nature of justice for a professor falls within the realm of dealing with academic honesty, plagiarism, and the consequences of these. These are watershed moments in working with students. Whether students are conscious or not of their actions, academic integrity and honesty are issues where the authority of the office of professor is most often demonstrated, and most often challenged. I believe that, while these challenges may be the worst moments to be a teacher, they are also the best opportunity to reflect the just nature of God in action.

The holding of a standard of integrity and behavior from students, whether it was a conscious decision on their part to plagiarize or cheat, or just a mistake or subconscious act, is an attribute of God revealed in Scripture. Jeremiah 9:23–24 says,

---

9   Veith, *God at Work*, 73.

Thus says the LORD: "Let not the wise man boast in his wisdom, let not the mighty man boast in his might, let not the rich man boast in his riches, but let him who boasts boast in this, that he understands and knows me, that I am the LORD who practices steadfast love, justice, and righteousness in the earth. For in these things I delight, declares the LORD."

God is a God of love, but he is also a God of justice and judgment. This "alien" action, as it is known by theologians (Isa 28:21), is seemingly counter to the loving nature that God also reveals to us in the Bible. But to overlook or dismiss that which goes against integrity or honesty is not God-like at all. There is a consequence for wrong doing, whether the act is consciously or unconsciously made, and whether forgiveness is extended and received. Many times students who have been academically dishonest will ask for "grace" or "mercy" for their situation, even acknowledging the wrong. Yet, we know while these are loving qualities of God as well, they are not shown apart from justice and consequences. The Law points people to the need for God's grace and mercy, not the other way around. The story of the cross is that God does not overlook or dismiss sin, but that Jesus paid the consequences for people's sins. Gene Veith says it this way in his book *Spirituality of the Cross*:

> To be sure, one response would be to deny it all, to insist that I really am a good person, that there is nothing wrong with my vices, and that God's Word isn't true at all. But the Bible speaks with an authority that is difficult to evade, and in one's heart of hearts, God's Law rings true. Admitting one's failure—and agreeing with one's condemnation—is the first step of Lutheran spirituality.[10]

The professor has the opportunity to model for students that while sin is forgiven through Christ's death and resurrection the consequences of sin are still real and felt in the world. This is maybe one of the most Christian and loving things a professor can do for students, provided that they point to the cross and the act of Christ taking that sin upon himself. He alone redeemed a fallen world, even a fallen academic world.

The secular realm of professor is one that God blesses both within a distinctively Lutheran university as well outside in state and private university settings. God provides knowledge and understanding of a field of study for the good of society and mankind. He blesses all of his creation through the understanding of the world, its cultures, and the various topics

---

[10] Gene Edward Veith Jr., *The Spirituality of the Cross: The Way of the First Evangelicals* (St. Louis: Concordia, 2010), 34.

found within academia. We dare not believe that these qualities alone are given to faith-based higher education institutions, but we can know, through faith, that God has called us into both kingdoms of his rule and authority and that we serve his people in our vocations as professor when we effectively teach that which is secular in nature.

The Kingdom of the Right

The kingdom of the right is a spiritual realm where Christ resides over those whom he has called to faith. The greatest part of teaching and working at a faith-based institution is that there are many opportunities to hear the good news of the Gospel and to be fed spiritually through Scripture. Weekly chapel, sacred concerts, and special services can all be places where God comes to us in his Word and reminds us of the grace we receive in Christ Jesus.[11]

While it seems that some believe the primary reason for faculty to attend chapel is to model or demonstrate the value of this time for students, I believe this notion is a confusion of the two kingdoms in many ways. While attendance may indeed serve as an example to others, this cannot be the primary reason for attending corporate worship on or off campus. We come into God's presence through his Word in order to be spiritually fed, for the strengthening of our faith, and for fellowship with the other members of God's family. These reasons are within the kingdom of grace and are truly blessings within a work environment, but they are God's work, not ours. Otherwise, we turn this time of worship into a law that brings resentment and distraction.

Since God has created his people to be with others in faith, the personal interactions in a university setting can be seen as related to this important function of the church. While it is true that not all our students may be members of God's family by faith, we are called in Scripture to be his witnesses "in Jerusalem and in all Judea and Samaria, and to the end of the earth" (Acts 1:8). Therefore, the opportunity to share and work with any individual student is an opportunity to witness to the grace we have received from God and to direct the student to the foot of the cross at every moment.

This close working relationship with individual students is referred to in many secular places as "mentoring." While mentoring can, and should, be available for any student, Christian or not, there is a unique mentoring relationship with those who profess faith in Christ Jesus. Mark William Roche, in his book *Why Choose the Liberal Arts?*, emphasizes that faculty

---

[11] For a discussion of chapel and other aspects of campus ministry, see Ruehs' chapter.

must do more in mentoring than just give advice or career counseling. Instead, Roche suggests that "as mentors, faculty members must both encourage and welcome the great questions that give meaning to a student's journey towards independence and maturity."[12]

Roche goes on to identify three types of questions that faculty can raise with their mentees. These range from enduring questions regarding the major facets of life (What is beauty? Where do we find truth?) to contemporary questions and possible solutions to them (Is cloning ethical? What is the role of family in the twenty-first century?) to questions regarding a student's existence and personal development (What gifts and talents do you have? What is the best way to use these talents in your vocations?).[13] These questions can be the framework for witnessing to the truth that we find in Christ Jesus and the grace we have received through faith in him.

Within the priesthood of all believers (1 Pet 2:9) we are called as Christians to serve God's people in prayer, teaching, and forgiveness. Luther says it this way: "[F]or as priests we are worthy to appear before God to pray for others and to teach one another divine things. These are the functions of priests, and they cannot be granted to any unbeliever."[14] Because of our calling to faith, Christian professors have the special opportunity to support their students in prayer and the teaching of God's Word when appropriate. The ability for faculty at a distinctively Lutheran university to witness to the gifts of faith, either to the non-believer as a "sowing of seed" (see Mark 4) or to the believing Christian as encouragement or strengthening of their already existing faith (see 1 Thess 3), is a special and unique portion of this vocation and office.

The existence of both kingdoms within the vocation of a professor is one that demands that we not confuse the two such that grace becomes law, or that law is not taken seriously, or that grace is not cherished. Both kingdoms have their proper place and both serve the purpose they are set forward to do within our lives. Seeing both kingdoms as present with this vocation will enable a professor fully to live out that vocation.

---

12 Mark William Roche, *Why Choose the Liberal Arts?* (Notre Dame: University of Notre Dame Press, 2010), 167.

13 Roche, *Why Choose the Liberal Arts?*, 167.

14 Martin Luther, "The Freedom of a Christian," in AE 31:355.

TENSIONS AND TIGHTROPES
WITHIN THE VOCATION OF PROFESSOR

In June of 2012, Nik Wallenda, a seventh generation member of the famous daredevil family, successfully crossed the Niagara Falls from Canada into New York on a tightrope. While I sat and watched him do that on television, with mist from the falls circulating around him and dripping from the wire, my thoughts were along the lines of "Is he nuts?" In spite of a safety harness, it seemed to me to be a pretty big gamble in the name of showmanship. Of course he seemed perfectly calm and at ease, probably because of the countless hours of practice and the sense of having done this all before, no matter what the surrounding environment was, and maybe because he was fully within his given vocation.

As I first entered into the vocation of professor, I had similar feelings watching those who were my colleagues balance and navigate the variety of tensions and tightropes they were walking on a daily basis, while at times I felt ready to fall off the rope into the freezing water of my own career. Teaching, family, research, graduate school, class prep, church . . . it all seemed to be too much at times.

Through the years of being a professor, it seems that a few of the tightropes that professors walk are unique to their vocation, even at a Lutheran university. While there is no watery grave if one should decide to move more towards one side or the other in these areas, they do represent practical areas that need to be carefully considered within our roles.

Teaching versus Research

Many Lutheran universities, as primarily liberal arts institutions for undergraduates and professional programs for graduate students, have made teaching the heart of what professors do. While faculty members at Lutheran universities do not typically live under the "publish or perish" model to earn tenure, professors are expected and supported by universities through sabbaticals, reduced course loads, fellowships, and the like to engage in research. The tension between these two areas seems to be growing as the desire of universities to gain prestige through scholarship clashes with their curricular and financial needs. Faculty have come to universities with the understanding that research opportunities and support would be present, yet growing student bodies coupled with delayed faculty hires have demanded that faculty teach four or more classes a semester and spend little to no time on scholarship.

One common trend to balance this tightrope is the use of undergraduate or student-focused research opportunities for faculty. This seemingly gives the faculty members the ability to do something in their area of expertise that may involve research, but to teach students along the way about the role of research and its foundational principles. The problem is that most research that can be done with students does not necessarily equate to the research faculty members have done in their field of study, or desire to do. It would make sense to connect the growing graduate student populations with faculty to work together on research, especially at universities with research degrees. But that may not be much of an option at institutions where most of the graduate students are working on professional degrees and may also be full-time employees with families.

The importance of professors continuing to do research and scholarly work, though, cannot be diminished. The knowledge and insights of scholar-teachers are beneficial gifts that God has bestowed on society, academia, and his church. The role of professor not only requires that they are "up-to-speed" on their field of expertise so that their teaching is sound and appropriate, it also encourages them to use these gifts to further fields of study into new arenas and discover new connections between fields of study. To be a static instructor, never changing and never growing, undermines the servant nature found in the vocation of a professor and weakens it to a point of being of no value. Scholarly work, either in the privacy of a professor's research or in connection with students, is an essential part of the whole vocation of professor along with excellent and inspiring instruction.

Content versus Relationships

Professors come into the vocation of teaching in higher education with a wealth of knowledge and, as just mentioned, extensive research within a given area or field. They are eager to share this information deeply and accurately so that others can use this knowledge and prepare themselves for their coming or continuing vocations. Students, especially younger students fresh out of high school, might be more interested in building relationships, not only with their peers, but with their professors. Here is another tightrope that professors walk.

For some faculty, this tension is seemingly diminished by taking the side of primarily content-focused instruction where the relationships are not built either within the class or between the student and professor. Instead, content is the only focus. In other situations, the classroom is run with a mindset that we are really here to just relate to each other, and there is less and less academic work that is done, or equally as dangerous, inaccurate content is shared. Is there a way to avoid both of these extremes? I not only believe there is, but I think it is expected of professors to do their best to know their students and relate to them while also instructing with the best and most accurate content.[15]

As mentioned previously, the opportunities for sharing your faith occur best in a relational context. While there is no doubt that higher education is built upon a solid discourse of content and the strengthening of student knowledge, there are opportunities, both inside and outside the class, for relationships to be developed that do not over-ride or supersede the content that needs to be taught. The first way to build relationships within a class seems fairly simple, yet is powerful. Promptly memorizing the names of your students sends a signal that they are important to you. Using student names will also help with class management and will enable those meetings out of class to be personal and meaningful.

Some have coined the term *ministry of presence* to model the acts of ministry done by just being visible and engaged with people.[16] This can apply to the vocation of professor very well and allows for balance in this tension between content and relationships. Being available during office hours, present on campus and in the cafeteria, and attending athletic, music, and theater events will give a professor those "connecting" points in the lives of their students. It may give the opportunity in a class situation to connect content directly to the students' lives or it may give opportunities for faculty to let students know that there is more to their lives than just what is in the class. Either way these kinds of connections can make a difference in the way that content is received in class and relationships are built.

Another important method to meet the goals of content and relationships is the use of "high-impact learning practices." For instance, classes that engage students in a seminar-style dialogue on seminal texts and exercise their minds with challenging questions and ideas foster personal interaction and intellectual development. The professor provides the necessary disciplinary knowledge and expertise to challenge the class, but also makes it a relational and encouraging environment for the students to grow intellectually and socially. Equally valuable is the exercising of students'

---

[15] Cf. Ken Bain who points out that "outstanding teachers know their subjects extremely well" and "often display openness with students and may, from time to time, talk about their own intellectual journey, its ambitions, triumphs, frustrations, and failures, and encourage their students to be similarly reflective and candid" (Ken Bain, *What the Best College Teachers Do* [Cambridge, MA: Harvard University Press, 2004], 15, 18). Reprinted by permission of Harvard University Press, Copyright © 2004 by the President and Fellows of Harvard College.

[16] Henri Nouwen, *Gracias: A Latin American Journal* (New York: Harper Collins, 1983), 147–48.

systematic inquiry and communication skills through writing-intensive courses and collaborative research.[17]

Whatever teaching methods the professor uses (seminar, problem-based lab, group project, lecture, etc.), the key factor in any effective practice is creating a "natural critical learning environment." In this environment, the professor motivates students to learn by "confronting [them with] intriguing, beautiful, or important problems, authentic tasks that will challenge them to grapple with ideas, rethink their assumptions, and examine their mental models of reality." The professor provides a challenging yet supportive setting where students have "a sense of control over their education," "work collaboratively with others," know that "their work will be considered fairly and honestly," have the freedom to try and fail, and are assured that they will "receive feedback from expert learners."[18] By setting up this kind of an environment, the professor can balance content and relationships to benefit student learning.

Teaching versus Administration

While it seems that this might be referring to the tensions between these groups of individuals, I am speaking of the tension that surrounds many faculty to "move up" into administrative offices, or conversely, to avoid it like the plague. As a professor progresses through the years, the opportunities for administrative duties or even a full-time administrative position may be available. How do we deal with the tension this creates within in our vocations? How do we know whether we should keep teaching or move into an administrative role?

The norm of higher education seems to be that "moving up" into administrative roles is the desired career path as pay increases and the day-to-day grind of the class wears on more "mature" professors. Dealing with students that are younger than their own children (or grandchildren in some cases) can begin to become less intriguing as the generation gaps widen. For others the thought of leaving the class or dealing with more meetings or the oversight of their colleagues is just as daunting and stressful.

Understanding the doctrine of vocation can help in making these decisions. If we fully believe that we are "called" by God into certain roles or positions and that God has prepared those he calls with the proper gifts and talents for those roles, some of the stress of "deciding" is removed. Our lov-

---

[17] For other examples, see George D. Kuh, *High-Impact Learning Practices: What They Are, Who Has Access to Them, and Why They Matter* (Washington DC: Association of American Colleges and Universities, 2009).

[18] Bain, *What the Best College Teachers Do*, 18 (also see pp. 99–109, 126–34).

ing Savior knows what is best for his people, including the person potentially being called into that role. If, and when, a person is called into an administrative role, apart from their pursuing or seeking it, then we must be open to the possibility that God has set this plan in motion and has given certain leadership gifts to an individual that others have noticed. If no opportunities in executive offices arise, then that may be God's way of informing a person about their vocation as well.

We also know that we can mess up God's callings by reaching outside and beyond our gifts and talents at times. Certainly this is true for some who have gone into administrative roles in the past. Some have sought administrative duties or been sought after when their real gifts and talents lie in the classroom and working with students. How do we know? How can we determine what God's calling is for us? Romans 12:1–2 gives us a piece of that answer as we consider how to determine God's will in our lives. Paul writes:

> I appeal to you therefore, brothers, by the mercies of God, to present your bodies as a living sacrifice, holy and acceptable to God, which is your spiritual worship. Do not be conformed to this world, but be transformed by the renewal of your mind, that by testing you may discern what is the will of God, what is good and acceptable and perfect.

God tells us that when we are connected to him by Scripture and the Sacraments of Baptism and Holy Communion we are transformed and that we may discern what God's will is for our lives. Finding God is not a mystery. God tells us where he is. He is present for us in his Word and Sacraments! The Christian professor connected to and fed by God has this promise.

Yet our human nature will still fail and our ego or "drive" will try to trump what God desires. There are many people that thought a move to administrative duties, or even a refusal of those duties, were the right decisions to make and found out that they were not. God surely works even then. The ability to see perfectly into the future is not given on earth, but the doctrine of vocation tells us to respond to the callings we receive in faith and grace. Those who have left administrative duties to return to the classroom, when done in faith in God's callings, have not erred or stepped outside their vocations, but have been faithful stewards of God's gifts.

But we also know that contentment in our present vocations, and service to God's people in whatever position we are in now, is also God-pleasing. We can be assured that doing our best today, and not worrying about the next step or next position, is something that God can and does bless. And should we be called into a position of administration at a later time, remembering that vocation is about serving one's neighbor in love, not serving ourselves or our egos, will enable us to move into that position as a representative of God in that position.

CONCLUSION

It has been joked that the university is full of doctors, just not the kind that can help folks. But in reality, the vocation of professor is one of the greatest opportunities to help young people (and sometimes more mature folks) reach their potential and strive for an intellectual, philosophical, and theological nature that they would not otherwise achieve. Helping students mature through discourse, intellectually stimulating content, and a foundation of faith in Christ is a high and important calling in service to the world and church. To fulfill this noble calling in a distinctively Lutheran university, professors need to be excellent in their academic content and fields of study. They need to be faithful to the God who has given them the talents and gift of teaching, reigns over society and the church, and commissions them to be his witnesses to the truth he shows in his creation and reveals in his Word. May God strengthen and guide you as you navigate your calling as a professor!

QUESTIONS

1. You have caught a student plagiarizing a paper and the student has confessed and apologized for this academic fraud. How does this incident reside in both the kingdom of the Law and the kingdom of the Gospel? How should you, the professor, respond to this incident?

2. How do professors confuse the two kingdoms of law and grace in their vocations? Why is it important to know which kingdom applies to a given situation as a professor?

3. Many professors feel a palpable tension between three aspects of being a professor: teaching, research, and service to the university or community. How do you think these tensions can best be navigated?

4. Identify some tensions caused by a professor having two simultaneous vocations, such as a professor and a spouse. What are we called to do in situations where two different vocations seem to be in conflict?

6

ONE VOICE OF ADMINISTRATION
AT A LUTHERAN CHRISTIAN UNIVERSITY

Mary Scott[1]

INTRODUCTION

I begin this essay with three confessions.

Confession number one: Despite years of teaching students the value of setting goals, I never, ever had a goal to enter into administration. Why would I? Administration is known in the world of education as "the dark side." In fact, when I accepted my first position with an administrative title, a faculty friend sat me down and told me all of the reasons why we could no longer be "real" friends. At Bible study another friend said to me, "You must not really care what people say about you." Obviously both were hurtful comments, which did not reflect favorably on what I thought was a prayerful and thoughtful decision.

Confession number two: There was a brief but intense period of time as an administrator when I literally prayed every day that God would provide a graceful way for me to exit my administrative role. It was during this time that, for the first time in my tenure, I actively searched for other positions.

Confession number three: Despite what was stated in confessions one and two, I know deep in my heart and soul that God has gifted me for administration. I know I am called into my role as provost at Concordia University Irvine. At this time in my life I am living fulfilled in my multiple callings as a wife, mother, and university administrator.[2] I have been known to tell new employees that, "I don't have two bad days in a row. I will have a bad day from time to time, but then I go home to a loving family. The next

---

[1] Mary Scott, EdD (Pepperdine), is Professor of Exercise Sports Science and Provost at CUI.

[2] Much can and should be written about the joys and struggles of each calling, but for purposes of this essay I have restricted my comments to that of administration.

day God's grace and mercies are new to me and to all of us. I return to this beautiful setting with faculty, staff, and students that I consider to be God's gifts to this institution at this time and I am blessed to serve another day."

The university where I work is an unabashedly Christian, distinctively Lutheran institution. Despite this, or perhaps because of this, my life in administration is filled with both tension and joy. Tension is defined in Oxford Dictionaries as "the state of being stretched tight" or "mental or emotional strain."[3] Often my sources of tension are the following: meetings, emails, strategic planning, emails, facilities, schedules, emails, agendas, curricular options, contracts, emails, budgets, decisions . . . did I mention emails? I usually get about 150 to 200 email messages a day during the regular semester. In addition, faculty, staff, students, regents, visitors, alumni, city council members, parents, or international guests can also create tension. However, the combination of all of these items also leads to the joy in my vocation: using my God-given gifts and skills to serve as an administrator.

Tension is a part of life on earth. As Lutherans we see the tension of life resulting from our sins, on the one hand, and the gift of amazing grace we find in our Lord and Savior Jesus Christ, on the other hand. How one serves or administers with the knowledge and understanding of sin and grace at an unabashedly Christian, distinctively Lutheran institution is the focus of this essay.

LUTHERAN THEOLOGY AND ADMINISTRATION

Simul Iustus et Peccator

As an administrator at a Lutheran Christian university, a proper understanding of Martin Luther's *simul iustus et peccator* ("simultaneously saint and sinner") paradox provides the context for work done in the academy.[4] The people administrators serve each day are saints and sinners. In his inaugural presidential address at Valparaiso University in 1940, the Reverend Otto Kretzmann defined a university as "a voluntary association of free men and women in a community which is dedicated to a two-fold task: the search for Truth and the transmission of Truth, free and unbroken, to those who are born later in time."[5] This association of truth

---

[3] Oxford Dictionaries, accessed September 19, 2014, http://oxforddictionaries.com/us/definition/american_english/tension.

[4] See Mueller's chapter for an overview of *simul iustus et peccator*.

[5] O. P. Kretzmann, "The Destiny of a Christian University in the Modern World," in *The Lutheran Reader*, ed. Paul J. Contino and David Morgan (Valparaiso, IN: Valparaiso University, 1999), 110.

seekers and truth transmitters—students, staff, and faculty—are in the residence halls, offices, classes, chapel, gymnasium, cafeteria, and online every day. Not only are they saints and sinners, but administrators are too. We all, like David, would do well to begin each day with verses from Ps 51 (especially verses 1–2, 10–12):

> Have mercy on me, O God,
>   according to your steadfast love;
> according to your abundant mercy
>   blot out my transgressions.
> Wash me thoroughly from my iniquity,
>   and cleanse me from my sin. . . .
> Create in me a clean heart, O God,
>   and renew a right spirit within me.
> Cast me not away from your presence,
>   and take not your Holy Spirit from me.
> Restore to me the joy of your salvation,
>   and uphold me with me with a willing spirit.

The knowledge and understanding of our sinful human nature allows us to approach our tasks in a spirit of humbleness. In humility we log on to our computers, review our calendars, enter our classrooms, prepare our agendas, and begin our meetings. Recognizing that as Christians we are simultaneously sinner and saint, we will struggle with our own humanness as we seek to serve and lead. In humility we enter into university planning with the knowledge that it is not our plans that we desire to put in place, but we seek to understand more fully God's plans for his institution. We approach each difficult personnel situation with the common platform found in Rom 3:23, "For all have sinned and fall short of the glory of God." We recognize that we too are sinful people, that all personnel problems are the result of our sinful nature, and that God's grace extends to the person I am working with as well as to me. While sin is not without its consequences, how one communicates the consequences during this stressful time is critical to living a life filled with an awareness of God's unbelievable grace.

Effective leaders have a deep understanding of their strengths and weaknesses. Leaders understand that what they bring to the organization each day is really much bigger than themselves. Our world is looking for "real." In a place where we are able instantly to see the brokenness of sin, perhaps today more than ever, a decidedly Lutheran university is poised to say, "Come join us. We are broken too!" Effective Christian leaders have an understanding of the dynamic realities of the present world while being grounded and framed through a deep connection to the incarnate Word. It is there that leaders find the source of guidance, vision, and purpose.[6]

Listening closely to the incarnate Word, an administrator at a Lutheran Christian university also rejoices in wonder at the free gift from God found in Christ Jesus. Because of God's work of salvation, we are able to approach each day as a saint (Rom 3:24)! With this knowledge of a strong foundation of forgiveness, we also enter into our offices, check and respond to emails, take telephone calls from angry parents, and pray with hurting colleagues. With thankfulness that I need do nothing—indeed I cannot do anything to earn this gift of forgiveness—I am able to approach each task rejoicing in the confidence of knowing that my God has prepared me and each believer to do the work that is in front of us today (Eph 2:8–10). As the apostle Paul writes in Rom 6:4, "We were buried therefore with him by baptism into death, in order that, just as Christ was raised from the dead by the glory of the Father, we too might walk in newness of life." The redemptive work of Christ is much bigger than the work of any individual. A deep understanding of the eternal promise of this free gift provides all Christians the opportunity to approach their tasks each day with a rich appreciation of living in newness of life.

One well-known example of leadership from way outside a Christian context is that of Adolf Hitler. In Dietrich Bonhoeffer's speeches and writings, he referred to Hitler's type of leadership as the "Führer Principle." It's a profoundly misguided concept of leadership that is dramatically different from a Lutheran understanding of real leadership. Bonhoeffer writes:

> Only when a man sees that office is a penultimate authority in the face of an ultimate, indescribable authority, in the face of the authority of God, has the real situation been reached. And before this Authority the individual knows himself to be completely alone. The individual is responsible before God. And this solitude of man's position before God, this subjection to an ultimate authority, is destroyed when the authority of the Leader or of the office is seen as ultimate authority. . . . [A]lone before God, man becomes what he is, free and committed in responsibility at the same time.[7]

It is inevitable for one to feel alone in many settings. This is true of administrators too. Our sins are ever before us and at times we wonder with the

---

6   Henri J. M. Nouwen, *In the Name of Jesus: Reflections on Christian Leadership* (New York; Crossroad, 1992), 31.

7   Quoted in Eric Metaxas, *Bonhoeffer: Pastor, Martyr, Prophet, Spy* (Nashville: Thomas Nelson, 2010), 142. Reprinted by permission of Thomas Nelson.

apostle Paul in Rom 7, "Why do we continue to do the very things we do not want to do?" The Lutheran understanding of sinner and saint places a leader alone before a jealous and gracious God. It is this comfort of companionship, of walking with our Savior who not only sees us in our sin, but saves us by his grace, that provides an administrator at a Lutheran Christian university with hope for the future when things seem dreary and joy in serving is gone.

James Kouzes and Barry Posner have researched and written extensively about the five practices of exemplary leaders. Their research indicates that effective leaders are able to challenge the process, inspire a shared vision, enable others to act, model the way, and encourage the heart.[8] Leaders must influence followers to dedicate their work to live out the mission of the organization. In a Christian organization, the leader who understands that daily they fail and fall short is one who will also understand, model, and encourage living by and with the grace of God.

A university administrator with the proper understanding of daily sinfulness and sainthood has an appropriate platform from which she is able to lead. Exhibiting this type of leadership at a Lutheran Christian university allows those who search for truth and transmit truth to be both cautious (as sinners) and bold (as saints). As Darrell Jodock says in this vein,

> [A Lutheran university] will be cautious about its intellectual claims, while at the same time valuing those claims as potential contributions to human wellbeing. It may proclaim those ideas widely and loudly but always with a sense that they can be challenged and never with a sense that they have exhausted the subject. Such a college or university will be wary of ideologies and receptive to paradoxes that point beyond ideas to something still deeper, still more complex, and still not well understood.[9]

Two Kingdoms

Left-hand Responsibilities

Leading a Lutheran Christian university today is an exciting and complex task. In addition to a deep love and appreciation for higher education, an administrator must keep current with federal rules and regulations, financial aid, scholarship, pedagogy, technology, human resources, deferred

---

8   James M. Kouzes and Barry Z. Posner, *The Leadership Challenge: How to Make Extraordinary Things Happen in Organizations* (San Francisco: Jossey-Bass, 2002).

9   Darrell Jodock, "Gift and Calling: A Lutheran Perspective on Higher Education," *Intersections* 34 (Fall, 2011): 15.

maintenance, financial margins, changing demographics, accreditation, enrollment data, licensure, and the like. At all times we are confronted with being in the world, but not of the world (John 17:13–16).

As an administrator at a Lutheran Christian university, proper understanding of Luther's kingdom of the law and the kingdom of grace provides a unique framework from which to operate.[10] The Lutheran understanding of two kingdoms is summed up in the understanding of the kingdom of the left (Law) where entities such as society, schools, and families are governed by rules, regulations, and authority, and the kingdom of the right (Gospel) where we find salvation and grace through faith in Christ Jesus.

Many of the daily activities of an administrator at a Lutheran Christian university are to fulfill the responsibilities of God's kingdom of the left. Although I am fortunate to have extremely competent colleagues who actually compile the data, complete the reports, and send the electronic submissions on or before the deadlines, my level of administration ultimately means that I am held accountable for making sure that all of this is accomplished. There are many items that fall under the heading of "kingdom of the law" in which I am fully engaged. The execution or termination of a contract, for example, is an item closely regulated by the laws of the state of California. Indeed, for the university to be able to keep its doors open to accomplish its mission, administrators at a Lutheran Christian university must operate competently within the kingdom of the law.

University administrators do not to work in silos. We believe that God has called all employees, including administrators, to work together to accomplish the mission of the institution using their God-given gifts to make appropriate recommendations and decisions. The way a president, provost, chief financial officer (CFO), and chief enrollment officer (CEO) reviews a draft budget for the new fiscal year is one example of an intersection of the work of the kingdom of the law with the kingdom of grace. While the board of regents (BOR) has ultimate authority for the university, the president may review the budget in light of deliverability. She will review the budget in order to determine if the right initiatives are in place to deliver a successful year to the BOR and keep the mission and ministry of the institution moving forward. While the provost is looking at the draft budget through the lens of investment in academics, instructional resources, staffing, and operations, the CFO is likely considering margins, bank covenants, investments, and cash flow. Finally, at a tuition-driven institution the CEO is reviewing the budget from the position of achievability. He will want to calculate risks and determine what the likelihood is that we can really bring

---

[10] See Mueller's chapter for a summary of two-kingdom theology.

a targeted number of students into the university or keep them here. To put it another way, are our enrollment and financial aid projections realistic and conservative? At the heart of each administrator is or should be a compelling drive to fulfill the mission of the institution. Despite this, in each budget review, people at various levels of the institution are normally disappointed or feel as if their requests were not considered. Some employees do not agree with the final budget and its allocations. Some do not care and others do not understand.

Right-hand Opportunities

While the university budget is a part of the kingdom of law, the administrator at a Lutheran Christian university will also pay attention to the budget's impact on the kingdom of the right. Administrators must ascertain how budget decisions help or hinder the work of a Lutheran Christian university in spreading the Gospel of Christ (Matt 28:19–20). Recognizing that we are sinners who err in our vocations, administrators remind each other that our God holds us and all people in his care. God is always at work in his world and his grace covers us all. We do our best in our vocations and extend his grace to all. We pray that our colleagues extend God's grace to us too!

Administrating a Lutheran Christian university means that there will always be tension between serving the kingdom of the left and the kingdom of the right. Recognizing God's two kingdoms at work on Christian campuses, Martin Marty rightly notes many tensions:

> This work of Christian higher education in church-related institutions occurs at the juncture of several sets of entities or descripts that we used to think of as opposites, antagonisms—but today, for good reasons and bad, and with both promise and threat, these zones tend to blur, fuse, overlap, and lose their distinctiveness. I have in mind tensions between the material and the spiritual, the secular and the religious, the privileged and the exposed, and vocation and Vocation.[11]

Administrators with an understanding of two kingdoms believe that God ultimately rules all and is concerned about what happens in the kingdoms of the left and the right. So, as they discuss and debate items such as social media and free expression or rules in the residence halls, administrators at a Lutheran Christian university recognize they are crossing the intersection

---

[11] Martin E. Marty, "The Church and Christian Higher Education in the New Millennium," in *Faithful Learning and the Christian Scholarly Vocation*, eds. Douglas V. Henry and Bob R. Agee (Grand Rapids; Eerdmans, 2003), 54.

of two kingdoms. Each topic touches on the rules and regulations of the kingdom of the left. However, "because God's greatest desire for human beings is that we hear the Gospel and come to faith" we not only seek to provide people at the university with God's protection and care in the kingdom of the left, we also use these topics as opportunities, when appropriate, to point people to God's grace in kingdom of the right.[12]

While competence in keeping the law is required of administrators at any university in America, the Lutheran context of the kingdom of the right allows us to acknowledge God's grace and use it as a model from which to function. Through the years, it has been my privilege to participate in and reflect upon the ways I have experienced the Holy Spirit working in the hallways, classrooms, and offices of our campus. What joy it has been to observe colleagues who were "at odds" for weeks, months, and sometimes years come to a deep appreciation of God's grace and be prompted to forgive in Christ and graciously reach an agreement. Likewise, it is a joy when difficult personnel decisions are concluded with dignity and respect for all involved. For example, when a valued employee needs to be repositioned into another role, colleagues join in supporting and praying for that individual offering her/him a fresh start and support in that change. Praying with students, colleagues, and their families when they are going through difficult times is a privilege as well. Because an administrator understands saving grace as a gift from our maker, the gracious and loving way an administrator treats those he serves with and for are marks not only of God's kingdom of the right, but also of effective Christian leadership.

Supporting Academics and the Gospel

Administrators at a Lutheran Christian university dedicate the institution to operate in such a way as to share the Gospel while upholding academic quality. To accomplish this, careful thought must be given to faculty hiring and academic program development. The days of hiring a faculty composed exclusively of Lutherans are gone. To maintain the Lutheran identity of the institution, care must be given to providing a rich development program for all faculty members, Lutheran and non-Lutheran. The vision and mission of the institution should provide a framework from which to build clarity around common theological understandings and a safe place to explore differences. In my experience, non-Lutheran Christian colleagues have made outstanding contributions to the institution and

---

[12] Steven P. Mueller, ed., *Called to Believe, Teach, and Confess: An Introduction to Doctrinal Theology* (Eugene, OR: Wipf and Stock, 2005), 428. For examples of such two-kingdom interaction in student affairs, see the chapter by Keith and Fugitt.

appreciated opportunities to understand its identity and culture on a deeper level. They feel the development program helped them in their disciplines and pedagogy, which, in turn, provided a richer educational experience for their students. At the same time, academic programs must also be thoughtfully developed, implemented, and refreshed within the deep understanding and framework of the liberal arts as well as God's work in our world today. Two examples of academic programs that reflect this understanding at my institution, Concordia University Irvine (CUI), are the Core Curriculum and the Around-the-World Semester.

The idea for the Core began with members of the faculty asking questions such as: "How could CUI continue to provide a true liberal arts education rooted in its Lutheran tradition?" and "How could the faculty and administration strengthen the entire academic experience, attract even better students, and create a shared intellectual foundation for the entire campus community?" Faculty and administrative colleagues shared ideas, addressed concerns, and provided perspectives in a thought-provoking manner. The result was the successful development and implementation of CUI's Core Curriculum.[13]

While the idea of a core curriculum is certainly not new, the timing of its implementation for CUI could not have been more challenging. Just as the dreams of the faculty members driving the Core Curriculum were becoming real, tangible plans, the institution went into a significant financial crisis. While we were literally looking at spreadsheets to find funds to cut, we were also encouraging and supporting the work of the faculty to develop the Core. (Many times administrators are accused of talking out of both sides of their mouths . . . this was probably one of those times.)

Why would administrators support such a bold and distinctive idea at such a difficult time in the life of the institution? Other administrators will answer this question differently, but for me, while there were many excellent reasons, the fundamental answer was found in my Lutheran understanding of the importance of the liberal arts in schools. Martin Luther was a prolific writer. While the majority of his works pertained to doctrinal rediscoveries of the Reformation era, several of his pieces on school are seminal works. In his essay, "To the Councilmen of All Cities in German That They Establish and Maintain Christian Schools," written in 1524, Luther goes on at some length about the value of a classical curriculum, for he was convinced that knowledge of the liberal arts provided the best context for the study of Scripture. Not only would ministers, theologians, teachers, and scholars educated in this manner best

---

[13] For details on CUI's Core Curriculum, see http://www.cui.edu/core.

serve the church, but all believers as members of Christ's body would better know God and better live out their vocations in both of God's kingdoms by means of such learning. As Luther states,

> [An illiberal education produces] blockheads, unable to converse intelligently on any subject, or to assist or counsel anyone. But if young people were instructed and trained in schools, or wherever learned and well-trained schoolmasters and school mistresses were available to teach [biblical and classical] languages, the other [liberal] arts, and history, they would then hear of the doings and saying of the entire world, and how things went with various cities, kingdoms, princes, men, and women. Thus, they could in short time set before themselves as in a mirror the character, life, counsels, and purposes—successful or unsuccessful—of the whole world from the beginning; on the basis of which they could then draw the proper inferences and in the fear of God take their own place in the stream of human events.[14]

The day the faculty passed the Core Curriculum I told one long-time fellow faculty member that this was one of the most important decisions the faculty had ever made. I believed this decision would significantly identify or brand CUI as a Lutheran Christian university for future generations to come. While the liberal arts content and design of the Core were significant in themselves, what was equally or perhaps more important for me was the commitment of the faculty to require *all* undergraduate students— freshmen and transfer—to engage with the Core.

As designed, one of the hallmarks of CUI's Core is the opportunity for students and faculty members to make connections in various ways. We aim to help students develop knowledge using the wisdom of the past as they learn to think clearly, read deeply, and communicate effectively. The Core allows faculty members to extend the reach of a specific discipline and bring in connections to the Christian faith while building intellectual habits. As faculty build relationships with students, they are able to find appropriate ways to bring in the knowledge of salvation through Christ. Indeed, it was the faculty's assurance of doing whatever is needed to support students in reaching a deep level of understanding of the liberal arts while finding appropriate connections to the saving work of Jesus Christ that influenced my support and commitment of the Core.

The Around-the-World (ATW) Semester also began with a question. The email I received said something to the effect of, "16 weeks, 10 countries,

---

[14] Martin Luther, "To the Councilmen of All Cities in Germany that They Establish and Maintain Christian Schools," in AE 45:369.

30 students . . . what to do you think?" Because I believe experiential education is very valuable and I could see the potential transformative value to the students, my initial response was something to the effect of "Sounds interesting. Tell me more." The faculty again went to work outlining objectives, developing the plan, interviewing the students, and we launched the first trip. What we learned from the first group was the trip was literally transformative for those involved. A quote from one ATW student at a board of regents meeting has stuck with me: "I don't know if I will ever be able to use my passport again. But I will never again look at things in the same way no matter where God calls me to serve."

As I write this we are preparing for ATW Semester III, faculty are building the budget, scheduling the itinerary, and developing their courses. Students are preparing their applications. The ATW Semester is an intensive learning, serving, and travel experience. It too is designed for students to find connections in the world. The connections may be to "great books," to each other, to the professors and their families, to others from different countries, or to cultural experiences. Through the ATW Semester they also build *koinonia*. As Gary Burge explains this Greek New Testament term,

> Christian community is not some passing association of people who share common sympathies for a cause. Nor is it an academy where an intellectual consensus about God is discovered. It cannot be so superficial. Christian community is partnership in experience; it is the common living of people who have a shared experience of Jesus Christ. They talk about this experience, they urge each other to grow more deeply in it, and they discover that through it, they begin to build a life together unlike any shared life in the world.[15]

Through the ATW Semester, students, faculty, and staff see the Gospel at work in their lives and the lives of others around the globe. At the same time, the visas that are required, the security checks, the communist states, and other regulations allow them to understand the broader workings of God's kingdom of the left in the world.

Pointing to the Cross of Christ

Administrators at a Lutheran Christian university understand that while they are called to serve others by excellently fulfilling their responsibilities in God's kingdom of the left, they are also called to serve others faithfully by pointing them to the cross of Christ. Henri Nouwen expresses

---

[15] Gary M. Burge, *Letters of John: The NIV Application Commentary* (Grand Rapids: Zondervan, 1996), 55.

this well in his book, *In the Name of Jesus,* when he encourages us to consider Christian leadership as an intimate relationship with and theological reflection about Jesus. The atoning work of Jesus provides the way to eternal life for each person. A leader that thinks, speaks, and acts in Jesus' name will seek to discern how human history and current events point us to the cross and the resurrection.[16]

Working in and through two kingdoms, administrators at Lutheran Christian universities can do more than point out temporary solutions to today's problems; they can direct people to God's eternal solution. While Christian leaders can and do make positive contributions to those around them through the daily practice of encouragement and comfort, their larger task is to recognize and proclaim the ways Jesus is leading, guiding, and empowering his people to move them from bondage to freedom. Christian leaders recognize the difficulty inherent in moving people through the conflicts, suffering, and uncertainties of this world, but know that the peace that passes all understanding is found in the freedom of the cross. This type of leadership requires an articulate faith, demonstrated in words and practice, that leans on God's real presence among us.[17]

It is faith in God's real, gracious presence that allows administrators at my university to approve a salary increase for a staff member going through a divorce even in the midst of significant institutional financial struggles or offer a reduced teaching load to a faculty member whose spouse is struggling with cancer. Indeed, we send students, faculty, and staff to serve in the local community after fires rage through canyons. We provide resources to send students to people and places that have been devastated, like New Orleans or Haiti. We teach and model for students how, in the midst of terrible situations, we can point people to Christ!

A Lutheran Christian university led by administrators who understand the tension and joy of operating within two kingdoms is one that attracts the finest students, employees, and donors. In today's world it stands apart from other institutions as it offers a model of competence and character in God's protection and grace through which truth seekers and truth transmitters are able openly and freely to engage in developing their habits of mind, understanding the truth, and serving their neighbor in God's two kingdoms.

---

[16] Nouwen, *In the Name of Jesus,* 66–67.

[17] Nouwen, *In the Name of Jesus,* 66.

Vocation

Betty Stanley Beene, former president and chief executive officer of the United Way of America, assumed leadership of the organization at a time when the nonprofit was reeling from the mismanagement and excesses of her predecessor. Beene successfully began to implement changes to the organization through national headquarters and local offices. As with any change, there were struggles. After five years, Beene felt she had accomplished as much as she would be able to, so she resigned. In explaining her decision, Beene said,

> I believe so strongly that God called me to this work. When I left, I felt just as strongly that He was calling me to go. Faith helps you understand that you are not the work and the work is not yours. God is in charge of it all, and if you will put your trust in Him, He will enable you to do amazing things, things you never dreamt possible.[18]

I do not know if Betty Stanley Beene is Lutheran, but her articulation of her calling acknowledges a strong commitment to God's work in and through her life. A Lutheran understanding of vocation is centered on the work of Jesus Christ and the Christian response, through which God works to fulfill his purposes in the world.[19] Simply stated, God created this world and all creatures. He uniquely and complexly created each person. Even after humanity sinned against God's callings for them, God, because of his amazing love for us, restored his relationship with us by sending his son, Christ Jesus, to die on a cross for our sins, descend victoriously into hell, rise from the dead for our resurrection, and ascend to heaven to rule over all his church and over us in grace. It is through Christ, and the new life he gives us, that God calls Christians to serve both his kingdom of the left and his kingdom of the right.

Understanding this deep, rich, profound gift provides us with the confidence to serve God with all of our capacities in all of our roles. It provides administrators with the assurance that God is daily at work in them as they carry out their duties. Even when we sin in our vocations, and we all do as the apostle Paul reminds us in Rom 7:7–25, God, in Christ, is still with and for us. As *The Lutheran Study Bible* says about this passage from Romans,

---

[18] Quoted in James M. Kouzes and Barry Z. Posner, "The Five Practices of Exemplary Leadership," in *Christian Reflections on the Leadership Challenge*, eds. James M. Kouzes and Barry Z. Posner (San Francisco: Jossey-Bass, 2004), 21.

[19] For a discussion of the doctrine of vocation, see Mueller's chapter.

> Our struggle with sin in not a past event; it is a present reality. We
> know God's will and desire to serve Him, but we cannot overcome sin.
> Even if we try, we fail. We cry out, "Who will deliver me from this
> body of death?" There is only one answer: "Thanks be to God through
> Jesus Christ our Lord!" Jesus rescues us. Though we sin daily, He
> continues to forgive and restore us.[20]

Indeed, God equips us with gifts and skills, calls us to serve him with our
talents, and forgives us in Christ when we fail to fulfill our vocations. With
these assurances of giftedness and grace, we are called to love God by serving our neighbor in all that we do. For an administrator at a Lutheran
Christian university, this service extends to those engaged in the university
community, on and off campus, in the city, and around the world. We cannot remove our calling when we leave the office and go home.

An administrator at a Lutheran Christian university also positions the
university to be a vehicle for students to explore their unique gifts and carry
out their callings. There are many fine colleges and universities where students are educated, but, as Marty observes,

> Only Christian higher education is committed to what Christians
> mean by *Vocation*. They mean lives that find their coherence in Christ,
> "in whom everything holds together." They learn that each of them is
> distinctively marked, irreplaceable, in God's scheme of things, and that
> they are not merely integers among the thrones and principalities and
> authorities.[21]

Because a Lutheran Christian university is committed to vocation, an
administrator will make sure that there are many opportunities for students
to discover and develop their God-given vocations. These opportunities will
extend from the classroom to chapel to student government to internships
to career counseling to mission trips to musical ensembles to athletics, and
much more.

The leadership practices cited by Kouzes and Posner include modeling
the way, inspiring a shared vision, challenging the process, enabling others
to act, and encouraging the heart. These practices are not restricted to only
a few select people. Rather, they are examples of how people will treat each
other when they live out their Christian vocation or calling in how they
lead. Leadership in light of vocation means moving an institution forward
by placing others before self. To do this requires a deep understanding of

---

[20] Edward A. Engelbrecht, ed., *The Lutheran Study Bible: English Standard Version* (St.
Louis: Concordia, 2009), 1923.

[21] Marty, "The Church and Christian Higher Education in the New Millennium," 60.

self in relationship to the saving work of Christ Jesus. Nouwen captures this notion well when he writes,

> The world says, "when you were young you were dependent and could not go where you wanted, but when you grow old you will be able to make your own decisions, go your own way, and control your own destiny." But Jesus has a different vision of maturity: It is the ability and willingness to be led where you would rather not go. Immediately after Peter has been commissioned to be a leader of his sheep, Jesus confronts him with the hard truth that the servant-leader is the leader who is being led to unknown, undesirable, and painful places. The way of the Christian leader is not the way of upward mobility in which our world has invested so much, but the way of downward mobility ending on the cross. This might sound morbid and masochistic, but for those who have heard the voice of the first love and said "yes" to it, the downward-moving way of Jesus is the way to the joy and the peace of God, a joy and peace that is not of this world.[22]

An administrator of a Lutheran Christian university with a deep understanding of Christ-like vocation does not need to be concerned with titles or organizational charts. They will not be blind to the advantages and disadvantages of movement in the institution, but they will hopefully be most interested in using their gifts and skills to serve others to the glory of God! By way of example, I have a colleague who expresses at times that he would rather be serving in a faculty role. Yet, because of his deep understanding of the cross and love of Jesus, he also finds true joy in using his gifts to serve others as an administrator.

There is freedom, too, in the proper understanding of vocation. Freedom to serve knowing that one is uniquely gifted for certain tasks and responsibilities means that an administrator does not need to do or know it all. The gifts and skills I have brought to the multiple administrative offices I have held at my institution through the years are different than what others have brought and will bring in the future. Knowing that God has called and gifted me, and that my unique gifts are complimented by those around me, provides me with the courage I need to use my gifts and skills in my current leadership position. Indeed, knowing what my vocation is gives me the courage and freedom to empower others to use their gifts and skills to fulfill their particular callings.

During my tenure I have been privileged to serve in administration for three presidents and one interim president. I have served alongside three

---

[22] Nouwen, *In the Name of Jesus*, 62–63.

chief financial officers. While I trust God truly called each man into his position, and each brought his own gift to the leadership team, when each person left the university, the executive team continued to function; the mission and ministry of the university continued. This occurred because leadership is much deeper than self. Leadership at a Lutheran Christian university today is a collaborative effort. While we each bring our gifts to the table, we also learn from and lean on each other. At times, we, like Peter, have had to go where we would rather not go (e.g., through a deep financial crisis, to the bedside of a dying colleague, into a meeting to tell loved and valued colleagues that their contracts will not be renewed, etc.). But we go knowing that God is using our unique gifts in administration and that we are growing in our understanding of being called to do both pleasant and unpleasant tasks for the sake of God's kingdoms of the left and the right.

LUTHERAN THEOLOGY AND INSTITUTIONAL LEADERSHIP: WHAT DOES THIS MEAN?

In his Small Catechism, Luther repeatedly asked "What does this mean?" to drive people into a deeper understanding of Scripture and its application to life. This question is worth repeating here. What does it mean to serve in administration at an unabashedly Christian, distinctively Lutheran institution?

Luther forthrightly acknowledged Scripture's tensions and paradoxes like saint and sinner, in the world but not of the world, and Jesus the baby in a manger and the Creator. At my institution, we also acknowledge tensions and paradoxes. Note the tensions outlined in the university's mission statement: "Concordia University Irvine, guided by the Great Commission of Jesus Christ and the Lutheran Confessions, empowers students through the *liberal arts and professional studies* for lives of learning, *service and leadership.*"[23]

As an administrator at a Lutheran Christian university, I live with these tensions every day. In fact, most often, I not only live but embrace the tensions found in my institution and the vocation of administration. As an administrator serving God's kingdom of the left, I am called to use my abilities—reason, experience, wisdom, and skill—to perform my vocation excellently. Regardless of whether I succeed or not (for we are all fallen and finite), I am also a child of God. This is not by my own ability, but purely by

---

[23] "Our Mission," Concordia University Irvine, accessed September 19, 2014, http://www.cui.edu/aboutcui (emphases added).

grace through faith in Jesus Christ (Eph 2:8). As Luther says in his Small Catechism about the third article of the Apostles' Creed, "I believe that by my own understanding or strength I cannot believe in Jesus Christ my Lord or come to him, but instead the Holy Spirit has called me through the gospel, [and] enlightened me with his gifts."[24] This tension of living by standards of excellence (Law), yet living as a child of God by grace (Gospel) puts everything about my life and this university into perspective. It allows me to challenge, inspire, and encourage excellence in an academic institution while also modeling and applying God's grace to colleagues and students.

It is under this banner of God's two kingdoms that we live out the tensions found at Lutheran Christian universities. We, as fallen and finite people, admit that we have limited knowledge and incomplete reasoning. Every person who enters our portals as truth seekers and truth transmitters must begin with the understanding that he could be wrong. This confession drives a serious academic institution and allows students to deeply question and richly understand their place in this world under the cross of Christ. Once we understand that we are incomplete and frail beings saved by God's grace in Christ alone, we can enter into serious intellectual and spiritual dialogue and study to develop the life of the mind for vocations of service in God's two kingdoms.

One of my favorite sayings is "Discussion changes things." It was collegial discussion among faculty members that lead to the development and implementation our Core Curriculum. It was recognizing that a deep understanding of other countries would enhance learning and bring greater opportunity to question the "American way" that lead to the development and implementation of the Around-the-World Semester. These discussions were firmly built upon Lutheran theology, including that of saint and sinner, two kingdoms, and vocation. This foundation provides wonderful resources to sustain the life of the mind for vocations of service in God's two kingdoms. From this administrative perspective, this means that, by God's grace and mercy, Christian colleges and universities that uphold these kingdoms and their tensions will continue to bring a clear, rich, and compelling voice to the table of American higher education for many years to come. To God be the glory!

---

[24] Martin Luther, "Small Catechism" in *The Book of Concord: The Confessions of the Evangelical Lutheran Church*, eds. Robert Kolb and Timothy J. Wengert (Minneapolis: Fortress, 2000), 355.

QUESTIONS

1. How do the notions of vocation and "simultaneously saint and sinner" help an administrator understand and live out her role at a Christian university? Why is the cross of Christ important for an administrator?

2. How is it helpful to speak about administration as having responsibilities in God's kingdom of the left and opportunities in God's kingdom of the right? What promises and threats are there to blurring these two kingdoms as an administrator?

3. How can administrators model, inspire, and enable faculty, students, and staff to be truth seekers and truth transmitters? What programs might administrators at Christian universities seek to develop that both uphold academic rigor and share the Gospel of Christ?

4. As an institution grows, what elements keep it grounded to its foundational Christian roots? How can administrators preserve and promote these key elements?

7

FULFILLING LAWS AND ADVANCING THE MISSION: THE VOCATION OF THE BOARD OF REGENTS

Cindy Steinbeck[1]

INTRODUCTION

Addressing the vocation of the board of regents is necessary to round out this work on Lutheran Christian higher education.[2] The governing board plays a significant role in the life of the educational institution. Unlike the president, faculty, or students, regents work behind the scenes doing work required by laws governing nonprofits. When functioning well, the board works together as one voice to promote the university's mission and, under the guidance of the president and his executive team, help set the vision for the future.

All nonprofits, including nonprofit colleges and universities, must be incorporated in the state in which they operate. A governing board is required by the law of that state. In order to understand the vocation of the board of regents we must take a brief look at why a governing board exists. Part one of this essay includes a brief overview of the history of not-for-profit corporations. Part two offers a specific example of one Lutheran university's governing board, on which I serve, by looking at Concordia University Irvine's articles of incorporation and bylaws as well as the Lutheran Church—Missouri Synod's (LCMS) bylaws pertaining to the university's board of regents. Parts three and four include brief explanations of the work of the board of regents from the vantage point of the articles of incorporation, bylaws, and the university's mission statement. Part five

---

[1] Cindy Steinbeck, MA (Concordia University Irvine), is a regent at CUI.
[2] For an explanation of the doctrine of vocation, see Mueller's chapter.

discusses the pitfalls to avoid and measures to implement for the board of regents to operate smoothly.

HISTORICAL ROOTS OF EDUCATIONAL INSTITUTIONS
AS NOT-FOR-PROFIT CORPORATIONS

Harvard College was the first nonprofit educational institution in the United States. Originally the legislature assigned a governing board of twelve. The first college president was Henry Dunster. As Peter Dobkin Hall explains,

> In 1650, Dunster obtained for Harvard a formal charter of incor-poration. The charter was an attempt to frame Harvard as a corporate entity distinct from the state: This would not only secure its control of properties that had been entrusted to it, but would also provide it with greater autonomy in managing its own affairs. The drafters specified the nature and extent of corporate powers, making a distinction between the persons who might serve as officials of the corporation and their role as *officers*.[3]

Originally the legislature appointed "fellows" to serve as corporate officers. Battles raged as to who would govern, how governors were elected, and the role they should serve.

Yale took a different approach, skirting the process of incorporation. The institution felt the impact of that decision, when no individual was legally responsible to the whole, thereby enabling the most powerful indi-viduals to make decisions and direct the educational system according to their individual biases. The whole was divided into parts very quickly.[4]

Incorporation of educational institutions as nonprofits run by govern-ing boards who spoke as one voice on behalf of the mission of the institu-tion, not the will of the legislature, became the norm by the mid-nineteenth century primarily due to the Dartmouth College vs. Woodward case.

---

[3] Peter Dobkin Hall, *A History of Nonprofit Boards in the United States* (Board Source, 2003), 5, accessed September 19, 2014, http://beech.ait.fredonia.edu/nfp/Reading Room/PDFs/BoardSource-AHistoryOfNonprofitBoardsInTheUnitedStates.pdf. Used with permission from *A History of Nonprofit Boards in the United States* by Peter Dobkin Hall, a publication of BoardSource. This source is no longer in print. For more information about BoardSource, call 800-883-6262 or visit www.boardsource.org. BoardSource © 2014. Content may not be reproduced or used for any purpose other than that which is specifically requested without written permission from BoardSource.

[4] Hall, *A History of Nonprofit Boards in the United States*, 6–8.

Dartmouth College argued before the Supreme Court that under the constitution of the United States major donors did not have the right to control operations of an incorporated institution. In the 1819 Supreme Court decision Chief Justice Marshall wrote:

> A corporation is an artificial being, invisible, intangible, and existing only in contemplation of law. Being the mere creature of law, it possesses only those properties which the charter of its creation confers upon it, either expressly or as incidental to its very existence. These are such as are supposed best calculated to effect the object for which it was created. Among the most important are immortality, and, if the expression may be allowed, individuality; properties by which a perpetual succession of many persons are considered as the same, and may act as a single individual.[5]

Even after this decision, arguments raged over the direction of institutions and dissension still took place, but the decisions of the whole governing body took precedence over the desires of individuals. Hall summarizes,

> The decision in the Dartmouth College case was perhaps the single most important judgment handed down by an American court. Marshall's decision did more than protect corporations from legislative interference: It advanced the notion that the will of the public could be expressed by other than electoral and governmental means. In doing this, it legitimated the idea of private associational initiative in the public interest. To this conception, perhaps more than any other, the nonprofit sector owes its existence.[6]

By law the governing board of nonprofit organizations takes action as a whole only when meetings are called. Outside of formal meetings the persons who serve on the board have no legal authority to act unless specifically given authority in a regularly scheduled meeting of the board. The governing board elects an executive committee—a chair, a vice-chair and secretary—that may be given authority by the whole board to act in certain capacities. Board members act on behalf of the corporation, on behalf of the members who comprise the corporation. The whole group of board members speaks for the whole corporation.[7]

---

[5] Quoted in Marion R. Fremont-Smith, *Governing Nonprofit Organizations: Federal and State Law and Regulation* (Cambridge: Belknap, 2004), 150.

[6] Hall, *A History of Nonprofit Boards in the United States*, 12.

[7] Harold Everson contends that our modern corporate concepts and structure have roots in the Christian theological understanding of the *Corpus Christi*, the "body of

By law the board of the corporation is the ultimately responsible "person." Person is singular, because as the whole board votes, its action is considered one vote. The board's decisions must always fall within the charter of the organization as spelled out in the articles of incorporation and bylaws. One additional point of clarification of the history of governing boards may prove helpful. The corporation states in the articles of incorporation the name by which governing board members are to be called. Board members might be called: curators, governors, overseers, regents, trustees, directors, or visitors.

THE WORK OF THE REGENTS AS SET FORTH
IN THE ARTICLES OF INCORPORATION AND BYLAWS

To illustrate the work of a governing board, the structure of Concordia University Irvine's incorporation and governing board, which is called the "board of regents" and on which I serve, will be used as an example. By law all other nonprofits, including educational institutions, have a similar structure.

Concordia University Irvine filed its articles of incorporation with the state of California May 22, 1972.[8] Article One states the name of the institution. Article Two, section "a" states: "The specific and primary purposes are to establish, conduct and maintain an educational institution in the County of Orange, State of California, offering courses of instruction beyond high school, and issuing or conferring diplomas and degrees." Additional sections list activities such as acquiring or selling property and soliciting donations for the express purpose of the university as stated in Article Two.

Additional articles state the section of the California Education Code under which the nonprofit corporation must operate and that the assets of the corporation must always be used for charitable purposes. Article Five

---

Christ." He states, "To incorporate means to create a body or corpus that in the eyes of the law is every bit as legitimate and real as flesh and blood." He explains that to incorporate means to "form one body," and thus to speak as one body (Harold Everson, *The Corporate Person: The Nature of Volunteer Boards, Their Culture, and Corporate Personality* [Minneapolis: Augsburg Fortress, 1998], 1).

[8] Concordia University Irvine was named Lutheran College at Irvine in the original articles of incorporation filed May 18, 1972. In 1973 the articles of incorporation were amended to rename the college "Christ College Irvine." The name was changed to Concordia University through an amendment of the articles of incorporation October 18, 2001. The use of the name took place well before these dates as per vote of the board of regents. The official amendments were filed on these dates. These legal documents are kept on file at Concordia University Irvine and are public documents.

states that "the minimum number of directors shall be five persons" and that number may be changed by amending the articles of incorporation or by amendment of the bylaws.[9] The original five directors signed the articles of incorporation.

The articles of incorporation were amended at various times (1973, 1981, and 2001) to change the name of the university, affirm that the corporation is a religious nonprofit corporation, organized exclusively for religious, charitable, and education purposes within the meaning of Internal Revenue Code Section 501(c)(3). In 2001 the articles of incorporation were amended to reflect an association with LCMS and that not only would the university's said purposes be accomplished, but also to further the objectives of Christianity as expressed by the LCMS.

In order to understand the vocation of the individuals of a governing board, it is critical to explore the bylaws, filed with the state of California, by which the corporation is governed. Additionally, Concordia has intentionally placed its operational activities within the context of the bylaws of the LCMS. Article Three states,

> The affairs of the Corporation shall be managed by a Board of Regents. The members of the Board of Regents and their successors in office shall consist of such number, shall be selected, removed and replaced, and shall serve for such terms as from time to time provided in the Constitution, Bylaws and resolutions of The Lutheran Church— Missouri Synod. The Board of Regents shall adopt Bylaws, rules and regulations which may be changed from time to time, said Bylaws not to be inconsistent with the Constitution, Articles of Incorporation, and Bylaws, resolutions, rules and regulations of The Lutheran Church—Missouri Synod.

The bylaws of the LCMS (from 2013) include regulations regarding membership of the board of regents and how individuals are elected for the LCMS's ten affiliated colleges and universities (the Concordia University System). These bylaws assure wide representation of board members (pastors, commissioned ministers, and lay people) who have differing life experiences that positively affect their ability to carry forward the mission and help drive the vision of the university. Some regents are elected by the national board, some by local districts of the church, and some by other regents. In particular, the bylaws of the LCMS regarding membership of the board and how the board is elected state that:

---

[9] Concordia University Board of Directors was renamed "Board of Regents" in the December 2005 Bylaws.

The board of regents of each college and university shall consist of no more than 17 voting members:

1. One ordained minister, one commissioned minister, and two laypersons shall be elected by the conventions of the Synod.

2. One ordained minister, one commissioned minister, and two laypersons shall be elected by the geographical district in which the institution is located.

3. No less than four and no more than eight laypersons shall be appointed as voting members by the board of regents.

4. The president of the district in which the college or university is located or a district vice-president as his standing representative shall serve as an *ex officio* member.

5. College and university boards of regents members may be elected or appointed to serve a maximum of three consecutive three-year terms and must hold membership in a member congregation of the Synod.

6. Not more than two of the elected members shall be members of the same congregation.

7. Persons elected or appointed to a board of regents should possess several of the following qualifications: be knowledgeable regarding the region in which the institution is located, possess an advanced academic degree, and have experience in higher education administration, administration of complex organizations, finance, law, investments, technology, human resources, facilities management, or fund development. Demonstrated familiarity and support of the institution is a desired quality in the candidate . . .[10]

The function of the board of regents falls within the bylaws of the LCMS. The vocation of regents at Concordia University Irvine must be explored, then, within the context of the job for which they are elected to serve. In general, the regents have responsibilities over the areas of governance, institutional planning, finances, academic programs, administration, faculty, staff, campus facilities, student life, and public relations. In particular, the bylaws of the LCMS regarding the function of regents state that:

---

[10] *Handbook: Constitution, Bylaws, Articles of Incorporation: The Lutheran Church—Missouri Synod 2013* (St. Louis: The Lutheran Church—Missouri Synod, 2013), 171.

The board of regents of each institution shall become familiar with and develop an understanding of pertinent policies, standards, and guidelines of the Synod and the Board of Directors of Concordia University System.

(a) It shall develop details of policies and procedures for governance of the institution, including but not limited to

  (1) attention to specific ways that the institution is confessing Jesus Christ in full accord with the doctrinal position of the LCMS (Constitution Art. II) and fulfilling His mission in our world;

  (2) annual certification of the institutions financial viability;

  (3) creation, modification, and abolition of administrative positions;

  (4) processes for filling and vacating administrative positions;

  (5) a clear plan for succession of administration to ensure that the institutions continues to function effectively in the case of incapacity or lengthy absence of the president.

(b) It shall coordinate institutional planning with other Concordia University System schools and approve master plans for its college or university.

(c) It shall review and approve academic programs recommended by the administration and faculty after assessment of system policies in accordance with Concordia University System standards and guidelines and institutional interests and capacities.

(d) It shall review and approve the institutional budget.

(e) It shall approve institutional fiscal arrangements, develop the financial resources necessary to operate the institution, and participate in its support program . . .

(f) It shall establish appropriate policies for institutional student aid.

(g) It shall participate fully in the procedures for the selection and regular review of the president of the institution and of the major administrators; approve of the appointment of faculty members who meet the qualifications of their positions; approve sabbatical and study leaves; and encourage faculty development and research.

(h) It shall take the leadership in assuring the preservation and improvement of the assets of the institution and see to the acquisition, management, use, and disposal of the properties and equipment of the institution within the guidelines set by the Board of Directors of The Lutheran Church—Missouri Synod.

(i) It shall operate and manage the institution as the agent of the Synod, in which ownership is primarily vested and which exercises its ownership through the Board of Directors as custodian of the Synod's property, the Board of Directors of Concordia University System, and the respective board of regents as the local governing body. Included in the operation and management are such responsibilities as these:

(1) Carrying out efficient business management through a business manager appointed on recommendation of the president of the institution and responsible to him.

(2) Receiving of all gifts by deed, will, or otherwise made to the institution and managing the same, in accordance with the terms of the instrument creating such gift and in accordance with the policies of the board of regents.

(3) Demonstrating concern for the general welfare of the institutional staff members and other employees, adoption of regulations governing off-campus activities, development of policies regarding salary and wage scales, tenure, promotion, vacations, health examinations, dismissal, retirement, pension, and other employee welfare benefit provisions.

(4) Determining that the Charter, Articles of Incorporation, Constitution, and Bylaws of the institution conform to and are consistent with those of the Synod.

(5) Serving as the governing body corporate of the institution vested with all powers which its members may exercise in law either as directors, trustees, or members of the body corporate, unless in conflict with the laws of the domicile of the institution or its Articles of Incorporation. In such event the board of regents shall have power to perform such acts as may be required by law to affect the corporate existence of the institution.

(6) Establishing and placing a priority on the capital needs of the institution and determining the plans for the maintenance

and renovation of the buildings and property and purchase of needed equipment, but having no power by itself to close the institution or to sell all or any part of the property which constitutes the main campus.

(7) Recognizing that the authority of the board of regents resides in the board as a whole and delegating the application of its policies and execution of its resolutions to the president of the institution as its executive officer.

(8) Establishing a comprehensive policy statement regarding student life that commits the institution to the principles of Christian discipline, an evangelical manner, and good order.

(9) Promoting the public relations of the institution and developing the understanding and cooperation of its constituency.

(10) Requiring regular reports from the president of the institution as the executive officer of the board and through him from other officers and staff members in order to make certain that the work of the institution is carried out effectively.[11]

The articles of incorporation and bylaws of Concordia University Irvine and the LCMS provide the framework for the work of the board of regents for the nonprofit universities in the Concordia University System. It is important to understand that state law mandates that the articles of incorporation and bylaws of nonprofits spell out the specific role of the governing board. Those documents also spell out the limitations of individual board members, apart from the whole. Within this framework we delve into the vocation of the board of regents.

THE VOCATION OF THE REGENTS IN LIGHT OF BYLAWS

Members of the board of regents have been elected as per the bylaws to serve in the capacity of regent. Election to the board serves as the call to a vocation that is clearly spelled out by the bylaws, which are filed with the state as well as the bylaws of the LCMS. The vocation of the individual as regent is very specific and is legally tied to the whole governing board acting on behalf of the nonprofit corporation.

---

[11] *Handbook*, 172–74.

The official work of the board is spelled out and clearly distinguished from the role of the university president. The president is the executive officer of the board of regents. He serves as "the spiritual, academic, and administrative head of the institution."[12] The president and the executive team carry out the day-to-day operations of the university. While the president is the executive officer of the board of regents, he has been interviewed, selected, and called by them to serve the university. The president is subject to annual review by the regents.[13]

This delicate structure provides an amazing opportunity to live out one's faith through this calling. Regents are required to oversee while stepping back; regents have opportunity to provide an optimum environment for the president and his executive team so that they can accomplish the work of operating a complex university. Authority over the president means giving him tools and support so that he can accomplish the mission and vision of the university as well as effectively carry out day-to-day activities.

The board of regents meets quarterly to tend to the official business of the university. The president and the chairman of the board set the agenda of the meetings based upon the business that needs attention and/or action. A quorum must be present for action to be taken. Regents are sent an agenda as well as materials to study in advance. Regents are expected to come to meetings prepared to listen, ask questions, comment, and make decisions.

Individuals step into the boardroom, but their authority comes only through the whole and only when the meeting is called to order. As Everson states simply, "Without the board you are not the board."[14] An individual is not the board; the whole board is the board. This is an important aspect of the vocation of the board of regents and regents as individuals. Once decisions are taken, the board turns over execution of daily activities to the president, who delegates responsibility to the executive team, faculty, and staff.

THE VOCATION OF THE REGENTS
IN LIGHT OF THE UNIVERSITY'S MISSION STATEMENT

The work of the regent is defined by the previously stated bylaws and yet it is so much more as the board works together to accomplish the mis-

---

[12] *Handbook*, 174.

[13] *Handbook*, 174–77.

[14] Everson, *The Corporate Person*, 9.

sion of the university. In this section we will delve deeper into the vocation of the regent through the eyes of the particular mission statement of Concordia University Irvine: "Concordia University, guided by the Great Commission of Christ Jesus and the Lutheran Confessions, empowers students through the liberal arts and professional studies for lives of learning, service and leadership."[15]

Meetings of the board of regents begin with this mission statement as a reminder that the reason for the existence of Concordia University Irvine is to empower students. From that perspective regents fulfill their vocation by living out their faith by serving their neighbor in love, specifically the student. In order to empower students for lives of learning, service, and leadership the president and executive team must be given tools and resources to empower faculty and staff to carry out the mission. Faculty and staff must be compensated fairly and shown regular appreciation for their work on the front lines with students.

With empowering the student in mind, regents step out of their primary vocation into a volunteer position as one member of a nonprofit governing board. The regent's primary vocation—whether an ordained or commissioned minister or a Christian serving in a secular position— qualified the individual to be elected to serve as a regent. The regent's primary vocation enables the regent to bring valuable life experience, professionalism, wisdom, and insight into the boardroom.

Clear understanding of the vocation of the executive team and the regents' vocation must be distinguished. The president and his executive team report to the regents. The president and the executive team carry out day-to-day operations. Regents are responsible to the whole for those operations, but delegate the authority to carry it out to the president. As Everson says about regents,

> The principle of *delegated authority/retained responsibility* dealt with the roles and relationship of board and staff. Practiced diligently, this principle enables the Corporate Person to "mind its own business"; that is, the business of governing, giving direction, dealing with the big picture and assuring the organization is well-managed.[16]

While tending to the business of the university, the regents' vocation is to allow the president to do his work, the executive team to do its work, and faculty and staff to do their work. The regents delegate authority while

---

[15] "Our Mission," Concordia University Irvine, accessed September 19, 2014, http://www.cui.edu/aboutcui.

[16] Everson, *The Corporate Person*, 47.

retaining responsibility within the mission of the university. Roles and responsibilities get blurred when the mission statement is not held in high regard. Roles and responsibilities also get blurred when regents cross the line and attempt to do the work that is properly delegated to the president.

Another helpful description of the role of regents comes from Robert Greenleaf, a pioneer in the concept of a trustee/regent serving on a non-profit board as a servant-leader. Greenleaf explains the legal power inherent in the vocation of regents when he says,

> Trustees have a kind of power that administrators and staffs do not have—they have the legal power to manage everything in the institution; they have all the legal power there is. They may delegate some of it, but they can also take it back. They cannot give any of it away, irretrievably, and still be trustees. ... This is the central issue of trusteeship: trustees hold ultimate power but they do not use it operationally. Yet they are responsible for its use.[17]

This powerful concept challenges the heart and mind of regents, all of whom are leaders in their primary calling. Regents are servants to the mission, to the president, executive team, faculty, staff, and students; regents are also leaders. Regents are ultimately responsible, but also have the high calling and responsibility to delegate.

Regents also delegate authority within their own ranks. Standing committees have been established according to specific work that needs to be accomplished outside regular board meetings and ad hoc committees are established as necessary. Committee work takes place in committee meetings because the work is too extensive for general regent meetings. Regents are asked to serve on sub-committees according to their particular interests, life experiences, and skill sets.

The various standing committees at Concordia University Irvine are: finance and audit, investment, philanthropy, academic enterprise, institutional identity, and membership. Committee work is reported back to the whole in concise summary form. Recommendations are made and, if necessary, action is taken. The larger group is not asked to do the detailed work, but asked to see and understand the broad picture. In order to operate in the best interest of the whole and for work to go smoothly, regents must trust one another.

For example, the finance and audit committee as well as the investment committee are comprised of people who have practical experience from

---

[17] Robert Greenleaf, *Trustees as Servants* (Cambridge: Center for Applied Studies, 1972), 11–12.

their primary vocation dealing with large budgets or nonprofit finances and investing. They pour over details, assess proposals, and approve concepts at the committee level that will be brought before the whole board. Some board members do not have this skill, so they trust the work to that sub-committee.

The academic enterprise, student experience, and institutional identity committees are comprised of people who have experience in these specific areas through their primary vocation. These committees meet regularly with the president and/or executive team in order to understand the intricacies of these specific areas. They pour over details specific to these categories and bring recommendations to the whole board.

Regents must take great care to bring personal expertise from the context of profession and life experience forward while carefully setting personal agendas aside. This challenge will always be faced by a nonprofit board. The corporate body is made up of individuals each having a voice, but their voice becomes one voice once decisions are made. Regents must focus on the mission of the institution they serve and the good of the whole. Vocationally that means that while members might have particular interests and passion, serving as a regent means keeping the big picture in mind at all times.

The mission statement of Concordia University Irvine states that the university is "guided by the Great Commission of Christ and the Lutheran Confessions." That statement provides insight into a parallel concept for the vocation of regent. The regent is guided by larger principles as well. Regents are guided by the institution's constitution and bylaws filed with the state of California. Regents are also guided by the bylaws of the LCMS. The work of the regents is also guided by the mission statement of the university, Scripture, and the beliefs of the LCMS.[18]

ACTING IN AND OUT OF VOCATION

In serving as a regent there are temptations to act outside of, or contrary to, the vocation of the board of regents. One potential pitfall of the board is that individual regents come to meetings believing that an agenda of a particular meeting drives the work. Vision narrows and creativity suffers when a narrowly focused board tries to operate from the narrow to

---

[18] For a summary of biblical faith and its applications at Concordia University Irvine, see "Lutheran Higher Education at Concordia University: Belief and Application," accessed September 19, 2014, http://www.cui.edu/aboutcui/heritage/index.aspx?id=20789.

the greater. Regents must operate from the greater mission and vision to the detailed work that serves the greater.

Regents must come to meetings prepared in order to fulfill their calling. The president and executive team write brief reports based upon day-to-day tasks and vision. Regents see only a tiny portion of the work of the team through their reports. Regents must come to listen, participate in discussions, and take action from the perspective of the mission of the university, which drives all decision making.

Another potential pitfall of the board is that individual regents speak on behalf of the board without the authorization of the board. The chair, vice-chair, and secretary of the board are granted limited authority by the board to speak or act in specifically identified circumstances. Individual regents step outside their vocation and misuse their role when they act as though they have power to speak on behalf of the board when that power has not been granted.

The temptation to speak outside of the specific vocation is always present and must be acknowledged. When all is going smoothly with the university, speaking outside of vocation may not be particularly harmful. When the university faces significant challenges, when dissention among regents arises, or when leadership problems arise, speaking outside of vocation causes great damage to the whole. Confidentiality is critical when board members interact with one another or with students, faculty, staff, or the community at large. Discussing board matters outside the boardroom is prohibited, even when the best intentions are present.

To ensure that the board of regents acts well together in its vocation, Everson points out that care must be taken to state and vision how a smoothly operating board functions together as a whole. Evaluation is important, but effective evaluation can only take place if regents understand how a board should and could operate.[19] Everson states, "The Corporate Person must continually attend to those needs. Health maintenance and management is an ongoing concern."[20] A healthy board welcomes self-assessment and intentional evaluation as part of the vocation of the servant-leader. A board that does not practice regular, honest assessment falls into this unhealthy practice:

---

[19] John Carver is a highly respected expert on board structure, development, and health. Everson quotes him numerous times in his book, *The Corporate Person*. One such quote from Carver is, "If you haven't said how it ought to be, don't ask how it is" (Everson *The Corporate Person*, 68 [taken from "Monitoring," a paper written by Carver in 1989]).

[20] Everson, *The Corporate Person*, 65.

What they don't realize is that if they neglect to intentionally and regularly evaluate themselves as a corporate body, evaluation will still occur. It will happen informally and erratically in the hallways and on the sidewalks after the board meetings. It will happen as individual members talk to each other about executive performance and board-staff interaction. It will happen as the board does its planning and critiques its progress or lack of progress. It will happen as community, staff, and client complaints filter back to the board.[21]

A board that submits itself voluntarily to evaluation practices servant-leadership and provides an example to the executive team, faculty, staff, and students, all of whom are subject to mandatory evaluation.

MISSION, VISION, AND VOCATION

The mission statement of the university sets the direction for all the activities and actions of individual regents as well as the whole board within the confines of the laws by which the university operates. This vision, at Concordia University Irvine, finds further articulation in a related heritage statement. Within this more broadly-articulated vision lies much food for thought regarding the vocation of regent:

Concordia University Irvine is committed to delivering a liberal arts education in the Lutheran tradition. We hope to prepare students to live as men and women whose Christian freedom inspires and enables service to others. We foster an intellectual pursuit of that which is true, a moral commitment to that which is good, and an aesthetic appreciation of that which is beautiful.

At Concordia University Irvine we are dedicated not only to teaching certain subjects, but to shaping a coherent and comprehensive view of the world, of humanity, and of the God who created and redeemed both. It is this faithfulness to this mission and this heritage which makes Concordia graduates *wise, honorable and cultivated citizens.* They become citizens prepared to serve God's world and proclaim God's word.[22]

Regents of Concordia University Irvine, as servant-leaders within this non-profit corporation, pursue this same broad vision. They too are called to be

---

[21] Everson, *The Corporate Person*, 66–67.

[22] "Faithful to the Lutheran Tradition," Concordia University Irvine, accessed September 19, 2014, http://www.cui.edu/aboutCUI/Heritage/index.aspx?id=18634 (emphasis original).

wise, honorable, and cultivated citizens as they serve God by serving their neighbor through their vocation as regent.

Direction for the vocation of the board of regents can also be found at other Christian universities. Regents of all Christian universities can find guidance for their activities and actions by looking to their university's foundational documents. The university's mission statement, articles of incorporation, bylaws, and the like all set a vision for the regents' role as servant-leaders who fulfill the university's legal responsibilities and advance its mission.

QUESTIONS

1. What is the vision for the vocation of regent at your university? How does it fulfill and advance the university's mission statement, articles of incorporation, bylaws, and other foundational documents?

2. A few examples were given regarding the vocational responsibilities of regents. What other examples from your experience help bring clarity to the vocation of regent?

3. The concept of servant-leader applies to all aspects of leadership in a Christian university. Reflecting on the role of regent, in what other ways can faith take action through that role?

4. There is an important, delicate balance in the overall operations of a university and the leadership of regent. How can that balance be honored and nurtured? Who is responsible for that task?

5. How much time should be dedicated in regent meetings to board education and development? How much time should regents be asked to spend outside regular meetings reading and reflecting on how things could be?

PART THREE

THE INTERACTION
OF FAITH AND LEARNING

8

LUTHERAN THEOLOGY AND PHILOSOPHY: FAITH AND REASON

James V. Bachman[1]

INTRODUCTION

Our topic is "faith and reason." Many today consider "reasons" to be public and, if not always agreed, at least worthy of argument and debate. But if these "reasons" happen to be relevant to questions about religion and "faith," contemporary intellectuals often dismiss them as private and not worthy of public argument and debate. British churchman Lesslie Newbigin comments concisely, "Questions of ultimate purpose are excluded from the public world."[2]

Arguments about the meaning of the world of nature provide an example. Contemporary Oxford chemist Peter Atkins asserts:

> The bare bones of the scientific explanation of the emergence, existence, and temporary persistence of persons are that the universe is sinking into chaos. . . . In the end there will be only dead flat space-time, our castles will have gone, as well as our libraries, our achievements, our selves. We, who will no longer be, will then listen in vain in the void for the Last Trumpet.[3]

Contemporary intellectuals may argue for or against Atkins' assertions, but Atkins' claims are considered rational and worthy of debate.

Contemporary Oxford philosopher Antony Flew, who was for most of his life an atheist, dismayed and angered many atheists with the following

---

[1]   Jim Bachman, PhD (Florida State), is Professor of Philosophy and Ethics at CUI.
[2]   Lesslie Newbigin, *Foolishness to the Greeks: The Gospel and Western Culture* (Grand Rapids: Eerdmans, 1986), 30.
[3]   Peter Atkins, "Purposeless People," in *Persons and Personality: A Contemporary Inquiry*, ed. A. R. Peacocke and Grant Gillette (Oxford: Blackwell, 1987), 12–32.

assertions concerning intelligent design of the universe. He begins with a quote from Darwin's *Origin of Species*:

> "[P]robably all the organic beings that have lived on the earth have descended from some one primordial form, into which life was first breathed." Probably Darwin himself believed that life was miraculously breathed into that primordial form of not always consistently reproducing life by God. . . . But the evidential situation of natural (as opposed to revealed) theology has been transformed in the more than fifty years since Watson and Crick won the Nobel Prize for their discovery of the double helix structure of DNA. It has become inordinately difficult even to begin to think about constructing a naturalistic theory of the evolution of that first reproducing organism.

Flew dismayed many modern intellectuals not only because he was flirting with some sort of deism, but because he claimed that natural theology continues to be a matter of public evidence and argument. He concluded his letter to *Philosophy Now* by asserting, "My own commitment then as a philosopher who was also a religious unbeliever was and remains that of Plato's Socrates: 'We must follow the argument wherever it leads.' "[4]

Many contemporary intellectuals in university settings consider Flew's line of reasoning to be private and ultimately entangled with "faith"-related questions and thus not worthy of public argument and debate. What Flew thinks "rational" and worthy of argument is no longer considered so in much popular thought today. This chapter takes up the interactions between faith and reason and attempts to shed light on the dismissal of faith-related reasoning in the contemporary academy.

The chapter explores a Lutheran perspective on the relationship between faith and reason. Traditionally, in the universities, this topic has also concerned the relationship between theology and philosophy. To do justice to modern universities, the word *philosophy* will be used in its broad, ancient meaning of reasoned, intellectual approaches to life. In this meaning, most disciplines of the modern university can be addressed under the umbrella of "philosophy."

---

[4] Antony Flew, "Letter on Darwinism and Theology," *Philosophy Now* 47 (2004), accessed September 19, 2014, http://philosophynow.org/issues/47/Letter_from_Antony_Flew_on_Darwinism_and_Theology. Where Flew, who died in 2010, ended up in regard to atheism, agnosticism, or deism is a controverted question that Christian apologists would do well to review before claiming Flew as an ally. Comprehensive (even if biased) details about the controversy are provided by Richard Carrier at http://infidels.org/kiosk/article/antony-flew-considers-godsort-of-369.html.

Plato's dialogue *Meno* will shed some initial light on our topics. In *Meno* Plato cautions that big questions like "Can excellence be taught?" must be taken apart into preliminary questions: "What is excellence?" and "What is teaching and learning?" Our big question is "How do faith and reason, theology and philosophy relate?" Preliminary questions include "How do philosophy and reason relate?" and "How do theology and faith relate?" Along the way we must not assume that we already know what "reason" is, nor what "faith" is, nor how each functions in the domains of theology and philosophy.

In the following I first examine Socrates' and Plato's competing notions of reason's function in philosophy as seen in Plato's *Meno*. Plato's distinction between opinion (*doxa*) and knowledge (*epistēmē*) provides one influential perspective on reason's role, but Socrates' alternative account, seen also in *Meno*, raises some questions that are best answered by examining more carefully what "reason" is all about. The next step, after examining Plato's *Meno*, will be to look at typical models of reason that will help us locate more precisely the disagreement between Socrates and Plato, a disagreement that can also inform disagreements about faith and reason today. Having examined typical models of reason, we can next examine the relationship of faith to daily wisdom and guidance in biblical thought. The goal will be to achieve an understanding of "faith" in biblical terms that can then be related to philosophical models of "reason." Lutheran distinctives concerning the role of faith in the Christian life will emerge in this study of a biblical perspective on "faith."

Having explored "reason" and "faith," each on its own terms, the larger question of relationships between reason and faith can then be addressed. Examination of this larger question will lead also into insights relevant to relating reason and faith in a modern university and will suggest implications for conversations today between Lutheran theology and philosophy, the reasoned, intellectual approaches to life found in the modern university.

Perspectives on Reason in Plato's Dialogue Meno

Before turning to the dialogue *Meno*, we need some background from Plato's dialogue *Apology*. *Apology* was written as a testament to Plato's mentor Socrates. Around 400 BC Socrates was put on trial in his native city of Athens at age seventy on charges of corrupting young people and being some sort of atheist. The jury of 501 Athenian citizens found Socrates guilty by a vote of 280 to 221. Socrates' accusers demanded the death penalty; Socrates, as a matter of principle, refused to propose the expected counter penalty of exile and instead proposed free meals in the city hall. He was subsequently condemned to death and two weeks later was executed by being required to take the poison, hemlock.

Plato was about thirty when Socrates was executed. Plato's *Apology* (in Greek *apologia* means "defense") is a dramatic reconstruction of Socrates' defense at his trial. Two famous lines from *Apology* are "the unexamined life is not worth living" (38a) and "surely it is the most blameworthy ignorance to believe that one knows what one does not know" (29b).[5] This latter point is often summarized as Socrates' insight that "knowing that one does not know" is the better part of human wisdom.

People in Socrates' day worried that his rigorous examination of life, leading to so much perplexity, might make people doubt whether any advice about life is reliable. Socrates himself, however, argued for an opposite conclusion. He said that his rigorous examination simply keeps individuals from the pride that claims to know better than the community what is right and wrong and bad and good in life. He was confident that the gods guide us through the morality and laws of society that have stood the test of time. He also thought that morality and law were intimately entangled with piety and religion.

Plato's *Meno* shows how Plato builds on Socrates' perplexity in a way that gives reason a different role in the interaction between individual citizens and the morality, religion, and laws of their society. In *Meno*, Plato argues that, while wisdom may begin in a healthy perplexity prompted by reasoned analysis, human reason also has the power to move beyond perplexity to defensible knowledge of its own that can stand the test of examination. Plato claims that disciplined conversation, in Greek *dialectic*, may first lead to perplexity but can also lead to knowledge.

The last third of *Meno* vividly contrasts Socrates' perplexity with Plato's own hope that perplexity can be overcome by disciplined use of reason. Socrates says that our reason mostly shows us we do not have knowledge, but he allows that some of us have a mysterious knack for coming to correct opinions (*orthai doxai*) when life models truth to us in exemplary citizens and in the traditions, religion, and laws of a well-ordered society. "Therefore, if it is not through knowledge [ἐπιστήμη], the only alternative is that it is through right opinion [εὐδοξία] that statesmen follow the right course for their cities" (99bc). Socrates concludes the investigation with these words: "It follows from this reasoning, Meno, that excellence appears

---

[5]   All quotations from Plato's *Apology* and *Meno* use the standard page numbers. The translation is from Plato, *Five Dialogues*, trans. G. M. A. Grube, rev. John M. Cooper (2d ed.; Indianapolis: Hackett, 2002). I use "excellence" rather than Grube's "virtue" to translate the Greek *aretē*.

to be present in those of us who may possess it as a gift from the gods" (100b).

Plato, however, thinks that correct opinions too easily escape us: "For true opinions [αἱ δόξαι αἱ ἀληθεῖς], as long as they remain, are a fine thing and all they do is good, but they are not willing to remain long, and they escape from a man's mind, so that they are not worth much until one ties them down by [giving] an account of the reason why" (98a). Disciplined conversation (dialectic) undertakes the task of giving "an account of the reason why" and of defending that account against all critiques. In this way reasoned thought and conversation can lead to knowledge. In Plato's words: "[After opinions] are tied down, in the first place they become knowledge, and then they remain in place. That is why knowledge (ἐπιστήμη) is prized higher than correct opinion (ὀρθῆς δόξης), and knowledge differs from correct opinion in being tied down" (98a).[6] Plato defends this account of how we come to have knowledge in full detail in his book-length dialogue *Republic*.

This brief summary of Socrates and Plato on human reason shows us two different accounts of how human reason seeks wisdom for guidance in life. Socrates argues that reason shows us the limitations of the mind striking out on its own. He counsels that reason more often than not refutes individual claims to knowledge and that the wise person will look to communal resources for guidance in life. Plato considers ordinary opinions drawn from communal resources to be too flighty to provide reliable guidance. Reason's most important task is to give "an account of the reason why," and Plato is confident that human reason is divinely equipped to pursue this task. In the *Republic*, Plato tips his hat toward Socrates when he writes that "if anyone is saved and becomes what he ought to be under our present [anti-intellectual] constitutions, he has been saved—you might rightly say—by a divine dispensation" (492e).[7] But Plato argues that when the education system has been rightly reformed, it will be "better for everyone to be ruled by divine reason, preferably within himself and his own, otherwise imposed from without, so that as far as possible all will be alike and friends, governed by the same thing" (590d).

---

[6]   I suspect that the church's use of the word *orthodox* has permitted careless enemies of the church to apply Plato's distinction between "orthodoxy" and "knowledge" to comfort them in their uncritical dismissal of any suggestion that knowledge rooted in faith could be knowledge.

[7]   All quotations from Plato's *Republic* use the standard page numbers. The translation is from Plato, *Republic*, trans. G. M. A. Grube, rev. C. D. C. Reeve (Indianapolis: Hackett, 1992).

MODELS OF HUMAN REASONING

Because he held such a high view of reason's capabilities, Plato labored to mark out the different tasks of reason. In the *Republic* he identifies two different tasks that reason undertakes in pursuit of knowledge. Reason must find reliable ways to gather information relevant to the guidance that we seek, and reason must also carefully process information in logical ways. Plato's student Aristotle further developed Plato's scheme in the part of his work called *Organon* or "Toolbox" for reasoning. Aristotle analyzes reason's two distinct tasks. In the *Prior Analytics* he provides a comprehensive and influential account of how logical processing works, naming his structure of formal deductive analysis the Syllogism. In the *Posterior Analytics* he investigates how reason finds reliable ways to gather foundational information for investigations in the many different domains of human interest.

Contemporary philosopher Jaakko Hintikka provides a convenient reference for relating the ancient models of reasoning to the present. All commentators on reasoning must account for the logical processing part of reasoning and for the ways reason seeks, gathers, and selects information to process. Hintikka models reasoning as the interweaving of steps that seek, gather, and select useful and reliable information (interrogative steps) with steps that logically process the information (logical inference steps). He calls his model an "interrogative" model of reasoning because, as we have already seen with Socrates and Plato, the main challenges for excellence in reasoning lie with strategies for interrogating appropriate sources, that is, for seeking, gathering, and selecting relevant and reliable information.

Hintikka's interrogative model helps us locate what is mainly at stake in disagreements between Socrates and Plato (and Aristotle and philosophers generally) about reason's capabilities. The logical processing part of reasoning is not where the main disagreements arise. Reason's task of logical processing is complex and has been exhaustively studied. For everyday purposes, very few disagreements arise about how reason can be deployed to process information logically. Socrates, Plato, Aristotle, and philosophers generally all agree that the human mind is admirably constructed for logical processing and that in daily work we are able to correct ourselves and one another when mistakes are made in logic.[8]

---

[8] Space does not permit a discussion of disagreements in contemporary models of reasoning concerning how to characterize non-deductive inferences. These inferences have often been treated in parallel with deductive inferences under the heading of "inductive" inferences, but the analysis has not led to consensus. Hintikka takes an approach used by several contemporary analysts. He argues that the uncertainty

We have seen, however, that Socrates and Plato have a significant disagreement concerning strategies for seeking, gathering, and selecting information to guide us in life. Socrates was skeptical of the ability of human reason to achieve independent knowledge on the central questions of life. He advised respect for communal resources of insight, including the traditions, religion, and laws of a well-ordered society. Socrates thought we can recognize valuable opinions about life, but we cannot independently defend the truth of these opinions. Plato worried that opinions, however valuable, are easily dislodged. He thought that reason can devise its own independent ways to get reliable information to guide us.

Hintikka's interrogative model is designed to highlight what is at stake in seeking good strategies for seeking, gathering, and selecting information. He argues that the complex challenges involved in finding good strategies is part of what obscures our ability to give a satisfactory account of when reasoning has led to "knowledge." He points out that most philosophers are agreed that if people claim to have knowledge, they must necessarily believe what they claim to know. Further, what they claim to know must be true. These two requirements can be summarized in the phrase "true belief." Philosophers also agree that something beyond "true belief" is needed for people genuinely to have knowledge, but they have had great difficulty analyzing what the further requirement(s) might be. The phrase "justified true belief" as an account of knowledge has been in use since the days of Plato, but precise specification of "justification" and related requirements has eluded philosophical analysis.

Hintikka comments that "there is no single definite meaning of the words 'knowing' and 'knowledge.' On different occasions, for different people, in the light of different purposes, these words will mean different things."[9] Hintikka is not here embarking on a subjective or relativist account of knowledge; he is simply observing that the relationship between knowers and what they know is so complicated that we should not expect a tidy account of how "true beliefs" become "knowledge" in the many different domains of human interest and inquiry.

Hintikka's analysis is closely related to his exploration of how people achieve knowledge. Knowledge is not simply beliefs that are justified; knowledge is achieved by finding the right questions to ask in the right

---

introduced by non-deductive inferences is better analyzed under the heading of strategies for seeking, gathering, and selecting information, that is, his "interrogative steps." For more details see Jaakko Hintikka and James Bachman, *What If? Toward Excellence in Reasoning* (Mountain View, CA: Mayfield/McGraw-Hill, 1991), 327–33.

[9] Hintikka and Bachman, *What If?*, 372.

circumstances and then by being able to discern reliable answers to the questions. In Hintikka's own words, what justifies applying the word *knowledge* "is *not* any binding or even particularly strong evidence that the inquirer has already found. Instead, what is offered as a justification of the knowledge claim are indications of the strategy the inquirer has used and will use" for seeking, gathering, and selecting information.[10] Thus, claims about knowledge lead us back to fundamental questions concerning strategies appropriate to what we want to know.

The disagreement between Socrates and Plato can shed light on Hintikka's claims about the multiple meanings of "knowing" and "knowledge." Socrates concentrated on fundamental questions about how life is to be lived; he wanted to understand human excellences like courage and piety and friendship. He thought he could show that humans do not command individual and independent knowledge of human excellences. Plato claimed that humans could command individual and independent knowledge, but his primary illustrations came not from fundamental questions about how life is to be lived but from instances of mathematical and technological knowledge. In *Meno* (82b–86b), Plato illustrates what he considers to be the independent power of human reason by analyzing how we solve problems in geometry. In the *Republic* (509d–511e), Plato's famous Diagram of the Line distinguishes different uses of reason by drawing our attention again to how we reason about geometry.

Hintikka prompts us to observe that strategies for gaining knowledge in mathematics are likely to differ in significant ways from strategies for gaining knowledge about courage or friendship. He warns us not to expect that a systematic application of strategies from mathematics to all human knowledge-seeking will necessarily produce insight.

The ancient philosophical tradition obscures this point somewhat. Socrates advises that a good strategy for finding reliable guidance in life includes attending to hard won communal truths entangled in the traditions, religion, and laws of society. He also seems to think that the gods gift at least some of us with insight as we pursue this sort of strategy. Hintikka would advise that, if Socrates persuades us that his is a good strategy for seeking guidance in life, then a "correct opinion" (*orthe doxa*) achieved in this way might be called "knowledge" (*epistēmē*). Socrates, however, and Plato both seem to reserve the word *knowledge* for application only to strategies of information seeking that the seeker fully controls independently of reliance on something or someone else that is not under the seeker's control. So, Socrates simply says he "knows that he does not know," because he

---

[10] Hintikka and Bachman, *What If?*, 372.

does not think we can achieve independent mastery of topics related to human excellence, though he cannot help from time to time claiming to "know" that his strategy for guidance in life is a good one.[11] Plato does not think that the strategy of asking questions of communal sources including religion can lead to reliable knowledge to guide us in life. He thinks Socrates is stuck with "correct opinions," and he worries that when we are not independently in control of our knowledge seeking, we will always be at risk for losing our way. Plato thinks we can achieve knowledge about human excellence, but he struggles to show how independent mastery of such topics actually arises in individuals. Not surprisingly, he often turns to topics in mathematics and cosmology to find cases where independent mastery of material seems more clearly to be seen.

We will not here investigate Plato's doctrine of the Forms in which he argues that human reason has independent access to ultimate truths about reality that can guide daily life. The important contrast for our purposes is between Socrates and Plato. Socrates thought human reason did not have independent access to ultimate truth and yet could be reliably guided. Plato and many other philosophers have argued that human reason does have independent access to ultimate truth about reality and that our duty is to cultivate and control rational insight defined in this independent way.

Contemporary understandings of "reason" often seem to try to coordinate insight from both Socrates and Plato. Like Plato, modern intellectuals are often inordinately confident in the independent access humans have to a significant range of questions about life. Close examination will show that mostly this confidence ranges over questions that can be answered by "impersonal information." The gold standard for contemporary knowing, developed over the last four centuries, focuses on ways of knowing the world that exclude categories of personal agency from our "accounts of the reasons why." Categories of personal agency include willing, choosing, planning, purposing, loving, hating, and so forth. Plato also tended to exclude categories of personal agency from our strategies for knowing, and part of the reason seems to be that categories of personal agency introduce elements that frustrate the goal of independent mastery and control that characterizes what many people understand "knowledge" to include.

Hintikka's scheme suggests that we should examine the fit between impersonal strategies for knowing and the topics about which we are curious. If our topics concern mathematics and the physical sciences, the fit may be very good. The exclusion of categories of personal agency from our attempts to understand physical science has a long and distinguished

---

[11] See, e.g., *Apology*, 29b, 29d–30b, and 36c.

history. Already in ancient Greek thought the human tendency to anthro-pomorphize, divinize, and personalize natural phenomena began to be held in check. When biblical faith encountered Greek thought, a significant part-nership developed. No matter how Christians read Gen 1, we all recognize that the text demystifies the natural world by taking personal benevolence and malevolence out of the account of sun and moon and other natural phenomena. The Psalmist knew that people worried about how the Sun might strike you by day or the Moon by night (Ps 121:6). But Gen 1 refuses to personalize these massive and troubling natural phenomena. God waits until the fourth day before getting around to hanging up the sun and moon, and the inspired author does not even dignify them by their names that evoked awe and fear among ancient peoples. The world in which we live has experienced a productive fit between impersonal strategies for knowing and effective research into the natural world.

Even as modern intellectuals extol impersonal knowing for a wide range of topics, they also despair of finding strategies for knowing phe-nomena that are fundamentally characterized by personal agency. In this regard they seem more like Socrates. Confining themselves to impersonal strategies for knowing, they discover that we do not "know" about God and personal meaning in life. Unlike Socrates, however, modern intellectuals are not prepared to turn to more personal, communal strategies for finding guidance in life.[12]

Modern dismissal of investigations concerning "intelligent design" in the universe provides an example. For the popular mind, this topic can be dismissed because it uses strategies of knowing that are to be rejected out of hand. The argument is very quick: discussion of intelligent design requires use of strategies for exploring possible personal agency in the world of na-ture. We have no use for such strategies. They do not lead to knowledge, because they threaten our mastery and control of our subject. Therefore, there is nothing for science to discuss regarding intelligent design. No rea-soned discussion of "intelligent design" can even begin.[13]

What seems to have happened is that people today gladly join Socrates in saying "we know that we don't know," and then they go on with Plato to

---

[12] Forensic science provides an intriguing counterexample to the way science confines itself to impersonal knowing. Reasoning about crime and criminals requires careful attention to matters of personal agency. This example reminds us that science is much more complicated than typical popular pictures of its methods suggest.

[13] I explore this feature of the refusal to debate intelligent design in James Bachman, "Self-Righteousness through Popular Science: Our Culture's Romance with Naturalism," *Concordia Journal* 35, no. 3 (2009): 279–90.

say that only strategies that provide us with independent mastery and control of our knowing can count. Unlike Plato, they think that many of the biggest questions about life will never be able to be addressed by approved methods. We are left able only to probe impersonal "accident" and "chance" when using the popularly approved strategies for knowing.

GUIDANCE FOR LIFE IN BIBLICAL FAITH

The next step for us is to explore the meaning of "faith" from a Christian, biblical perspective. Lutheran Christians have more familiarity with questions about "faith" than about philosophy and "knowledge." Still, questions about faith are quite complex. The theological tradition addresses such questions by carefully distinguishing different topics that come under the heading of "faith." When the topic is "faith and reason," we must carefully distinguish between the faith that grasps the Gospel and brings salvation (*fides directa*) and reflection on that faith that provides reasoned guidance for Christians (*fides reflexa*). This chapter is exploring how reflection on our faithful relationship with God in Christ provides rationally defensible guidance for daily life. This exploration is not claiming that a process of independent reasoned reflection is the foundation for the Christian's faithful relationship with God.[14]

Our exploration of "reason" thus far will already have alerted us why so many find conflict between "faith" and "reason." Hintikka has prompted us to ask how strategies for seeking information can be evaluated, and we have seen that all the way back to Socrates and Plato, the emphasis in philosophy has been on strategies that leave knowers independent and in control of the processes by which they know. Faith in Jesus Christ raises questions con-

---

[14] The tradition of systematic reasoning by Christians about faith provides a useful distinction. Francis Pieper helpfully summarizes the tradition:

> The distinction between *fides directa* and *fides reflexa* must be carefully observed. . . . The *fides directa* designates that act of faith (*fides actualis*) by which the Christian directly lays hold of the divine promises of grace set forth in the Gospel, desiring and seizing it. The *fides reflexa*, reflex faith, is found in those who by reflecting on the effects and fruits of faith are conscious of the existence of their faith. In all cases believers accept the promises of the Gospel with *fides directa*, whether they are awake or asleep, whether they are adults or infants (Luther, St.L. XI:495), even when in trials and afflictions (*in statu temptationis*) they fear that they no longer believe. . . . However, the importance of the *fides reflexa* must not be minimized. The Christian can and should know that he has faith (*Christian Dogmatics* [St. Louis: Concordia, 1953], 2:443–45).

cerning how much we humans are independent and in control of the most important things we would like to know.

Genesis 3 and Rom 4 provide useful biblical reference points for our exploration of "faith" (Greek, *pistis*). Genesis 3 famously and familiarly illustrates lack of faith. The serpent raises the question whether Adam and Eve are getting the most reliable guidance they could get concerning their lives. Would not you rather be a "god," independently controlling and confirming the knowledge by which you will guide your life? Adam and Eve find themselves wondering whether the strategy of trusting God and faithfully listening to his Word is good enough for human knowledge and wisdom. They adopt the serpent's strategy and break their trusting relationship with God.

In Rom 1–3, Paul traces the terrifying consequences of faithless lives under the wrath of God, but God's judgment that all are faithless is countered by God's faithfulness in Jesus Christ. As Paul proclaims in Rom 3:23–25, "[F]or all have sinned and fall short of the glory of God, and are justified by his grace as a gift, through the redemption that is in Christ Jesus, whom God put forward as a propitiation by his blood, to be received by faith (πίστεως)." God's gift of faith in Jesus sheds light on what counts in a human life. In Rom 4:1–3, Paul elucidates what the gift of faith meant for Abraham and what it means for us:

> What then shall we say was gained by Abraham, our forefather according the flesh? For if Abraham was justified by works, he has something to boast about, but not before God. For what does the Scripture say? "Abraham believed (ἐπίστευσεν) God, and it was counted to him as righteousness" [Gen 15:6].

By this gift of faith Abraham entrusted his life to God. (Note that, because the faith that saves is God's gift and not our achievement, Paul omits the all too human wavering and doubts of Abraham and Sarah as reported in Gen 12–25.) Paul continues in Rom 4:18–25:

> In hope he believed against hope, that he should become the father of many nations, as he had been told, "So shall your offspring be." He did not weaken in faith when he considered his own body, which was as good as dead (since he was about a hundred years old), or when he considered the barrenness of Sarah's womb. No unbelief made him waver concerning the promise of God, but he grew strong in his faith as he gave glory to God, fully convinced that God was able to do what he had promised. That is why his faith was "counted to him as righteousness" [Gen 15:6]. But the words "it was counted to him" were not written for his sake alone, but for ours also. It will be counted to us

who believe in him who raised from the dead Jesus our Lord, who was delivered up for our trespasses and raised for our justification.

Humans have been created for a faithful, trusting relationship with God. Though we all are faithless, God in Christ restores us to faith, and that is what counts in our renewed relationship with God. This is the "faith" that we are trying to coordinate with our understanding of "reason" and "knowledge." We have seen that philosophers struggle to provide an account of "justified" in knowledge understood as "justified true belief." Hintikka helpfully points out that accounts of what is "justified" will vary depending on the type of true belief being sought. If Christians can give an account of why they reason that their faith and trust in God is defensible, then their strategy for finding guidance in life is not opposed to reason. Yes, Christians struggle both intellectually and in daily life to give an account of why they are wise to trust God, but such struggles do not make them irrational. In his Allegory of the Cave (*Republic*, 514a–518d), even Plato vividly depicted the journey to justified true belief as a challenging, uphill struggle. A brief review of Augustine and Luther can help us see some of the ways Christians defend their strategy of putting faith in God.

Early in his life, Augustine (AD 400) turned to philosophy first by way of Cicero and then through Neo-Platonism. In his early thirties God drew him to faith in Christ. He continued to admire Plato, but he diagnosed a fundamental problem in Plato's program of tying down opinions by "giving an account of the reason why." Plato and Aristotle had both noticed a "weakness of will" that led people, even while knowing the reason why, not always to act on the knowledge they achieved. Augustine saw that the biblical account of sin as choosing against God provided an explanation of "weakness of will," and he elaborated this insight to argue that sin makes reason deliberate and choose wrongly on the most important questions in life.

God has created us to be in a trusting relationship with him so that human reason will choose what God says as the first trustworthy source for gaining information to guide us in life. Genesis 3 vividly depicts us turning away from what God says toward sources that let us first trust ourselves and only secondarily trust God. This "original sin" of making ourselves the independent judge of trustworthy information to guide us in life breaks our trusting relationship with God. When the questions are about the meaning and purpose of human life, "original sin" dooms our reason to processing defective information drawn from non- and anti-godly sources. Paul describes a similar derailing of human reason in Rom 1:18–31. "And since they did not see fit to acknowledge God, God gave them up to a debased mind to do what ought not to be done" (Rom 1:28).

When Christ restores our trusting relationship to God, then human reason again will begin from what God says and will break the cycle of basing life on false, God defying information about humanity, the world, and our Creator. This is the meaning of Augustine's famous slogans *credo ut intelligam* ("I believe in order to understand") and *fides quaerens intellectum* ("faith seeking understanding"). The first says that when I believe and trust God, I become able to use my reason and understanding rightly. The second says that faith and trust in God frees me to use my reason to seek truth.

In our exploration of philosophical models of "reason" we noted the bias toward an imperative for reason to be the independent judge, in control of its strategies of knowledge seeking. Augustine highlights the contradiction that arises when humans designed for trusting relationship with the creator choose against the creator and design strategies for knowing that omit trust in God.

Luther, an Augustinian monk, shares Augustine's analysis of the relationship between faith and reason. When he was on trial for his life in Worms in 1521, he articulated the relationship between faith and reason this way: "Unless I am convicted by Scripture and plain reason—I do not accept the authority of popes and councils, for they have contradicted each other—my conscience is captive to the Word of God."[15] Here, like Augustine, Luther trusts what God says, and he boldly claims to use "plain reason" to elucidate what he finds in the most reliable source, the Word of God.

What brings Augustine and Luther to the claim that reason should take what God says in Scripture to be the primary authoritative reference for guidance about humanity, the world, and our Creator/Redeemer? Luther answers this question simply in the Small Catechism explanation of the Third Article of the Apostles' Creed:

> I believe that I cannot by my own reason or strength believe in Jesus Christ, my Lord, or come to Him, but the Holy Spirit has called me by the Gospel, enlightened me with His gifts, sanctified and kept me in the true faith. In the same way He calls, gathers, enlightens, and

---

[15] Translated and quoted in Roland H. Bainton, *Here I Stand: A Life of Martin Luther* (Peabody, MA: Hendrickson, 2010), 180. As Bainton notes, the exact record of Luther's words is a matter of scholarly research and debate. For example, the famous "Here I stand" does not seem to be well attested. See http://de.wikipedia.org/wiki/Reichstag_zu_Worms_(1521) and http://www.specialtyinterests.net/luthersworte.html.

sanctifies the whole Christian Church on earth, and keeps it with Jesus Christ in the one true faith.[16]

Luther is not rejecting reason which, in the explanation of the First Article, he calls a gift of God—God "has given me my body and soul, eyes, ears, and all my members, my reason and all my senses, and still takes care of them."[17] Luther is instead rejecting the common sinner's claim that I can independently control my choice of God and my relationship to Jesus Christ. When reason begins, apart from what God says, to attempt its own assessment of humanity, the world, and God, it begins where no reliable information can be found. But, God has chosen us in Christ and has taken us captive to his Word. When reason begins from that trustworthy, reliable source, it succeeds in understanding who we are and where we stand.

Critics of Luther, and often Lutherans themselves, misunderstand Luther's account of God's good gift of reason. Yes, Luther spoke harshly against reason when it functions as "the devil's whore." Roland Bainton rightly locates Luther's vivid critique as a critique of how "common sense" thinking would guide us about God. "The reason why faith is so hard and reason so inadequate is a problem far deeper than logic. . . . [W]hen Luther railed against the harlot reason, he meant something else. Common sense is perhaps a better translation."[18] We have already seen that common human thought wants to make itself judge of God. Common sense demands that God hold still for our independent accounts of the possibilities of our relationship to him, so that we, independently, can make a judgment whether God is worthy of us or not.

FAITH AND REASON IN THE MODERN UNIVERSITY

We have been following Hintikka's advice to explore the fit between strategies for reasoned knowing and the topics about which we wish to know. Lutherans are adamant that, if the topic concerns God and our relationship to him, then the only strategy that can succeed for theological knowledge is one that starts from God's initiative that puts us in a faithful, trusting relationship with him. Trust God and that will count for righteousness (Rom 4 and Gen 15). Quenstedt, one of the old Lutheran theologians, speaks of "reason held locked within the circle of the divine

---

[16] Quoted in The Commission on Worship of the Lutheran Church—Missouri Synod, *Lutheran Service Book* (St. Louis: Concordia, 2006), 323.

[17] The Commission on Worship of the Lutheran Church—Missouri Synod, *Lutheran Service Book*, 322.

[18] Bainton, *Here I Stand*, 221–22.

Word and kept under discipline."[19] Such discipline embodies the strategy of starting from trust in God and his Word.

But Lutherans freely note that God has given all humanity the gift of reason, and many topics of study do not require reasoning strategies that begin from a trusting relationship with God. Lutherans are not surprised to find that, in many disciplines of the modern university, leading scholars are not people of faith. Earlier in this chapter we noted a productive fit between impersonal strategies for knowing and effective research into the natural world. Both atheism and faith in God are well served by a demystifying of the natural world.

We must also carefully discern sophistries that arise when people characterize a debate as one between reason and faith. This chapter began by contrasting two Oxford intellectuals—chemist Peter Atkins and philosopher Antony Flew. Atkins confidently eliminates any hint of intelligent design from his account of the world around us. Flew, having spent a lifetime dissecting and dismissing arguments about intelligent design, found that the intricacies of DNA raised significant challenges to explanations based in impersonal chance and accident. Atkins and many other university sorts today too easily rely on popular dismissal of strategies of knowing that may bring us into the presence of God. It is ironic that, in the absence of plain evidence and persuasive argument, popular thought today tries to justify its beliefs against God as more "reasonable" than religious faith.

Many contemporary intellectuals have learned the sophistic technique of characterizing the disagreement between Christians and nonbelievers as a conflict between reason and (blind) faith. This sophistry spares them the hard work of constructing arguments. But Flew claims that he does not need nor does he have a faithful relationship with God. He claims that he is providing reasoned argument for his new appreciation of the reasoning involved in design arguments that go all the way back through Aquinas to Aristotle. He does not write that he has found faith. Instead, as we have seen, he wrote the editor of the Journal *Philosophy Now* in 2004 that "my own commitment then as a philosopher who was also a religious unbeliever was and remains that of Plato's Socrates: 'We must follow the argument wherever it leads.' "

People can only characterize Flew as irrational in his new appreciation of design arguments if they have already successfully categorized all references to personal agency and intelligence as illegitimate strategies for

---

[19] Johannes Quenstedt, *Systema* 1:55ff. quoted in Francis Pieper, *Christian Dogmatics* (St. Louis: Concordia, 1950), 1:199.

explaining the natural world. But the intellectual record shows that no one has succeeded in demonstrating that reference to impersonal, naturalistic processes are the only legitimate strategies for explaining everything encountered in the natural world. The refusal of many contemporary intellectuals even to debate this question shows an impoverished understanding of "reason," and Augustine would likely raise the question whether original sin is playing a role in how people desperately defend themselves from ever having seriously to debate questions that might pertain to a living God. Paul is more blunt: those who blithely turn to agnosticism and atheism "are without excuse" (Rom 1:20).

Two further observations press the question of what justification people today can give for not even examining the arguments. The decades long, scientific search for extraterrestrial intelligence (SETI) shows that scientists are quite capable of raising questions about whether intelligent design can be discerned in the complex patterns of the universe. And, the sophisticated methods of forensic science indicate that, when appropriate, "science" can be quite reasonable in the patient search for planning, purpose, motive, and intelligence when reasoning about crimes.

Trusting God and his gift of reason, Lutherans are not afraid to examine where strategies crafted by atheists may lead on specific issues in the physical sciences, the social sciences, business, economics, education, the arts and the humanities. But Lutherans, as people of faith, stay alert to the ways in which faithless people, expert in the specifics of their disciplines, begin to encroach on questions about God and humanity that require research strategies rooted in a stance of faith. Christianity has long been criticized for imposing a one-size-fits-all approach to knowledge on the world; ironically, popular veneration of science in the modern university is now at risk for imposing its one-size-fits-all approach on the world.

The chapter in this book on "Cultural Anthropology and Theology" provides examples that contrast strategies for knowledge in the social sciences with strategies for theological work. Other chapters provide examples relevant to other disciplines. In the chapter on anthropology, Jack Schultz helpfully speaks of "interaction" between theology and anthropology rather than "integration" of the two. We have been observing how different disciplines and topics of study require different strategies for effective, reasoned inquiry. Some strategies are fundamentally shaped by faith in God, but many others operate well without reference to faith in God. Thus, "interaction" of faith and reason may be a better description of their relationship in a Lutheran university than "integration" of faith and reason.[20] It is true that "integration" rightly points to how Lutheran professors integrate within themselves a faithful relationship to God alongside a variety of strategies for seeking knowledge in their disciplines. But the strategies themselves cannot be said to be integrated. Strategies of knowing relevant to studying change over time in a population of fish will be very different from strategies of knowing relevant to an understanding of a faithful relationship with God. Hintikka is correct that "there is no single definite meaning of the words 'knowing' and 'knowledge.'"[21] Neither theology nor philosophy should claim a monopoly on effective deployment of reason.

A faith-based university in the Lutheran tradition can be a great gift to the world. Lutherans have the resources thoroughly to appreciate how God has given and preserved valuable knowledge throughout the many cultures of the world. Commenting on political science, Luther asserts that non-Christians "can speak and teach about this very well, as they have done. And, to tell the truth, they are far more skillful in such matters than the Christians."[22] So he advises: "Let whoever wants to be wise and clever about earthly government read the pagan books and writings. . . . [I]t is my conviction that God has given and preserved such pagan books as the poets and histories, as Homer, Virgil, Demosthenes, Cicero, Livy and also that fine old lawyer Ulpian" so that we might think wisely about earthly government.[23] This same attitude saved the Lutherans of the seventeenth century from making the mistake other Christians made of condemning scientists like Copernicus and Galileo.

Because Lutherans see a close tie between love of God in Christ and love of neighbor, they resist the encroachments of impersonal and faithless strategies of knowing into topics that touch on the dignity and worth and significance of human lives. The foundation of biblical faith is a trusting relationship with God. When, like Abraham, we put our faith in God, we have a powerful strategy for knowing God and also for knowing each other. Strategies that seek knowledge from impersonal sources of information are different from strategies that explore the dynamics of a trusting relationship with a person. Reason is involved in both types of strategy. A living faith in

---

[20] For further discussion on the interaction of faith and learning compared to integration, see Ashmon's chapter.

[21] Hintikka and Bachman, *What If?*, 372.

[22] Martin Luther, "Psalm 101," in *Selected Psalms II*, trans. Alfred von Rohr Sauer (St. Louis: Concordia), 13:198.

[23] Quoted in E. Gordon Rupp, *The Righteousness of God: Luther Studies* (London: Hodder and Stoughton, 1953), 297–303.

God will typically encourage university scholars to maximize the benefits of interpersonal relationships in scholarship, teaching, and mentoring.

Lutherans expect to find a healthy interaction between faith and reason, theology and philosophy. They are well placed to create universities where faithfulness to God and excellence in academic studies together flourish.

QUESTIONS

1. This chapter has criticized philosophical approaches to "knowledge" that presume that the knower must be independent and in control of what is claimed to be known. Hintikka argues that we need different strategies to account for our knowledge that acorns produce oak trees than to account for our knowledge of a friend's trustworthiness, since we are not in control of a friend's character. What strategies are appropriate for accounting for "knowledge" in your academic discipline? In the process of seeking, gathering, and selecting information, how do you discover the most important questions to ask?

2. Lutherans stress the sole work of the Holy Spirit in bringing us to Christ. Yet, in Rom 1:19, Paul says about all humans that "what can be known about God is plain to them, because God has shown it to them." Can we today more thoroughly explore natural knowledge of God as a way to put our generation on notice about their broken relationship with God, their creator?

3. The media frequently presumes that science knows that there is no need to speak about God in connection with questions about the origins of the universe, biological life, or humans. For many people, this popular and reductionist view of science has become the gold standard of "knowing." How can we prepare ourselves to contend against this popular conceit without immediately quoting Scripture? For the sake of those who have rejected God's Word, can we undermine their secular confidence by being better prepared to discuss what exactly science has and has not established?

4. Lutherans distinguish between *fides directa* (saving faith) and *fides reflexa* (the Christian's reflection upon his or her faith). This chapter explores how *fides reflexa* enters into the way that Christians seek guidance in life. The tradition plainly encourages reasoned reflection on the effects and fruits of faith. When Lutherans converse about "faith," are they sufficiently alert to the place of *fides reflexa* in the Christian life? How can we highlight such reflection when non-believers challenge us to give an account of the hope that is in us?

9

CULTURAL ANTHROPOLOGY AND THEOLOGY:
DEFINING THEIR LIMITS AND INTERACTION

Jack M. Schultz[1]

INTRODUCTION

I am Lutheran.

I assume "Christian" as an unmarked feature of the appellation Lutheran—to be Lutheran is to be Christian. Neither can I view "Lutheran" as an "add-on" to Christianity. I see Lutheran as a "from-the-ground-up" understanding of and response to Christ's Gospel. As such, Lutheran and Christian are inseparable in my mind and I will use them interchangeably in this essay.

I am mindful and appreciative of our rich Lutheran heritage of faithfulness to our Lord, Jesus Christ, the Word of God, our insistence on recognizing Christ as the beginning, center, and end of all Scripture, and our clear proclamation of salvation by grace through faith alone. I value our careful distinction between Law and Gospel in handling Scripture, and our "two kingdom" approach to life where Christians live simultaneously in God's penultimate, temporal society ruled by law and reason, and God's ultimate, eternal church ruled by grace and faith.[2] I am Lutheran and have been as long as I have known myself to be anything.

I identify myself as Lutheran, not as *a* Lutheran. For me, it is an identity, not an affiliation. That must not imply in your minds a simple "He thinks it really important." Rather, being Lutheran (and recall, I can replace Lutheran with Christian here) is fundamental to who I am and how I view the world. It defines my values, goals, roles, and relationships. The funda-mental relationship I participate in is one with our Lord. God has revealed

---

[1] Jack M. Schultz, PhD (Oklahoma), is Professor of Anthropology at CUI.

[2] For an explanation of Law and Gospel and two-kingdom theology, see Mueller's chapter.

himself and come to me (and each Christian) in Jesus, the incarnate Word. In Jesus, I recognize that God seeks to be known and seeks to be known by me (and each Christian). It is this Word I seek to know and serve. That Word of God, revealed and active, continues to draw all mankind to God. I am part of that process.

I am also a cultural anthropologist, and have been for a much shorter time than I have been Christian. I am Lutheran and an anthropologist. I am not a Lutheran anthropologist. I resist such an identification. To identify myself as a Christian anthropologist, to me, implies that I am doing anthropology as a kind of apologetic enterprise (perhaps there is a place for such an enterprise, but not for me). Rather, I am doing anthropology as an academic pursuit in fulfillment of what I understand to be my God-given vocation—that is, I am investigating the human factors involved in the development and expression of cultures, including my own. I am especially interested in how culture and religion interact, including my own.

I am Lutheran and I am an anthropologist, not one then the other. I am one person and embrace both identities. Each informs the other and at times the two identities are incommensurate. As a Christian and an anthropologist I live with that tension. I am careful to "properly distinguish" the role of each. I am Lutheran; I do anthropology.

THE ACADEMIC DISCIPLINE OF ANTHROPOLOGY

To understand the full sweep and complexity of cultures across all of human history, anthropology draws and builds upon knowledge from the social and biological sciences as well as the humanities and physical sciences. A central concern of anthropologists is the application of knowledge to the situation of human problems.[3]

In preparation of a discussion regarding theology and anthropology, it is perhaps useful to overview the discipline of anthropology. Anthropology is a social scientific investigation of human being and the human processes that are responsible for this thing we call culture. Anthropology is foremost a "way of looking," rather than a body of knowledge. It begins with the assumption that "people are people." This means that human beings are fundamentally similar in their biological makeup and moral and cognitive capacity. This also means that the great diversity of traditions and practices people groups express will be explained in reference to cultural learning rather than in reference to inherent, organic, or biological differences. As a

---

[3] "What Is Anthropology?," American Anthropological Association, accessed September 19, 2014, http://www.aaanet.org/about/whatisanthropology.cfm.

vital component of the liberal arts, anthropology seeks to broaden our understanding of human being.

We, as humans, have a variety of needs. We need a regular supply of food; we need clothing and shelter to protect us from the elements. We need to govern ourselves; we need to express beauty. We need to reproduce ourselves and our systems. We need to know what is worth living for and what is worth dying for. And just how do humans go about meeting those needs? How have people around the world, at varying times, solved these problems? How have these solutions developed into tradition? How should one account for the many differences between culture groups? Why are some groups so much more "advanced" than others?

These are the kinds of questions that anthropology is interested in answering. As (post-) modern Americans we know *our* answers, our "common sense," but what about those *others,* what of their answers? It is the answers of *others* that anthropology is particularly interested in. "Anthropology," Robert Borofsky aptly summarizes, "broadens the conversational frames of reference regarding the human experience. It stretches us beyond our everyday, parochial perspectives by drawing into the conversation other humans, separated from us by space and time."[4]

Anthropology is heir to the positivist tradition that emphasizes "tested and systematized experience rather than. . . undisciplined speculation."[5] In other words, anthropology seeks to investigate questions of human diversity scientifically. Anthropology identifies itself as a social science. The adjective "scientific" is significant. By defining itself as scientific, the discipline seeks to limit its investigations to empirically verifiable data and the interpretations of that data are limited to material (empirical, non-spiritual) forces. For the scientist, "ideas must abide by rules of uniformitarianism (i.e., the rules of the natural world) and be explained with reference to those rules. Science works only with the known or the potentially knowable. It admits nothing that is ultimately unexplainable."[6] Anthropology is an academic enterprise that limits itself to knowable, humanly significant, empirically verifiable forces.

These are the self-imposed limitations of the discipline. Therefore, the discipline is limited, admittedly. It is partial, admittedly. Anthropology is an investigation of knowable human forces and processes that allows an understanding and perhaps manipulation of these human forces to meet

---

[4]   Robert Borofsky, "Public Anthropology," *Anthropology News* 40, no. 1 (1999): 6–7.

[5]   Kaplan, Abraham Kaplan, "Positivism," in *International Encyclopedia of the Social Sciences*, vol. 12, ed. David Sills (New York: Macmillan, 1968), 389.

[6]   Mark Nathan Cohen, "Correspondence," *Anthropology News* 52, no. 2, (2011): 3.

human needs. It is an investigative discipline: data are collected and interpreted; theories are generated, tested, and revised. As a science, anthropology is by its nature a tentative business, always subject to revision. "What we know now is not fact or truth;" rather, "[i]t is the present state of our understanding, always potentially to be refined by new contributions."[7] In the sciences, the scientific process is believed to be self-corrective—errors will be revealed through the process—and knowledge is viewed as be being built up. Anthropology is practiced in an attempt to get a clearer picture of the human world and the human forces at play in the development and maintenance of social worlds.

As a science, anthropology assumes a material, closed reality. The reality that science investigates is a purely material reality. Spiritual forces are not amenable to empirical investigation and so they are ignored (if not denied). As such, in its ontological assumptions (its "big picture" narrative about origins) it is contradictory to and incommensurate with a Christian understanding (which is probably also true for any strictly materialist discipline; perhaps individual scientists will acknowledge a reality of non-material dimensions; however, the scientific method does not). Even while as a Christian I recognize that an exclusively materialist view is inadequate, I will approach a research subject "as if" it were nothing but material in make-up. And I am not alone in that approach. Christian researchers investigating the tensile strength rates of aluminum alloys, or changing population figures of white-tailed deer in Oklahoma forests will not likely conclude that God broke the metal or killed the deer, but rather look for empirical, repeatable forces to explain the phenomena in question.

CONTRASTING THEOLOGY AND ANTHROPOLOGY

Theology and anthropology are two academic disciplines that have markedly different approaches to some overlapping questions. The two approaches use different criteria to determine what is accepted as valid data and valid conclusions. It should not be surprising that they arrive at radically different conclusions and answers to those overlapping questions. I offer two references to demonstrate the contrast of anthropology to theology. Excuse their hubris, but the two excerpts provide a sampling of the contrasts. The first, from Abdul el-Zein, clearly assumes the superiority of a scientific approach:

> The anthropological positions claim to be more objective than both
> the folk and the theological traditions. With respect to the folk

---

[7] Cohen, "Correspondence," 3.

expressions [anthropologists] assume their scientific analyses to be more reflective and systematic. And although theology is recognized as highly reflective, it is not critical and therefore remains subordinate to the authority of anthropology which, being scientific, is critical as well. Anthropological analyses then establish their validity not only on the necessity of particular assumptions concerning the nature of reality but also on the epistemological criteria of scientific rationality. Theology, to the contrary, establishes truth on the incontestable basis of faith. So at the level of the content and form of knowledge, faith is opposed to science, theology and anthropology deny each other's capacity to grasp the final truth. Yet from the perspective of the structure of knowledge, their opposition is only apparent, for they both begin from and impose preconceived and positive meanings which necessarily frame their understanding of other experiences. . . . [W]hen reviewed collectively, these studies reveal the incredible diversity of possible definitions and descriptions.[8]

Interestingly, the theology referenced and held in contrast to anthropology here is Muslim theology, not Christian theology. In the second excerpt, from Vassos Argyrou, there is an even more startling assertion and hubris. Here anthropology is presented as the keeper of the assumed "truth" of a universe randomly generated by non-spiritual, non-intelligent, evolutionary forces and assumes that lens to investigate humanity:

In all ethnological paradigms that take a hermeneutic approach, what we know and what the natives do not is an ontological truth—the truth of the human condition. It is that the world is intrinsically arbitrary and that whatever meaning, sense, and purpose we find in it exists only because we have constructed and placed it there beforehand. The division that this disenchanting realization effects, then, is between those who forget the truth of the human condition because they cannot bear it and turn to the metaphysical to protect themselves and those who cannot forget because they would be deluding themselves.[9]

Such is an anthropological orientation, and clearly such an orientation is incommensurate with Christian theology. The two approaches, anthropology and theology, are primarily interested in vastly different realms and

---

[8] Abdul H. el-Zein, "Beyond Ideology and Theology: The Search for the Anthropology of Islam," *Annual Review of Anthropology* 6 (1977): 249.

[9] Vassos Argyrou, "Sameness and the Ethnological Will to Meaning," *Current Anthropology* 40, no. 1: (1999): S33.

the questions they ask are most often very different, but there are some overlapping questions that each claims to answer definitively. As was already acknowledged, the "big picture" narrative of anthropology is irreconcilable with a Christian understanding.

I will maintain, however, that there is "little picture" value to an understanding of human forces at play, even for Christians. For even if we are unaware of these forces, we are still subject to them. I will maintain that in consideration of religious motivations, institutions, explanations, and sensibilities there are unacknowledged human forces at work. Perhaps we Christians jump too soon to a spiritual explanation when other, empirical forces may more fruitfully explain and predict human predicaments. For example, the Lutheran Church is the least racially diverse (i.e., has the greatest proportion of "white members," 96 percent) of all mainline American denominations.[10] This is better explained and remedied by looking to social forces rather than spiritual forces. It is here that a nuanced understanding of social mechanisms contributes. Certainly, we are justified in speaking about the many social issues we experience as consequences of sin and a fallen world, but that does not abdicate responsibility in seeking to rectify injustices.

THE LIMITS OF A SCIENTIFIC APPROACH TO TRUTH

The apostle Paul speaks about the "full assurance of understanding and the knowledge of God's mystery, which is Christ, in whom are hidden all the treasures of wisdom and knowledge" (Col 2:2–3). In Christ the Truth is revealed. He is the "big picture" that God himself has revealed to us and *that* Truth is not available to science (empirical verification). The Word informs me, and warns me of the limits of my discipline. It reminds me of the "biggest picture," the always True. It is all his, made by and for him. That, again, is the "big picture."

The anthropological approach requires scientific investigation, but clearly there are humanly relevant questions that are not amenable to scientific investigation. Science has its place, but there are things that can be understood only partially via a scientific method. What science can do, it

---

[10] Barry A. Kosmin, Egon Mayer, and Ariela Keysar, *American Religious Identification Survey, 2001* (New York: The Graduate Center of the City University of New York, 2001), 35, accessed September 19, 2014, http://www.gc.cuny.edu/CUNY_GC/media/CUNY-Graduate-Center/PDF/ARIS/ARIS-PDF-version.pdf. Also see Barry A. Kosmin and Ariela Keysar, *Religion in a Free Market: Religious and Non-Religious Americans: Who, What, Why, Where* (Ithaca, NY: Paramount Market Publishing, 2006).

does very well. The answers it provides appear very compelling primarily because science, with its rules for obtaining knowledge and its tendency to self-corrections, has been a very effective tool for allowing prediction and control. However, prediction and control does necessarily mean proof of understanding (consider the now obsolete scientific teaching of "spontaneous generation;" it was predictive, and wrong). A scientific, naturalistic understanding is limited.

As a believer and as an anthropologist I must always be mindful of the "big picture." We are not the products of natural, random forces. As human beings we have basic needs, motivations, structural needs—all of which anthropology investigates and explicates. But humans are *more than that*. We are created for purpose. We are made to be in relationship with the Creator, and in relationship and service to our neighbor. The ultimate is already settled.

As academics we pursue a penultimate at best. There are plenty of competing "big pictures" and claims of ultimate. We who have been called by our Lord hear his voice above the din. This "more than that," however, is generally not amenable to empirical or scientific investigation. But even Christians should be interested in those usually hidden forces that influence, determine, and shape our human experiences. And while it is quite unlikely that anthropology will look to theology to provide direction or contribution, anthropology does have something to offer to a theological understanding, or more precisely, an understanding of theological praxis.

INTERACTION OF FAITH AND DISCIPLINE

John Calvin noted almost 500 years ago that "true and substantial wisdom principally consists of two parts, the knowledge of God, and the knowledge of ourselves. But, while these two branches of knowledge are so intimately connected, which of them precedes and produces the other, is not easy to discover."[11] While I'm not asserting that we need to recognize social science as an equal to theology, I will nonetheless maintain that a nuanced understanding of the human is essential to a genuine, broadly applicable theology.

In the Lutheran doctrinal declaration of *sola Scriptura* ("Scripture alone") we do not posit that the Bible answers every question, but that "Holy Scripture is recognized as the only source and standard of faith, from

---

[11] John Calvin, *Institutes of the Christian Religion*, trans. John Allen (Philadelphia: Westminster, 1936), 1:47.

which alone the theologian must draw his teachings."[12] When Lutherans say that the Bible is the only infallible source of faith and practice (2 Tim 3:15–17) we do not mean that it addresses every issue in life.[13] The Bible is not everything about all things. While Scripture is completely true, it is not the complete truth. The Bible is not intended to have an answer to every question, but it is intended to answer some questions unequivocally. It may be argued that it does consider every *meaningful* issue in life and that will not be disputed. There is, however, much that needs to be known that is not included in the Bible. Scripture reveals quite clearly who created us and why we were created, but we do not have the details on how and when. It also clearly demonstrates that humankind is fallen and in need of restoration, but it does not provide many details on how we are to feed, clothe, shelter, organize, and govern ourselves.

I suggest that it is not helpful to speak of the *integration* of theology and anthropology, rather a much better image is one of *interaction*.[14] I don't think that my task as a Christian and social scientist is to develop a harmonic synopsis of the Bible and the social sciences. While I will uphold that "all truth is one" and that we aspire to be a *university* (where knowledge is "turned into one [whole]"), we don't need to bring into harmony the biblical account and an anthropological account under the rubric of "truth." Such would require a complete understanding of both theology and the processes of culture. I would argue that by attempting to harmonize these divergent approaches, theological and anthropological, we unnecessarily distort and lessen each. Neither understanding is complete. All the data are not yet in. We should not expect a premature agreement. We can live with the tension between these different ways of knowing different kinds of things. The Truth of the Word does not need science to verify it. It is what judges all things; it does not receive judgment. We can live confidently trusting our Creator even while admitting "I don't know (yet)."

---

[12] John T. Mueller, *Christian Dogmatics: A Handbook of Doctrinal Theology for Pastors, Teachers, and Laymen* (St. Louis: Concordia, 1955), 85.

[13] See sections 16 and 20 of Preface to the Book of Concord (1580) and Formula of Concord, Solid Declaration, Rule and Norm 3 and 9 (1577) in Robert Kolb and Timothy J. Wengert, eds., *The Book of Concord: The Confessions of the Evangelical Lutheran Church*, (Minneapolis: Fortress, 2000), 10, 13, 527–28.

[14] For a discussion on the distinction between an integration and interaction approach to faith and learning, see Ashmon's chapter.

CONTRIBUTIONS ANTHROPOLOGY CAN MAKE
TO THEOLOGICAL APPLICATIONS

As a Christian I know some things that science cannot know. Setting aside "big picture" questions, there is much that can be gained from a "little picture" investigation of human, knowable forces. Where my two roles meet is in the recognition that even true faith is manifested in a particular cultural context. My discipline informs me of the limits of my culture. It reminds me that even my *understanding* of the "big picture" is "under the influence of culture," and I think it imperative that each Christian be aware that theirs is too. We need to acknowledge that our cultural contexts (e.g., our citizenship, our participation in democratic or socialist system, pluralism, consumer capitalism, media, and technology) affect our relating to God. Unless I understand these forces I may confuse them for my unique relationship with God; our cultural preferences may be misunderstood as divine requirement.

The place I see the interaction of anthropology and theology most clearly is in the contributions anthropology can make in the application of theology. How might our current cultural context influence our understanding of eternal things and the practices those understandings generate? How might "our understanding" (our doctrinal statements, practice, and identity) be a reflection of our time and place and not "an eternal mandate?" I recognize that there is no such thing as a culturally neutral church or a culturally neutral theological expression. Indeed, I have contended elsewhere using the example of my own church body, The Lutheran Church—Missouri Synod (LCMS), that,

> The LCMS is a "cultured" church. We have a way. We have an identity. We are not simply a group of diverse people gathered around the Word; there is a way we do things. When we bring others into our fold we expect them to make the adjustments and accommodate our conclusions and practices. It is not, a, many of us understand, that we are "just regular" and the "others" are the ones with the accretions of culture. We, too, have characteristic ways to think and speak. We have a *common* sense. We privilege the head over the heart. We have our values (especially regarding work, education, and home ownership). We have our mores, and foodways (with regional iterations to be sure), and dress (I am told by non-Lutherans that we have a look; and once an airport shuttle driver picked me out of a crowd of 30 as the Lutheran). We have our traditional songs (some of which are only a decade old), and indispensable vocabularies. We have our recognized authorities. We know our heroes and our villains. We are prone to a

slightly self-congratulatory ethos at our Reformation Festivals. We are mindful that the "mispronunciations" of Synód and Cóncordia often mark those who were raised outside our church. We have a set of shared and unexamined institutionally supported assumptions. We have our gate-keepers and our institutions of enculturation and sanction (whether they be our seminaries, our Sunday schools, or doctrinal review). We have an underlying, organizing framework whose potency lay in its concealed ubiquity and assumed structures. And these traits we can explain *theologically*—but that does not preclude their being a contextual (cultural) expression that may not be the only acceptable theological manifestation of the theological truth. Even if denied or spiritualized, we still have an identity. This identity structures our social relations, provides social cohesion, perpetuates our systems, organizes our ways of acting and interacting, and distinguishes *us* from *them*. It is an identity that functions, in effect, as ethnicity.[15]

The LCMS, like any denomination, is a visible church that is part of the church invisible. It is in understanding a church's visible manifestation that an anthropological understanding can contribute. We, as Lutherans Christians, are something spiritual and something very human. Our Lutheran "two kingdom" approach to Christian life acknowledges this tension. Unless we properly divide the two we will likely confuse one for the other with dreadful consequences. Therefore I continue in my God-given vocation of anthropology to explicate the relationship between the eternal and the contextual.

CONCLUSION

At creation God placed in the animals clear directions or instincts to govern their lives. Humans were created without those built-in, defining directives for feeding and sheltering themselves. We use tools to transform nature into humanly useful commodities, and even a cursory overview reveals a wide array of human solutions to the problems of living. Many of those solutions have a direct influence on our religious sentiments and understandings. For the Christian, the motivation to understand social processes and the often hidden dimensions of these forces is in our desire to more effectively serve others in our vocations. I recall here that curious prayer of Paul that identifies an increase of knowledge and insight with an

---

[15] Jack M. Schultz, "Dealing with Theology Culturally," *Missio Apostolica* 20, No. 2 (2012): 161–62.

increase of love: "And this is my prayer that your love may abound more and more, with knowledge and all discernment, so that you may approve what is excellent" (Phil 1:9–10).

Our "human condition" includes a variety of underlying forces that circumscribe us at every turn: we are social beings created to be in relationship, we need social structures and institutions in order to divide labor make and enforce group decisions; provide enculturation and education; produce food, clothes, and shelter; organize thought; and provide a system of meaning and values. It is these inescapable forces that profoundly impact our being in ways we are mostly oblivious to. The task of anthropology, and all other social sciences, is to disclose and explicate these forces. For believers, with an increase of knowledge about and insight into these forces, we may become better prepared to serve others whom we are called to love and proclaim the Eternal Word (Christ) to.

As a Christian and an anthropologist I assert an ongoing dialogue between theology and anthropology is needed to contextualize our understanding and communications of the Word. Each generation needs to ask and answer many of the same questions the church has always asked and answered. Sometimes we'll get the same answers; perhaps sometimes they will be different. A responsible anthropology is, I have argued, essential to a genuine, broadly applicable theological expression. Divine revelation is essential for a genuine understanding of the nature of reality and the implications that understanding has in the life of individuals. Without an acute awareness of human forces one can mistakenly conclude that "our" preferred ways of doing things is conterminous with the will of God.

Questions

1. How do the methodologies of the social sciences (e.g., psychology, sociology, etc.) limit and shape their investigations and conclusions?

2. What are some of the ways that your cultural context shapes your understanding of the Christian faith?

3. Is there a difference between an interaction versus integration approach to the social sciences and theology? If so, what is it and what difference does it make to relationship of faith and discipline?

4. What common questions do the social sciences and theology share? How can the social sciences interact with theology to serve the church?

10

METHODOLOGICAL COHESION IN THE BIOLOGICAL SCIENCES AND LUTHERAN THEOLOGY

Roderick B. Soper[1] and Michael E. Young[2]

INTRODUCTION

The topic of theology and science is as vast as the history and data associated with both areas of study. Consequently, narrowing this topic from the extremely broad to the somewhat specific should be the first order of business. This chapter is intended to elucidate the way in which the biological sciences are taught at a Lutheran university (in particular, Core Biology courses at Concordia University Irvine, which we both have taught). Biology courses at Concordia function under the following mission statement: "Concordia University, guided by the Great Commission of Christ Jesus and the Lutheran Confessions, empowers students through the liberal arts and professional studies for lives of learning, service and leadership." This statement provides a platform upon which the biological sciences build a curriculum that focuses on the "Great Commission of Christ Jesus and the Lutheran Confessions" and gives students the tools necessary to become, as the university's motto says, "wise, honorable, and cultivated citizens."[3]

The mission statement and motto are a part of our opening curriculum and provides the platform from which Core Biology (a science class that

---

[1] Roderick B. Soper, PhD (Curtin), is Professor of Biology at CUI.

[2] Michael E. Young, PhD (Washington University), is Associate Professor of Natural Science at Concordia University Wisconsin.

[3] "Our Mission," Concordia University Irvine, accessed September 19, 2014, http://www.cui.edu/aboutcui. The motto comes from "Faithful to the Lutheran Tradition," Concordia University Irvine, accessed September 19, 2014, http://www.cui.edu/aboutcui/heritage/index.aspx?id=18634.

every freshman takes linked with Core Theology) is taught. We explain the mission, motto, and linked nature of the Core Biology course this way for students in the syllabus:

> It is our goal to help you on the path of becoming an educated person (wise, honorable, cultivated). An educated person, as it relates to biology, is someone with the ability to think and articulate their thoughts on biological topics as viewed from a distinctly Christian worldview, scientific worldview, and a combination of the two.
>
> Terms defined:
>
> **Wise** = Knowing when to speak and when to listen.
>
> **Honorable** = Respectfully engaging those with whom you disagree in such way that they know you respect them, but you disagree with them.
>
> **Cultivated** = You seek knowledge more than wealth.

In this chapter we will show how Core Biology at Concordia University Irvine educates students to realize how a Christian (particularly a Lutheran) worldview can epistemologically speak to matters of nature and God.

THE PROCESS

Undergirded by this platform, we begin each Core Biology course by asking three questions: What is truth? How do you know truth when you have it? Why do you believe what you believe? Answers to these questions are central to understanding what science is and how science answers questions about the natural world.

What is Truth?

Truth is relational. That is to say, each individual has a relationship with a concept called truth. The word *truth* is used in society today in such way that it is difficult to understand whether truth is subjective or objective. Using the term *relational* provides a useful definition of truth that helps students understand how society uses the word in the vernacular. To illustrate this concept, truth is presented on a continuum with subjective and objective on opposite ends:

TRUTH

SUBJECTIVE   OBJECTIVE

One can use this diagram to place various truth statements somewhere along the continuum. For example, a subjective truth statement like, "The Minnesota Vikings are the best professional football team in the NFL," is presented to the students for their consideration. This truth statement can be supported by some facts, but primarily reflects the instructor's selective choice of facts, subjective opinion regarding these facts, and a burning desire for the Vikings to finally win a Super Bowl. An objective statement is also presented. For example, "All things living will die." This truth statement is obviously more objective and universally true for all things regardless of the facts used or one's understanding of the phrase. Interestingly, both statements can be said to be true.

How Do You Know Truth?

Truth is determined with a method of knowing or epistemology. For science that method is usually termed the Hypothetic Deductive Approach. In this approach, a hypothesis is first made regarding an observation in nature using induction. Then a prediction is made with the use of deduction, which is tested by means that are as objective as possible (using some sort of statistical or more quantitative than qualitative method). Students are required to apply simple statistical analyses to simple problems. For example, students analyze provided data using a t-test to determine efficacious methodologies for habitat management to obtain a real-world feel for this method. They are additionally challenged to think about their own epistemological method and become aware that the question of knowing truth has an answer for the individual as well as the group.

Truth is only known within the context of culture, and science is not immune to this fact. Science, however, has a difficult time acknowledging its own culture because the concept of culture is rarely explicitly taught or explained in a science curriculum.[4] As a result, Core Biology classes have worked over the last three years with the guidance of the professors to define culture in the following way (with characteristics of the culture of science to follow): "Culture is a common paradigm that influences our behavior, which we may not be aware of fully unless our attention is drawn to it. Culture changes over time and cannot be replicated outside of the con-

---

[4] For more discussion of the issue of culture in science see Fernando Espinosza, *The Nature of Science: Integrating Historical, Philosophical, and Sociological Perspectives* (Lanham, MD: Rowman and Littlefield, 2012), and Jonathan Marks, *Why I Am Not a Scientist: Anthropology and Modern Science* (Berkeley: University of California Press, 2009.)

text in which it occurs." Using this definition we delineate the following characteristics of Western scientific culture:

1. It is methodologically naturalistic/materialistic
2. Searches for the Truth (probabilistic)
3. Has a problem with being wrong
4. Exists within a "publish or perish" environment
5. Can be arrogant and insecure

The first characteristic is the primary operating paradigm of science. Or, a better way of saying it is that science will not operate outside of a naturalistic/materialistic worldview. Students observe that one of the most important guiding principles of science's culture is a principle that was not generated from the scientific method, but from history.

Core Biology students learn how the origins and paradigms of Western science can be traced from early Greek philosophers, primarily Aristotle. Aristotle's practice of observing nature to answer questions about nature is contrasted with that of Plato who looked to the heavens. This proto-naturalistic paradigm made its way throughout areas of Hellenistic influence (geographically around the Mediterranean and culturally from Greeks to Romans to Arabs to Europe), and was eventually incorporated into the church in Europe by the Scholastics, primarily Aquinas. However, the church's failure logically to separate observations of nature from scriptural texts and its failure to separate Scripture from interpretation of Scripture lead to a shift of authority regarding nature away from the church. This paved the way for reason to be of more use to understand the world than the Bible. Consequently, when Charles Darwin's *On the Origin of Species* (1859) seemingly answered the age old question of where we come from without the use of any sort of deity a naturalistic worldview gained wide acceptance in the nascent modern science community. This is how a modern naturalistic/materialistic principle removed the possibility of non-natural explanations for observed phenomena because of culture—not data.

Why Do We Believe What We Believe?

This question is answered by using what has become known as the "light bulb effect" diagramed below:

UNKNOWN | KNOWN

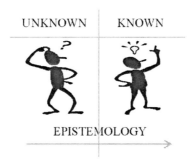

EPISTEMOLOGY

In this intuitive diagram, students are made aware that all forms of episte-mology take us from the unknown to the known in varying fashions. Regardless of how simple, complicated, natural, or supernatural a concept is, a decision is ultimately made when one crosses the line and says, "Now I know, where before I did not." An awareness of when and how this decision is made (or what epistemology is used) allows one to understand why (or how) they have come to know anything and, hopefully by extension, why they know what they know. Using this awareness for the individual, we broaden that understanding to the scientific method (Hypothetic Deductive Approach).

Examples of Cultural Impacts on the Scientific Method

Introducing and teaching the topic of evolution allows us to show how the culture of science has changed and impacted the interpretation of scien-tific data. We do not use this opportunity to show how evolution is wrong; rather, we use topics like homology (using comparative anatomy to show evolutionary relationships—such as similarity of human hands and primate hands—to show how they are evolutionarily related) to show how data that exists is interpreted using the scientific method (Hypothetic Deductive Approach) and how the interpretation of the data is influenced by the op-erating scientific paradigm (naturalism/materialism). Students are expected to know that evolutionary theory is an accurate scientific theory based upon the operating paradigm that is used to interpret the data. From this we show how a change of the operating paradigm causes a change in the interpretation of data that itself remains unchanged. Teaching the history of scientific development allows students to see that when operating para-digms change (or culture changes), paradigms will shift and so will how nature is understood. Other scientific topics are used in a similar way.

Teaching Science

After a thorough review of evolutionary theory (including readings from *Origins of Species*) we teach typical biological topics such as genetics, mitosis, meiosis, and proteins synthesis. We do this for two primary reasons. The first is it to make sure that students are knowledgeable and literate in current biological topics and technological advances. The second is to show students that the majority of scientific information comes to them in the form of axioms (a concept accepted as true and taught by an authority without the physical evidence to support an objective truth decision).

It is important to make students aware that knowing science axiomatically is not a problem, and that axiomatic truths are actually the bulk of knowledge in any topic. For example, when taught protein synthesis, students will understand enzymatic proteins are made by DNA, or genes, instructing the order of amino acids without actually seeing the process or the original research used to document the process. Knowing information axiomatically is not problematic unless one has confused axioms with reality and accepts information generated from the scientific method as producing an unquestionable and wholly objective understanding of reality.

APPLICATION OF THE PROCESS

Current generations of students will be exposed to technological advances that will force them to answer many questions with sophistication, resolution, and precision that previous generations have not had to do. For example, advances in genetics, implantation of prosthetic microchips in humans, cloning, genetic engineering, and the like, will require a definition of what it means to be human as the line between machine and mankind becomes blurred. Situations such as these, and more like them, require educated people in society to rely on answers about nature that span beyond nature. Showing students how culture can affect the scientific method gives them an opportunity to begin to question scientific information that they previously assumed was an objective description of reality. Then students must make use of the increasingly abundant data available on any particular topic to thoroughly reason through that scientific topic before making precise truth claims.

One way to provide students with the tools to question science is to give them a clear understanding of the difference between data and theory. In general, data is considered the information collected by the scientific method and theories are those conclusions extrapolated from the data. When these are confused, the theory that the origin of deoxyribonucleic acid (DNA) was random, even though it is statistically very improbable and cannot be supported by data, become accepted as objective truth. The theory of randomness is a reasonable extrapolation from the paradigm of naturalism/materialism, but if no distinction is made, the theory of randomness is treated as if it were empirical data.

Once accepted as empirical data, these theoretical claims take on a life of their own and become difficult to question unless one is prepared to run afoul of established scientific dogma and potentially suffer scientific reprobation. If one can see that the claim of randomness in the origins of DNA is a theoretical product of a naturalistic/materialistic paradigm inculcated by a scientific culture rarely acknowledged or recognized, then one can see that the statistical data does not support the theory of randomness and can intellectually be satisfied that an alternative explanation should be investigated. If asked why one might make this claim, students would know to look to the data with an acknowledgment of the operating paradigm guiding the interpretation that is external to the data.

These sorts of epistemological "light bulb" moments allow bridges into theology and how theology's method of understanding is similar to science's method. Acknowledging their similarity in epistemology is what we have termed "methodological cohesion." In other words, we bring to the student's attention that moving from the unknown to the known ("light bulb effect") is something that is done when humans try to understand something as small and apparently natural as DNA or as big and apparently supernatural as God. Information is gathered about what we know of God and his creation through words and through our senses (much like DNA). Once enough information is gathered and accepted as true (somewhere in the continuum of truth), we then live our lives as if the conclusions are reality. Once sufficient data or evidence is gathered we believe the truth statement and then live our lives as if the statement is at least close to the objective end of the truth continuum. This process applies to a student's view of the existence of DNA in each of their eight trillion somatic cells just as well as it applies to the existence of a soul housed within the organism that those cells comprise.

CAN METHODOLOGICAL COHESION BE CONSIDERED LUTHERAN?

Lutheran Theology Emphasizes God Working through Means

While God can work to accomplish his will immediately, directly, and "miraculously," more frequently he chooses to work through means. In what the church calls sacraments (specifically Baptism and the Lord's Supper), he chooses to work through water, wine, and bread (Acts 2:38–39; Matt 26:26–28). He brings his Word to us through the spoken words of pastors and teachers (Jer 1:4–10). And most significantly, he brought himself, incarnate into the molecules, cells, organ systems and body structures of our physical world (John 1:1–3, 14).

Thus, Lutherans are accustomed to seeing God precisely where the culture of science sees something purely "natural." Where science observes carbohydrates in a communion wafer, there is Christ's body. Where science sees actin and myosin contracting within a sarcomere (muscle cell), there is Jesus, God incarnate, stretching out his arms. Where science sees differential methylation as a mechanism for DNA (gene) repair, there is God sustaining us every day of our lives.

Of course many varieties of Christians (and theists in general) have for hundreds of years seen science as a way of knowing God's mind or seeing how God works. But today's culture so strongly favors natural explanations that it takes a lot of practice to see how deeply this culture affects our thinking. If I drop a pen and ask people of most religious traditions why it fell, virtually everyone will answer "gravity." Virtually no one will say it fell because I wanted it to fall. In fact, many people will question whether my will is actually a valid explanation at all. But most will come to realize that the natural explanation (gravity) and the supernatural explanation (my will) are not contradictory even though modern science only studies the former. Thus, any perspective that is not purely naturalistic provides more freedom to explore possibilities (e.g., how humans will interact with nature) that are outside the exclusively naturalistic/materialistic explanations permitted by the culture of science. The Lutheran tradition of considering both natural explanations and supernatural explanations is a useful way of thinking when studying science.

Lutheran Theology Carefully Distinguishes Between Data and Interpretation

Lutheran theology treats Scripture with great care and authority in a manner very similar to how the scientist treats observations and data. Just as science starts with observations and data (of the natural/material world), and then uses reason to develop theories that explain observation from the data, so do theologians start with observations and data (the text of Scripture) and use reason to develop systems of theologies. One major strength of Lutheran theology is the ability to know the extent to which conclusions are based on text and the extent to which they are based on reason. For example, Lutheran theology asserts that God predestines people to heaven, but does not take the logical step of asserting that God predestines people to hell because this is not taught in Scripture.[5] Of course Lutheran theology uses and honors logic and reason, but it is very careful to not let them lead one too far from the data (Scripture).

The very strong commitment of Lutheran theology to data is perhaps clearest seen in what are often called "paradoxes." These Lutheran "paradoxes" are concepts that are held as true even though they are logically inconsistent. Paradoxes occur when using logic results in apparent contradictions in Scripture. For example, it is logically difficult to comprehend how people can be both saints and sinners at the same time even though both are scripturally true (Rom 7:14–24). This willingness seen in Lutheran theology to constrain logic by external data (Scripture) is also necessary for science to constrain theories to external data (observations of nature). Of course reasoning beyond the data is a crucial part of the scientific method, but a fastidious dedication to the data is necessary to recognize if a theory is being treated as data, and at what point that occurred.

Lutheran theology, based on scriptural passages like 1 Cor 9–10, allows for a distinction between what is scripturally important and what is culturally mandated. The term *adiaphora* (Greek for "indifferent things") is a part of Lutheran culture that is used when trying to understand whether a practice is scripturally articulated (commanded or prohibited) or culturally practiced ("We have always done it that way"). For example, when baptizing, should the individual be sprinkled with water or immersed in a local river? Scripture does not require one over the other, consequently either practice is consistent with Lutheran doctrine (or the choice is considered *adiaphora*). This type of thinking helps one to potentially be aware when culture is having a direct effect on the interpretation of the data or when theory is being treated like data.

Thus, understanding the relationship between data and theory is crucial when studying science. While the priority, significance, and importance of data versus theory is known, they are not generally distinguished very well on a day-to-day basis in our culture. Most people would claim that both of the following statements are "scientifically proven facts": (1) I have five fingers on my right hand and (2) I have forty-six chromosomes in each cell of each of those five fingers. However, the former is a direct observation (data), and the latter is based on very reasonable logic from studies of DNA in many other people and organisms (theory). Of course just because something is based on reasoning or theory does not

---

5   For more discussion of predestination, or election, in Lutheran theology, see Steven P. Mueller, ed., *Called to Believe, Teach, and Confess: An Introduction to Doctrinal Theology* (Eugene, OR: Wipf and Stock, 2005), 281–96.

mean that it is wrong or that one should not believe it. The point here is that Lutheran theology presents a good framework to help establish a mindset that can recognize and appreciate both logical reasoning and data when coming to a conclusion regarding a truth statement.

Is Methodological Cohesion Uniquely Lutheran?

While the previous sections have shown how methodological cohesion fits within the framework of Lutheran theology and education, these concepts are in no way unique to Lutherans or even Christians in general. All people and academic disciplines make observations in many areas, which they then incorporate into relevant theories and explanations. Most of them also feel as though they are getting at some kind of "truth" in the process after some critical amount of evidence has been reached ("light bulb effect"). Similar processes are employed routinely in science. Moreover, understanding features of our current scientific culture (e.g., having a problem with being wrong or existing with a "publish or perish" environment) require integration of subjective and objective material via a method that is very similar to theological integration of supernatural and natural explanations.

Interestingly, many scientists, as well as theologians, would not acknowledge that culture or paradigms played any role in reaching a conclusion regarding a truth statement. Rather, scientists routinely claim that their truth statements are supported solely by naturalistic/materialistic data, and theologians routinely claim that their truth statements are supported solely by Scripture. Methodological cohesion is a useful tool to deconstruct how culture can affect one's epistemology.

In theology, taking the step from learning data and theories to personally accepting them as true is often called "faith." In science, taking the step to decide something is objectively true generally means deciding the probability that one is wrong (often calculated using statistics) is small enough that it would not be productive to continue questioning it. The difficulty lies not in getting people to use this reasoning, but in recognizing what kind of reasoning they are using, and then seeing that this kind of reasoning for deciding what is true is nearly universal. So, while Lutheran theology provides a useful framework to help students understand these issues, the descriptions and discussions of the issues themselves are not limited to a "Lutheran" or even a "Christian" or "Theist" perspective. Rather, an understanding of methodological cohesion opens one's mind to natural and supernatural explanations and an understanding of the various ways in which the veracity of truth statements is determined.

Is Methodological Cohesion a Method to Refute Evolution?

Unfortunately, for many people when science and theology are discussed, the immediate questions are about creation vs. evolution vs. design. For others the immediate pointed questions are ethical, often pertaining to the beginning or end of life, or ecological concerning the environment or sustainability. However, discussing these issues directly without trying to get at the more fundamental reasons for the disagreement is often divisive and unproductive. It is much more important that all our students be able to explain the interplay among data, theories, paradigms, and culture that leads people to very different conclusions or truths when presented with the same observations. Thus, methodological integration does provide insights into evolution, but it is by no means limited to being an approach to deal with this one issue.

Therefore, when we do address the issue of evolution, we are not usually focused on whether it happened or not. Instead, we want to ask fundamental questions like: What are the data everyone is trying to explain? What paradigms are shaping how they interpret the data? What data, if any, would it take to get them to change their mind? Why do people have the paradigms that they do? Why would someone interpret the data from a natural or supernatural perspective? What data are available, or could be made available, so that someone could develop a theory about which paradigm is right? The point is not to end up in a post-modern relativistic morass, but to get students to recognize how they are thinking, what the similarities are between how they are thinking and how the people they disagree with are thinking, and finally, how you could then go about addressing the points on which you disagreed.

CONCLUSION

We often tell our students in Core Biology that our goal is for them to be able to know that God is real in the same way that they know their DNA is real. Often, what they first hear from that statement is that we want them to know God is an observable, tangible part of reality just as surely as they already know their DNA is an observable reality. We hope that by the end of the semester they are able to articulate that neither is their DNA as objectively true as they thought nor is God as non-empirical as they may have thought. Even more, we hope they are able to articulate how their belief in both is shaped by their own theories and paradigms, and why they have chosen those theories and paradigms for themselves. In doing so, we hope they are convinced that it is possible to have objectively true knowledge not only about biological science, but also about theology and all other disciplines. More importantly, our objective is that students will be able to explain how they obtain this knowledge and why they consider it to be true.

QUESTIONS

1. Science is currently limited to natural explanations. Describe ways in which this may be helpful and/or problematic.

2. Do you think that theology is limited by paradigms and culture? Why?

3. Can you think of examples (either personal or historical) where theories were treated like data and incorrect conclusions were the result?

4. How was the timing of the publication of Darwin's *Origins of Species* important to the development of modern science?

5. How would you describe the similarities in scientific and theological reasoning and, conversely, the dissimilarities?

11

LUTHER ON TRADE AND COMMERCE

Christopher "Kit" Nagel[1]

"I shall say nothing here about the pure pleasure a person gets from having studied. . . . he can read all kinds of things, talk and associate with educated people, and travel and do business in foreign lands."[2]

—*Martin Luther*

INTRODUCTION

The world is a complicated place; events and philosophies don't stand in isolation but need to be understood in context. Luther, the great reformer, likewise needs to be seen in the historic context of a pre-industrial age economy. Luther's theologically-rooted perspective on trade and commerce, the topic of this chapter, can be seen as part of an unfolding continuum of economic, social, and political analysis from those Mercantilist times to the current era of Keynes, Friedman, and Chandler.

While best remembered as a doctor of theology, Luther was nonetheless keenly aware of the forces changing Europe and the lives of common people. The 1500s were a time of great change—and not only because of the Reformation. Within Luther's lifetime (1483–1546), voyages were made to the New World and trade routes were expanded to the Indies. There was a great rise in commerce and economic growth—an era often referred to as the Age of Discovery.

In examining Luther's views on economics, there should be no expectation that Luther could comprehend or predict the extent of today's trade and finance. Even in his era, Luther's views on economic matters were at times ambiguous. That being said, it is also good to note that even the study of what became known as economics was not a recognized area of inquiry

---

[1] Christopher "Kit" Nagel, MIM (American Graduate School of International Management), is Professor of Business at CUI.

[2] Martin Luther, "A Sermon on Keeping Children in School" in AE 46:243.

until centuries later; the world's first professional economist (someone who actually got paid for such work) was Thomas Malthus in the nineteenth century.

We should also be slow to credit Luther with supporting one or another form of economic model. As Max Weber wrote, "Luther cannot be claimed for the spirit of capitalism."[3] Further, many seek to define Luther in a way that fits into their own agendas and philosophies. One recalls how the officially atheist East German government sought to "adopt" Luther—hailing him as an early socialist, a man of the people, and being part of the dialectic that would oppose established, elite, and corrupt powers. Just as Christian missionaries build upon the work of those who have gone before them—all the way back to Timothy and Titus—so too economists build upon the writings and analyses of their predecessors. In addition to seeing how Luther's views on economics fit into the broad sweep of economic history, business professors should also reflect on the abiding truths that he provides, and so help both business executives and students navigate the increasingly competitive global marketplace. With these caveats in mind, let us look at Luther in his own words, commenting on his own economic era, how those words relate to economic life today, and how to prepare students at a Christian university for an ethical career.

LUTHER AMONG THE MERCANTILISTS

The focus of Luther's work was on the redemptive power of the Gospel, yet his extensive writings include commentary on such economic issues as pricing, cross-border trade, the role of government in the marketplace, and the thorny issue of usury—something he roundly and frequently condemned. Basic to understanding Luther's economic views is his promotion of a foundational behavior in both commerce and life—that of *Nächsten-liebe* (loosely translated, the love and care for those around us, our neighbors). In his Luther biography, Roland Bainton quotes Luther's treatise "On the Freedom of the Christian Man" to explain this behavior: "When God in his sheer mercy and without any merit of mine has given me such unspeakable riches, shall I not then freely, joyously, wholeheartedly, unprompted do everything that I know will please him? I will give myself as a sort of Christ to my neighbor as Christ gave himself for me." Bainton calls this "the epitome of Luther's ethic, that a Christian must be a Christ to his

---

³ Max Weber, *The Protestant Ethic and the Spirit of Capitalism*, trans. Talcott Parsons (New York: Charles Scribner's Sons, 1958), 82.

neighbor."[4] And so, maintaining this sense of *Nächstenliebe* should remain one's guide in commercial life.

Luther did not condone (nor could he fully understand) the changing economic environment of sixteenth century Europe. This was a time of growing merchant power and the rise of trade and commerce. Luther's major economic writing, "On Trade and Usury" (1524), promotes an economics based on the Christian virtue of charity and *Nächstenliebe*, not the "enlightened self-interest" of Adam Smith. And while Luther acknowledged that trade was necessary, he remained skeptical of commerce, noting that "those do much better who till the soil and seek their living from it."[5]

Luther was troubled with the rise of the merchant class and merchant capital, which consisted of ownership of the means of buying, transporting, and selling. As cross-border trade grew, local prices that had hardly increased in centuries were changing. Between 1520 and 1538, prices in Wittenberg doubled, but net wages were static.[6] Local markets were connecting to regional and foreign markets, and the question of price and value was increasingly tied to unfamiliar concepts of supply and demand, availability, and proximity. A trader could buy cheap in areas of surplus (low prices), transport the product, and sell dear in areas of shortage (high prices); profits would derive from the act of exchange, in the commercial process, not from the product's innate "value."

A key competitive factor in business is pricing, and Luther is both naïve and ambiguous on how prices should be set. For students, an important question to think through is "What is value and what is price?" In much of his writing, Luther looks to have products derive their price from their intrinsic direct cost. And here Luther is not too far afield from classical economists who sought to determine pricing by the costs of productive inputs, principally labor, and less upon the economic principles of supply and demand.

Yet at other times, and absent governmental intervention, Luther suggests that goods be valued at the price that is given and taken for them in the local common market (*wie sie der gemeyn marckt gibt und nympt*). Luther notes, "Any profit made in this way I consider honest and proper,

---

[4] Roland H. Bainton, *Here I Stand: A Life of Martin Luther* (Peabody, MA: Hendrickson, 2010), 230–31.

[5] Martin Luther, "Schriften 1519/1520," in *D. Martin Luthers Werke: Kritische Gesamtausbage* (Weimar: Böhlau, 1883–1986) [hereinafter WA], 6:466–67.

[6] Carter Lindberg, "Luther on Poverty," in *Harvesting Martin Luther's Reflections on Theology, Ethics, and the Church*, ed. Timothy J. Wengert (Grand Rapids: Eerdmans, 2004), 143.

considering the fact that you will be in danger of suffering loss in terms of merchandise and cost, and that you will be unable to earn great riches."[7] This comment follows the line of argument that free markets can be self-regulating, and that supply and demand will drive fair and competitive pricing for the consumer. However, while interesting and useful for classroom discussion, it would be wrong to stretch Luther's sixteenth century words on pricing to suggest any prescient view about the modern world. Luther also observed how markets could be manipulated, and he would decry the acts of merchants in those same common markets where "The poor are defrauded every day, and new burdens and higher prices are imposed. They all misuse the market in their own arbitrary, defiant, arrogant way, as if it were their privilege and right to sell their goods as high as they please without any criticism."[8]

Any basic college marketing class will talk about the four "Ps" of the Marketing Mix: product, price, promotion, and place. Of the four, the P of pricing is perhaps the most difficult to get right (and the easiest to get wrong). In a market economy, there is no pure, pristine, elegant, correct price. Attributes change, perceived values evolve. Why will consumers pay a premium for an iPhone over a Samsung? Sales and prices are negotiated; values are imputed. Quantitative analysts (our beloved "Quants") try to build econometric pricing models, but the world is volatile and "event driven" and seldom conforms to expectations. Earthquakes in Asia led to shutting down nuclear energy production in Japan and so raised the demand for imported oil to produce electricity—with the knock-on effect on global pricing. So what is price and what is value? In the late 1990s, Russia defaulted on its sovereign debt—which ultimately contributed to falling share prices and a market crash in Brazil—remarkable since the underlying Brazilian economy was sound. So what is price and what is value? The heavy equipment company Caterpillar sells bulldozers that command a premium in the marketplace. Why? Not because of the cost of labor, steel or rubber, but because of less tangible but very real values of superior design, reputation, and the best service network on the planet. So what is price and what is value?

A hundred and fifty years after Luther, the economic writer Nicholas Barbon in his *A Discourse of Trade* famously noted that the market is the best judge of value; set by the meeting of buyers and sellers and based upon

---

[7] WA 15:296.

[8] Martin Luther, "Large Catechism," in *The Book of Concord: The Confessions of the Evangelical Lutheran Church*, eds. Robert Kolb and Timothy J. Wengert (Minneapolis: Fortress, 2000), 418 (part I:240).

the quantity (supply) and the need (demand). Things are just worth as much as they can be sold for, according to the old rule, *Res Tantum Valet Quantum Vendi Potest* ("a thing is only worth what someone else will pay for it"). There is a corollary in financial markets today, "If there is no market, there is no value." How much is your house worth if no one will buy it?

As noted, Luther's life bridged decades of great change, from the Mercantilist era to the broad openings of world trade. This era gives context to engage students with economic history and trade development. The Mercantilist economic approach reflects the common national view in Luther's time that a nation's wealth is measured by its reserves of precious metals. Trade theory held that nations benefited from accumulating such metal reserves by encouraging exports and discouraging imports. Having a trade surplus was seen as vital to a country's success (trade deficits were to be avoided) and governments would intervene in international trade through banning or restricting imports and subsidizing exports. The basic flaw in this theory is the belief that the world's wealth is finite and that one's own success can only be achieved at the detriment of one's trading partners—a zero-sum game.

Many in Luther's time also assumed that poverty and rising prices were due to the Age of Discovery and the increase in international trade, which presumably was denuding Germany of its precious metals through payment for imported goods. Luther's concern for the poor and needy, his *Nächstenliebe*, led him to agree with this view, plus the general belief that government should intervene to manage and control trade. Thus Luther was no "free trader" when he wrote,

> But foreign trade, which brings from Calcutta and India and such places wares like costly silks, articles of gold, and spices—which minister only to ostentation but serve no useful purpose, and which drain away the money of the land and people—would not be permitted if we had proper government. . . . God has cast us Germans off to such an extent that we have flung our gold and silver into foreign lands and make the whole world rich while we ourselves remain beggars.[9]

This is a classic Mercantilist view. And, like his contemporaries, Luther saw trade as a zero-sum game with little consideration for the balancing effect of exports. It is important to note that the nation-states of Europe followed such policies well into the eighteenth century.

---

[9]   Luther, "Trade and Usury," in AE 45:246.

LUTHER AND LATER ECONOMISTS

Moving forward two hundred and thirty years after Luther's death, Adam Smith published the *Wealth of Nations*. This classic included the deceptively simple insight that if an exchange between two parties is voluntary, it will not take place unless both believe they will benefit from it. The size of Smith's economic pie is not fixed; exchange is not a zero-sum game where one party can benefit only at the expense of the other. In contrast with Mercantilism, Smith believed that real wealth should be measured by the standard of living of households (bags of gold do not necessarily translate into bags of food); real wealth should be measured from the viewpoint of a nation's consumers, and individual motivation and innovation lead an economy to greater prosperity. Smith's case against Mercantilism rested on the assumption that free competition will maximize growth. In contrast, and in his era of great change, Luther looked at trade and the new free markets as destructive of social harmony and a source of hardship.

Smith argued that economic expansion brings benefit to all, and all humans want to live better than they do. He wrote that humankind has a natural drive, "a certain propensity in human nature . . . to truck, barter, and exchange one thing for another . . . it is common to all men." And in perhaps the most cited passage in the history of economic thought, Smith proclaims: "It is not from the benevolence of the butcher, the brewer, or the baker, that we expect our dinner, but from their regard to their own interest." If all seek to promote their self-interest, the whole society prospers. The individual "neither intends to promote the publick interest, nor knows how much he is promoting it. . . . [H]e intends only his own gain, and he is in this, as in many other cases, led by an *invisible hand* to promote an end which was no part of his intention."[10]

A twentieth century comment from free market proponent Friedrich Hayek (Nobel laureate 1974) adds that if the free market had not arisen naturally, it would have been proclaimed the greatest invention in human history. For market competition leads a self-interested person to wake up in the morning, look outside at the earth, and produce from its raw material not what he wants, but what others want (a true marketing perspective). Not in the quantities he prefers, but in quantities his neighbors prefer. Not at the price he dreams of charging, but at a price reflecting how much his neighbors value what he has done.[11]

---

[10] Adam Smith, *An Inquiry into the Nature and Causes of the Wealth of Nations* (1776) (New York: Modern Library, 1994), 14–15, 484–85

[11] Todd Buchholz, *New Ideas from Dead Economists* (New York: Penguin, 2007), 22.

The *invisible hand* is, of course, the iconic symbol of Smith's economics and represents the true orchestrator of social harmony, the free market.[12] In a free market, prices and profits signal to entrepreneurs what to produce and what price to charge. It is such "self-interest," not Luther's social conscience or charity which leads to enlarging a nation's economic pie.

Of more than passing interest is Luther's recognition of such "self-interest" in writing to the "Beloved rulers, wise and sagacious men" of Germany on the need to establish and maintain schools. He writes, "For it is a great and solemn duty that is laid upon us, a duty of immense moment to Christ and to the world, to give aid and counsel to the young. And in so doing, we likewise promote our own best interests."[13] Here Luther is basing his argument not on altruism or charity that in the kingdom of God's grace comes as a faithful and self-less response to God's mercy in Christ, but on an appeal to individuals' self-interest. Luther was a realist when dealing with matters of society, the left-hand kingdom of God.[14]

Smith's approach to international commerce is often referred to in trade theory as the Law of Absolute Advantage—where if Nation A can produce a good (wine, linen, etc.) more efficiently than Nation B, then Nation A will benefit from trading that good for some other good that Nation B produces more efficiently—so there will be mutual gain from specialization and trade. Trade is not a Mercantilist zero-sum game.

While this seems quite understandable, not so obvious is the insight developed in 1817 by David Ricardo in his *Principles* and known in trade theory as the Law of Comparative Advantage. Here, even if a nation does not have an absolute advantage in producing a specific good over another nation, it can still benefit by specializing in producing and trading those goods that it produces relatively more efficiently (with a lower opportunity cost) than its other goods—so there is still incentive to trade even if one nation's products are produced at an absolute disadvantage compared to its trading partners. The broader point is that free trade enables nations and households to consume more goods regardless of the level of development of their trading partners. Ricardo also demonstrated that government interference in trade, such as with protectionism, is almost always bad for an economy as a whole, though often good for a particular faction. As we

---

[12] Buchholz, *New Ideas from Dead Economists*, 21.

[13] This quote can be found in several sources like, Ellwood Patterson Cubberley, ed., *Readings in the History of Education* (Cambridge: The Riverside Press, 1920), 241. Also see Luther, "To the Councilmen of All Cities in Germany that They Establish and Maintain Christian Schools," in AE 45:350.

[14] For an explanation of the Lutheran doctrine of two kingdoms, see Mueller's chapter.

need to move on, we will not here further develop Ricardo's nuanced analysis, something Harvard Economist Buchholz calls "perhaps the most complex and counterintuitive principle of economics . . . [and] key to modern economic understanding" and laments how "few politicians then or now can follow the analysis. As a result, quotas, tariffs, and trade wars mar the world's economic history."[15]

Imparting to students an appreciation for the continuum of economic thought is vital to producing global citizens. And while Luther could not anticipate future economic theories, his Mercantilist views help inform students' understanding of trade today. For all its success, China is regularly criticized for being *neo-mercantilist* because of its government's manipulation and undervaluation of the Renminbi (the official currency of the People's Republic of China) to support exports (concurrently making imports more expensive), and the aiding of export companies via direct subsidies and Bank of China credits. Much of economic thought since Smith has recognized the inefficiency and counter-productiveness of protectionism and government intrusion in markets and trade (Marxist-Leninism and the Chinese model not withstanding); the espousal of a *laissez faire* approach to free trade runs to the current era.

Just as the initial followers of Luther did not call themselves Lutherans, the term *Mercantilism* was used not by the "Mercantilists" themselves, but by those who derided such views as archaic. Even today, economists such as John Maynard Keynes make a point of adding their own criticism. In his famous tome, *General Theory*, Keynes comments,

> [T]he mercantilist argument is based, from start to finish, on an intellectual confusion. . . . Contemporary experience of trade restriction in post-war Europe offers manifold examples of ill-conceived impediments on freedom which, designed to improve the favorable balance, had in fact a contrary tendency. [Such an] immoderate policy may lead to a senseless international competition for a favorable balance which injures all alike. And finally, a policy of trade restrictions is a treacherous instrument even for the attainment of its ostensible object, since private interest, administrative incompetence and intrinsic difficulty of the task may divert it into producing result directly opposite to those intended.[16]

---

[15] Buchholz, *New Ideas from Dead Economists*, 71–72.
[16] John Maynard Keynes, *The General Theory of Employment, Interest and Money* (1936) (Amherst, NY: Prometheus Books, 1997), 334, 338–39.

LUTHER ON PRICING

Now let us move away from issues of trade theory and return to Luther's thoughts on pricing. Luther believed a merchant's pricing should be *billich*, meaning fair. Given the broadly-held perception of merchant greed and avarice, Luther said the best solution would be to have official price limits set on all goods by "some wise and honest men" appointed by governmental authorities.[17] However, Luther recognized the impracticality of this ideal and that merchants themselves would need to price their goods. He noted the almost incalculable number of issues that reasonably affect costs and therefore prices: quality, seasonality, transportation, road tolls, and the like.

Luther says it is fair and right that a merchant make as much profit on his wares as will cover his costs and pay him for his efforts, work, and risk, but not to "overcharge your neighbor by your greed but seek your modest living."[18] Here (surprisingly), imbedded in Luther's commentary, is recognition of the key business concept of risk (*Gefahr*) as it relates to pricing, and the recognition that merchants can legitimately "price-in" such risk in selling their products.

College instructors take pains to explain "risk" in pricing, not just in financial instruments but in everyday products. The greater the risk, the greater an individual or firm needs to be compensated or rewarded for taking on such risk, and thus the concept of "risk and return." An instructive case is to have students think through how the oft-maligned pharmaceutical industry needs to set its prices at a level to cover the extensive costs, time, and risks of developing medicines (the majority of which never make it to market). Such firms are not charities (charities cannot afford to take such risks), and such benefits to society are not free. Pricing and cost allocation are complex; medicines have a limited patent life, and firms need to recoup the heavy research and development (R&D) and regulatory costs plus compensate their stockholders with a reasonable return for putting their capital at risk. So, how then should medicines be priced when it can take fifteen years to bring a product to market, and where only two drugs in ten recoup their R&D costs? Even before selling one pill, hundreds of millions will have been spent developing the drug.[19] So

---

[17] WA 15:296.

[18] "*Nun ist's aber billich und recht, dass ein Kaufmann an seiner Waare so viel gewinne, dass seine Kosten bezahlt, seine Muehe, Arbeit, und Gefahr belohnt werde*" (WA 15:296–98).

[19] The author is grateful for the generous assistance of Dieter Weinand, President, Bayer Healthcare Pharmaceuticals.

ultimately pricing cannot simply cover direct costs but must also cover earlier "sunk costs" and capital risks. The reality is that the odds of successfully developing a new medicine and bringing it to market are extremely low, while the upfront investment is extremely high. With long lead times and high costs, firms need also to factor in the "time-value-of-money." This concept is foundational to any finance course and includes the issues of discounted cash flows, hurdle rates, and internal rates of return. We will return to this shortly.

Today's market reality is that value is determined by what someone is willing to pay for something, not what the product costs to produce. Today, we may consider this self-evident. The harsh yet efficient reality is that if there is no market, there is no value. Pricing is a "market mechanism" that can efficiently find an equilibrium level between supply and demand—and optimally allocates scarce resources.

Nobel economist Milton Friedman comments that prices perform three functions in organizing economic activity: first they transmit information; second they provide an incentive to adopt those methods of production that are least costly and thereby use available resources for the most highly valued purposes; and they determine who gets how much of the product— the distribution of income. Prices that emerge from voluntary transactions between buyers and sellers can coordinate the activity of millions of people, each pursuing their own interest, and in such a way as to make everyone better off.[20]

Luther bemoaned how volatility in pricing was unsettling lives and traditions, especially for the common man. He blamed the greed and avarice of merchants in manipulating pricing, controlling supplies, and price gauging. Undoubtedly, there were many merchants that coerced customers and committed fraud. Yet, in a market economy, prices fluctuate and a free market is not a pain free market. Luther shared the common lack of understanding, and indeed, mistrust of rising prices—though such confusion was understandable given that Germany was moving from a tradition-bound agrarian society to the brave new world of open markets with the challenges of opportunity and risk.

Skepticism that rising prices (inflation) can be part of a legitimate economic order and not a malicious ploy by sharp operators has resonance in our day. In the late 1970s, Chinese leader Deng Xiaoping reopened China to international trade and investment. This caused consternation among Chinese managers trained to operate within a command economy. The

---

[20] Milton Friedman, *Free to Choose: A Personal Statement* (New York: Harcourt, 1990), 14.

previous Maoist government had decided every detail of life: where one would live and work, and what one would consume (the iron rice bowl). Managers followed central directives on what to produce, in what volume, and at what price they should be sold. They had no frame of reference to deal with foreign firms that would as a matter of course incorporate price-escalator clauses in agreements to accommodate future inflation. The Chinese managers were sure that the unreasonable and greedy capitalists (what Luther would call "knaves and scoundrels") were simply finding clever ways to cheat them. Times of economic turmoil can be hard to comprehend—whether in the sixteenth century or today.

LUTHER ON MONOPOLIES

Moving beyond pricing, Luther also looked at the market manipulation of monopolies. In his 1524 "Trade and Usury" treatise, Luther talks of economic coercion, when a merchant takes advantage of customers to reap unfair profits—especially the manipulation brought on by monopoly power. His concern remains every bit as valid today, as monopolies wreck the beneficial efficiency of free markets. Luther noted that

> there are some who buy up the entire supply of certain goods or wares in a country or city in order to have these goods entirely under their own control; they can then fix and raise the price and sell as dear as they like or can. . . . Even the imperial and secular laws forbid this; they call it *monopolia*. . . . For such merchants act as if God's creatures and God's goods were created and given for them alone, as if they could take them from others and set on them whatever price they chose.[21]

While monopolies in Luther's time were illegal, the laws were not enforced against the great trading houses. A case study from Luther's time is the Augsburg family of the Fuggers, a major banking house that held monopolies in mining, commerce, and finance. With no legal limitations or competitive constraints from what Luther called the common market (*gemeyn marckt*), the Fuggers amassed a huge fortune. Resonating with the lamentable state of American politics today, the Fuggers also made enormous cash outlays that secured the imperial election of Emperor Charles V. The *quid pro quo* was sufficient to ensure that the authorities would not move against the Fuggers or limit their monopoly power.

Tied to this case, and as the Luther story always includes his strident opposition to the sale of Papal Indulgences, we should also note the

---

[21] Luther, "Trade and Usury," in AE 45:262.

Fuggers' role in this commercial transaction. It gets ugly. In 1517, Albert of Brandenburg aspired to be the Archbishop of Mainz, which would make him the primate of Germany. Knowing he would need to pay Rome a princely sum to buy the office, he retained the Fugger banking house to negotiate with Pope Leo X (not coincidentally, the Fuggers already held a monopoly on papal finances in Germany). The pontiff and the Fuggers settled on a figure of ten thousand ducats, and Albert had to pay Leo before receiving the papal appointment. He borrowed the ducats from the Fuggers. To enable Albert to recoup the huge cost, Leo granted him an eight-year privilege to sell Papal Indulgences. The deal stipulated that beyond the ten thousand ducats already received by the pope, half of the Indulgence revenues would go to Leo for building the new St. Peter's, the other half going to the Fuggers to service the loan and as added compensation for handling the transaction.

It is small wonder that Luther was so disgusted with the connivance of the secular, political, and religious powers. Luther was surely including the Fuggers when he condemned "the great, powerful archthieves with whom lords and princes consort and who daily plunder not just a city or two, but all Germany." He also called the pope in Rome "the head and chief protector of all thieves."[22]

Beyond monopoly pricing by the likes of the Fuggers, Luther was concerned that even if merchants did not control a market, their self-interest would likely injure others:

> Merchants have a common rule which is their chief maxim and the basis of all their sharp practices, where they say: "I may sell my goods as dear as I can." They think this is their right. Thus occasion is given for avarice and every window and door to hell is opened. What else does it mean but this: I care nothing about my neighbor; so long as I have my profit and satisfy my greed, of what concern is it to me if it injures my neighbor in ten ways at once? There you see how shamelessly this maxim flies squarely in the face not only of Christian love but also natural law. How can there be anything good then in trade? How can it be without sin when such injustice is the chief maxim and rule of the whole business? On such a basis, trade can be nothing but robbing and stealing the property of others.[23]

Harsh words for a harsh, corrupt, and abusive time. However, Luther's underlying social concern—which was motivated both by reason's natural

---

[22] Luther, "Large Catechism," 417 (part I:230).
[23] Luther, "Trade and Usury," in AE 45:247.

law and faith's love toward one's neighbor in response to Christ's love—remains instructive today. Pricing should be market-driven—and at the same time not exploitive or coercive. Today, freely fluctuating prices in a competitive marketplace are a necessary and beneficial underpinning of a market economy. The role of business and trade can and should be to improve the quality of life in society. Both parties, the buyer and the seller, should gain from exchange—perhaps not in some elegant theoretical balance, but trade should lead to mutual benefit.

LUTHER ON USURY AND FINANCE

The final section of this chapter will briefly discuss Luther's views on usury and what some call the vagaries of finance. Students who read Luther learn to appreciate how his views were in line with church and cultural prohibitions on usury (flowing from the traditions of Aristotle and Thomas Aquinas) that it is wrong to make money from money.[24] This ancient legacy still resonates today. Deuteronomy 23 says that one should not charge one's brother interest, and Biblical usury focuses on unjustly charging someone for a loan when they are in dire straits. Though Luther generally took this as a blanket prohibition on interest, he was pragmatic enough to allow that modest levels of interest of 4 to 6 percent were permissible. Such low interest loans had been incorporated into canon law and are one of the few sections in canon law with which Luther did not argue. For Luther, low interest loans had a social appeal as they helped the poor and needy refinance existing debts carrying exorbitant rates from the public usurers (which could range over 40 percent).[25]

Naturally, usury and abusive finance are not unique to Luther's time. Today's "payday loans" are small loans marketed as an easy way to tide borrowers over until their next payday. However, the typical payday loan borrower is indebted for more than half of the year with an average of nine payday loan transactions that compute to a mind-numbing effective annual interest rate of over 400 percent.[26] Just as in Luther's day, the poor and least capable in society are the ones targeted and exploited.

---

[24] An Elizabethan era (1558–1603) view on usury is shown in Shakespeare's *The Merchant of Venice*. When lending three thousand ducats to merchant Antonio, Shylock relates the biblical story of Jacob working for Laban (Gen 30) to the charging of interest so that as with ewes and rams, money breeds money (Act 1, Scene 3).

[25] Luther, "Trade and Usury," in AE 45:305.

[26] "Payday Lending: How a Short-Term Loan Becomes Long-Term Debt," Center for Responsible Lending, accessed September 19, 2014, http://www.responsiblelending.org/payday-lending.

Our intent here is not to condemn all bankers. The reality is that a functioning banking system is vital to the global economy and the increase of living standards around the world. Harvard historian Niall Ferguson says it well:

> Far from being the work of mere leeches intent on sucking the life's blood out of indebted families or gambling with the savings of widows and orphans, financial innovation has been an indispensable factor in man's advance from wretched subsistence to the giddy heights of material prosperity that so many people know today. The evolution of credit and debt was as important as any technological innovation in the rise of civilization, from ancient Babylon to present-day Hong Kong. Poverty is not the result of rapacious financiers exploiting the poor. It has much more to do with the *lack* of financial institutions, with the absence of banks, not their presence.[27]

In the study of developmental economics this rings true. A key "marker" in a developing country's growth or renewal is the appearance of small banks—whether providing microfinance in Bangladesh or rural banks making small loans to farmers' cooperatives in strife-weary Rwanda. Banks are a social good—when they serve society.

Economic historians note that to help fund the expanding trade of the sixteenth century, merchants would borrow capital from investors, who would be paid for the use of their funds. In our day, this is self-evidently sensible and common practice. In Luther's day, this transaction was known as a *zinse*. The merchant would receive a loan from an investor. Later, after paying off the investor's principal and *zinse*, whatever was left over was kept by the merchant as profit. Luther correctly noted, "The merchant is doing the citizen a great service, for his money would otherwise lie idle and bring him no return. The citizen does the merchant a great service, for the latter anticipated a profit at least above the fixed *zinse* payment." However, Luther then went on to say, "That common practice is wrong and is in fact usury." He continues to criticize the *zinse*, saying, "What some greedy-bloated fellows do: they collect their *zinss* (plural of *zinse*) at stated times and immediately reinvest it in more *zinss*, so that one *zinse* is always driving the other along, as water drives the mill wheel."[28] Albeit rather colloquial, such language could be part of an introductory business text today on what one *should* do, not the opposite.

---

[27] Niall Ferguson, *The Ascent of Money* (New York: Penguin, 2009), 4.

[28] Luther, "Trade and Usury," in AE 45:268, 298.

Luther here shows an understanding of the benefits of maximizing a firm's financial return by not letting surplus funds sit idle. Today, publicly-held companies have a fiduciary obligation to maximize the use of investor capital, and corporate treasury departments have extensive processes to ensure that this does happen. Additionally, we earlier touched on the concept of time-value-of-money, and Luther's writing on *zinse* shows an implicit recognition of compound interest, the building-block of modern finance. He noted the benefit (though he decried it as usury and sin) to the investor of reinvesting profits from investment capital into further investment capital—a concept that is central to today's calculation of compound interest, discounted cash flows, and corporate "hurdle rates"— all vital take-aways from any college-level finance course. On this matter it is interesting to note that even five centuries after Luther, two thirds of Americans still do not understand how compound interest works.[29]

While Luther's views on the correct use of debt are archaic, his harsh criticism of financial houses still resonates today. While vital to a modern economy, finance presents great opportunities for avarice and excess, and the biblical stigma of usury (the taking advantage of others) continues to affect those who work with money. Among senior non-financial managers, there remains both grudging admiration and resentment of those who just move around money for a living. This compares to those who actually work in the real economy—you know, the economy that produces real stuff like food, raiment, packaging, wind turbines, or flies you across the country or fixes your plumbing. And this is not a peripheral view. In 2011, Wolfgang Schäuble, the Finance Minister of Germany, in a speech to financiers, expressed his disdain for the financial culture of making money from money (harkening back to Aristotle, Aquinas and Luther), noting that the vast majority of financial transactions "do not serve the real economy."[30]

In his Large Catechism, Luther's commentary on the commandment "You are not to steal" says that theft is

> taking advantage of our neighbors in any sort of dealings that result in loss to them. . . . taking advantage of someone in the market . . . wherever business is transacted and money is exchanged for goods or services. . . . Furthermore, at the market and in everyday business the same fraud prevails in full power in force. One person openly cheats

---

[29] Alexander Conrad, "Finance Basics Elude Citizens," *The Harvard Crimson*, February 29, 2008, accessed September 19, 2014, http://www.thecrimson.com/article/2008/2/29/finance-basics-elude-citizens-americans-are.

[30] Charlemagne, "Keep the Fire Burning," *The Economist*, October 1, 2011, accessed September 19, 2014, http://www.economist.com/node/21531032.

another with defective merchandise, false weights and measurements, and counterfeit coins, and takes advantage of the other by deception and sharp practices and crafty dealings. Or again, one swindles another in a trade and deliberately fleeces, skins, and torments him. Who can even describe or imagine it all? In short, thievery is the most common craft and the largest guild on earth. If we look at the whole of the world in all its situations, it is nothing but a big, wide stable full of great thieves.

Luther calls many merchants *Stuhlräuber* ("seated thieves"). For "[f]ar from being picklocks and sneak thieves who pilfer the cash box, they sit in their chairs and are known as great lords and honorable, upstanding citizens, while they rob and steal under the cloak of legality. . . . In short, this is the way of the world." Luther also adds the admonition that

all people [should] know, then, that it is their duty, on pain of God's displeasure, not to harm their neighbors, to take advantage of them, or to defraud them by any faithless or underhanded business transaction. Much more than that, they are also obligated faithfully to protect their neighbors' property and to promote and further their interests, especially when they get money, wages, and provisions for doing so.[31]

MODERN-DAY LESSONS FROM LUTHER

Students benefit from connecting this admonition of "sharp practices and crafty dealing" with the private-sector-induced market meltdown of 2008. This was a time when many financial houses succumbed to avarice and greed, while knowing full well that what they did was unsustainable. Abusing a trusted role in society, many bankers and financiers, what Luther would call greedy-bloated fellows (*Geytzige blassen*), grew recklessly wealthy. Their behavior became so profitable that, while driving the economy into ruin, financial sector profits spiked to over 40 percent of the profits in the *entire* U.S. economy. This compares to the financial sector's average share of profits from 1970 to 2000 of 20.2 percent.[32] Few would argue that financial services contribute 40 percent of the well-being of the country. Key poster children of this nonsense are the managers at the failed Lehman Brothers. They absolutely knew their actions were dangerous and added risk not only to their company but to society at large, yet the *Geytzige*

---

[31] Luther, "Large Catechism," 416–17 (part I:224, 227–33).

[32] U.S. Department of Commerce, Bureau of Economic Analysis, Corporate Profits by Industry 2012, accessed June 19, 2013, http://www.bea.gov/national/index.htm #corporate.

blassen would "get theirs." Their attitude was: "Let's get our cash out, park it in T-Bills, and let the thing crash." In Lehman, this was called IBG-YBG. When a middle-level manager approached his boss with a concern that what the firm was doing was unsustainable, the response was, "Don't worry IBG-YBG" (I'll Be Gone and You'll Be Gone). The firm was led by Richard Feld, who, while flying his company into failure and helping to crater the US economy, "got his"—taking out earnings of $71.9 million. Tragically for the country, greed and avarice prevailed with a pathetic lack of concern for *Nächstenliebe*.

We should add here that Luther did not single out bankers and financiers as the only ones driven by greed. He condemned greed in members of all classes (*Stände*); no social or professional calling was any greedier than another. Nevertheless, bankers have a unique role in society, and therefore must take that responsibility seriously and act ethically. Unfortunately, we all have witnessed too many professional failings in those who lost their ethical rudder and had no latent appreciation of the social purpose of commerce. Greed and avarice became the norm.[33]

Especially troubling is that many of the financial managers who pushed the economy into deep recession were graduates of elite business schools. So it is incumbent on us, whose vocation it is to teach business as a profession, to reflect on our collective failure to produce ethically sensitive managers and citizens. We need to have graduates who achieve what the Dean of the Harvard Business School, Nitin Nohria, says society expects of business leaders: the creation of broad prosperity. Nohria ruefully notes that the days are past when the measure of a good business person was whether he or she was as good as their word, the days when the local banker was the most respected person in town. Today the word *bank* has become a four-letter word. Harvard Business School is aware of business education's shortcomings and Nohria is working to revamp the curriculum. He asks students always to reflect on their decisions. He pushes them to be truthful and both recognize and acknowledge when they have acted immorally, such as being dishonest or taking a bribe, and then address the question of why that happened.[34]

---

[33] Of particular annoyance are the financial sector apologists on cable television. Such "journalists" blithely comment that the hugely destructive actions of the financial houses were simply mistakes and, surely, being stupid is not a crime. The only trouble with this defense is that those at Lehman Brothers were regarded as the smartest of the smart.

[34] Joyce Lau, "Harvard Business School Dean on Ethics and Global Education," *The New York Times*, March 26, 2013, accessed September 19, 2014, http://www.nytimes.com/

Uplifting a business culture will take time, and as yet few lessons from the recent financial experience have been absorbed. In some ways we have not progressed much since Luther looked out at his world. A recent article in *The Economist* summarized where we stand today:

> During the financial crisis, governments used oceans of public money to rescue banks from the consequences of their own folly and greed. Bankers quickly went back to paying themselves fat bonuses. Inequality is growing in many countries. Plutocrats wax richer as the middle class is squeezed and the poor are trodden underfoot. Hedge-fund moguls and casino kings spend fortunes to sway American elections—and the Supreme Court tells them to carry on spending.[35]

Here *The Economist* is alluding to conservative mogul Sheldon Adelson who said he was willing to spend $100 million to defeat President Obama. Regarding the Supreme Court, this is in reference to the court's ruling in the Citizens United case that "money equals speech" or again, as with the Fuggers, money talks. Senator McCain called this, "The worst decision by the Supreme Court in the twenty-first century; uninformed, arrogant, naive." One can almost hear Luther again rising to assail "the great, powerful archthieves with whom lords and princes consort and who daily plunder not just a city or two, but all Germany."

CONCLUSION

So where do we go from here and how can we benefit from the caring perspective of the great reformer? Christian universities—especially Lutheran ones—should show that Luther's theologically-rooted perspective provides students with an important understanding of ethical moorings in natural law and faith active in love during times of economic change and transition. Swedish theologian Bo Giertz notes that we are free to decide how we should act, but "the limit to our freedom is the fact that we live in a fallen world." Our "fatal inheritance makes it impossible for man to love God with all his heart and his neighbor as himself." We will fall short. Yet with the sure knowledge of our redemption, we can go out with good

---

2013/03/27/education/harvard-dean-on-ethics-and-global-
education.html?pagewanted=all&_r=0.

[35] Schumpeter, "The Transience of Power," *The Economist*, March 16, 2013, 70.

courage knowing that, while we cannot be perfect as our heavenly Father is perfect, we have "the power to choose the good and do it."[36]

Luther's legacy in the economic sphere is an emphasis that our focus as economic agents should not be a simple impersonal calculus, but one that incorporates fairness (*billich*) to others as a guide and constraint on one's actions, and doing much more than simply what is legal. Impersonal markets and legalities should not have the final say in determining our actions or our neighbor's welfare. To close with a quote from Bainton's great Luther biography: "In the realm of economics [Luther] considered less [the] abstract laws of supply and demand than the personal relations of buyer and seller, debtor and creditor."[37] The appropriate admonition for students, our society's rising cohort of managers, is that they consider their impact on others with whom they will deal—and so follow Luther's *Nächstenliebe*, the necessary love and care for those together with us in society, our fellow citizens, our neighbors.

QUESTIONS

1. How can Luther's Mercantilist era inform business students today?

2. The director of Pratt & Whitney International notes that, for long term success, the outcome of a business negotiation should benefit all sides. How does this view relate to the perspectives of Luther, Smith, and Friedman?

3. What companies do you think incorporate a sense of *Nächstenliebe* in their approach to markets?

---

[36] Bo Giertz, *The Freedom We Have in Christ* (London: Concordia, 1962), 1, 3, 5. This is the lecture Giertz delivered at the inauguration of Westfield House as a Lutheran House of Studies in Cambridge, England.

[37] Bainton, *Here I Stand*, 236.

12

MIRROR, IMAGINATION, AND CREATION: A LUTHERAN APPROACH TO LITERATURE

Kerri L. Tom[1]

"How I regret now that I did not read more poets and historians,
and that no one taught me them!"[2]

—*Martin Luther*

INTRODUCTION

The study of literature has become awash with "isms"—e.g., Marxism, feminism, new historicism—to such a point that some scholarly articles rarely refer to the text they are purportedly analyzing. Indeed, it is not unusual to plod through an analysis, littered with the latest literary jargon, only to discover that the author's seeming erudition leads him to the conclusion that Hamlet has issues with his mother or that Scout is a child navigating a complex world. For those of us who entered this field because we love to read and who spend the majority of our professional career in sharing that passion with undergraduates, such scholarship offers very little to us or to our students.

I am, of course, fearful of adding yet another "ism" to the pot, of creating an approach to literature that we might call Lutheranism. What I would like to suggest, however, is that the Lutheran approach is nothing new, but rather a refocusing on close reading with a view towards the central Lutheran conception of grace.

---

[1] Kerri L. Tom, PhD (Massachusetts), is Professor of English at CUI.
[2] Martin Luther, "To the Councilmen of All Cities in Germany that They Establish and Maintain Christian Schools," in AE 45:370.

LITERATURE AS A MIRROR

As recently as 2012, Alan Jacobs advises Christian students to ask of each book read, "Through it, can I see into my own heart—is it a mirror for me?"[3] In doing so, Jacobs is building on a long tradition that finds full voice in the sixteenth century. Hamlet, rather famously, tells the players what Shakespeare himself undoubtedly believed about "the purpose of playing, whose end, both at the first and now, was and is, to hold, as 'twere, the mirror up to nature, to show virtue her own feature, scorn her own image, and the very age and body of the time his form and pressure." (Hamlet then, remarkably, criticizes bad actors for not "having th'accent of Christians.")[4] We may extrapolate from this observation about staged plays an oft accepted observation about all literature and its role as a mirror in which we see our own qualities reflected, both as individuals and as societies.

Sir Philip Sidney, another product of the English Renaissance, applies this same concept to the biblical account of Nathan's fictitious tale of the "beloved lamb," which he used to show King David his own wickedness regarding Bathsheba: this story caused David "as in a glass [to] see his own filthiness" and repent.[5] This simile is evidence in Sidney's greater argument that fiction is a good and useful thing (an argument to which we will return later); Martin Luther pre-empted Sidney some sixty years earlier by making a similar argument for the humanities:

> [I]f children were instructed and trained in . . . the languages, the other arts, and history, they would then hear of the doings and sayings of the entire world. . . . Thus, they could in a short time set before themselves as in a mirror the character, life, counsels, and purposes—successful and unsuccessful—of the whole world from the beginning; on the basis of which they could then draw the proper inferences and in the fear of God take their own place in the stream of human events.[6]

Luther's "education as a mirror" allows students to see themselves in relation to the whole of human history, not just as participants in the here and now of the twenty-first century.

---

[3] Alan Jacobs, "How to Read a Book," in *Liberal Arts for the Christian Life*, eds. Jeffry C. Davis and Philip G. Ryken (Wheaton, IL: Crossway, 2012), 130.

[4] William Shakespeare, *Hamlet*, ed. Willard Farnham (New York: Penguin, 1970), 3.2.19–23, 29.

[5] Philip Sidney, "The Defence of Poesy," in *Sir Philip Sidney: Selected Prose and Poetry*, ed. Robert Kimbrough (Madison: University of Wisconsin Press, 1983), 126.

[6] Luther, "To the Councilmen of All Cities in Germany," in AE 45:368–69.

In reality, however, undergraduates often do not understand the texts we ask them to read. If students are to see themselves and their world in these textual mirrors, then it is our job to clean and polish them; the spots and smears of misreading must be wiped away through close reading. Interpretation is necessary, not just of the language's meaning but of its presentation. Luther biographer H. G. Haile notes that "Luther's very first lectures as a university professor, on Psalms (1513), are distinguished by their sensitivity to the poetic devices and poetic qualities of the Old Testament."[7] Simply put, one must understand how a metaphor works before one can understand what a metaphor means. The clearer we make the mirror for the students, and, more importantly, the better we teach the students how to clean the mirror for themselves, the more they will discover about themselves and their world.

In his "Defence of Poesy," Sidney argues that literature is the best way to educate the English, and he has a very specific goal for such an education:

> This purifying of wit, this enriching of memory, enabling of judgment, and enlarging of conceit, which commonly we call learning, . . . the final end is to lead and draw us to as high a perfection as our degenerate souls . . . can be capable of. . . . So that, the ending end of all earthly learning being virtuous action.[8]

As a Protestant, Sidney embraces this concept of virtue in action, and he longs for his contemporaries to write sound fiction that will both entertain and instruct their countrymen.

The danger, of course, is that "virtuous action" can quickly deteriorate into piety, Christianity that tallies up good deeds. But the mirrors of literature can also, as Thomas Sluberski notes in his list of the uses of literature, "indicate our true situation, the ways in which we have fallen short as human beings."[9] In either case—the former in which we believe falsely that we are living up to the Law's demands, the latter in which we recognize our failure to achieve righteousness on our own—the shortcomings of the mirror metaphor, as our only way of approaching literature, are made apparent as its focus on humanity reveals an incomplete picture because it cannot comprehend the divine. We need something more.

---

[7] H. G. Haile, "Luther and Literacy," *Publications of the Modern Language Association* 91, no. 5 (1976): 821.

[8] Sidney, "The Defence of Poesy," 112–13.

[9] Thomas R. Sluberski, "Lutherans and Literature: The John the Baptist Function of Literature," in *Christian Wisdom in Service to God's World*, ed. Robert Kolb (St. Paul, MN: Concordia College, 1984), 109.

LITERATURE AS IMAGINATIVE PARTICIPATION

H. G. Haile, translating Luther, describes his "intense imaginative participation" as he interprets the Bible.[10] Luther, for example, feels Gideon's fear and Abraham's paternal love, using his own experiences to imagine theirs. Today, we might call this Reader-Response Theory, a theory that argues for an individualized interpretation of the text. This "intense imaginative participation" depends, however, not only on each reader's own experience, but on the skill of the author to create a new experience for the reader, to take her far beyond her own mundane life. And I have found, in my own reading, that the most powerful works of literature are those that demonstrate God's grace, either in divine form or through human agency, and I do not believe that I am alone in this. I cannot help but think that *Les Misérables* is so hugely popular because of its remarkable moments of grace when we least expect them, when we, in fact, might be smugly satisfied with punishment for sins committed against characters with whom we sympathize.

Sola gratia—grace alone—is one of the foremost tenets of Lutheran Christianity: "The grace of God is his undeserved love of people who deserve only punishment. This grace is not ours because of our merit but only because of Christ."[11] This concept is easy to verbalize, but sometimes difficult for us to understand deeply. Intense imaginative participation in great literary texts can bring us closer to such an understanding. How might we feel, what might we discover, if we imagine ourselves in Jean Valjean's place, first as one forgiven and then as one who forgives?

As a Lutheran English professor, I feel that it is of utmost importance to guide our students towards experiencing God's grace as it is expressed in literature. This does not mean that we choose our texts based on this expression nor does it mean forcing a "Christian" reading out of a non-Christian work. Rather, it means grabbing those opportunities as they present themselves to us.

CHRISTIAN TEXTS

I would like to provide two examples of how this might be done, beginning with an openly Christian text that often appears in American literature survey courses: Anne Bradstreet's "As weary Pilgrim, now at rest."

---

[10] Haile, "Luther and Literacy," 824.

[11] Steven P. Mueller, ed., *Called to Believe, Teach, and Confess: An Introduction to Doctrinal Theology* (Eugene, OR: Wipf and Stock, 2005), 169.

Anne Bradstreet was a Puritan in colonial Massachusetts, and thanks to a heavy dose of Nathaniel Hawthorne's *The Scarlet Letter* and Arthur Miller's *The Crucible* in high school English classes, the term, "Puritan," has a decidedly negative ring to it in the American student's ear. A stern figure clothed in black, morally upright on the outside but inwardly seething with hypocrisy: that is the commonly held perception of the Puritan and his religion. We forget that neither Hawthorne nor Miller was around during the seventeenth century nor were they really trying to describe early American life so much as the issues of their own day. Thus, we make a grave error if, as modern Christians, we summarily dismiss the remarkable faith of the Puritans who first populated our country.

In his study of *Puritan Radicalism in New England*, Philip Gura points to the place of grace in the Puritan belief system: "While the doctrine of salvation by God's free grace assuredly was one of the linchpins of the Protestant Reformation, it was even more important to the development of English Puritanism." Or, as Thomas Shepard, minister of Newtown, Massachusetts (1635–49), explained to his parishioners, "when we break our Covenant, and that will not hold us, He takes a faster bond and makes a sure and everlasting Covenant, according to Grace, not according to Works; and that shall hold His people firm unto Himself, and hold Himself close and fast unto them, that He may never depart from us."[12] Unlike the common image of the smug Puritan, sure of his salvation based on a strict observation of a moralistic code, we see a church dependent on God's grace for faith and subsequent salvation.

Grace boils down to this: "God is no passive force. God is the one who is active, not human beings. The issue is not our ascent to God, but God's descent to us."[13] The Puritans were acutely aware of this. Jesus Christ, of course, is the chief means by which God's grace is enacted. As true God and true man, Christ lived the perfect life, was punished for our sins on the cross, and rose from the dead to give us eternal life. Christ is active, man is passive in salvation.

Now that we have a better picture of early American Puritan faith, we can see how Bradstreet conveys beautifully the relationship between Christ and man in "As weary Pilgrim, now at rest," a forty-four line meditation on her death, half of which describes a pilgrim who has, at last, reached his destination. The pilgrim has suffered a variety of physical hardships, but

---

[12] Philip F. Gura, *A Glimpse of Sion's Glory: Puritan Radicalism in New England, 1620–1660* (Middletown, CT: Wesleyan University Press, 1984), 6, 50.

[13] Gene Edward Veith Jr., *The Spirituality of the Cross: The Way of the First Evangelicals* (St. Louis: Concordia, 1999), 23.

"means in safety now to dwell." The first-person pronoun "I" at last appears in line 19, where we come to understand that the pilgrim is actually Bradstreet:

> A pilgrim I, on earth perplexed
>   With sins, with cares and sorrows vexed,
> By age and pains brought to decay,
>   And my clay house mouldering away,
> Oh, how I long to be at rest
>   And soar on high among the blest!
> This body shall in silence sleep,
>   Mine eyes no more shall ever weep;
> No fainting fits shall me assail,
>   Nor grinding pains my body frail,
> With cares and fears ne'er cumbered be,
>   Nor losses know, nor sorrows see.
> What though my flesh shall there consume?
>   It is the bed Christ did perfume;
> And when a few years shall be gone
>   This mortal shall be clothed upon.
> A corrupt carcass down it lies,
>   A glorious body it shall rise;
> In weakness and dishonor sown,
>   In power 't is raised by Christ alone.
> Then soul and body shall unite,
>   And of their maker have the sight;
> Such lasting joys shall there behold
>   As ear ne'er heard nor tongue e'er told.
> Lord, make me ready for that day!
>   Then come, dear bridegroom, come away.[14]

Certainly, there is nothing "Puritanical" in the poet's description of her life, no catalogue of virtues or of good deeds accomplished. Rather, she presents a figure who brings nothing to the salvation equation, or, perhaps, less than nothing. "[P]erplexed / With sins," her body is "mouldering away" towards its inevitable fate: a "corrupt carcass." Remarkably, Bradstreet does not even mention her soul in relation to her life on earth (although she

---

[14] Anne Bradstreet, "As weary Pilgrim, now at rest," in *The Poems of Mrs. Anne Bradstreet (1612 –1672)* (n.p.: The Duodecimos, 1897), 346–47 (lines 18–44).

refers to it in her description of the afterlife), thereby erasing any possible suspicion that she might deserve a heavenly reward.

Heaven, it would seem, is indescribable ("Such lasting joys shall there behold / As ear ne'er heard nor tongue e'er told") except for one crucial element: the presence of God, father and son. All action, all energy, emanates from the divine. God the father is the "maker" of Bradstreet's "soul and body," and that body "In power 't is raised by Christ alone," not in response to Bradstreet's faith, but as a gracious miracle upon a person of "weakness and dishonor."

That body is to be buried in "the bed Christ did perfume," a beautiful image that works in two directions. First, it points backwards in time to Jesus' actual burial on Good Friday. Saint Luke tells us, "But on the first day of the week, at early dawn, they went to the tomb, taking the spices they had prepared. And they found the stone rolled away from the tomb, but when they went in they did not find the body of the Lord Jesus. . . . they were perplexed" (Luke 24:1–4). Bradstreet implies that Christ's dead body did not need spices or perfumes because it itself "perfumed" all tombs in his death and resurrection. We may also note here that the King James usage of the word *perplexed* to describe the women at the tomb may have been the source for Bradstreet's own "perplexed / With sins."

Second, the image points forward to the final couplet and culminating metaphor of the poem in its use of the word *bed* rather than *grave* or *tomb*: "Lord, make me ready for that day! / Then come, dear bridegroom, come away." That "bed" is no longer a grave at all, but the meeting place of bride and bridegroom. This poem invites Christ to delay no longer and to turn her funeral graciously into her wedding day.

By speaking in the first-person singular, Bradstreet creates two "I"s: the poet herself, and the reader who hears himself cataloguing his own "sins" and "sorrows" and imagines his own death and physical dissolution. Bradstreet paints the mundane experience to serve as a foil to the experience of grace promised by Christ. We move from dreading our end to anticipating joyfully a new life.

NON-CHRISTIAN TEXTS

By utilizing the literary tools of close reading and historicism, we can easily illuminate the evidence of God's grace in decidedly Christian texts such as the works of Anne Bradstreet and Edward Taylor, Edmund Spenser and John Milton, Christina Rossetti and Gerald Manley Hopkins. With a little more work, we can find it in texts produced in Christian cultures, such as the novels of Cervantes or of John Steinbeck. But what of works produced in pre- or non-Christian contexts?

Many medieval (i.e., Catholic) scholars believed that although God revealed himself completely in Holy Scripture, he revealed glimpses of himself in the classic texts of the Greco-Roman world. This supposition rescued these texts from the flames but also led to an overly moralized reading of some amoral works such as Ovid's *Metamorphoses*. Again, as Lutheran educators, we should be wary of this brand of Christian interpretation. Too often, I have read student essays that conclude in this manner: "If so-and-so had been Christian, he would not have done this terrible thing or ended his life in despair." This type of reading is all too facile and without validity unless the text itself hints at such a possibility. We cannot read a text anachronistically or a-culturally, subjecting its characters and attitudes to our own world view and rendering judgments upon them. This could easily lead to the same sort of book burning or banning that many Christians have been (and continue to be) guilty of. Rather, as educated Lutherans, we have the freedom to engage opposing views; it is often by encountering opposition that we see the Truth with greater clarity. Furthermore, the medieval idea of seeing glimpses of God in non-Christian literary works is a useful one if we look for examples of love, grace, and sacrifice.

Let us take as our sample text Homer's *Iliad*, that peerless epic poem of the ancient world. The poem is expressly about rage: the wrath of Achilles primarily, but also that of Agamemnon, Menelaus, Hector, and of that never-satisfied goddess, Hera. How could anyone expect to see undeserved love amidst such a whirlpool of revenge?

In Book 16, the Greeks are being slaughtered by the Trojans while their greatest warrior, Achilles, sits on the sidelines, nursing his grudge against Agamemnon. Neither Agamemnon's offer of bountiful gifts, Odysseus' eloquent speech, nor the imminent destruction of the Greek ships has the least effect upon Achilles. As all hope seems lost, Achilles' dearest companion, Patroclus, pleads with him to save their friends. Finally, Patroclus begs,

> At least send *me* out, let *me* lead a troop
> Of Myrmidons and light the way for our army.
> And let me wear your armor. If the Trojans think
> I am you, they'll back off and give the Greeks
> Some breathing space, what little there is in war.[15]

Achilles agrees, Patroclus fights valiantly but is killed; Achilles rejoins the war to avenge his death.

As many another reader, I have always taken this action of Patroclus to be a tremendous act of courage and compassion for his fellow brothers-in-

---

[15] Homer, *Iliad*, trans. Stanley Lombardo (Indianapolis: Hackett, 1997), 16.42–46.

arms, but a student of mine taught me to read this passage in a more pro-found way. Concordia University Irvine sophomore Faith McAllister argues quite effectively that,

> Patroclus knows that he has to die. He knows it is the only way to win the war. He believes Achilles is sick and believes he [Patroclus] is the only cure. . . . This [speech in Book 16] is not a conversation of war tactics and pleading for military assistance. Rather it is Patroclus' desperate attempt to save his best friend in any way possible before giving up the ultimate sacrifice to his friend to "cure" him of his insanity.[16]

McAllister's close reading of Patroclus' speech provides ample evidence for her thesis.

What I wish to point out here is that McAllister's argument elevates Achilles' best friend's character above all the others in *Iliad*. If he is courageous, so are countless others; if he is compassionate, so are many; but if he is *gracious*, he is unique. Achilles does not *deserve* to be "cured" of his selfishness and vanity, his stubbornness and blindness, yet Patroclus deems this cure to be greater than his own life. Without Patroclus' recognition of Achilles' weakness—despite Achilles' self-perception that he is a strong hero whose actions are justified by the injuries he has suffered at Agamemnon's hand—Achilles would be incapable of doing the right thing by helping his fellow Greeks in their hour of need. Achilles is saved from his sin by Patroclus' death in his place. It would be terribly anachronistic to call him a Christ-figure; as Lutheran professors, however, we are free to call attention to this act of grace to show our students just how powerful God's grace towards us is.

I have chosen grace as my primary example because of its power and significance, but English professors are free to look for other biblical themes woven into literary works. In fact, *because* we teach in Lutheran colleges, we have the freedom to explore any and all themes—those taught in public schools and those considered inappropriate in a secular setting. Baptism, for instance, a washing away of foulness, appears in many texts that are not necessarily Christian, demonstrating the human need for cleansing and rebirth. Francis Rossow's *Gospel Patterns in Literature* provides many specific examples of "familiar truths in unexpected places," including such widely divergent works as *Crime and Punishment*, *Measure for Measure*, and *Tom Sawyer*. He writes,

---

[16] Faith McAllister, "Patroclus' Speech" (unpublished essay, Concordia Irvine, 2012), 5.

> That central event of history called the Gospel event (the Son of God's incarnation, life, death, damnation, and resurrection for our salvation) has had so profound an impact on our world that it has spilled beyond the bounds chosen by God to contain it and convey it, namely divine revelation, the Holy Scriptures; that many aspects of the Gospel, such as God becoming man, the Creator sacrificing himself for the creature, the God-man dying and rising again, are in varying degrees of accuracy and completeness foreshadowed or reflected in literature.[17]

Even authors who seem to reject or ignore the Bible often struggle with its ideas and themes, revealing the plight of this fallen world. One might even argue that all essential literary themes find expression in Scripture; although I would frown upon any student who dragged biblical quotations into an essay where they did not belong, such comparisons do provide rich food for thought and discussion.

LITERATURE AS CREATION

If Sir Philip Sidney looked to his contemporaries to write good literature for future generations, then we have marvelous opportunities to mentor and nurture our students as creative writers. Sidney saw that creativity itself is a gift from God, a way in which humans reflect the fact that we are made in his image and by which we honor and extend the beauty of his creation:

> Neither let it be deemed too saucy a comparison to balance the highest point of man's wit with the efficacy of Nature; but rather give right honor to the heavenly Maker of that maker, who, having made man to his own likeness, set him beyond and over all the works of that second nature, which in nothing he showeth so much as in Poetry, when with the force of a divine breath he bringeth things forth surpassing her doings.[18]

This does not mean forcing our students to write "religious" poetry, stories, or essays, (especially since many of our students are not Christian or are Christian in name only) but teaching them to write beautifully. Indeed, there are thousands of terrible "Christian" works out there, a circumstance with which I am sadly familiar, due to my experience working at a vanity press. In the year between college and graduate school, I served as a proof-

---

[17] Francis C. Rossow, *Gospel Patterns in Literature: Familiar Truths in Unexpected Places* (Minneapolis: Lutheran University Press, 2008), 6–7.

[18] Sidney, "The Defence of Poesy," 109.

reader and judge, slogging through doggerel that may have been written through faith but which offered only clichés and unsurprising rhymes. This is what we want to avoid.

No, what we want is not to assign "Christianity" but rather create an atmosphere where students feel free to express their faith naturally. I offer, as an example, a poem by my colleague, Thea Gavin:

Late Summer, Morning, Dad is in Hospice

Down here in the chill
rock-carcass path
that was winter's river,
I am filled with the green
sighs of arroyo willow.
Although their root-toes
disappear in the dust
trees somehow remain
until rains return.

My feet flex around
morning-cold stones
to follow a trail
that leaps out of shadow:
the half-gold hills speak
how light follows gray—
the rocks and I wait,
listen and pray.

The only obvious reference to a religious context is the final word, but a careful reading shows subtle echoes of Ps 23. Additionally, many of the images evoke a feeling of hope—hope that is linked to nature and, through the last line, to God.

As we help our students find their own voices in writing, we need to teach our students not to be afraid of including their faith. This might be directly, as C. S. Lewis does in the Chronicles of Narnia where his "strategy" was to present "vital Christian truths . . . in a new manner—in an imaginary world—[so] they might be viewed more objectively. The stumbling blocks of presentation might be avoided and the events themselves truly seen in their full power."[19] Thus, for example, aspects of Christ are demonstrated by

---

[19] Steven P. Mueller, *Not a Tame God: Christ in the Writings of C. S. Lewis* (St. Louis: Concordia, 2002), 106.

the writer in Aslan, then contemplated by the reader. Or, faith may be expressed indirectly, in that the student writers, by virtue of their Christianity, cannot help but imbue their work with that very faith. This need not be theological per se and may be as simple as a poem written in response to a hummingbird's flight or a child's laugh. As our world becomes inundated with information and misinformation, with poorly crafted books and abusive screenplays, these sorts of Christian writings become ever more important.

CONCLUSION

Let me reiterate my caution against Christianizing non-Christian texts, overly moralizing any work of literature or of history, or demanding written expressions of faith. But if we emphasize close readings, "Literature can be used to make us better students of Holy Scripture, better interpreters, better theologians. . . . Our understanding of metaphor, simile, image, and genre are all honed by reading secular literature. . . . Exegesis and explication are basically literary skills."[20] Luther saw clearly the ways in which the Humanities "worked both ways," as it were, creating stronger citizens in both the secular and the divine kingdoms: "Languages and the arts, which can do us no harm, . . . are actually a greater ornament, profit, glory, and benefit, both for the understanding of Holy Scripture and the conduct of temporal government."[21] And as our students study the Word of God, they will both see for themselves and express to others, ever more clearly, the unmatchable act of grace that gave us the Word of Christ incarnate.

QUESTIONS

1. Which texts have you found to be the most reflective mirrors for your students?

2. Which is your favorite Christian text to teach? Does it illustrate God's grace?

3. Can you think of a non-Christian text that may point to God's grace? How so?

4. What other biblical themes have you discovered in teaching literary works?

5. What type of writing assignment can you envision that would encourage an expression of faith without requiring it?

---

[20] Sluberski, "Lutherans and Literature," 108.

[21] Luther, "To the Councilmen of All Cities in Germany," in AE 45:358.

13

THE ARTIST'S VOCATION: LUTHERAN HIGHER
EDUCATION, THE ARTS, AND THEATRE

Peter Senkbeil[1]

INTRODUCTION

The 1981 film *Chariots of Fire* depicts the true stories of Eric Liddell and Harold Abrahams, two athletes who competed for Great Britain in the 1924 Paris Olympics. Liddell, a record-breaking sprinter nicknamed "The Flying Scotsman," spent time in Scotland training for missionary service in China as well as for the Olympics. In one of the film's early scenes, Liddell's sister Jenny berates him for missing an opportunity to give an evangelistic talk because his training run went long. Liddell replies, "I believe God made me for a purpose—for China. But he also made me fast. And when I run, I feel his pleasure."[2] Liddell went on both to Olympic victory and to a lengthy missionary career in China.

Liddell's statement and his life reflect an understanding of God's callings on him that Lutherans describe as the concept of vocation. Liddell acknowledges that God calls him to love and serve his neighbor as a citizen of God's kingdom of grace, in which his calling is to reach out to others with the Gospel of Jesus. He also celebrates the fact that God has gifted him athletically, and that he serves God with that gift by cultivating and using it to its utmost in God's kingdom of power, in civil society.[3]

Applying a similar understanding of vocation in two kingdoms to the visual and performing arts can clear away many misunderstandings

---

[1] Peter Senkbeil, PhD (Northwestern), is Professor of Theatre and Associate Provost at CUI.

[2] *Chariots of Fire*, directed by Hugh Hudson (1981; Burbank, CA: Warner Brothers Home Video, 2001), DVD.

[3] See Mueller's chapter for an overview of the doctrines of vocation and God's two kingdoms.

241

involving Christianity and the arts, and it can provide a solid foundation for artists and arts educators who are Christians as they seek to live out their callings. The Bible provides numerous examples of God's people making art, using a variety of art forms, genres, and styles, and for a variety of purposes. In his landmark book *Art Worlds*, sociologist Howard Becker describes and analyzes art as "the work some people do"—that is, "artist" is a job like many other jobs.[4] In an effort to shed light on the vocation of artist, I will begin by examining both God's Word and God's world for an understanding of the nature and purposes of art and art-making. I will then consider the vocation of artist in general terms before turning to my chosen discipline, theatre, for some reflections and applications of these concepts to that specific art form.

THE NATURE OF ART: REVELATION AND REASON

Creativity is the first attribute of God revealed in the Bible. In Gen 1, the first thing we learn is that God is a creative being—the one who made the heavens and the earth. By the end of Gen 1, we have learned that God created human beings in his own image and made them stewards of the earth. If we are truly created in God's image, then we are creative beings too, and our stewardship of God's world involves exercising our God-given creativity. After all, the first task God gives to Adam in Gen 2 is essentially creative—in naming the animals, Adam uses his creative gift to choose a set of sounds that take on symbolic value in reference to part of God's creation.

Humans don't create the way God does. I cannot turn on the lights in my house by walking through the front door and saying, "Let there be light." Instead, I have to flip a switch. By flipping that switch, I take advantage of hundreds of acts of creativity by the people who discovered electricity, figured out ways to generate it, and developed the various scientific breakthroughs and pieces of technology that enable the power generated miles away to be transported to my home where it can be activated with one finger, or (if I'm willing to spend $20) a voice-activated light switch.

Humans exercise creativity by discovering things about God's created universe, by organizing and reshaping things found in nature—that is, by creating culture. This has been described by sociologist and theologian H. Richard Niebuhr (quoting Malinowski) as "the 'artificial, secondary environment' that humanity superimposes on the natural. It comprises language, habits, ideas, beliefs, customs, social organization, inherited artifacts, technical processes, and values."[5] Culture, then, includes not only the crea-

---

[4] Howard S. Becker, *Art Worlds* (Berkeley: University of California Press, 1982), ix.

[5] H. Richard Niebuhr, *Christ and Culture* (New York: Harper and Row, 1951), 32.

tion of tangible physical objects, but also conceptual structures—political, social, artistic, and military systems, for example. Some human creations can best be described as innovations that make our lives easier—for example, tools, buildings, clothing, communication devices, and manufacturing techniques. We typically refer to these as "applied arts." Their usefulness is generally apparent. Some human creations can best be described as making our lives richer—for example, poetry, fiction, drama, music, and dance. We typically call these the "fine arts." Their usefulness is not immediately apparent. All human creations can be described in terms of both form and function, and can be called ugly or beautiful or something in between.

Scripture describes a surprising range of artistic activity. In the Old Testament, God's people created and performed vocal and instrumental music, painted and sculpted works of visual art, created buildings of great architectural beauty, told stories using various genres, danced singly and in groups, enacted various kinds of rituals with symbolic elements, and even, in a few cases, carried out behaviors commanded by God that might be described today as performance art (more on this shortly). While the Bible makes no overt mention of drama, some scholars have argued that the oral reading of the Hebrew Scriptures may well have involved multiple voices, and the books of Job and Song of Songs are both largely structured like dramas.[6] Four key examples reflect important biblical concepts related to art.

1. In Exod 25–30, God gives Moses detailed instructions for the design and construction of the tabernacle that will serve as a mobile house of worship during the Israelites' time in the wilderness. In Exod 31:4, God tells Moses that he has called two artists, Bezalel and Oholiab, to "devise artistic designs" for the tabernacle and its furnishings. When the time comes to complete this work, Moses tells the Israelites that God has commanded him to ask them for contributions of raw materials, but also for contributions of their time and skill in making the various parts of the tabernacle and its contents, all under the guidance and supervision of the two artists named above. This is described in detail in Exod 35–40.

Several important concepts emerge here. First, God calls human beings to serve as artists in accord with his will, using their skill and intelligence.

---

[6] See Thomas Boogaart, "Drama and the Sacred: Recovering the Dramatic Tradition in Scripture and Worship," in *Touching the Altar: The Old Testament for Christian Worship,* ed. Carol M. Bechtel (Grand Rapids: Eerdmans, 2008), 35–61; see also Calvin Seerveld, *The Greatest Song in Critique of Solomon* (Toronto: Tuppence, 1967).

Next, the art they make adorns a house of worship; it consists of both decorative and functional elements, in both realistic (e.g., carved pomegranates, almond blossoms) and abstract (e.g., curtains, the priests' breastplates) styles. Third, this project involves the participation of the whole community; members contribute the raw materials and help construct parts of the tabernacle under the supervision of those called to lead the work. The line between "artist" and "non-artist" is very blurry here. In *Art Worlds*, Becker points out that all art is made in social contexts, and that it involves not only those whom we typically call artists and audiences, but also many other people who participate in an art world as producers of raw materials and equipment, patrons and donors, critics and reviewers, landlords and gallery/theatre owners, most of whom we don't think of as "artists." Becker argues:

> Whatever the artist, defined as the person who performs the core activity without which the work would not be art, does not do must be done by someone else. The artist thus works in the center of a network of cooperating people, all of whose work is essential to the final outcome.[7]

Reason and revelation both acknowledge that it takes a community to make and receive art, whether that art is part of a house of worship or is presented to some other part of society.

2. Between the two sections of Exodus described above, while Moses is on Mount Sinai receiving the Ten Commandments, the children of Israel grow restless and persuade the high priest Aaron to create a golden calf for them to worship. Once Moses returns from the mountaintop, he calls the people to repentance, invokes God's punishment upon the idolaters, and destroys the calf (Exod 32). God announces his mercy and commands Moses to make two new stone tablets that contain the law in a renewal of his covenant with his people. Centuries later, when Solomon oversees the building of the temple in Jerusalem, in keeping with God's instructions, its furnishings include an enormous bronze basin, called "the sea," that rests on the backs of twelve bronze oxen (1 Kgs 7). Clearly, the creation of a metal statue of an animal is not inherently sinful; rather, the purpose to which the statue is put plays a critical role.

While some Christians have argued against some or all art-making on the grounds that it is idolatrous, Lutherans have joined with other Chris-

---

[7] Becker, *Art Worlds*, 24–25.

tians (most notably Roman Catholics and Eastern Orthodox) in distinguishing between art and idolatry and arguing for a place for art in worship services and their venues as well as in society. Martin Luther rejected the more iconoclastic elements of the Protestant Reformation, asserting that stained glass and religious images should be preserved in Protestant churches: "Nor am I of the opinion that the gospel should destroy and blight all the arts, as some of the pseudo-religious claim. But I would like to see all the arts, especially music, in the service of Him who gave and made them."[8] Luther repeatedly commended music, which, he said, "next to the Word of God . . . deserves the highest praise."[9] In *Luther on Music*, Carl Schalk argues that Luther's education, worship life, and personal activities included sacred and secular music of many styles and genres. He not only developed a German Mass that combined liturgical chant with vernacular hymns, he also sang and played the lute in his own home, and he was well acquainted with the composers of his day.[10] Again, the Lutheran tradition has embraced the arts, rejecting only that which is rejected explicitly in the Bible.

3. In Ezek 4, God calls the prophet Ezekiel to perform symbolic acts that today might best be described as performance art. God tells him to make a diorama of sorts, using a carved brick and an iron griddle, to set it up in public and lie down next to it for 430 days while bound with cords, in a symbolic enactment of the siege of Jerusalem. God even tells Ezekiel what to eat (mixed-grain bread) and how to prepare it—over human dung, which is not only gross but also ritually unclean (Deut 12–14). Ezekiel protests and God relents on the cooking instructions, but the fact that God commands his prophet to perform an act that violates the ceremonial law in order to make a point is striking. This is one of the most theatre-like events in the Bible, and it is worth noting that God commands it, not for the purposes of worship or celebration, but as a critique of his disobedient people and a prophecy of their fate.[11]

---

[8] Martin Luther, "Preface to the Wittenberg Hymnal," in AE 53:316.

[9] Luther, "Preface to Georg Rhau's Symphoniae iucundae," in AE, 53:323.

[10] Carl F. Schalk, *Luther on Music: Paradigms of Praise* (St. Louis: Concordia, 1988), 18–24.

[11] For other examples of God commanding his prophets to perform symbolic acts, see Ezek 12, 37; Jer 13, 19, 27, 28, 32, 36, 43, 51; and most notably Hos 1–3, in which Hosea's literal marriage to a prostitute functions as an extended metaphor for God's love for an unfaithful people.

4. Jesus' earthly ministry as recorded in the Gospels relies heavily on storytelling in the form of parables. In Matt 13:34–35, after Jesus tells a series of stories, including the parable of the sower, we read: "All these things Jesus said to the crowds in parables; indeed, he said nothing to them without a parable. This was to fulfill what was spoken by the prophet: 'I will open my mouth in parables; I will utter what has been hidden since the foundation of the world.' "

Jesus' parables are a fulfillment of Old Testament prophecy; they are a revealing of God's hidden mysteries. Sometimes they are difficult to understand. When the disciples ask Jesus why he teaches in parables, his answer is, "To you is has been given to know the secrets of the kingdom of heaven, but to them it has not been given" (Matt 13:11). He explains two parables in this chapter, but in general, all four Gospels present most of Jesus' parables without explanation. While many Christian churches today prize clear expository preaching—a particular emphasis during the Protestant Reformation and in the churches that developed from it—Scripture records that Jesus approached the matter differently, using stories rich in symbols and allusions whose meanings were not always clear.

To summarize, the Bible suggests a number of principles of art that are consistent with reason and experience:

1. All humans are creative beings and therefore capable of both artistic expression and aesthetic appreciation.

2. Art is "the work some people do"—that is, some people are called to the vocation of artist as a profession, or as an integral part of their profession.

3. Art happens in community, and it is shaped, at least in part, by the interaction between artists, audiences, and support personnel.

4. Art may fulfill one or more of a number of purposes, including instruction, beautification, worship, celebration, prophecy, and/or social criticism.

5. Art functions differently than rhetoric; to criticize an art work because its message or meaning is insufficiently clear is to misunderstand the nature of art. Those who want to criticize works of art for their opacity or ambiguity may want to consider God's words to Isaiah (6:9–10), quoted by Jesus (Matt 13:14–15; Mark 4:11–12), which indicate that not all people will understand God's Word.

6. Art, like every other human endeavor after the fall, is susceptible to the corrupting effects of sin, and it may be used for idolatrous or destructive purposes. This is not an indictment of art itself; it is a

reality of all human activity and culture in a fallen world. While human reason may not choose the word *idolatry* to describe such corruption of art, studies of fascist and other totalitarian art demonstrate that one need not be religious to assert that sometimes artists create works that glorify corrupt individuals and destructive regimes.

7. Art combines symbols and images in ways that are not always easy to understand or easy to take. Art is polysemic (literally, "many-meaninged") in nature, so what may be clear to some audience members may be opaque to others, and members of the same audience take away very different sets of meanings from the same art experience.

THE VOCATION OF ARTIST

Contemporary Challenges to the Arts

If it is true that all humans are creative, then it stands to reason that a significant part of the vocation of the artist is educative. Those who have learned to express their artistic gifts with greater skill can serve their neighbors by helping them experience, understand, and appreciate many forms of artistic expression.

The challenge in doing so in the U.S. today is threefold. First, though our culture is awash in entertainment of many kinds, most of us have received a very poor arts education. American K–12 school systems have tended to regard education in the arts as at best a nice extra feature, to be included in affluent schools if the budget permits, but to be cut in tough budget times in favor of more fundamental knowledge and skills. Colleges and universities fare slightly better, but by the time students begin their first year of college, most of them are hopelessly behind in any sort of arts education. My colleagues in the university's music department, for example, report that they regularly encounter prospective students who are gifted singers, but who have never been taught the fundamental skill of reading music. Unfortunately, the "arts as extras" approach ignores the body of literature that demonstrates a high correlation between engagement with the arts and academic success in other areas—the documented links between childhood music lessons and cognitive development in spatial intelligence and mathematical ability, for example.[12] Luther's recommendations

---

[12] For recent studies and meta-analyses, see Frances H. Rauscher and Sean C. Hinton, "Music Instruction and Its Diverse Extra-Musical Benefits," *Music Perception* 29, no. 2 (2011): 215–26; E. Glenn Schellenberg, "Music and Cognitive Abilities," *Current*

that music be integrated into education at all levels have been ignored in American education for the most part, and students receive a poorer education as a result.[13]

The second challenge facing arts education in the U.S. today is that our culture has absorbed the idea that it should be unnecessary. Most Americans seem to have embraced the notion that any work of art should be accessible to any audience member, and that historical and philosophical background should be irrelevant. This view tends to reduce art to decoration and popular entertainment ("I don't know much about art, but I know what I like"). The idea that one should have to work to appreciate a particular work of art seems alien in that context. At best, arts education is considered the province of those few who want to work in these obscure and largely unprofitable fields—all while popular music, film, and television churn out a nearly endless supply of performances for popular consumption. Likewise, serious visual art is seen as something for museums and art schools, completely unrelated to its daily application in advertising, fashion, domestic, and industrial design. Why should I care about developing a sophisticated visual aesthetic when I can just go to a discount store and pick up some trendy new clothes and a colorful picture for my wall? I am not arguing for some sort of high art vs. low art competition; rather, I am suggesting that our society could benefit greatly from approaching the art and design that fill our daily lives with greater understanding and discernment. Philosopher and art historiographer Calvin Seerveld, in his seminal work *Rainbows for the Fallen World*, argues eloquently that Christians are called to "obedient aesthetic life" in both the church and the world, hinting broadly that kitsch is not only in bad taste, but also that it may be a sin.[14]

A third, and perhaps the most insidious, challenge facing arts education today is the myth of professionalism. Our nation and our dominant culture

---

Directions in Psychological Science 14, no. 6 (2005): 317–20; and Gottfried Schlaug, Andrea Norton, Katie Overy, and Ellen Winner, "Effects of Music Training on the Child's Brain and Cognitive Development," *Annals of the New York Academic of Sciences* 1060 (2005): 219–30.

[13] See Luther, "Instructions for the Visitors of Parish Pastors in Electoral Saxony," in AE 40:314–20. Regarding the education of pastors and teachers, Ewald Plass quotes Luther as saying, "Necessity demands that music be kept in the schools. A schoolmaster must know how to sing; otherwise I do not look at him. And before a youth is ordained into the ministry, he should practice music in school" (Ewald M. Plass, ed., *What Luther Says: A Practical In-home Anthology for the Active Christian* [St. Louis: Concordia, 1959], §3092). See also Schalk, *Luther on Music*, 28–30.

[14] Calvin G. Seerveld, *Rainbows for the Fallen World: Aesthetic Life and Artistic Task* (Toronto: Tuppence, 2005), 42, 63–67.

tend to reinforce the notion that the arts, like athletics, should be the domain of a few highly talented performers, while the rest of us are merely spectators. Our economic system also reinforces this notion—entertainment, like sports, is a consumer commodity, and bigger is better. The only arts and entertainment news regularly reported in the mass media is the list of top-performing movies each weekend in terms of box office gross. We would be a physically healthier nation if, instead of dividing our society into athletes and spectators, we were to promote the idea of lifelong fitness and amateur participation in sports and exercise. We would also be an aesthetically healthier nation if we promoted the idea of lifelong artistic participation along the same lines. Art is for everybody, not just the elite and the experts, and art can be made by everybody in ways that benefit them and their neighbors. Furthermore, artistic participation is a critical stepping-stone to thoughtful art criticism; just as an athlete who once played the game understands it more deeply than a fan who has not, those who have created or performed in art works bring a more comprehensive perspective to analyzing and criticizing art than do those who have never made visual art works, written a story or a poem, or performed a piece of music or a play.

A Calling in Two Kingdoms

These may not seem like spiritual issues, but they are. If we permit an impoverished aesthetic culture, we are ignoring part of God's call on our lives. This may not be as important as carrying out the Great Commission or feeding the poor and hungry, but we are still ignoring part of whom God made us to be. Thus one calling of the artist, particularly in educational settings, is to help their neighbors access and celebrate their own inherent creativity, learn to perceive and understand various styles and genres of art by acquiring knowledge and skills to help them do so, and thereby become more aesthetically aware members of society—"cultivated citizens," to borrow a phrase from Luther.[15]

A second calling of the artist—and the one that generally comes to mind first for most people—centers around the idea that some people are, in fact, called to be artists by profession, in the same way the people are called to any profession. A major challenge related to this calling springs from a set of myths about artists that seem to have crept into Western civilization around the time of the Romantic period. These have to do with the notion of the artist as inspired and tortured genius; the popular images of

---

[15] Luther, "To the Councilmen of All Cities in Germany that They Establish and Maintain Christian Schools," in AE 45:356.

Mozart, Van Gogh, Franz Kafka, Sylvia Plath, and Kurt Cobain all reflect these myths. While it is true that some artists have led tortured lives, plenty of those who make their living through the arts lead fairly ordinary, well-adjusted lives, with spouses, children, homes, and networks of friends and family—but their personal stories are less memorable. In addition, these myths tend to mystify art as the result of spontaneous inspiration, rather than as hard work based on a set of specific knowledge and skills acquired over time. Again, Becker's description of art as the work some people do, in which they collaborate with and rely upon the labor of many other people, most of whom are not labeled "artist," is a helpful and welcome corrective. The Old Testament example of Bezalel and Oholiab, described earlier, depicts just this sort of art world, and the Lutheran concept of vocation leads to an understanding of making art in social context. Some people are called to make houses for a living; some are called to make spreadsheets; others are called to make plays or concerts or paintings. In each case, the making can either be a joyful response to one's calling, lived out so as to serve one's neighbor, or it can dwindle into something self-serving and short-sighted, lived out primarily for personal gain or with grudging resentment at one's lot in life.

The vocation of professional artist is lived out in both of God's kingdoms. As in other forms of human work, its expression in each kingdom may differ somewhat, depending on the nature and purpose of the artistic task. When we think of art in God's right-hand kingdom of grace and faith, we may be inclined to focus on art in the context of Christian worship—and the arts have a critical role to play here. The Lutheran tradition affirms the place of the visual arts in adorning houses of worship, and it affirms the place of the performing arts—most notably music—in the worship service itself. Artists can also contribute to the right-hand kingdom in other ways, of course. For many centuries in the Western tradition much of the art produced was religious in theme and context—paid for by the church, exhibited and performed in worship, or for the purpose of evangelism or education. Even as classical art, music, and theatre appeared with increasing frequency in non-church settings, they frequently retained religious themes and images. It is worth noting that Handel's beloved *Messiah* was first performed in a concert hall, not a house of worship; that medieval morality plays such as *Everyman* were written for performance in schools, not churches; and that Renaissance artists like Leonardo moved back and forth between "religious" and "secular" subjects in their work.

In discussing this work, I am deliberately avoiding the phrase "Christian art" for two simple reasons. First, the word *Christian* appears in the New Testament only as a noun describing people, never as an adjective applied to objects or concepts. Second, the term *Christian art* is prone to very vague and slippery definitions, as C. S. Lewis points out when describing a similar term:

> [I]f we enlarge the idea of Christian literature to include not only literature on sacred themes but all that is written by Christians for Christians to read, then, I think, Christian Literature can exist only in the same sense in which Christian cookery might exist. . . . Boiling an egg is the same process whether you are a Christian or a Pagan.[16]

I am following Lewis in arguing that the key distinction between art created for the kingdoms of the left and right hand has less to do with content than it does with context—that is, the venue and audience for which the art work is prepared. This distinction is particularly important in the live performing arts in which audience members have a collective shared experience of the art work as it is presented in real time by the artists. Each venue/audience combination comes with its own expectations regarding the nature and purpose of the art it will experience, and its response to a particular art work derives at least partly from those expectations.

As a Christian is always a citizen of both kingdoms, these artistic vocations are not mutually exclusive. However, it is important to note that, since all art involves interaction between the art work and the consumer or audience, groups of consumers organized primarily in one kingdom or the other will have differing expectations for art, and they will evaluate and respond to it differently. A congregation's expectations for music in worship may be quite different from those same people's expectations for music in a concert in a secular setting.

Nigel Forde, a Christian who works as a director, writer, and actor, describes this as the issue of "register," pointing out that worship services are a special case in this regard. A congregation that is expecting one sort of music, but gets another, may react against musical style as much as lyrical content. The same holds true in visual art, dance, and theatre. The problem of register applies when artists create work for civil society as well. The famous riot that attended the opening night of Stravinsky's 1913 ballet *The Rite of Spring* is a well-known example.

The calling of the professional artist also involves creating art in and for God's left-hand kingdom of law and reason—that is, for civil society. In doing so, artists bring their knowledge, skills, and education to bear on artistic tasks that are carried out on the context of specific social settings, generally in collaboration with many others, and with an awareness of likely

---

[16] C. S. Lewis, "Christianity and Literature," in *Christian Reflections*, ed. Walter Hooper (Grand Rapids: Eerdmans, 1967), 1.

audiences. In this way, the Christian who is an artist carries out her work just like any other artist. A key distinction for her is that she is aware of her calling from God to exercise her creative gifts and skills in just and loving service to others. That artistic service may take many forms. William Romanowski describes four main functions of the popular arts—cultural communication, social and cultural critique, social unity, and collective memory—that may be applied to the fine arts as well.[17] A quick review of the biblical examples explicated above reveals that all these functions are carried out by art in the Bible. With this in mind, "art for art's sake" is a misnomer; art is *always* for the sake of something besides itself, since it always carries out one or more of these functions. Those who ask the question, "Are you making art for art's sake or art for God's sake?" are posing a false choice. Since God created us as creative, artistic beings who function in social and cultural contexts, when we make art—even if we state that we're making "art for art's sake"—we are reflecting our nature as God's creatures. Furthermore, since civil society consists of both Christians and non-Christians, it is difficult for artists to compartmentalize their art into "religious" and "secular" works. The Lutheran perspective suggests the good news that is indeed unnecessary to do so. Art is not good only insofar as it fulfills a worship function or can be interpreted as an individual's act of worship. Rather, the visual art, music, and drama that artists create for civil society is an expression of their vocation and is, for the Christian, loving service to God and neighbor just as surely as is the art created for the purposes of worship, evangelism, and religious education.

Sin, Truth, and Art

That said, all art is not necessarily good just because it is art. Lutherans acknowledge the radical effects of sin in damaging all aspects of God's created order. In acknowledging this, Lutherans follow the apostle Paul, who not only points out that sin came to all humankind as a result of the fall (Rom 5:12), but also states:

> For the creation was subjected to futility, not willingly, but because of him who subjected it, in hope that the creation itself will be set free from its bondage to corruption and obtain the freedom of the glory of the children of God. For we know that the whole creation has been groaning together in the pains of childbirth until now (Rom 8:20–22).

---

[17] William D. Romanowski, *Eyes Wide Open: Looking for God in Popular Culture* (Grand Rapids: Brazos, 2001), 59–63.

Sin has radical effects on the arts, just as it has radical effects on creation and on every human endeavor and vocation. Works of art can be created to serve an idolatrous purpose (e.g., the golden calf in Exodus), and works created to inspire sincere religious devotion can be misused as idols (this was criticism leveled by Reformation-era iconoclasts against much pre-Reformation religious art in churches). Art works focused more on civil society than religious worship can also idolize either the subject (e.g., ten-story banners depicting athletes that hang on buildings in major cities) or the artist (much of modern pop music performance tends in this direction, but this tendency goes back at least as far as Liszt, and perhaps as far as Mozart). C. S. Lewis describes a subtler form of artistic idolatry: "Every poet and musician and artist, but for Grace, is drawn away from the love of the thing he tells, to the love of the telling till, down in Deep Hell, they cannot be interested in God at all but only in what they say about Him."[18] Small wonder, then, that in the Ten Commandments, God's injunction against graven images follows immediately after the prohibition of idolatry.

Sin's distortions should not prevent Christians from living out their artistic vocations, but it is critical that they consider the nature and extent of the effects of sin on the arts, and then go on to live a free, joyful, and faithful artistic life in response to God's love in Christ. In "The Freedom of a Christian," Luther suggests that,

> as our heavenly Father has in Christ freely come to our aid, we also ought freely to help our neighbor through our body and its works, and each one should become as it were a Christ to the other that we may be Christs to one another and Christ may be the same in all, that is, that we may be truly Christians.[19]

Such artists create the art they are called to make for the audiences they are connected with and, in doing so, joyfully serve God by serving their neighbor. For Christians living out a vocation in the arts, this entails creating art works based on the biblical understanding of the nature and purpose of the arts described above, coupled with the awareness that human understandings of God's Word and world are, by their very nature, imperfect and limited and therefore prone to both error and correction.

A common error Christians make regarding the arts is to confuse artistic expression (particularly in theatre and literature) with rhetorical communication, which tends to lead down the path of valuing works of art only

---

[18] C. S. Lewis, *The Great Divorce* (New York: Harper Collins, 1946), 85. Reprinted by permission of The C. S. Lewis Company Ltd., Copyright © C. S. Lewis Pte. Ltd. 1946.

[19] Luther, "The Freedom of a Christian," in AE 31:367–68.

insofar as they communicate a particular meaning or message. Art is a form of expression and therefore communicative, but it does not function—and should not be judged—in the same manner as rhetorical communication. Signal-to-noise ratio is important in rhetorical communication—was the message communicated clearly, with a minimum of interference?—but it is not nearly as important in poetic expression. Ambiguity, allusion, symbolism, evocation of multiple meanings—all these are inherent parts of artistic expression, not flaws in a communication system. Christians occasionally regard such art as failed, or perhaps even sinful, when they may in fact be missing key elements expressed in the art work or attempting to hold it to a standard not articulated in Scripture, thereby confusing aesthetics with, say, morality.

A critical question for all artists (whether or not they are Christians), and one that nearly all artists will agree has value, is: Does my art work express or reveal truth? Is it, in some way, an expression of things I understand to be true about the world and the way it works? Note that "what is true" is not necessarily the same as "what is nice," "what is pleasant," "what is realistic," or "what is inoffensive." It is critical that we not confuse our own cultural perceptions regarding artistic styles, or even the sources of particular art works, with our perceptions of the truthfulness of those works. In Acts 17, the apostle Paul speaks to some philosophers in Athens and mentions that in their city, he has seen a number of altars, including one "to the unknown god." Rather than excoriating the Athenians for their failure to honor the God of Abraham, Isaac, and Jacob, Paul seizes upon this altar as an opportunity to describe the unknown God to them. In doing so, he quotes their own poets back to them as evidence that all people are the offspring of God, then proceeds to share the Gospel with them. Paul takes truth where he finds it and builds a rhetorical argument upon it. Christians in the arts can certainly do the same. It is also worth noting Paul's famous exhortation to the Philippians: "[W]hatever is true, whatever is honorable, whatever is just, whatever is pure, whatever is lovely, whatever is commendable, if there is any excellence, if there is anything worthy of praise, think about these things" (Phil 4:8). Paul calls God's people to think about things that are pure, lovely, commendable and just—but before all these things, he points them to "whatever is true." Truth is not always pleasant; sometimes it is very uncomfortable indeed, as both Pilate during the trial of Christ and Sophocles' fictional Oedipus discover to their dismay.

Lutherans point out that the two principle doctrines of Scripture are the Law and the Gospel. Both are described as beautiful in the Bible, but both also include difficult and unpleasant elements.[20] When the Law shows human beings their sinful condition, the sight is not a pretty one. The Gospel, for all the beauty of its message of God's unconditional love and forgiveness, reminds us that divine mercy comes as a result of blood sacrifice—God's own Son, offered up to horrific suffering and crucifixion for our salvation. Some of the more disturbing images in religious art, literature, and drama depict precisely these events. Sometimes telling one's neighbor the truth is a very disturbing and unpleasant experience. But Christians are called to speak the truth (especially, perhaps, the difficult truth) in love. Christians whose vocations lie in the arts are called to do the same. They may, in fact, be called to speak difficult truths in the face of criticism or opposition. Despite such hostility, both the Old and New Testaments (e.g., Ezek 3:18–20; Acts 18:6) suggest that those who do not warn the wicked of their impending destruction may be held accountable for their failure to speak.

THE VOCATION OF THE THEATRE ARTIST: ENACTING STORY

Unique Aspects of Theatre

As I seek to apply these principles to the vocation of creating art in a specific art form—theatre—I find it important to begin by acknowledging several unique aspects of that form:

1. Theatre involves conflict expressed through story. As American actor James Earl Jones once put it, "Drama is about people in trouble."[21] Tension and struggle, disagreement and hostility are inevitably part of such stories. The enactment of such stories inevitably involves matters of morality and ethics, good and evil, commendable and reprehensible behavior. These elements are necessary to effective story-telling; a paper villain or a thin conflict make for weak drama. Dressing up an event with sets, lighting, and costumes may make it theatrical, but that does not make it theatre.

2. Theatre is a time-based art form that includes (as Aristotle noted in *Poetics*) a beginning, a middle, and an ending. A work of visual art can be perceived in its entirety with a single look, though many paintings and sculptures reward long and careful visual study. By contrast, theatre (like music) unfolds over time, and the audience

---

[20] For an example of this beauty, see the discussion of Ps 1 in Ashmon's chapter.

[21] James Earl Jones and Penelope Niven, *Voices and Silences* (Pompton Plains, NJ: Limelight, 1993), 227.

member who misses the start or the end may miss critical parts of the work. In fact, since many plays incorporate reversal and climax into their dramatic structure, the last few minutes may require the audience to alter completely its understanding of everything that has come before. M. Night Shyamalan's film *The Sixth Sense* provides an obvious example. As an audience member at a live event, I cannot skip ahead to the final scene, nor can I go back and review an earlier one; I go on a journey with the actors. Furthermore, the conventions of live theatrical performance dictate a maximum length to the event. Victor Hugo's *Les Misérables* may run to a thousand pages in novel form, but the musical needs to clock in somewhere between two and three hours. The novelist may linger over detail and narrative description; the theatre artist must structure an event of manageable length for both performers and audience, or break the story into shorter parts. For instance, David Edgar's eight-hour stage adaptation of Dickens' *Nicholas Nickleby* is typically performed over two consecutive days, or as a matinee separated by a dinner break from an evening performance. Such time limitations raise the question, "How much of a given story can be depicted? How can one best structure the story, given the amount of time available and the need to attract and retain the audience's attention throughout?"

3. Theatre is collaborative. It involves a number of artists working together, both in preparing and giving the performance. Moreover, these artists often do very different kinds of work from one another. The actor's performance is shaped by the director, but both make creative contributions, and each is very different from the work of those who design the set, lighting, costumes, makeup, properties, and sound. The actors' performances are affected by the costumes they wear, just as the costume designer's choices are affected by the body types and movement patterns of the actors, not just by the script and the director's production concept. Even a one-person show typically involves dozens of people in its preparation and performance.

4. Theatre is interpretive, consisting of a series of acts of interpretation that are sequential, but also mutually influencing. The playwright chooses to write about a specific subject and set of characters. The director typically chooses the playwright's script and develops an overall concept to guide her specific production, casting actors who fit that concept. The actors collaborate with the director and each other in interpreting not only their roles, but the

text as a whole. In some forms of theatre (e.g., improvisation or development of new plays), the actors help create or revise the text. The designers work with the director to develop a look and sound for the entire production that is consistent with all the other interpretive acts. Technicians interpret the designers' blueprints and plans as they build sets, prepare lighting, construct costumes, and build sound cues. Finally, the cast, the stage manager, and the running crew bring the sum total of these interpretive choices before an audience, whose members commit their own acts of interpretation—collectively and individually—as they view the production and respond to it, both during and after the performance. Most of the interpretive work has been hashed out before the first performance begins. The audience sees the result of the artists' collaborative interpretation, but not the process that led to that result.

5. Theatre is incarnational, requiring the physical presence of the actors, unlike the visual arts and printed literature, which result in tangible art objects that exist independent of their creators. Film and television require the image (though not the presence) of the performers, which may be heavily manipulated, but they still involve the actors' body, voice, intellect, and emotions. I do not mean to equate the incarnational quality of theatre with the incarnation of Jesus Christ, in which "the Word became flesh and dwelt among us" (John 1:14). However, in *Theater and Incarnation,* Max Harris argues that applying an incarnational hermeneutic to the process of turning script into performance, and applying a theatrical hermeneutic to Christ's Incarnation, sheds additional light on both. Harris points out that

> a play script is much less precise than an architectural blueprint, serving more to suggest possible performances than to delineate a single option. . . . [T]he nature of a particular performance will be shaped as much by the interests and outlook of the players and of the audience for which it is performed as it will be by the text.[22]

The performers incarnate or "enflesh" the text as they assume the play's roles, moving through spaces in light and shadow, wearing clothing, and handling objects selected and prepared by designers, perhaps accompanied by sound and music. Theatre alone of all art forms has the potential to engage all five senses; it

---

[22] Max Harris, *Theater and Incarnation* (Grand Rapids: Eerdmans, 1990), 14.

also engages our kinesthetic sense as we watch actors move through space and respond to the presence and movement of their bodies. A script can best be understood as an instruction manual for performing that play; it includes the words to be spoken by the actors, together with some information describing movement, emotion, and characterization. The play is not fully realized, however, until it is performed—until it becomes, in the words of my friend Ron Reed, a director and playwright, "a story that gets up and walks around." The subtext of a given scene or moment is created through a combination of scripted dialogue, movement, the actors' physical presences and delivery of their lines, and the overall look and sound of the play at that point. The actors' bodies thus play a critical role in "incarnating" the script.

Harris also points out that the Bible is a record of God's actions in human history, and as such it consists largely of written transcripts of texts meant to be spoken and/or sung, as well as narrative descriptions of historical events that were enacted. He argues that this has profound implications: "Christians who pay attention only to the medium of the written word and resist imaginative reconstruction of the very palpable events to which it claims to bear witness will miss much of the fully sensual and even theatrical nature of God's self-revelation."[23]

God chose to enter human history in the form of the Incarnate Christ, a living human being, and we would do well to consider, reconstruct, and perhaps even perform imaginative imitations of his presence. In this light, the medieval church's development of mystery plays depicting everything from the creation of the world through the life of Christ and on to the final judgment become compelling attempts to understand the full impact of the Incarnation through theatrical enactment.

6. Theatre is live, involving the physical presence of performers and audience in the same space in real time and in three dimensions. It has the potential for great power and immediacy of impact, as well as for unpredictability through improvisation, accident, or surprise. One of my most vivid theatrical memories is from a 1986 performance by a South African theatre troupe, in which the performers left the stage and walked down into the audience. I was sitting in an aisle seat. One of the actors stopped and looked at me, came and stood over me, and talked directly to me individually

---

[23] Harris, *Theater and Incarnation*, 7.

while drops of his perspiration landed on me. For me as a Cauca-
sian American audience member, listening to a black South
African describe his people's experiences under apartheid (which
was still the law of the land at that time), the surprise and immediacy of this experience gave it a profound impact.

7.   Theatre is an amalgamation of the arts. It involves writing, oral
performance in both epic and lyric styles, singing, instrumental
music, dance, painting, sculpture, textile work, and (frequently
today) use of electronic technology related to sound, light, and/or
movement. We tend to think of theatre as primarily about acting,
and the actors undoubtedly serve as the primary conduit for the
audience's experience of the play. But these other arts, and the artists who create them, also affect that experience.

I find, then, that my vocation as a theatre artist—primarily, these days, as a
director, the person most responsible for choosing a play and shaping its
production—is shaped by the biblical and theatrical principles I have described thus far.

The Interaction of Principles, Production, and Performance
in Theatre

A major part of my job involves selecting for production a script that I
understand to be worth everyone's time and energy—the months of preparation by director, designers, cast and crew, plus the time and money
invested by the audience members who come to the performance. I believe
that I am called to choose plays that depict the human condition truthfully.
Such plays may be comedies or tragedies or something in between. They
may or may not address religious issues directly, though I would argue that,
in the same sense that all plays are political because they presuppose a political order (or lack thereof), so also all plays are religious because they
presuppose a worldview that reflects the presence or absence of God. As
director, I seek plays that I understand to depict the nature of God in the
world in a truthful manner, acknowledging that elements of Law and Gospel, sin and grace, and the fallen and redeemed human condition may appear in the script and production in varying proportions. Choosing a play
is, for me, less a matter of finding something entertaining and appealing
that would receive a G or PG rating if it were a film, and more a matter of
finding a script that speaks powerfully to me and my artistic collaborators.
The same approach applies when working with Scripture; it also contains
scripts that are not "safe for the whole family," to borrow an advertising
slogan adopted by a Christian radio station in California. Mel Gibson's *The
Passion of the Christ,* which hewed fairly closely to the New Testament

accounts of Jesus' suffering and death, deserved its R rating, and if other parts of the Bible were filmed, they might earn a similar or worse rating.[24]

Selecting plays also involves choosing scripts that can speak powerfully to the audiences I am in a position to serve. All theatre is produced in a specific context, as part of a particular art world. I may not know every audience member personally, but I am called to an awareness of venue and register. I am called to serve the groups of people who come, or are likely to come, to the theatre settings in which I work. Many plays are what Calvin Seerveld calls "incapsulated events;" that is, they do not stand alone as theatrical performances, but function as part of a larger event or environment.[25] Most short plays performed in worship services fit this description, and it is precisely for this reason that choosing the right five-minute sketch for a church service can be trickier than choosing a full-length play for a professional theatre season. Plays produced in educational settings, including both public and private universities, also function as "incapsulated events." Much of the audience that attends plays at my university comes because they are associated with the university, and they bring with them various (and often widely differing) expectations based on that association. I am a foolish director, or at least a poorly trained one, if I neglect to take these audience dimensions into account. More importantly, I am called to serve this multi-faceted audience through what I choose to direct and how I choose to direct it. I may seek to serve them by celebrating with them, by entertaining or instructing them, reminding them of shared history or experiences, or by engaging them with social or cultural criticism. Through such artistic choices, I have the opportunity to share Law and/or Gospel with them as I lead an artistic ensemble that seeks to live out our vocations in God's two kingdoms, serving the neighbors who form our audience. What I dare not do is choose plays as though the audience did not matter.

Once the play is selected, I am called as a theatre artist to be a faithful collaborator in the artistic community in which I currently work, for whatever length of time I work there. American theatre today is particularly transitory in nature. Typically a cast and crew are assembled for a particular project, then disbanded once the play closes. This is true on Broadway, but it is also largely true in regional professional theatre, community theatre,

---

[24] See, among other examples, Noah's drunkenness and nakedness (Gen 9), Lot's incest with his daughters (Gen 19), the rape and dismemberment of the Levite's concubine (Judg 19–20), and the text of the Song of Songs.

[25] Calvin G. Seerveld, "God's Gift of Theatre in Our Hands" (paper presented at the annual conference of Christians in Theatre Arts, Chicago, IL, June, 1996), 12–14.

and educational theatre. In the latter setting, and in some church settings, a relatively stable community of theatre artists serves as the nucleus of each cast and crew, and they may work together on a series of productions over the course of a year or more. But even in such situations, individuals come and go with each production. Contrast this with a university choir or instrumental ensemble, whose membership may remain unchanged for a full year, and the *ad hoc* nature of modern American theatrical production becomes more readily apparent. Christians working in the arts can and should bring some important ideas about community-forming and mutual service into the collaborative process, whether or not they are working with fellow believers. I have met many directors and actors who value developing a strong sense of ensemble when doing theatre. As a director who values ensemble, I often share with my casts and crews these words from the apostle Paul: "Do nothing from rivalry or conceit, but in humility count others more significant than yourselves. Let each of you look not only to his own interests, but also to the interests of others" (Phil 2:3–4).

Actors are faced with ethical choices and challenges unique to their art and craft, due partly to the demands of portraying specific characters, and due partly to the nature of theatre as a conflict-based art form.[26] Artists and audiences will sometimes need to cope with unsavory and difficult subject matter onstage, if plays and actors are doing their jobs as "the abstract and brief chronicles of the time."[27] This includes depiction of various kinds of sinful behavior. Ironically, audiences are frequently least comfortable with depiction of sin that is difficult to distinguish from the actual sin itself (e.g., profanity and sexuality). An actor playing a character who commits murder

---

[26] In my experience, most Americans have little idea of how actors actually create characters and prepare for performances. Most popular depictions of the creative process simply perpetuate stereotypes of last-minute or spontaneous artistic inspiration and obscure the process further. (Most episodes of *Glee* illustrate this point.) High-quality preparation for theatrical performance involves grinding hours of rehearsal and repetition, singly and together, under the supervision of skilled leadership, in order to create the illusion of spontaneous, natural performance. In music, dance, and sport, the audience at least tends to watch the final event and marvel at the performers' virtuosity. By contrast, since realism continues to dominate the American stage, the theatre audience sometimes sees actors doing things that look like everyday behavior and may think, "They're just walking and talking. That's easy; anyone can do that." The reality is vastly different; well-trained actors spend hours analyzing their characters, practicing specific physical, vocal, emotional, and performance skills required to create convincing depictions of their roles, and coordinating their performances with the work of other actors and crew members.

[27] William Shakespeare, *Hamlet*, ed. Willard Farnham (New York: Penguin, 1970), 2.2.481–82.

onstage rarely hears moral objections to such behavior since performers and audience are well aware that the murder is illusory. On the other hand, an actor playing a character who uses profane and blasphemous language onstage may well hear objections voiced by well-meaning Christian friends—after all, she spoke words that, spoken by someone else in an everyday context, would in fact be blasphemous, profane, or offensive. Making the point that the character is swearing, not the actor, may not satisfy those easily offended by profane language and themes. Similar points of discomfort may arise regarding display of the body and physical intimacy onstage. Again, the actor may argue that this behavior is that of the character as written by the playwright, but a stage kiss looks very much like a real kiss, and in either case, two pairs of lips are meeting. The actor is simultaneously "me" and "not-me" onstage—undeniably present physically, yet engaging in behaviors dictated at least in part by his role and his interpretation of it, not solely the result of personal choice.

This last distinction is important. Done right, acting is imaginatively depicting a fictional character, not becoming another person. Many of the negative reactions of some Christians to the theatre can be traced back to this point. But it is important to remember here that Christianity does not teach that the body is inherently evil—it was created "very good" before the fall. As such, sins of the flesh do not deserve some special, worse category. Sin is sin, the Bible indicates, and no sin (save the sin against the Holy Spirit) is potentially more or less damning than another. Some sins (e.g., murder) have far greater temporal consequences than others (e.g., petty theft), but in the Sermon on the Mount, Jesus goes to great lengths to point out the spiritual consequences of sins that may seem minor to some. Most importantly, all sin is covered by Christ's atoning sacrifice, and all repentant sinners receive God's forgiveness and mercy. It is important in general for Christians to disentangle biblical teaching about the body from Puritan discomfort regarding dance, movement, and sexuality. Clearer understandings in this area may also reduce Christians' squeamishness regarding onstage depiction of various behaviors—both those that depict sin, and those that do not, but may make us nervous anyway. Again, the Motion Picture Association of America (MPAA) rating a play would receive if it were a film may be less significant than its overall expressive impact for an audience.

As I have argued above, Christians have been granted the freedom to follow their artistic calling where it leads, bearing in mind that a joyful response to the Gospel involves loving service to their neighbor through artistic expression as well as through other means. An important theological concept here is that of *adiaphora*—things about which Scripture is silent, and which may therefore be morally neutral.[28] Beyond some general principles, Scripture may not speak directly to any of the choices I make regarding playscript, colors in the design palette, theatrical style, or cast and crew members. In these situations, I follow the example of Luther, who (as one scholar put it) "was inclined to allow anything not condemned by the Bible."[29]

This approach does acknowledge that Christians exercise such freedoms in the context of community and culture. For example, in 1 Cor 8 and 9, the apostle Paul addresses a local disagreement—whether church members in Corinth are free to eat meat offered to pagan idols—and points out that while eating such meat is not a sin, a larger issue is at stake: concern for fellow believers whose faith may be weakened by seeing such an action. Paul writes, "Food will not commend us to God. We are no worse off if we do not eat, and no better off if we do. But take care that this right of yours does not somehow become a stumbling block to the weak" (1 Cor 8:8–9). As a Christian, I have tremendous freedom under the Gospel; I also have a desire and a calling to use that freedom to serve others (rather than my personal satisfaction or aggrandizement), particularly if my free expression might weaken the faith of others. I am called to use my artistic gifts creatively, to express truths about God's Word and God's world, in ways that engage and enlighten my neighbor. Paul concludes his discussion of giving and taking offense with the following:

> For though I am free from all, I have made myself a servant to all, that I might win more of them. . . . To the weak I became weak, that I might win the weak. I have become all things to all people, that by all means I might save some. I do it all for the sake of the gospel, that I may share with them in its blessings. (1 Cor 9:19, 22–23)

CONCLUSION

Regardless of the details of any particular production and the accompanying artistic process, my vocation as a theatre artist calls for me to love and serve my neighbors in the cast, crew, and production team. I frequently tell my theatre students that for me as a Christian, *how* I do theatre is just as important—or perhaps more important—than *what* I do in the way of

---

[28] For a discussion of *adiaphora*, see Steven P. Mueller, ed., *Called to Believe, Teach, and Confess: An Introduction to Doctrinal Theology* (Eugene, OR: Wipf and Stock, 2005), 72–73, 163–64.

[29] Leslie P. Spelman, "Luther and the Arts," *The Journal of Aesthetics and Art Criticism* 10, no. 2 (1951): 166.

theatre. If I am directing the play, typically I serve by leading the production process. If I am a designer, technician, or actor, I am called to serve as part of an ensemble engaged in a challenging task, usually short of time and financial resources. In any of these roles, I am called to bring my skills, knowledge, and expertise to contribute to the production process. I am also called to treat my artistic colleagues with kindness, compassion, and respect—professionally and personally. In short, if I choose a brilliant script and direct it skillfully but have not love, "I am a noisy gong or a clanging cymbal" (1 Cor 13:1). In the making of art, as in the living of my daily life, I am called to be a servant, and I find it helpful to recall Jesus' words about servanthood: "If anyone would be first, he must be last of all and servant of all" (Mark 9:35).

QUESTIONS

1. Based on the principles outlined in this chapter, how would you go about choosing a season of plays for a theatre in your university or your community? Which principles and elements do you find most critical in shaping such decisions? Why?

2. Some Christians have made much of the fact that the New Testament describes far fewer instances and kinds of artistic activity than does the Old Testament. Does this represent a shift in the role of the arts among God's people? Why or why not?

3. This chapter contrasts rhetorical communication with artistic expression. To what extent should works of art be judged on communication of content? Are such judgments moral, aesthetic, or both? What is the relationship of artistic form to content in such matters?

4. What are the implications of Christ's Incarnation for an understanding of theatrical performance? What are the implications for acting in particular?

5. In your view, what role (if any) might theatre play in the worship life of congregations with which you are familiar? Which kinds of theatrical performance might be considered beneficial and appropriate, and why?

PART FOUR

UNIVERSITY LIFE
IN A LUTHERAN CONTEXT

14

FROM CHURCH TO CAMPUS TO WORLD:
LUTHERAN THEOLOGY AND CAMPUS MINISTRY

Jonathan Ruehs[1]

INTRODUCTION

*"I make bold to ask you whether strong belief in [evolution] is
compatible with belief in God, or whether one has only the choice
between your theory and belief in God, or whether those who believe
in your theory can and should also believe in God as well?"[2]*

—*W. Mengden*

The above quote comes from a letter written in 1879 by an angst-ridden
young man to the aging naturalist Charles Darwin. Although the letter was
written over 125 years ago, a similar struggle of faith faces many college-age
students today. James Fowler, who is known the world over for his work on
faith development, describes this particular stage as a time when a person
"must undergo a sometimes painful disruption of their deeply held but
unexamined world view or belief system."[3] Current social science research
probes why this faith stage contains moments of "painful disruption" for
today's college student. In his research, Christian Smith notes that "the
transition to adulthood today is more complex, disjointed, and confusing
than in past decades."[4]

Cultural conditions certainly have evolved or devolved, depending how
you look at it, since the days of Mengden. We no longer live in a world of

---

[1] Jonathan Ruehs, MA (Biola), is Residential Coordinator of Spiritual Life at CUI.

[2] Quoted in Stanley L. Jaki, *The Savior of Science* (Grand Rapids: Eerdmans, 2000), 4.

[3] James W. Fowler, *Faith Development and Pastoral Care* (Philadelphia: Fortress, 1987), 68.

[4] Christian Smith and Patricia Snell, *Souls in Transition: The Religious and Spiritual Lives of Emerging Adults*, (New York: Oxford University Press, 2009), 6.

"epistemological certitude" where people believe that the world they see around them can be completely verified with human reasoning and/or scientific empiricism. The epistemological center or starting point has shifted from certitude to doubt.[5] The world doubts the ability of reason to bring satisfactory answers or the ability of scientific investigation to solve all the mysteries of the universe. Long gone are the days when it was believed that the Milky Way was the center of the universe. With the advent of Einstein and others, our "eyes have been opened" to the vastness of the universe, which leaves us to wonder where the center might be or if there is a center.

As many cultural commentators have proclaimed, we live in a time when modernism has been replaced by postmodernism, a postmortem philosophy that declares that the "Age of Reason" is dead. Its probable founding prophet, the late nineteenth-century German philosopher, Frederick Nietzsche, also sang a similar dirge against religion with his declaration that "God is dead," therein adding another "post"—that of "post-Christian"—to the cultural malaise.[6] The medieval world built the church at the center of the town, village, and city to communicate that God was to be at the center of civilization.[7] Amidst the sprawling and crawling metropolises of today one finds street after street filled with synagogues, mosques, and store front churches, which leaves one to wonder who is God and whether any one religion can rightfully claim to have the ultimate answer to that question.

This is the culture from which today's young adults are emerging. While they might face a time, in the words of Christian Smith, of "unparalleled freedom," they are drowning in a sea of choice.[8] Burger King's motto, "Have it your way," no longer just applies to hamburgers, but to religion and morality too.

Today's Lutheran liberal arts university should be a beacon of light in this cacophonic sea. Other Christian universities might seek to steer people safely through the tumultuous sea by requiring all students to sign a statement of faith. Typically Lutheran universities do not require this, even if they proclaim themselves to be a confessional-based university.

---

[5] Matthew Lee Anderson, *The End of Our Exploring: A Book about Questioning and the Confidence of Faith* (Chicago: Moody, 2013), 47ff.

[6] For argumentation that Nietzsche was the premier postmodern prophet, see Stanley J. Grenz, *A Primer on Postmodernism* (Grand Rapids: Eerdmans, 1996), 88–98. For the Nietzsche quote see, Friedrich Nietzsche, *Thus Spoke Zarathustra*, trans. Graham Parkes (Oxford: Oxford University Press, 2008), 11.

[7] James. K. A. Smith, *Desiring the Kingdom: Worship, Worldview, and Cultural Formation* (Grand Rapids: Baker Academic, 2009), 113.

[8] Smith and Snell, *Souls in Transition*, 6.

At first glance, the practice of not requiring incoming students to sign a confession of faith seems only to contribute to the sinking of the university into the postmodern deluge resulting in the loss of identity. Yet Lutheran universities do not require a faith statement because their two-kingdom theology makes it clear that a Lutheran campus is not a church.[9] The Lutheran campus exists primarily as an educational entity, an entity grounded and rooted in the Scriptures, the ecumenical creeds, and the Confessions, but an educational entity located in God's left-hand kingdom of society, not God's right-hand kingdom of the church. While it may be a great desire of many administrators, faculty, and staff that non-believing students come to faith in the salvation found in Christ Jesus at college, it is not a graduation requirement that students tick the box "Christian" when they leave.

This means that Lutheran universities are free to accept students of all creeds. They do not require students to acquiesce, for instance, to the Apostles' Creed. In doing this, the university can still be a church-based institution with a strong Lutheran theological identity. For by welcoming the Christian, Muslim, atheist, or agnostic to study for their future vocations in life, the university is directly engaging in God's left-hand kingdom work to serve society.

Contemporary philosopher, James K. A. Smith, in quoting Pope John Paul II, argues that "the Christian university should not only be born but also nourished *ex corde ecclesiae*, 'from the heart of the church.' "[10] In short, Smith argues that Christian practices should form the core of the Christian university. In Lutheran language, this means that the church—identified in the Lutheran Confessions as the place where the Gospel is purely taught and the Sacraments are administered in "harmony with the gospel of Christ"—is also at the core of the Lutheran university.[11] But the question needs to be asked, "How is this to be accomplished if the university is not a church?" One important answer to that question is the establishment of a campus ministry.

WHAT IS MINISTRY?

Prior to understanding what constitutes campus ministry we need to have an understanding of what we mean by the term *ministry*. Francis Pieper in his book on Christian doctrine defines ministry this way:

---

[9] See Mueller's chapter for a summary of two-kingdom theology.

[10] Smith, *Desiring the Kingdom*, 221.

[11] Philip Melanchthon, "The Apology of the Augsburg Confession," in *The Book of Concord: The Confessions of the Evangelical Lutheran Church*, eds. Robert Kolb and Timothy J. Wengert (Minneapolis: Fortress, 2000), 174 (art. VII/VIII:5).

> The term "ministry" is used both in Scripture and by the Church in a general, or wider, and in a special, or narrower, sense. In the wider sense it embraces every form of preaching the Gospel or administering the means of grace, whether by Christians in general, as originally entrusted with the means of grace and commissioned to apply them, or by chosen public servants (*ministri ecclesiae*) in the name and at the command of Christians.[12]

Pieper echoes what the reformers taught in the Lutheran Confessions concerning the nature of ministry: that it is defined as focusing on the Gospel, which is delivered to people through preaching and the administration of the Sacraments. In contemporary Christendom there is much confusion regarding what constitutes ministry. From a Lutheran perspective, not any type of service can be interpreted as ministry, despite the fact that the Greek word for ministry *diakonia* can also be translated as "service."[13] Only that service connected to the Gospel can be considered ministry. So, for example, while it might be tempting for someone working in alumni relations to refer to their work as "ministry" since they work for a Christian university, it does not necessarily follow, from a Lutheran perspective, that her work is rightly understood as ministry.

A corollary to this understanding of ministry is whether everyone can rightly be called a minister. Pieper's definition might seem to indicate that if Christians, in general, engage in ministry when it deals with Gospel proclamation, then everyone must be a minister. Despite the apparent logic of this argument, we do not see Scriptural indicate this.[14] First Peter 2:9 affirms that all baptized Christians are part of the priesthood of believers. No longer do God's people need a special tribe of priests to act as intercessors on their behalf as was the case in the Old Testament. With the work of the great High Priest, Christ, all Christians—student, administrative assistant, professor, or pastor—have the same access to their Heavenly Father. In this sense all Christians are called to be priests before God, serving one another in the love of Christ. What might this look like? Imagine that Betty, who works in the education department, comes to work feeling awful. She shares with her colleague, Carol, that she had a fight with her husband that morning. Betty talks about how she said some things that she wishes that she could take back. Speaking words of comfort, Carol shares with Betty the forgiveness that she has in Christ Jesus for the sinful words that she used

---

12 Francis Pieper, *Christian Dogmatics* (St. Louis: Concordia, 1962), 3:439.

13 Steven P. Mueller, ed. *Called to Believe, Teach, and Confess: An Introduction to Doctrinal Theology* (Eugene, OR: Wipf and Stock, 2005), 408.

14 Mueller, *Called to Believe, Teach, and Confess*, 408.

with her husband, further assuring her with the words of the psalmist that her sin is removed from her "as far as the east is from the west" (Ps 103:12). This is an example of how Christians engaging in their ongoing priestly work have a direct connection to the ministry of the Gospel.

As said above, not all acts of service are acts of ministry, even though non-ministry acts of service are still good works that benefit others. For example, in a university context we can say that such tasks as helping students enroll for classes, supervising a call center, engaging in judicial affairs, serving meals in the cafeteria, teaching a philosophy class, and the like are all tasks that are very valuable to the life of the university. These tasks are all related to supporting God's left-hand kingdom work.[15] They are all God-pleasing works that service others.

In order to ensure that the work of ministry is done in a right and proper order, God has established the office of the public ministry. The office of the public ministry is the ministry done publicly on behalf of a church, primarily by a pastor. The pastor, from a biblical and confessional Lutheran perspective, is a man, a fellow priest, who has been called by a congregation to publically serve God's people.[16] The public ministry to which the pastor is called is the proclamation of the Gospel and administration of the Sacraments of Baptism, Absolution, and the Lord's Supper as a servant of God's Word to the church. In this sense public ministry can also be referred to as pastoral ministry, which is the narrow sense of ministry as defined above.

The public ministry of the church can be a daunting task, so in order to help with the large task of ministry the church has established other ministry roles. In the Lutheran Church, roles such as Directors of Christian Education (DCEs), Directors of Parish Music (DPMs), deaconesses, called teachers, and Directors of Christian Outreach (DCOs) are examples of auxiliary offices that help, under the leadership of the pastor, in the task of ministry to the church. While these auxiliary roles have limitations in the way they engage in ministry, the work they do is vital. These auxiliary roles illustrate the giftedness of different ministers for engaging the work of public ministry.

CAMPUS MINISTRY

One of the biggest challenges to understanding or defining ministry in a Lutheran university context is that the public ministry is not done in a

---

[15] For further understanding regarding left- and right-hand kingdoms, see Mueller's chapter.

[16] Mueller, *Called to Believe, Teach, and Confess*, 408.

congregational setting. What does it mean, then, for a Lutheran university not to have a campus church, but desire to call a pastor and other auxiliary offices to engage in the task of public ministry? For the Lutheran Confessions state, "For wherever the church exists, there also is the right to administer the Gospel. Therefore, it is necessary for the church to retain the right to call, choose, and ordain ministers."[17] How then is public ministry on a Lutheran campus legitimate without the presence of a congregation?

The way that one Lutheran church body, The Lutheran Church—Missouri Synod (LCMS), has worked out answers to these questions is to require that the campus ministry be sponsored by a local congregation. In this respect the campus ministry works on behalf of the church at large as well as rooting it in a nearby parish, which is why campus ministry can be seen as a continuation of the Lutheran ministry that a student will receive regardless if her church is in California, Wisconsin, or Japan. In other words, the Word and Sacrament ministry she received in her own home church is, in a sense, the same Word and Sacrament ministry she will receive on campus. Although that ministry might look different, based upon context, it is rooted in the same Lutheran theological identity. It is in this sense that campus ministry can be viewed as working on behalf of the church at large. Rooting the ministry in a local church helps to maintain the understanding that public ministry is primarily done in and through local parishes.

In the midst of postmodern doubts that assail the Christian faith, some theologians suggest that we should return to using the ancient image of the church as an ark, a place of safety in the deluge.[18] This image can also be useful for campus ministry working with emerging adults. As students deal with this time of transition and wrestle with new ideas and new experiences, they can find a safe place in campus ministry to weather the storms. They can find a firm foundation, not based on doubt or the certitude of reason or empirical thinking, but on the solid rock that is Christ Jesus (Matt 7:24-25), the "Word made flesh" and revealed to us in God's Word (John 1:14).

---

[17] Philip Melanchthon, "Treatise on the Power and Primacy of the Pope," in *The Book of Concord: The Confessions of the Evangelical Lutheran Church*, eds. Robert Kolb and Timothy J. Wengert (Minneapolis: Fortress, 2000), 340–41 (sect. 67).

[18] See, for instance, Leonard Sweet, *Aqua Church 2.0: Piloting Your Church in Today's Fluid Culture* (2nd ed.; Colorado Springs: David C. Cook, 2008), 32. Concerning the ancient image of the church as ark, see Rudolph F. Norden, *Symbols and Their Meaning*, (St. Louis: Concordia, 1985), 51.

THE WORD

Lutherans believe that God's Word centers on the person and work of Christ Jesus. This is graphically stated by what Martin Luther reportedly said: "Wherever you cut the Bible it bleeds the blood of Christ."[19] What this means is that the verses of Scripture, from Genesis to Revelation, course with the message of Christ and the Gospel of salvation. The Bible might be similar to other books in that it has paper, ink, and is bound, but it differs in that it is God-breathed and makes us "wise for salvation through faith in Christ Jesus" (2 Tim 3:15–16). It is the "blood of Christ," the Gospel, then, that should also course through preaching, teaching, witnessing, Baptism, Absolution, Communion, and worship in campus ministry.

Preaching

Given a Lutheran university's religiously diverse population, the task of preaching can be a daunting one. Not every ministry setting, especially chapel, is attended by Christians alone. Add to this mix the fact that chapel tends to be a key location where the entire community comes together from administration, faculty, staff, and students, and the challenge of determining one's audience when preaching in chapel becomes quite complex.

Despite this diversity, context should not be ignored in preaching. We see examples of this in the Bible. For example, the apostle Paul, in the book of Acts, engaged audiences differently depending upon if they were Jewish (having a biblical background) or Gentile (no biblical background). Yet what both types of preaching had in common was evangelistic proclamation. The central goal of preaching to a non-Christian audience was the proclamation of the Gospel. Sermons to a Christian congregation taught believers how God's Word applied to contemporary situations in their lives.[20] Here, too, the Gospel was at the core of preaching since the Gospel forms the hub of the whole Christian life.

---

[19] This statement is, so far as I can determine, unattested. It is, however, wholly in keeping with the Christ-centered view Luther had of Scripture: "What purpose other than proclamation does Scripture have from beginning to end? Messiah, God's Son, was to come and through his sacrifice, as an innocent Lamb of God, bear and remove the sins of the world and thus redeem men from eternal death for eternal salvation. For the sake of Messiah and God's Son Holy Scripture was written" (quoted, with attestation, in Ewald M. Plass, ed., *What Luther Says: A Practical In-Home Anthology for the Active Christian* [St. Louis: Concordia, 1959], §204).

[20] These insights come from an unpublished essay by Mike Middendorf titled, "Preaching and Teaching in the New Testament."

In designing a weekly chapel message series, then, the campus pastor should consider the audience attending chapel. If a chapel time is made up primarily of Christians, then it is important to preach messages that apply God's Word to the university setting. In other words, what does it mean to be a Christian in this context? Topics, whether they flow from a topical series or arise from the lectionary, could consider such themes as: "How might love of mind replace love of God?"; "What does it mean to love your neighbor in a residential hall situation?"; "How can we live faithful lives in all of our vocations as student, professor, staff, spouse, child, etc.?" Because college tends to be a time when faith questions crop up, chapel messages should also address perennial issues like suffering, doubt, and the goodness of God.

If a particular chapel time tends to draw larger crowds of non-believers, then the pastor should seek to avoid using "insider" language, phrases, or images that are largely common to Christians (e.g., justification, atonement, etc.). Instead, the pastor should create a message that communicates the Gospel in terms that might be more broadly understood. It is important, therefore, for the pastor to be a student of the university's culture and the broader culture around the university. By listening to the language of those in his midst, by paying attention to the images all around him (in all the various forms of mass media) the pastor is able to find words and pictures that can communicate the unchanging Gospel message to an ever-changing culture.

Teaching

A church setting is a common place to find Bible studies. In a typical church there are usually Sunday morning and mid-week Bible studies that are generation or gender specific. Given the hectic schedule of a typical college student, limiting Bible studies to one particular type or one particular time is unhelpful. Yet, it is important that a campus ministry consider establishing a small group ministry that is gender specific. These Bible studies provide a safe time and place for young men and women to talk about sensitive issues surrounding their gender. For example, given the proliferation of problems related to internet pornography, which is unfortunately a typical struggle for men, having a group of emerging adult men gather for a time of Gospel-focused study and prayer can foster an environment of grace-based support.

But it is also important for emerging adult men and women to gather together for Bible study and prayer. While a larger group study would not typically be a comfortable environment for individuals to share their specific struggles, it is important for men and women to learn with and from one another on topics that impact them all. For example, issues like gender roles, sexuality, marriage, vocations, spiritual warfare, and doubts should be explored together as well as a host of other topics that have a direct impact upon young men and women.[21]

Catechesis should also be present at a Lutheran university. Catechesis is a specific type of teaching oriented around the fundamentals or basics of the Christian faith. In fact, when it comes to teaching, one of the most commonly used books in Lutheran churches, next to the Bible, is Martin Luther's Small Catechism. The Small Catechism is a helpful tool that instructs a person in the Ten Commandments, the Apostles' Creed, the Lord's Prayer, on Confession/Absolution, Baptism, and Holy Communion. The simple question and answer format is an often overlooked, but powerful, tool of repetition designed to help a student absorb the content in a simple way. Yet, catechesis is not meant to be regurgitation; rather, it is a way to "think God's thoughts after him" so as to ponder the Christian faith more deeply and its application to life today.[22]

Although core Christian truths, or doctrines, are covered in general education theology classes that students are (typically) required to take at a Lutheran university, these theology classes, while teaching right-hand kingdom beliefs, occur in a left-hand kingdom context of deadlines, tests, and grades. This is why it is important to establish opportunities for catechesis to occur on campus in non-academic settings. It is in these settings, whether intimate gatherings or large inquiry-based experiences, where students are free to ask and dialogue over questions that they may not be comfortable asking or have the time to wrestle with in a classroom setting. In this respect, catechetical teaching may look a bit more free form, using Luther's catechism as a means to absorb the information, but then coming together in community to meditate on what it means for the Christian life. The focus of catechesis in this setting functions in four ways: (1) as an opportunity for new Christians to learn more about the basics of the Christian faith, (2) to provide a chance for non-believers, who have an interest in Christianity, to learn more about the faith, (3) for interested non-Lutheran Christian students to explore more of the Lutheran teaching of the Christian faith—especially if they desire to become members of a Lutheran

---

[21] Marva Dawn speaks to this when she says that the church needs to help young men and women learn how to support one another in their "social sexuality" (all aspects of a person's identity not related to genital union) rather than seek affection and acceptance in their "genital sexuality" (Marva J. Dawn, *Sexual Character: Beyond Technique to Intimacy* [Grand Rapids: Eerdmans, 1993], 11).

[22] Anderson, *The End of Our Exploring*, 78–79.

church, and (4) for Lutheran students to deepen their faith and understanding.

Witnessing

In Acts 1:8, Jesus gives the call for his church to be witnesses of him "in Jerusalem and in all Judea and Samaria, and to the end of the earth." The early church were witnesses of Jesus because they were "eyewitnesses" of the miracles he performed, the greatest being his resurrection from the dead. What does it mean, then, for contemporary saints, removed two thousand years from the resurrection, to be witnesses of Jesus in the world? A great illustration of what it means is found in the story of the demoniac in Mark 5:1–20. After the man possessed by "legion" is set free from the power of darkness, he asks Jesus if he can go with him. Jesus tells the man in verse 20, "Go home to your friends and tell them how much the Lord has done for you, and how he has had mercy on you." While the word *witness* (*martyr* in Greek) is not referenced in this passage, we see that this man indeed engages in witnessing as "he went away and began to proclaim in the Decapolis how much Jesus had done for him."

Lutherans tend to shy away from "personal testimony" stories because these stories often tend to bring focus and glory upon the converted in place of a Christ-centered proclamation. But witnessing is really telling the story of "subjective justification," that is, how Christ has personally shown you mercy and grace through his crucifixion and resurrection. This kind of witnessing puts the focus and glory where it should be: on Christ, his cross, and empty tomb and Christ's transformation of your life.

The idea of being a witness for Christ on a Lutheran campus might sound odd at first. However, since students who attend a Lutheran university are not required to sign a faith statement, students from all walks of life are welcome on campus. Christians on campus does not need to look too far, then, to share Christ with their neighbors. Lutheran campuses with international communities even have the chance to engage in "foreign missions" in their own midst. In this respect, a Christian can engage in the "Great Commission" (Matt 28:18–20) without even leaving the campus.

Evangelistic proclamation should occur in corporate worship settings that contain a majority of non-Christians; but witnessing should also happen outside of chapel. As Christian students build relationships with the non-Christians in class, in the residential halls, in the cafeteria, and the like they will have opportunities to talk genuinely and authentically about their Christian faith. The various discipling activities available on a Lutheran campus such as chapel, small group Bible studies, and the like provide many opportunities for Christian students to connect their non-believing friends to the Christian faith on a communal level.

Christian professors and staff should also see the positive influence that they can have on students. Professors, for example, can initiate relationships with their students in and out of class and open up opportunities to develop, in the words of Michael Cartwright, "wise friendships."[23] These "wise friendships" can provide opportunities for a professor to give a Christian witness and connect their non-believing students to the Holy Scriptures that make them "wise for salvation" (2 Tim 3:15).

SACRAMENTS

What are sacraments? They are referred to as "rites, which have the command of God and to which the promise of grace has been added."[24] The two primary sacraments celebrated in the Lutheran Church are Baptism and the Lord's Supper. In both sacraments we see God's Word combined with visible elements (water, bread, and wine). A lesser understood sacrament is Absolution. Since sacraments are "commanded by God" and have the "promise of grace," the Lutheran Confessions state that this makes it "easy to determine what the sacraments are, properly speaking."[25] Why is it easy to determine? The reason is that although they are rites, they are not human in origin; they come to us solely from the hand of God.

Baptism

Baptism is a sacrament that involves a new birth. Although our world gets caught up in celebrating the physical birth of babies, in the Christian church the celebration focuses on the new birth of babies, teenagers, and adults. The baptismal new birth can happen at any age and in any circumstance. In Baptism God washes us clean of our sin by his grace and calls us as part of his family by placing his Triune name upon us. All Christians, therefore, are rightly understood as brothers and sisters in the faith because they all share the same family name: Father, Son, and Holy Spirit (Matt 28:18–20).

In a Lutheran campus community, Baptism is also an important part of Christian identity. For example, in the worship center at my institution, Concordia University Irvine, when the faithful enter through the front

---

[23] Michael G. Cartwright, "Moving beyond Muddled Missions and Misleading Metaphors: Formation and Vocation of Students within an Ecclesially Based University," in *Conflicting Allegiances: The Church-Based University in a Liberal Democratic Society,* eds. Michael L. Budde and John Wesley Wright (Grand Rapids: Brazos, 2004), 197–201.

[24] Melanchthon, "The Apology of the Augsburg Confession," 219 (art. XIII:3).

[25] Melanchthon, "The Apology of the Augsburg Confession," 219 (art. XIII:4).

doors for chapel, they first encounter the baptismal font. The placement of the font is symbolically significant, because it states to the believer that we come into the sanctuary as baptized children of God. It is here where all the various vocations—president, professor, administrative assistant, student, etc.—give way to the prime vocation of being a Christian. Here the saints of God, the priesthood of all believers, the family of Christ, gather to hear God's Word proclaimed to them in preaching and song, and respond to that Word in singing and prayer. It is equally significant that as the saints exit the sanctuary they once again pass by the baptismal font. As they, in a sense, take back up their various vocations they are reminded that whatever left-hand kingdom call they maintain their primary vocation of being a Christian is part and parcel of who they are and what they do.

Baptismal identity is also the great equalizer when it comes to social stations in life. While in the left-hand kingdom we use titles such as president, professor, director, and student, we understand from a baptismal perspective that there is a different title placed upon all of us. For example, the student might refer to his professor as "Dr. Jones," but their common baptismal identity also makes them siblings to one another. In Christ we all belong to the same bloodline and are reborn into the same royal family. Why might this be important for the Christian student to remember? For while the professor is tasked to give out grades on academic work done or not done, the Christian student needs to remember that his professor is also his brother or sister in Christ, and that God calls us to be reconciled to our brothers and sisters in the faith. The same can be said of the professor's relationship to a particular Christian student, who may or may not be holding their own in class. That student is not just another mind to be molded, but is also a fellow, reconciled sibling in Christ.

Baptismal identity is also a place where students can understand the nature of their relationship with one another. Young men and women, while obviously navigating through natural feelings of physical attraction, should not just view the opposite sex as a potential mate. Christian male and female students should view each other as siblings in Christ. Seeing each other through the "watery lens" of the font can guide students away from "eros" to "agape" (unconditional) love where they care for and are reconciled to each other as brothers and sisters in Christ.

Absolution

Talk of reconciliation brings us to Absolution. Absolution, although not containing a physical component like water, is instituted by God and called a sacrament in the Lutheran Confessions.[26] The reason for its inclusion as a sacrament is because it is a means of grace. Prior to hearing the comforting words of Absolution we first confess our sins. Confession is an act whereby we tell back to God what he has already told to us. In this case, we confess the sins that we have done—in thought, word, and deed—against others and God.[27] The comforting word of the Gospel in Absolution frees us from the burden of the Law. Absolution is the sure, complete forgiveness that the pastor announces to the church in the "stead" of Christ; it is something that we can speak to one another too.

Receiving and giving forgiveness is part of the new identity practiced in the body of Christ (John 20:23). A Christian campus rooted in the Lutheran tradition should be a place that liberally practices Absolution. In the words of Paul, "all have sinned"—from president to freshmen—"and fall short of the glory of God" (Rom 3:23). Thus, for instance, when a student confesses to her professor the sin of plagiarism, the professor has the right-hand kingdom privilege of forgiving that student—even though the left-hand kingdom penalty of a failed assignment remains the academic consequence.

Pastoral counseling is another area where Confession and Absolution can occur. Unlike the Catholic tradition, where there is the belief that a Christian must go to the priest to engage in penance, in the Lutheran tradition of the "priesthood of all believers" one can receive forgiveness from a pastor or a fellow Christian. Yet, it is a good practice for people, especially those racked with guilt over sin, to come to a pastor to confess that sin and hear the words that Christ has died "for them" and forgives them of that sin (John 20:21–23). While the declaration of forgiveness may not change temporal consequences for acts committed (e.g., plagiarism may still result in a failed grade), the forgiven believer can stand firm in their eternal forgiveness in Christ Jesus. In turn, God's grace empowers them to face whatever consequences they may face at the university concerning their sinful actions.

Christianity in American society is viewed primarily as a system of morality.[28] Given the context of Lutheran universities in America, it is no surprise that many non-Christians (and, sadly, many Christians) on those campuses hold a similar erroneous view of the Christian faith. The visible

---

[26] Melanchthon, "The Apology of the Augsburg Confession," 219 (art. XIII:4).

[27] Ultimately all sin is against God as David writes in Ps 51:4.

[28] See, for example, David Kinnaman and Gabe Lyons, *Unchristian: What a New Generation Really Thinks about Christianity . . . and Why It Matters* (Grand Rapids: Baker, 2007). This book does a good job of showing the moralistic view of Christianity that is prevalent in American society, especially among millennials.

practice of Confession and Absolution, then, seeks to eradicate the works righteous or moral merit understanding of the Christian faith. When non-believers witness Christians asking one another for forgiveness and hearing the sweet words of forgiveness being spoken in the name of Christ, it communicates the reality of the *simul iustus et peccator* ("simultaneously justified and sinful") existence of the Christian life.[29] This should help demolish the "moral" definition of Christianity and spur further dialogue concerning the Christian faith with the non-believer.

The Lord's Supper

The practice of Communion on a Lutheran campus offers its own challenges. These challenges are directly related to the Lutheran understanding of the Lord's Supper. The Lutheran faith teaches that Christ is truly present in the bread and wine. Lutherans reject a merely symbolic understanding of the meal (i.e., the bread and wine only represent Jesus' body and blood); they also reject a spiritualized view of the meal (i.e., Jesus is present in the meal through the Holy Spirit). Lutherans take seriously Jesus' words that the bread *is* his body and that the wine *is* his blood offered for the forgiveness of sins (Matt 26:26–29). Lutherans speak of Jesus' participation in the meal as his "real presence."

Since the days of the New Testament the practice of Communion has been one that was not to be entered into lightly given the nature of the meal. Paul gives a stern warning against having a cavalier attitude about Communion practices in 1 Cor 11. Given the Christian diversity on a Lutheran campus, the question naturally arises whether this is an appropriate place for this Sacrament to be offered. While the meal is an opportunity for the body of believers to gather around the body and blood of Christ, the serious nature in which the meal should be entered means engaging in a somewhat restrictive approach to the meal (the approach the early church took), based on one's agreement with what Scripture says about it. In this respect, it is probably better to connect students to local Lutheran congregations where they can participate in the meal with others who share a common confession about the Lord's Supper and thereby avoid some of the delicate issues associated with serving this sacred meal in a religiously heterogeneous setting. Yet, if there is a desire for the Lutheran campus to participate in the Lord's Supper, then it will be very important to educate people on the Lutheran understanding of Communion. Here is where catechesis will play an important role.

---

[29] See Mueller's chapter for a brief discussion of *simul iustus et peccator*.

WORSHIP

Lutherans believe that worship is centered in God coming to us in love and that we then respond to his gracious gifts. This is a contrast to some other traditions that make worship a human work of praise for God's benefit. Worship is a reflection of our theology, especially our understanding that it has always been God's movement in history to come down first to meet us sinners in grace, a movement which was fully realized in the incarnation of Jesus. This is why it is important, especially in the midst of a diverse Christian student population, to get worship right. At a Lutheran university, worship should communicate its theological and liturgical identity, which is rooted in the Gospel of Christ. To do otherwise would be to communicate something that is not true about the core of the university and, in the end, could betray the Gospel.

The chapel setting is a time for the people of God to gather together. This time should be communicated across campus as a "sacred" time when offices are closed, and colleagues and students invite one another to come and be fed with God's Word. Chapel is the primary setting on a Lutheran campus where the saints of God—from president to student—can gather together for worship. In worship the vocational distinctions of administrator, professor, student, etc. should be left behind. A way in which a campus community can honor this equality before God is for students, faculty, staff, and administration to freely mix and mingle with one another. The image of professor and student, staff and provost receiving forgiveness and then singing praises to God next to one another reflects the reality that all those gathered are children of God.

MISSIONS

Much of the focus regarding campus ministry so far has been on internal ministry needs. Since university life is a transitional life stage that prepares emerging adults to enter life on a larger scale, it is also important that they are trained to think about ministry beyond the academy. One common way that this is accomplished is through mission work done on a local or global scale. Students should spend time sharing the Gospel in both "word and deed" in the world beyond the university. Being involved in contexts outside the university helps students to experience the greater world beyond the "bubble" of the campus. What might this look like? For starters, other local public universities can provide opportunities where student-to-student witnessing can occur. Ministry outreach of this sort can also become a safe place where students can practice the art of evangelism with strangers in order to become more comfortable with witnessing to their non-Christian classmates back on campus.

Connecting students to local Lutheran churches engaged in mission work is another way to help students see that mission is—first and foremost—the work of the local church. Many churches, for instance, host a food pantry or are involved in some type of food distribution program, especially in poorer communities. While not all food distribution programs can rightly be called "missions," those that intentionally provide opportunities for the Gospel to be shared are a great example of how a local church can provide "daily bread" (Matt 6:11) for those in their community while also connecting them to the "Bread of Life," who is Christ Jesus (John 6:35). Many churches also are involved in annual short-term mission trips to ministry partners in various parts of the global. Again, connecting students to these "vetted" church mission projects helps students to see how the local church can make a difference in the international community.

MINISTRY MENTORING

Campus ministries should also be places where students—whether preparing to enter into a future in church work or some other important vocation—can play an important role in the work of the campus ministry. Since Lutherans believe strongly in the church being the "priesthood of all believers," campus ministry should provide a place for the priests to be raised up and mentored for service in the church. Students preparing for a vocation in church work should actively seek out student ministry leadership positions to round out their classroom education by participating in a ministry in a safe, mentoring environment. Students preparing for work in other vocations should also be encouraged to be involved in student ministry leadership. Training and raising up students as servants and providing a positive grace-based experience for them, shows to them that the church needs all of her priests to be involved in work for the kingdom.

CONCLUSION

"You will be my witnesses to the ends of the earth" (Acts 1:8).

The ministry that takes place on a Lutheran university campus is an extension of the larger public ministry that goes on in local congregations strewn about the globe. While the goal is to provide a ministry that is indeed contextualized to the university setting and to the ever-changing generational milieu of the college student, it is never meant to leave the student in this transitional stage. Students need to graduate and move out into the world. Transitioning from the safe environment of the university setting out into the wider world means a return back to the local church, wherever that might be. As students transition out into the world to become leaders in various fields of study, it is hoped that they will also become servants in their churches. For in the end, the goal for Lutheran campus ministry is not only to provide Gospel-centered Word and Sacrament ministry for the student, but also to play a part in forming them into Gospel-centered servants for the world and church.

QUESTIONS

1. What ministry challenges do Lutheran and other Christian universities face in today's contemporary setting?

2. In what ways does campus ministry function as the "church" on a university campus? In what ways does it differ from the "church" in this setting?

3. What does it mean for baptized Christians to be part of the family of God at a Lutheran or other Christian university? How does this understanding transform the nature of our relationships with one another in the classroom, the office, the dorm room, the chapel, etc.?

4. What challenges and opportunities does campus ministry have with students who are not on campus, e.g., commuters, adult students at extension sites, and online students?

15

TOWARD A LUTHERAN VIEW OF STUDENT AFFAIRS: DEVELOPING LEARNED PIETY IN COMMUNITY UNDER THE CROSS OF CHRIST

Scott Keith[1] and Gilbert Fugitt[2]

LUTHERAN HIGHER EDUCATION AS COMMUNITY

From inception, the goal of the Lutheran university has been to develop citizens holistically meeting their future vocations under the cross of Christ. In "In Praise of the New School," Philip Melanchthon, Martin Luther's colleague and collaborator in reform, deals with the role of education as preparing good citizens. "In the well constituted state," says Melanchthon, "the first task for schools is to teach youth, for they are the seedbed of the city." A holistic well-rounded, liberal education is crucial for this task, since without it "there could be no good men, no admiration of virtue, no knowledge of what is honest, no harmonious agreements concerning honest duties, no sense at all of humanity."[3]

Melanchthon provides a helpful view of education as integral to religious and civic life. By focusing on the training of the individual, Melanchthon sought to unite the academic, religious, and community-related responsibilities of each student. According to him, education should be seen as contributing to the formation of the human being, rather than as performing distinct functions in two spheres of activity. Moral and intellectual developments are connected, and religious piety is linked to civic responsibility. In short, Melanchthon applies education to the whole

---

[1] Scott Keith, PhD (Graduate Theological Foundation—Foundation House Oxford), is Associate Dean of Residential Education and Housing Services at CUI.

[2] Gilbert Fugitt, EdD (Pepperdine), is Dean of Students at CUI.

[3] Philip Melanchthon, "In Praise of New Schools," in *A Melanchthon Reader*, trans. Ralph Keen (New York: Peter Lang, 1988), 60, 63.

person rather than to two aspects of one person. Thus, there ought not be two distinct silos at a Lutheran university. Since, according to Melanchthon, the goal of education is "learned piety," the guiding vision of the Lutheran institution of higher education ought to be to prepare students to live under the cross of Christ and live with one another as citizens in community until Christ calls them home.[4]

Countering the prevailing attitude that young adults should acquire only abilities and skills whereby jobs could be obtained, Lutheran universities have consistently encouraged students to look beyond the obvious but simple goal of getting a job.[5] Virtuous and noble citizens, who seek to promote the wellbeing of the community in which they live, are those who have studied the subjects that teach them about social life and have learned to live vocationally under the cross. Going beyond the practical advantages granted by schooling, Lutheran universities should encourage learning about community, ethics, virtues, and ideas in and out of the classroom. The students who will best contribute to society are those who understand the higher goals of their current and future vocations. Thus, they ought to learn the virtues of their chosen professions as well as the virtue of life in a community, and see their own tasks in the context of the larger purposes of God's earthly realm.[6]

Approaching education like Melanchthon did, this chapter will examine a way for today's Christian institutions of higher education to engender a sense of good citizenship within a community through the vocation of student affairs and its co-curricular endeavors. Such co-curricular activities typically involve six main areas: (1) student conduct, (2) residential education, (3) first year experience, (4) civic engagement, (5) student leadership, and (6) student health and wellness. Each area will be examined as a way to foster learned piety in students within the campus community under the cross of Christ.

THE VOCATION OF THE STUDENT AFFAIRS PROFESSIONAL

As students begin their journey at Christian university and professionals examine their role in student affairs, it is important that they realize that God has set all Christians free on account of Christ, yet has

---

[4] See Ashmon's chapter for further exploration of the purpose of Lutheran higher education.

[5] See the chapter by Dawn and Mallinson for a history of Lutheran higher education from Wittenberg to America.

[6] For more on this, see Riemer Faber, "Philipp Melanchthon on Reformed Education," *Clarion: The Canadian Reformed Magazine* 47, no. 18 (1988): 428–31.

called all Christians to serve others freely. This is what Paul states in Eph 2:8–10: "For by grace you have been saved through faith. And this is not your own doing; it is the gift of God, not a result of works, so that no one may boast. For we are his workmanship, created in Christ Jesus for good works, which God has prepared beforehand, that we should walk in them." A right relationship with God has nothing to do with our good works, but is totally God's work.[7] This truth allows student affairs professionals at a Christian university to work with a group of students who may have always been told how special they are and help them realize that it is possible to serve others because of what Christ has done in their lives.

Moreover, if the material principle within Lutheran higher education is the sharing of the Gospel and promoting a lifelong relationship with Christ, then, within a Lutheran context of *sola Scriptura*, the formal principle can only be the truth, Christ, as we know it from God's Word.[8] This, then, is ultimate in a Lutheran student affairs context: sharing the truth of Christ Jesus as the way, truth, and the life in the co-curricular environment (John 14:6). Many aspects of student affairs are penultimate to that, including: teaching life skills in housing and residential education services, first year academic and social transitioning in the Office of First Year Experience, and even community relational lessons that come from the Office of Student Conduct. All of this is guided, as it were, by Scripture, with the ultimate aim of being in a trusting relationship with Christ and a loving/serving relationship in community. This is as Luther stated in "The Freedom of the Christian": "A Christian is a perfectly free lord of all, subject to none. A Christian is a perfectly dutiful servant of all, subject to all."[9] This is what it means to live within a community under the cross of Christ.

Theologian and educator George Forell notes that the Christian university is distinguished from the public institution by its sense of community.[10] Engendering and nurturing a healthy and appropriate Christian community is the vocation of student affairs professionals at a Christian institution of higher education. Cultivating a sense of Christian community, however, need not entail promoting an unrealistic environ-

---

[7] Gene Edward Veith Jr., *God at Work: Your Christian Vocation in All of Your Life* (Wheaton, IL: Crossway, 2002), 37.

[8] For an overview of the material and formal principles, see Steven P. Mueller, ed., *Called to Believe, Teach, and Confess: An Introduction to Doctrinal Theology* (Eugene, OR: Wipf and Stock, 2005), 7.

[9] Martin Luther, "The Freedom of a Christian," in AE 31:344.

[10] Ernest L. Simmons, *Lutheran Higher Education: An Introduction* (Minneapolis: Augsburg Fortress, 1998), 78.

ment on a Christian campus. Indeed, such approaches often backfire as students find that they are unable to live up to expectations and hide their self-destructive struggles. Christians, like all other humans, are sinners. Promoting a Christian community thus involves promoting a lively interaction with non-Christians and their personal struggles to live healthy and responsible lives.

Students are the reason campuses exist. Since students are not one-dimensional creatures, Christian campuses need to educate the whole student. For colleges and universities that take this seriously, the concept of education needs to include the development of students physically, socially, emotionally, morally, spiritually, and intellectually. For this reason, many student affairs departments include offices dedicated to recreation, housing, residential education services, wellness and psychiatric health, student conduct, and campus ministry. Additionally, the program of co-curricular activities on the average North American Christian campus is quite extensive, including student self-government, religious programming, debates, musical performances, departmental clubs, recreational sports, and inter-collegiate athletics. Christian education gives special attention to connecting many of these programs under the umbrella of campus ministry. This means that the ministry of the Gospel, Christ as the Truth, and the preparation for life as citizens happens during counseling sessions, judicial appointments, recreational activities, and choir practice, as well as in roommate conflict meetings. Developing the student's full and balanced Christian maturity is the major objective of co-curricular education and student affairs professionals at a Christian university.

Within the realm of the university experience, some of the greatest lessons a student learns often occur outside of the classroom: in the dorms, lounges, coffee shops, and sports fields, or in a rare moment of quiet while sitting and reading Scripture on a bed. Student affairs departments, then, seek to provide and promote safe and engaging venues for such experiences and lessons to occur. For this to happen, student affairs and academic affairs need to work hand in hand to provide coherent educational experiences that combine the values of the institution (educational, behavioral, moral, and theological) with opportunities for students to become engaged in and out of the classroom. It is true that "the younger generation has preferred intuition to cognition, discussion to lecture, involvement to dispassionate investigation."[11] Yet, as Arthur Holmes states in *The Idea of a Christian College,*

---

[11] Richard E. Koenig, *A Creative Minority: The Church in a New Age* (Minneapolis: Augsburg, 1971), 60–61.

A community that argues ideas only in the classroom, a teacher whose work seems to be a chore, a student who never reads a thing beyond what is assigned, a campus that empties itself of life and thought all weekend, an attitude that devaluates disciplined study in comparison with rival claimants on time and energy, a dominant concern for job-preparation—these can never produce a climate of learning.[12]

Higher education is often minimized to include only the mastery of information and perfection of techniques; it is too infrequently viewed as serving the higher goal of assisting students to develop a worldview, preparing them to answer real world questions of ethical import, helping them discern their vocations, and live in community.[13] But higher education ought to be about articulating ideas of responsibility and character, and the vocations of professor and student affairs professional ought to work together to form such virtues within students in all aspects of life. This is especially true within the Lutheran framework where vocation (in all its many and varied aspects) plays such an important theological role.[14] Higher education should be about "the asking of great questions and the development of new capabilities" and understanding the "kind of person one is and what kind of person one wants to become."[15]

COMMUNITY AND STUDENT CONDUCT

A community is a group of people living together who share a common purpose. This purpose is identified by common values, goals, and responsibilities. Within a Lutheran context, community standards will reflect biblical values and will strive to enforce those standards with a good understanding of both God's Law and Gospel as well as the two-kingdom theology of God's left-hand kingdom of power and right-hand kingdom of grace.[16] Standards of community interaction will be seen as essential to the growth and development of the student and the community. The disciplinary process in a Lutheran university will, therefore, be both corrective (Law) and restorative (Gospel). The goal will be to correct and redeem individuals as well as to restore relationships with God and one another. Such loving discipline is a just and gracious balance of Law and Gospel.

---

[12] Arthur F. Holmes, *The Idea of a Christian College* (Grand Rapids: Eerdmans, 1975), 88.

[13] Mark William Roche, *Why Choose the Liberal Arts?* (Notre Dame: University of Notre Dame Press, 2010), 103.

[14] See Mueller's chapter for a discussion of the doctrine of vocation.

[15] Roche, *Why Choose the Liberal Arts?*, 103.

[16] See Mueller's chapter for an overview of Law and Gospel and two-kingdom theology.

For those within student affairs whose responsibility it is to ensure the wellbeing of students, the safety of each individual member of the campus community becomes a critical component to supporting the university's overall academic and co-curricular mission. To that end, universities must do what they can to create an environment that is free of acts of violence, harassment, and infringement of rights of privacy and property. Lutheran universities understand that respect and civility are characteristics that help build a Christ-centered community. Being an active participant of an academic community, students are expected to accept and abide by particular student codes of conduct as adapted by each university. These codes of conduct ought not be too cumbersome and should reflect those laws under which we all live in the civil realm, that is, the second table of the Decalogue (Exod 20:12–17). "Administrative controls," such as those sometimes expressed in the realm of student conduct, "become excessive when they no longer express any underlying community of interest and purpose nor allow for individual differences that are compatible with the common purpose."[17]

These codes of conduct ought to include sections that specifically outline students' rights and responsibilities, the disciplinary process as well as opportunities for appeal, and university policies and procedures. As in the home, Lutheran universities will often view the disciplinary process as a learning experience that can result in ethical and spiritual development. In addition, these universities believe that this process is a catalyst for understanding one's responsibilities and privileges within the university community and the greater society. A Lutheran institution will have as a core value the belief that instilling a sense of Christian freedom within students is of paramount importance. Again, this principle is found in God's Word time and again (e.g., 1 Cor 9:19; Rom 13:8; Phil 2:6–7) and was reiterated by Luther: "A Christian is a perfectly free lord of all, subject to none. A Christian is a perfectly dutiful servant of all, subject to all."[18] This freedom allows students to grow spiritually, to learn to make moral decisions, which affect themselves and others, and, in the case of mistakes, to receive the grace that Jesus Christ has given to them so abundantly.

These policies at Lutheran universities also ought to acknowledge that students live in two kingdoms, the civil realm and the realm of the Gospel or grace. For students, the administration of the university often acts as their branch of local government or at least governance. The workings of administration in the context of student conduct (kingdom of the left) have

---

[17] Holmes, *The Idea of a Christian College*, 80.
[18] Luther, "The Freedom of a Christian," 344.

different aims than the ministry of the church or even campus ministry (kingdom of the right). Nonetheless, Christians, and thus students, are called to be subject to both realms.[19] Student conduct works specifically to ensure safety and security within the civil realm. The church and its branch as represented by campus ministry, serve to preach the Gospel, administer the Sacraments, absolve sins, and evangelize with the Gospel of Christ.[20] It is important to remember here that, "People who serve in the kingdom of the left, and those who serve in the kingdom of the right are apt to confuse their authority and their role."[21] Thus, to say that the Office of Student Conduct works in the kingdom of the left is not to say that it does not serve a purpose for which God intended. Rather, it is to say that it can serve as an instrument of God working in the lives of students for the purpose of benefiting and supporting them as they learn to live together civilly and peaceably in society and community.

COMMUNITY AND RESIDENTIAL EDUCATION

Residence Life

The popularity of college residential living has sparked a crisis on many college campuses.[22] Students flocking to live on campus are doubling (sometimes tripling) up in college residence hall rooms and, when room runs out, even being housed in local hotels. Campus housing, residential living, and residential education are realities that seem to be here to stay, even in the age of the Internet and online education. Lutheran universities therefore ought to have a holistic vision for residential education and housing.

When approaching the development of a plan for moving forward on this topic, we need to first ask how values are transmitted. In answering this question, Arthur Holmes says that,

> Young people assimilate [values] more from example than precept, more from their peers than from their elders, and more by being involved than by being spectators. Values can be caught from a contagious example of a community at work; in this case a community

---

[19] See Rom 13 for more on the Christian's obligation to earthly authority.

[20] For a discussion of campus ministry, see Ruehs' chapter.

[21] Mueller, *Called to Believe, Teach, and Confess*, 430.

[22] Elsa Brenner, "Solutions to Dorm Crowding," *The New York Times*, August 13, 2010, accessed September 19, 2014, http://www.nytimes.com/2010/08/15/realestate/15wczo.html?_r=2&adxnnl=1&ref=education&adxnnlx=1391735112-vrKWmhGZAOGLqfnlHQ9j4Q.

of well-equipped scholars who inflect their students with a love for learning and involve them in disciplined work.[23]

Within a Lutheran campus community, the instilling of values should extend to all of campus life. It should be a holistic, curricular, and co-curricular effort.

Again, the heart and life-blood of any Lutheran university is community. These communities exist in many forms: a diverse community of faith, an extraordinary academic community, and a vibrant residential community. Lutheran universities ought to maintain a steadfast commitment to a residential, co-curricular environment in order to enhance and deepen the academic integrity and faith of the community. Residential living should be an integral part of any undergraduate experience because it provides more opportunities to instill and cultivate values in students.

A Lutheran residence life community will promote the reality that those who are free in Christ are free to serve one another. Redeemed and esteemed by Christ's gracious love under the cross, each member of a Lutheran residential community is free to be treated with respect, dignity, integrity, and compassion, reflective of Christ's love. In turn, each member is also free to treat others with respect, dignity, integrity, and compassion, reflective of Christ's love. This may look like a law of some sort, but it is not. This is the gift of freedom, and as Gerhard Forde liked to put it: "All you can do is begin to live the life it grants you."[24] This is what James Nestingen, Forde's student and colleague, has called "the free obedience bestowed by the Spirit of the living Christ." This entails "daily looking after the things that God gives—loving your wife or husband, giving yourself for your family and friends, doing your job fully and well, sharing what you have with those who need it. It's loving simple—like Jesus." [25] According to this standard, it is the mission of these departments that students leave their residential community as developed individuals, confident in their relationship with God on account of Christ and in their call to the world, able to serve their community vocationally under the cross.

Students arrive at American Lutheran universities from every state in the union and quite frequently from many different nations, providing a diverse, eye-opening, and new life experience. At its best, living in community encourages the collision of new ideas, student development,

---

[23] Holmes, *The Idea of a Christian College*, 82.

[24] Gerhard O. Forde, *Where God Meets Man: Luther's Down-to-Earth Approach to the Gospel* (Minneapolis: Augsburg, 1972), 122.

[25] James A. Nestingen, *The Faith We Hold: The Living Witness of Luther and the Augsburg Confession* (Minneapolis: Augsburg, 1983), 77.

dialogues, and personal growth. Students should be challenged daily to balance their personal heritages, life stories, experiences, and beliefs with others in the community who have likewise been redeemed by the blood of the Lamb (John 1:29). And yet, at its worst, life in community can also exacerbate anti-social tendencies and unbiblical behaviors. Issues such as drug and alcohol abuse, suicidal ideation, and extra-marital sex, while typically not new to students upon arriving at college, can worsen in an atmosphere that is finally free from parental constraint. This makes living in community under the cross of Christ—where students are daily called, reminded, instructed, and encouraged in their new life in Christ (Rom 6:1–14)—even more important. A Lutheran approach would thus take residential living and learning seriously. Students need to learn how to respond to conflict with humility and maturity, develop integrity and take responsibility for their actions, balance the strenuous demands of university life with callings from God to be students and to serve family, friends, and neighbor through faith in Christ.[26]

Living Learning Communities and Faculty in Residence

Learning communities are small, defined groups of students who come together with faculty and usually student affairs professionals to engage in a holistic and intellectually interactive learning experience within the context of community. As has been stated, in order for any university truly to accomplish its vision of developing citizens who are ready to fulfill their vocations in the world, learning environments ought to extend beyond the traditional lecture hall and laboratory and into the informal learning spaces

---

[26] One specific issue of sexuality that will soon be on the forefront of student affairs discussions is how to respond to transgender students who identify as being the opposite gender of their "birth gender" and want to live on campus with students of their self-identified gender. The Education Department, in accord with Title IX of the Education Amendments of 1972, has already granted a few Christian universities exemptions from admitting or housing transgender students in their place of choice because that would violate the university's stated religious beliefs. But this issue has only begun. How can Lutheran universities use a two-kingdom, Law and Gospel approach with students who self-identify as transgender? What if the federal government declares that a student has transitioned successfully from one gender to the other? These and other issues of sexuality that conflict with God's Word (e.g., homosexual acts and heterosexual sex outside of marriage) must be addressed clearly and carefully. For two recent examples of this issue, see Scott Jaschik, "The Right to Expel," *Inside Higher Ed*, July 25, 2014, accessed August 31, 2014, https://www.insidehighered.com/news/2014/07/25/2-christian-colleges-win-title-ix-exemptions-give-them-right-expel-transgender.

of the residence halls, recreation areas, and gathering places. The importance of supporting a seamless learning environment was documented by George Kuh in his 1991 landmark critique of effective higher education strategies, *Involving Colleges: Successful Approaches to Fostering Student Learning and Personal Development outside the Classroom.* Kuh's major insight is that, "Students do not think of their lives as bifurcated by the classroom door. For students, college is a stream of learning opportunities."[27]

Many important life challenges and character building opportunities are encountered when students live in a community. Because the residential environment has historically been and, in fact, is an integral part of the Lutheran educational experience, the Lutheran university ought to be intentional in creating and supporting distinctive, subject-based or even topically-based residential learning environments that: (1) promote faithfulness to God, neighbor, and vocation; (2) encourage students to exercise their Christian freedom by encouraging choice and design; and (3) cohere with the mission and vision of each Lutheran university. That is, Living Learning Communities should prepare students to live under the cross of Christ and live with one another as citizens in community until Christ calls them home.

Conventional residence halls are on-campus facilities intended to provide low-cost, attractive, safe, and convenient living quarters for undergraduate students in close proximity to academic buildings. Residents often participate in dining plans provided by centralized dining facilities and services. Conventional halls are usually supervised by undergraduate resident advisers and professional staff members trained in student affairs administration. Staff members are trained to assist students with adjustment and developmental issues or to make appropriate referrals to other campus professionals. Conventional residence halls may offer a range of social, recreational, and educational programming organized by their staffs.[28]

The contemporary vision of residence education programs attempts to connect more out-of-class experiences with in-class learning. In a 1998

---

[27] See Chun-Mei Zhao and George D. Kuh, "Adding Value: Learning Communities and Student Engagement," *Research in Higher Education* 45, no. 2 (March 2004): 115–38.

[28] See Frances Arndt, "Making Connections: The Mission of UNCG's Residential College," in *Gateways: Residential Colleges in the Freshman Year Experience,* ed. Terry B. Smith (Columbia, SC: National Resource Center for the Freshman Year Experience, 1993), 49–54. See also Gregory S. Blimling, "The Benefits and Limitations of Residential Colleges: A Meta-Analysis of the Research," in *Residential Colleges: Reforming American Higher Education,* ed. F. King Alexander and Don E. Robertson (Lexington, KY: Oxford International Round Table, 1998), 39–76.

opinion paper, the Residential College Task Force of the Association of College and University Housing Officers presented a number of models of existing residence education programs. There is considerable overlap among these models; the differences are often matters of emphasis. Somewhat ironically, what emerged in many ways reflects the values this chapter has already discussed as key components to Lutheran collegiate life. That is, these new models encourage residential education settings, which are generally the result of partnerships between student affairs professionals, academic staff, and faculty. These venues have been dubbed Living Learning Communities. Living Learning Communities value interaction in and out of the classroom with faculty and professional staff who can model a vocational life, address deeper questions, and are accessible in real life scenarios. This is the model that Lutherans have followed since the inception of the Lutheran university. Luther's famous *Table Talk* emerged from conversations that Luther often had with his students around the dinner table.[29] Also, Luther and Melanchthon were both well-known for providing housing in their homes for students.[30] By way of example, Martin and Katie Luther housed up to thirty students at a time in their home, the Black Cloister, a refurbished monastery turned *de facto* dormitory complex.[31] The Lutheran view of higher education was never intended to stop at the classroom door. The Lutheran view of vocation would never allow for such a limited set of interactions with those whom we are called to serve.

Living Learning Communities have been shown, by multiple studies, to improve academic achievement, overall student success, and retention and persistence rates.[32] To succeed in these areas, on campus learning commu-

---

[29] Smith describes how "The Luthers kept open house and entertained not only their poor relatives such as old 'Muhme Lehne' and their nieces, but many students as well, to say nothing of the distinguished strangers who visited Wittenberg" (Preserved Smith, *Luther's Table Talk: A Critical Study* [New York: Columbia University Press, 1907], 10).

[30] Joseph Stump, *The Life of Philip Melanchthon* (New York: Pilger Publishing House, 1897), 81.

[31] Roland H. Bainton, *Women of the Reformation in Germany and Italy* (Boston: Beacon, 1971), 30. As Stjerna explains, "Katharina partnered in Luther's ministry of teaching by providing material sustenance, managing a house full of people, running a boarding school for theology students, a hostel for visitors, a symposia for theological conversations, centered around her husband, occasionally turning her house into a hospital, receiving refugees, providing meals and beds for all, and finding money to cover all of the costs" (Kirsi Stjerna, *Women and the Reformation* [Oxford: Blackwell, 2009], 60).

[32] See Stephanie Baker and Norleen Pomerantz, "Impact of Learning Communities on Retention at a Metropolitan University," *Journal of College Student Retention:*

nities need to incorporate three integral factors: (1) they need to be faculty driven; (2) they need to incorporate faculty involvement in the class and in the residential/community setting; and (3) they need to be geographically locatable and centered, that is, students need a place that is theirs to call a home away from home. The key to all of this is faculty involvement.

With this in mind, a truly residential Lutheran campus will provide desirable residential communities that include ample opportunities for students to engage with faculty beyond the classroom. Thus, the best model will likely include a Faculty in Residence program. A Faculty in Residence program might exist to assist student affairs departments by providing live-in faculty who could foster and shape the social, cultural, and educational life within the Lutheran residential living communities. As such, these faculty members would work collaboratively with student affairs to nurture a heightened sense of community that fosters academic excellence, promotes faculty-student interaction, increases a sense of vocational life, and enriches the student living and faith-building experience. Live-in faculty would be tasked to develop avenues for: (1) community development, (2) student interaction, (3) co-curricular learning opportunities, and (4) academic success and intellectual development of students living on campus.

Lutheran student affairs divisions need to strive to develop all aspects of the human character—the intellectual, faithful, personal, moral, and religious life—so that students may be fully prepared for lives of service in the world. If residential learning communities are to be recognized for their contributions to the Lutheran higher education experience, each community must be shaped in accordance with the overall vision of Lutheran universities toward living examined lives, replete with grace toward the goal of responsible citizenship in community with one another.

COMMUNITY AND FIRST YEAR EXPERIENCE

The changing landscape of higher education has brought a greater focus to the idea and reality of student retention. In many universities this has spawned the creation of departments known as First Year Experience. Typically this department will run an orientation program for new freshmen and transfer students. This department will also help coordinate a freshmen seminar course, which attempts to assist the students as they transition from being high school students to successful college students. This office is critical because, according to Tinto's theory, a university has

Research, Theory and Practice 2, no. 2 (2000–2001): 115–26. Maureen S. Andrade, "Learning Communities: Examining Positive Outcomes," *Journal of College Student Retention: Research, Theory and Practice* 9, no. 1 (2007–2008): 1–20.

six weeks before a student decides if she wants to remain at a certain university.[33] Once this decision is made, either for or against a university, the decision will impact the student's involvement with the campus as a community, as well as her retention and persistence to graduation.

Working with first-year students is an interesting world because one finds students at extreme ends of a given spectrum. Some students are incredibly academically and socially capable and need very little attention as they transition into the university. In fact, these are the leaders, and the challenge here is to find positions of leadership that will inspire their faith development and provide competence as they take more responsibility in leadership. The other end of the spectrum, and where universities often end up focusing most of their time and attention, is with those students who need close advisement and are unsure if this university is the right "fit" for them.

Often what students need in their first year is a readjustment away from a narcissistic view of, "What job will I choose that will make me the most money for the least amount of work?" Responding to this self-centered, occupational view, the Lutheran university will attempt to instill in students an understanding that the vocation of a student, while they attend university, is simply to be a student. It is certainly not simple, but they should focus intently on the academic tasks at hand, along with getting involved with co-curricular activities that connect them to the campus community in a holistic fashion. All of this will prepare them for the many vocations they will have after graduation as they live in community with friends, spouse, neighbors, employers, co-workers, etc.

The difficulty of this task is exacerbated by the reality that the world puts stressors on students, almost constantly, which encourages them to split their focus. There are many students who work full-time to support their family and pay for school. This does not allow them to participate in the campus community and often causes them to lose focus on their academic life altogether. Although these students may participate in many vocational endeavors, they ought not lose sight of their primary vocation, the vocation of being a student.[34] In the Office of First Year Experience, it is critical to build relationships with these students so that when they go through life-changing moments they feel comfortable sharing and exploring where God is calling them with those he has set in place to assist them.

---

[33] For more information on "Tinto's Theory," see Vincent Tinto, *Leaving College: Rethinking the Causes and Cures of Student Attrition* (Chicago: University of Chicago Press, 1993).

[34] See Maas' chapter for an account of the vocation of a student.

COMMUNITY IN THE CONTEXT OF CIVIC ENGAGEMENT

The current college student has been involved with community service projects throughout their high school experience. In 1990, 63 percent of college students reported being involved with volunteering in their senior year of high school; in 2000 this increased to 81 percent of college students.[35] The advent of the Internet has also thrown a new wrinkle into an ever-increasing passion for students not only to participate in community service, but to do it globally. When they come back from missionary trips to South Africa, Haiti, China, etc., they can stay connected with their new friends through Facebook, Twitter, Instagram, or other social media outlets. This connection allows students easily to see the impact of their mission work, a possibility that did not exist in past generations. In the past, staying connected to far-flung populations across the globe meant writing letters. Now, this communication is instantaneous. Unfortunately, the current global connectedness of students makes it difficult to get students involved locally in their own community because they do not sense a need in their own community. Students who volunteer locally, for instance, in the context of a reading program, will report back that those they helped youth who had better cell phones than they did. This does not produce a sense within them that they are serving a "greater good."

As students wrestle with being locally or globally focused, it is important to point them back to a two-kingdom perspective: "Christians are citizens in both of God's kingdoms. In His spiritual kingdom we rest in Christ; in His earthly kingdom we serve our neighbors."[36] The purpose of serving the neighbor is because Christ called us to do so. As Matt 20:25–28 says,

> Jesus called them and said, "You know that the rulers of the Gentiles lord it over them, and their great ones exercise authority over them. It shall not be some among you. But, whoever would be great among you must be your servant, and whoever would be first among you must be your slave, even as the Son of Man came not to be served but to serve, and to give his life as a ransom for many."

---

[35] Lori J. Vogelgesang, Elaine K. Ikeda, Shannon K. Gilmartin, and Jennifer R. Keup, "Service-Learning and the First-Year Experience: Outcomes Related to Learning and Persistence," in *Service-Learning and the First-Year Experience: Preparing Students for Personal Success and Civic Responsibility*, ed. E. Zlotkowski (Columbia, SC: University of South Carolina, 2002), 29.

[36] Veith, *God at Work*, 38.

This call to service is further clarified by Jesus in Matt 22:39: "You shall love your neighbor as yourself." In this biblical way of thinking and acting comes the realization that "your neighbor," the one(s) you are called to serve, is more often than not the person that is closer, or closest, to you. Service to neighbor begins with those already in your sphere of influence—your community—and extends outward from there. This biblical approach means that service and civic engagement at a Christian university should start first in the residential halls and the campus community.

COMMUNITY AND STUDENT LEADERSHIP

Students today are inundated from the time they walk onto campus to get involved. Although at many schools less than 10 percent of the students actually participate in student leadership, there is much time spent on promoting these positions and training students for the various tasks in the context of student government, student life/activities, intramurals, diversity, or a myriad of other leadership positions. The vocation of being a student-leader lands in the arena of the fishbowl concept at most Lutheran universities because of their small size. It is difficult not to know most of the students on campus, and so once a student gains a leadership position, more is expected of them in the eyes of the student body, faculty, and administration.

Certainly we are all sinful people, but if a student wants to take on the added responsibility of being a leader, that role does not end with correctly filling out the application or running a successful campaign. The vocation of being a student-leader lands not only on words but on actions. Too many students have underestimated the responsibilities that come with being student body president and are often distraught upon realizing that other students have real expectations of them in this role.

Thankfully, within the realm of the Lutheran university, it is quite natural to remind student-leaders of the graciousness of God shown upon them even, if not especially, in their vocational failures. It is also quite easy to remind them that even though student leadership can be stressful, they are truly building leadership and teamwork skills that will be valuable in their future vocations once they leave college. This means that student affairs personnel need to equip students with "tough skin" because the world is not always interested in making sure that their self-esteem bucket is full. As Christians, our esteem does not come from self. Rather, our value comes from knowing that while we are yet sinners, Christ died for us (Rom 5:8). Having died and risen with Christ daily in our Baptism, he now calls us into a new life, which includes all those things that he has prepared for us to do (Eph 2:8–10).

Helping a student decide on a student leadership position, or if helping them to discern if they should even apply, is an interesting and time consuming journey. One theory on leadership comes from Robert Greenleaf's essay in 1970 entitled, *The Servant as Leader.* Summarizing Greenleaf's view, Komives and Woodward explain that, "The servant leader takes care to ensure that other people's greatest needs are met and that they therefore 'become healthier, wiser, freer, more autonomous, more likely themselves to become servants.' "[37] Jesus talks about being a servant leader in Matt 20:28 when he states, "even as the Son of Man did not came not to be served but to serve, and to give his life as a ransom for many." It is paramount as we look at the vocation of leadership under the cross of Christ with our students that we realize they might not have thought that being a leader involves serving those whom they are expected to lead. This concept seems to have been lost in the narcissistic worldview in which many students grew up.

A COMMUNITY THAT IS WELL

The landscape of higher education and student life has changed drastically over the last twenty years in the area of psychological counseling and wellness services. In many universities there might have been one person, probably a part-time therapist, who was dedicated to providing psychological services. This is no longer the reality. In many universities, there are large departments of full-time licensed therapists who have a waiting list of students seeking counseling services. As Holley Belch notes, "One of the fastest-growing categories of disability in the college student population is psychiatric disabilities: bipolar disorder, anxiety disorders, and borderline personality disorders, among others."[38] These challenges make it increasingly important to work with these students in an intentional way. If not, the result may be that they simply leave the university or cause countless other students to leave by making the community an unhealthy place. What is worse, failing to put an appropriate action plan into place can result in catastrophic consequences for the student and the university.

A university wellness center, then, is another aspect that is of paramount importance in the area of student life. It is important to have the center staffed with competent medical practitioners that are able to work

---

[37] Susan R. Komives, Dudley B. Woodward Jr., and Associates, *Student Services: A Handbook for the Profession,* 4th ed. (San Francisco: Jossey-Bass, 2003), 452.

[38] Holley A. Belch, "Understanding the Experience of students with Psychiatric Disabilities: A Foundation for Creating Conditions of Support and Success," *New Directions for Student Services* 134 (2011): 73.

with the student population. It is common for a student to come in with a minor medical condition that leads to the realization that they need counseling too. It is critical that the wellness center staff and the psychological counselors have a good relationship.

In order to respond as a college community to these significant mental health issues, each university needs to have specific protocols in place that address the mental, physical, spiritual, and academic concerns of the student. Such protocols, Brett Sokolow and Scott Lewis show, often include intentional prevention measures: "The post-Virginia Tech era shows a dramatic shift to proactive prevention as the majority of campuses move to implement or update behavioral intervention team practices."[39] A Behavioral Intervention Team (BIT) is a critical component in responding to and documenting the needs of some of the most challenging students on a college or university campus. A BIT is critical in putting together all of the information about a certain student and creating an official and intentional action plan designed to address each student's unique needs.

The BIT should also have the power to impact a student's status as a student at the university. The struggle within the BIT is balancing the concept of helping a student as opposed to enabling that student to remain in a pattern of behavior that is not healthy or beneficial to the university community. This is why the BIT needs to be comprised of student affairs professionals and faculty members that bring various perspectives from around the campus and help to create an action plan.

Bringing a biblical and Lutheran perspective to bear on this issue means that, as a community, we should care for our neighbors. First Corinthians 13:4–7 states: "Love is patient and kind; love does not envy or boast; it is not arrogant or rude. It does not insist on its own way; it is not irritable or resentful; it does not rejoice at wrongdoing, but rejoices with the truth. Love bears all things, believes all things, hopes all things, and endures all things." This passage is a key aspect to the BIT at any Christian institution. Students will need to have difficult conversations about unacceptable behavior such as stalking, drug and alcohol abuse, suicidal ideations, etc., that may be connected to other chronic mental health issues and need to be treated properly. Ultimately, when a professional staff member is dealing with multiple issues at 3:00 am involving the same student, it is pivotal that they rely on passages like 1 Cor 13 to remind them of love for neighbor in

---

[39] Brett A. Sokolow and W. Scott Lewis, *2nd Generation Behavioral Intervention Best Practices* (National Center for Higher Education Risk Management, 2009), 2, accessed September 19, 2014, http://www.nabita.org/docs/2009NCHERMwhitepaper.pdf.

community. If not, it can be easy to dismiss these students that desperately need help in their darkest moments of their young lives.

Parents are a critical piece in working with the student population and addressing their mental health concerns too. However, universities and their administrators must be aware that some students will only give an emergency contact person who is not their parent. A good policy is, when a student is sent to the hospital, to contact their emergency contact person. It is a balancing act because a parent might exacerbate the situation; however, if a parent is the emergency contact, then s/he needs to have contact with the university. It is not uncommon to find out that this student has been struggling with these issues for years. The disheartening situations are when you realize the parents felt they could not handle the students so they simply decided to ship them off to a nice "Christian" college thinking that their mental health issues would disappear; this is rarely, if ever, the case. Therefore, clear and consistent contact with the parents is critical. This shows care for the student and seeks to insure the student's best success.

There are certainly challenges to the new world of mental health. Lutheran universities need to rely on the firm foundation of Christ's love when developing a plan designed to serve a population that is hurting and needs the highest level of service possible—even when those who are called to provide that care may feel emotionally drained in the process.

CONCLUSION

In many colleges and universities in the United States, the department of student affairs has changed significantly over the last twenty years. This is because the culture has demanded it. Higher education is entering a time when parents and students demand a level of customer service that must be balanced with developing the students into productive members of society. Lutheran universities have a difficult task ahead of them explaining how God can indeed call students to a vocational life that might be in conflict with their parents' dream.

This puts additional stressors on Lutheran universities as they try to stay true to their vision and mission of teaching students to live out all their vocations in life under the cross of Christ. Though all hope is not lost, as one impartial observer, James Burtchaell, notes, "For although it is the vocation and mission of the Lutheran venture in higher education that most counts, Lutherans are likely to be the only people who could be committed to it enough to dedicate their careers and their lives to it." Burtchaell also notes that Lutherans ought not lose sight of the reality that in order to pull this off, it will take actual Lutherans to do it. As Burtchaell, himself a Catholic, observes: "And such Lutherans would seem to be the critical resource which the Lutheran colleges and universities have lost."[40] Put into simpler terms, this means that if Lutheran universities are to accomplish the mission of educating students who understand their calling under the cross of Christ as citizens of God's two kingdoms—free before God on account of Christ and free to serve one another on account of Christ—they will need to hire Lutherans to do this in the classrooms, in the residential halls, and in student affairs offices.

Even as a Lutheran university devoted to the concept of the freedom of the Christian, we cannot simply hand a student a key at the beginning of the year to their residence hall room and collect it again in May. Instead, we must continually engage these students in vocational conversations in the residence halls, in the dining hall, when they want to take on a leadership role, and whenever a teachable moment occurs. The students that we have on our campuses today need a whole campus community dedicated to their success, some of which will come by saying "no" to students or challenging them to strive for excellence when they have repeatedly be given artificial praise for subpar work. As Tim Elmore states, "There is no comfort in the growth zone, but there's no growth in the comfort zone. With the right perspective, failure and stress aid the growth process."[41] The challenge of helping students understand that God has called them to "learned piety" and a life of service in community using the gifts he has given them can be challenging when they refuse to enter the growth zone because the muscles that help them take on a challenge have atrophied or were never exercised to begin with. It is imperative that any Lutheran university has the opportunity to connect and care for these students in ways that will fundamentally change the course of their lives and enable them to live out their vocations in the forgiveness given to them on account of what Christ has accomplished for them. To achieve this holistic educational goal, it will take a holistic effort at each university.

QUESTIONS

1. What are some out of classroom challenges faced by students at the modern university?

2. What are some services that have developed in student affairs to deal with these challenges? Have student affairs services gone too far? What should be the role of faculty in this arena?

---

[40] James T. Burtchaell, *The Dying of the Light: The Disengagement of Colleges and Universities from Their Christian Churches* (Grand Rapids: Eerdmans, 1998), 538.

[41] Tim Elmore, *Artificial Maturity: Helping Kids Meet the Challenge of Becoming Authentic Adults* (Hoboken: Jossey-Bass, 2012), 80.

3. In what ways can the curricular and co-curricular sides of the university, faculty and student affairs personnel, work together to foster "learned piety" in students to live as citizens with one another in community under the cross of Christ?

4. What is the proper role of Law and Gospel as well as the two kingdoms in the realm of student conduct? How can these be applied to student conduct issues that you have addressed recently?

5. What are some of the ways that students learn about their current and future vocations during their out of classroom experiences at the university?

16

THE ROLE OF ATHLETICS
ON A LUTHERAN LIBERAL ARTS CAMPUS

Timothy Preuss[1]

INTRODUCTION

Sports are taken very seriously in America, and not just by those who twirl "terrible towels" in support of the Pittsburgh Steelers. Other countries take sports very seriously as well. A tragic example occurred in 1994, when Columbian soccer star Andres Escobar was murdered after he inadvertently deflected a ball into his own goal during the World Cup finals. But, no other country has anything resembling our country's collegiate athletic programs; these are a uniquely American phenomenon.

In this chapter, I am less interested in how seriously Americans take sports *as sports* than in the question of how the athletic (and other co-curricular programs) on campus can support, complement, and accomplish the mission and vision of the university. Taken a step further, I am particularly interested in how the Athletic Department on a Lutheran liberal arts campus can support, complement, and accomplish the academic mission of the institution. Considering this question, I am cognizant that decisions in this arena send unmistakable signals to current and prospective students, their parents, faculty and staff, alumni, and other constituents of the university.

In their book, *The Game of Life: College Sports and Educational Values*, James Shulman and William Bowen assert that

> some people love college sports and some hate them. Some who feel passionately about colleges and universities regard their athletic programs as among their best features; others regard them as "part of

---

[1] Tim Preuss, PhD (Nebraska), is Professor of Exercise Sports Science, Dean of Arts and Sciences at CUI.

the scene"—something accepted and appreciated, but not of primary importance. Others may categorize athletics as irrelevant or even detrimental to the accomplishment of educational objectives. One fact is clear to all: however one feels about them, intercollegiate athletic programs have become institutionalized within American higher education.[2]

If this assertion is accepted, it begs several questions: How and why did this "institutionalization" occur? Has the relationship between the academy and athletics changed over the years and, if so, how? And most importantly for the purposes of this chapter, how has the institutionalization of athletics on the college campus supported the educational mission of the university?

A BRIEF HISTORICAL OVERVIEW:
THE ROLE OF SPORT IN SOCIETY

A brief historical overview will help answer the first two questions. Sports may be among the most powerful human expressions in all history (along with art, music, literature, and theatre). Not all expressions were positive (think gladiators in the Coliseum), but were powerful, nonetheless. Organized games and sport are evident dating from the ancient Greek's contests and games, throughout the period of the Roman Empire and the medieval period up to the time of the Reformation. In *The Republic*, Plato recommended gymnastics as a major component of education. The motto "a sound mind in a sound body" was a goal of Roman education. During the Protestant Reformation, two schools of thought emerged toward games and sport activities. Calvinists and Puritans came to view sports as "profane and licentious—they were occasions of worldly indulgence that tempted men from the godly life; being rooted in pagan and popish practices, they were rich in the sort of ceremony that poorly suited the Protestant conscience."[3] Martin Luther had a different perspective. In his work, "The Freedom of a Christian," he wrote that physical training ("caring for the body") is valuable so that people can be more physically able to serve their neighbors. Faith active in love comes through physical means, so the physical needs to be taken care of for them to work well as means.[4] Thus, in areas where Luther's ideas dominated, lawful recreational pursuits were not dis-

---

2 James D. Shulman and William G. Bowen, *The Game of Life: College Sports and Educational Values* (Princeton: Princeton University Press, 2001), 1.

3 Jay Coakley, *Sports in Society: Issues and Controversies* (New York: McGraw Hill, 2004), 71. Reprinted by permission of McGraw-Hill Education.

4 Martin Luther, "The Freedom of a Christian," in AE 31:365.

couraged. By 1633 Charles I issued *The King's Book of Sports,* which emphasized that Puritan ministers in England should not discourage recreational pursuits among the people. Growth in activities like cricket, horse racing, yachting, crew, fencing, golf, and boxing followed (with significant variation by social class). By the time of the Enlightenment, sports of this sort had been accepted as diversions—interesting and often challenging ways to pass free time. They were not yet seen as having utility for athletes in particular or society in general.[5]

Organized sports as we know them today began to emerge during the Industrial Revolution. Initially, games and sports activities existed despite the Industrial Revolution, not because of it. People took opportunity to indulge in games and sport activities during seasonal holidays and festivities with family and neighbors, but economic survival required long working hours and little time for leisure pursuits. Around the middle of the nineteenth century this began to change as people became concerned about the physical health of workers. On the one hand, there was growing awareness that workers were being exploited; on the other hand, the reality that weak and sickly workers were not productive. Fitness became highly publicized and there was an emphasis on calisthenics, gymnastics, and outdoor exercises.[6]

By the late nineteenth century there was a growing emphasis on organization of sport in American society. This began with the establishment of clubs that sponsored and controlled sport participation. Clubs initially were limited to wealthy people in urban areas and college students at select Eastern schools. British boarding schools provided some of the impetus for this development.[7] Underlying the growing organization of sports activities during the second half of the nineteenth century was a new emphasis on the seriousness of sport. People gradually came to see physically strenuous, organized competitive games as tools. Many began to link sport participation with economic productivity, national loyalty, and the development of admirable character traits.[8]

This line of thought continued to develop so that by the early twentieth century sports were beginning to be defined as potential educational experiences—experiences with important consequences for individuals and society as a whole. For the first time in history, people saw sports as tools

---

[5] Coakley, *Sports in Society,* 74.

[6] Coakley, *Sports in Society,* 76.

[7] Brenda L. Bredemeier and David L. Shields, "Sports and Character Development," *President's Council on Fitness and Sport Research Digest* 7, no. 1 (March 2006): 1.

[8] Coakley, *Sports in Society,* 77.

for changing behavior, shaping character, building unity, and cohesion.[9] And the church, which had previously taken either a negative or neutral position regarding sports, began to embrace sports as well. "Muscular Christianity" began to be espoused by influential Christian men in the northeastern United States. They promoted the idea that the body was an instrument for good works and that meeting the demands of godly behavior and good works required good health and physical conditioning. The idea that the body was a temple and that moral character was associated with physical conditioning became embodied in the Young Men's Christian Association (YMCA) and the Young Women's Christian Association (YWCA), both of which grew rapidly between 1880 and 1920; these organizations built athletic facilities in many communities and sponsored teams in many sports. In fact, James Naismith invented basketball in 1891 while a student at the Springfield, Massachusetts YMCA and William Morgan invented volleyball while he was activities director at the YMCA in Holyoke, Massachusetts in 1895.[10]

By the end of World War II, the prevailing attitude toward sport had become that reflected in the words of General Douglas MacArthur:

> Sport is a vital character builder. It molds the youth of our country for their roles as custodians of the republic. It teaches them to be strong enough to know they are weak, and brave enough to face themselves when they are afraid. It teaches them to be proud and unbending in honest defeat, but humble and gentle in victory.[11]

This change in societal views on the value of sport was a necessary precursor for sport to become part of the academy. We next turn our attention to that chain of events.

The Institutionalization of Sport
on the American College Campus

What began as student initiated, student funded clubs was, over several generations, brought under institutional control. The first intercollegiate athletic contest in America was a crew race between boats from Harvard and Yale in 1852. (This first contest was sponsored by a real estate promoter who was selling land in the area—commercialism has been with us the

---

[9] Bredemeier and Shields, "Sports and Character Development," 1.

[10] Coakley, *Sports in Society*, 538.

[11] Quoted in Ryan Miller, "The Role of Athletics in Higher Education," *Major Themes in Economics* 5 (Spring 2003): 34, accessed September 19, 2014, http://business.uni.edu/economics/Themes/miller.pdf.

entire journey.) In 1859, Williams lost to Amherst in the first intercollegiate baseball game (by a score of 73–32!) and in 1869 Princeton lost to Rutgers in the first football game.[12]

The new sport of football developed rapidly in the 1870s. Harvard, Yale, Princeton, and Columbia gradually formulated common rules and by the 1890s 40,000 fans would gather to watch the championship game, played in New York City on Thanksgiving Day. To understand this enormous popularity developing so rapidly, recall that the Olympics had only just been revived in 1896, the first World Series took place in 1901, and there were no professional football, basketball, or hockey leagues. There were no movies, no television, and no Internet. In many ways, the twenty-five colleges and universities that had intercollegiate football clubs in the late nineteenth and early twentieth century had stumbled into a sports-entertainment market, somewhat by accident, and had it nearly all to themselves.[13]

By 1905, the game had taken on a brutal tone. Plays such as the Harvard-invented "flying wedge" (the modern equivalent would be today's offensive line taking a twenty-five yard run and slamming en masse into a designated member of the opposing team) had escalated the level of violence in the game. People were literally dying for their school; in 1905 alone eighteen players died playing football. Shocked by the level of violence, President Roosevelt summoned the presidents and football coaches from Harvard, Yale, and Princeton to the White House. The result of the meeting were some rule changes (including the institution of the forward pass—designed to relieve some of the pressure of the rugby-like scrums) and a mandate for college presidents to gather. Gather they did, and they formed the group that would eventually become the National Collegiate Athletic Association (NCAA). Although some schools chose to drop football altogether (Northwestern, Stanford, Columbia, and New York University banned it), others worked to reform it.

With the immense popularity of the sport, two other issues emerged in addition to the threat to life and limb. Outside interests quickly began to exploit popularity with the public and place commercial pressure on student sports, which threatened academic integrity. Both of these issues were clear to Howard Savage, author of the 1929 study, *American College Athletics*. He identified several questions (all of which are still with us over eighty years later): "[W]hether financial aid should be given based on athletics, whether athletics builds moral character, how institutions should pay

---

[12] Shulman and Bowen, *The Game of Life*, 6.

[13] Shulman and Bowen, *The Game of Life*, 7.

for facilities, and how much influence outside interests (like boosters) should be permitted in the management of athletic programs."[14]

In response to these grave challenges, faculties at the various institutions voted to exert faculty control. By this they hoped to retain what had by now become a very popular program, attracting positive publicity (and students) for the university, while at the same time addressing the very real challenges. The solution seemed to lie in appointing leaders from the faculty to coach the various teams and/or supervise others who coached. Thus the "scholar-practitioner" model arose in collegiate coaching, as well as the antecedents of the modern-day athletic director. Almost from the outset, the new concept of faculty control seemed to create as many problems as it was supposed to solve. As Savage noted in his report,

> The final test for the presence or absence of true faculty control would seem to be these: First, is the guiding influence that of a man whose chief activities and interests lie in the academic fields, or of one to whose income athletics contribute directly or indirectly? Secondly, are the coaches immediately responsible to a faculty representative whose principle concerns are academic, or are they subordinate to another or former coach now elevated to faculty status, or of a former business manager or an alumni secretary who is under appointment for the sake of the good that may accrue to athletics from his connection with them? Certainly in the institutions where faculty control exists at its best there appears to be little truckling to special interests or privileged groups, because the director is not in any way dependent upon athletics for success in his professional career.[15]

It is clear from Savage's report that the well-meant concept of faculty control brought athletic clubs into the institution. At different rates on different campuses oversight shifted from tenured faculty to non-tenured faculty to non-faculty. In higher education today (at all levels) athletic directors are much more likely to be drawn from the ranks of former coaches or those with business, management, or marketing backgrounds. As Shulman and Bowen note:

> No other historical development in intercollegiate athletics has been as influential, or as subtle, as the progressive institutionalization of the athletic clubs that students once ran. . . . This act of assuming ownership of the enterprise has led to tacit or implicit endorsement of

---

[14] Shulman and Bowen, *The Game of Life*, 8.

[15] Howard J. Savage, *American College Athletics* (New York: The Carnegie Foundation for the Advancement of Teaching, 1929), 101–2.

the goals, values, and norms associated with college sports in a way that has allowed the athletic enterprise to have access to the inner chambers where the educational mission of the school is defined and pursued.[16]

The issue of faculty control has also reared its head on my campus. Concordia University Irvine is a relatively young academic institution. By the time the doors opened to receive the first students in 1976, the landscape of higher education in America had firmly embraced intercollegiate athletics. But, this was not the intent of the founding president and faculty. The intent was to establish a "fine liberal arts institution with a robust intramural program."[17] And for five years that is what Concordia (then Christ College) did. Then in 1981, Concordia entered the arena of intercollegiate athletics, fielding club teams in men's basketball and men's soccer. These two teams became Concordia's first varsity teams in 1983. The next year saw the addition of club teams for women's basketball and women's volleyball with both entering varsity competition in 1985. In 1985 the first (and current) gymnasium was opened. The building of an athletic facility with a seating capacity of two thousand was viewed as visionary by some (since there were only three hundred students at the time) and as a betrayal of the mission and vision of the institution by others who felt it was a step toward embracing varsity athletics at the expense of a liberal education and a robust intramural program.[18]

THE PREMISES FOR THE INCLUSION
OF ATHLETICS IN THE ACADEMY

The historical record shows that highly popular athletic clubs have presented institutions of higher learning (including my own) with a dilemma since the early twentieth century. Should we embrace them and their potential for attracting positive public attention and students to the institution or should we not? Either choice had attendant risks. In the end, the majority of institutions chose to embrace athletics with an eye toward reforming and controlling athletics in a manner that would align with the mission of the institution.

---

[16] Shulman and Bowen, *The Game of Life*, 9.

[17] Provost Mary Scott, interview by Tim Preuss, Concordia University Irvine, CA, May 22, 2013.

[18] Provost Mary Scott, interview by Tim Preuss, Concordia University Irvine, CA, May 22, 2013.

It will be informative at this point to examine the rationale for including athletics as part of a Lutheran institution and its implications for institutional mission. Let us start with my institution as an example. While the relationship between a liberal and useful education has seen shifts in curricular balance over the centuries, throughout history liberal education has consistently served as the foundation for vocations.[19] This line of thought is clearly reflected in Concordia University Irvine's mission statement, which reads, "Concordia University Irvine, guided by the Great Commission of Christ Jesus and the Lutheran Confessions, empowers students through the liberal arts and professional studies for lives of learning, service and leadership."[20] This statement captures some of the tension between the liberal arts and professional studies as well as the balance to be had by putting them in juxtaposition.

How, then, does intercollegiate athletics relate to the educational mission? At the outset, it must be conceded, as others have pointed out, that there is no direct connection between participating in organized sport and the pursuit of learning. But that does not mean there is no connection at all. At Concordia, the connection is based on the premise that intercollegiate athletics teams provide a "laboratory" for character development, spiritual formation, competitive excellence, and motivation for academic achievement. The vision for Concordia Eagle's athletics is clearly stated in the Concordia University Irvine Student-Athlete Handbook:

The Vision of CONCORDIA UNIVERSITY ATHLETICS

We are a City on a Hill. We are changing the world, one life at a time, through the vehicle of athletics. As coaches we do this by **transforming** lives. Our players will come to us as average people but graduate as extraordinary men and women. The average person influences 10,000 people in their life. Our outstanding student-athletes will impact many more! Eagle graduates will become leaders of their families, businesses, churches, communities, and their nation as they pursue faithfulness and excellence in their relationships and endeavors.

Concordia University Athletics is anchored in one **primary purpose: serving the long-term welfare of the players God has placed in our programs.**

---

[19] See Ashmon's chapter for a historical sketch of this topic.

[20] "Our Mission," Concordia University Irvine, accessed September 19, 2014, http://www.cui.edu/aboutcui.

Our first priority is to create and foster a *Christ-based family* where the love of God and of people is constantly evident. This includes sharing the Gospel with those whom God places in our care and path. Our next priority is the molding of *indomitable Character* to secure the base needed for a life that makes a difference. Thirdly, we want to ensure that our students receive an *exceptional education*—one that opens doors for them to serve according to their talents and calling. Finally, we want them to experience *competitive excellence* as measured by Christian standards.

The four core objectives are captured in our program's Mission: *Sharing Jesus Christ and winning on and off the field.*

We share Jesus as part of the Great Commission. When Jesus said, "Go, and make disciples" a literal translation would have been, "As you go, make disciples . . ." As we undertake this journey together as coaches and athletes, disciples are made. In other words, spiritual growth and development is intentionally woven into every aspect of the shared experience.[21]

GOD'S TWO KINGDOMS AND SPORT

One might ask, "Is this four-fold premise legitimate, and if so, on what grounds?" It is here that two aspects of Lutheran theology are of benefit. The first of these is the doctrine of God's two kingdoms. Let us consider what this doctrine has to tell us about the idea of using athletic programs as a vehicle for the Gospel. In "One Kingdom Teaches the Other," Russ Moulds examines Luther's doctrine of the two kingdoms as one of the Reformation's central insights about the Gospel. Before considering the implications of this doctrine, Moulds helpfully points out that Scripture informs us of a two-fold strategy that "God is using to free humanity from its captivity to the devil: one strategy sustains the present world, thereby providing *opportunities* for the Gospel, the other *advances* the Gospel in the world."[22] To expand, Luther taught that God's left-hand strategy is to create temporal arrangements like marriage, government, the church (and by extension, universities of the church and their various programs) to promote order, maintain the common good and justice, and provide

---

[21] Dave Bireline and Tim Preuss, *Concordia University Student-Athlete Handbook* (Irvine, CA: Concordia University Irvine, 2012), 4.

[22] Russ Moulds, "One Kingdom Teaches the Other," in *Learning at the Foot of the Cross: A Lutheran Vision for Education*, eds. Joel D. Heck and Angus J. L. Menuge (Austin, TX, Concordia University Press, 2011), 82.

opportunities by which any person can contribute to promoting that common good and justice. Intercollegiate athletics on a Christian campus does this to the degree that it helps develop "wise, honorable, and well-educated citizens,"[23] men and women of character who understand and fulfill their left-hand vocations as student, team, and campus community member. This strategy does not "defeat the devil, redeem creation or accomplish anyone's righteousness and salvation before God. Not even the church as an institution can do that. But this strategy does sustain the present age—the 'kingdom' of this world, God's left-hand kingdom—as the campaign zone for his right hand work."[24] And, of course, this right-hand strategy is to spread the great good news of the Gospel that without our contribution or cooperation, Jesus' birth, life, death, and resurrection have restored us to a right relationship with God. This news changes people's hearts and lives through his pledge, promise, and power.

Moulds rightly notes that this two-fold strategy differentiates the Lutheran teaching ministry from all other kinds of education and distinguishes it as a ministry of the church, rather than merely a rehash or replication of public or private education. The proclamation of the Gospel is itself the intersection between the two kingdoms. And this leads to an inherent tension: we do not leave the two kingdoms separate and compartmentalized (if we do, our rationale collapses). We also do not merge them, trying to transform a team, department, or university into God's right-hand kingdom here on earth. Rather, we keep the two kingdoms intersecting with each other and use the tension this generates to draw attention to the difference between the ways of God and the ways of the world so that others may be drawn by God's promises to himself.[25] If this teaching is true (and I believe it to be so) we have a responsibility to employ the typical left-hand activities common to higher education—curricular and co-curricular—to call attention to another realm. Done rightly, we can and should do the teaching of *both kingdoms*, in *both arenas*, that public and private education cannot do.

Before moving on to the foundation for our second premise, I must offer a caveat. By "done rightly" I mean that in this model it is incumbent upon coaches, trainers, athletic administrators, and student-athletes to use meetings, practices, games, and every appropriate opportunity to make disciples. Failing that, we are merely mimicking what we see others doing

---

[23] This educational vision comes from Luther, "To the Councilmen of All Cities in Germany that They Establish and Maintain Christian Schools," in AE 45:356.

[24] Moulds, "One Kingdom Teaches the Other," 83.

[25] Moulds, "One Kingdom Teaches the Other," 85.

elsewhere and abdicating our responsibility for promoting spiritual formation in those entrusted to our care. As a case in point, my institution is deliberately open to non-Christian students. If we represent clearly who we are (and whose we are) in the recruitment of a student-athlete that is not a Christian and they choose to come to Concordia University Irvine, we interpret that to mean the Holy Spirit has business to transact with that student. The audience for a positive witness to Jesus Christ can be to a teammate, faculty or staff member, official, opponent, fellow student, or anyone with whom we come in contact. And, while making the sign of the cross on the court, or "giving the glory to God" in an interview, is helpful as a testimony, it is conveying saving knowledge of Christ as Lord and Savior that is the ultimate expression of the Great Commission.

VOCATION AND SPORT

The foundation for our second premise flows from the doctrine of vocation. Society today equates vocation with occupation. We ask young children, "What are you going to be when you grow up?" and we have in mind a job. We ask students entering university, "What are you planning to major in?" and the follow up, "What are you planning to do with that major when you graduate?" and again we have a job in mind. Vocation is never singular for the Christian; each Christian has multiple vocations in life.[26] Gene Veith likewise reminds us that Luther taught that our vocations are multiple and fall into four realms, or estates.[27] The first estate is the family with the vocations of husband, wife, mother, father and child. There are subsidiary vocations in the family as well, like brother, sister, aunt, uncle, and grandparent. The calling that each of us has in the workplace (our occupation) was included by Luther *as what people do to provide for their families.* Together this constitutes a household (economy, in Latin). God has further called each of us to be citizens, and he expects us to be actively and constructively engaged in our society. Thirdly, Christians are part of another God-formed estate: the church. We have been "called by the Gospel," in the words of Luther's Small Catechism, into faith in Christ. Finally, Luther speaks of a fourth estate, an over-arching realm in which people from all walks and callings interact and come together:

> Above these three estates and orders is the common order of Christian love, by which we minister not only to those of these three orders but

---

[26] See Mueller's chapter for a discussion of the doctrine of vocation.

[27] Gene Edward Veith Jr., *The Spirituality of the Cross: The Way of the First Evangelicals* (St. Louis: Concordia, 2010), 96–99.

in general to everyone who is in need, as when we feed the hungry and give drink to the thirsty, etc., forgive enemies, pray for all men on earth, suffer all kinds of evil in our earthly life, etc.[28]

By extension, it must be concluded that, strictly speaking, we do not serve God; rather, God graciously invites us into his work, which always involves serving others. Thus, vocation becomes, in all our various roles, loving and serving others. Admittedly, this is not the message of our culture, which says (at least to some student-athletes), "Athletics is your way into college, it's your path to the pros" or other self-focused messages. Jesus' words in Matt 20:28, that he "came not to be served but to serve," are just as counter-cultural and revolutionary today as ever. The fact that this application of vocation to the student-athlete is counter-cultural simply reinforces the earlier point that we can use differences between the two kingdoms to point people to how God's ways differ from our ways.

So, how do we know our vocation? And, how do we know when we are acting in accord with it? In contrast to the way we badger young people to "decide" what they want to be when they grow up, vocation is not something we choose for ourselves. God has given each of his children unique talents, skills, abilities, inclinations, and opportunities. Since vocation is not self-chosen, it can be revealed through the actions of others. As a case in point, I cannot decide to become a student-athlete; the coach has to offer me a spot on the team. Essentially, your vocation is always to be found in the roles you occupy in the present.

Since God is at work in vocation, observes Gustaf Wingren, the devil seeks to thwart vocation. One way he does this is to turn the focus from sacrificial service and love of neighbor to a "theology of glory," to self-aggrandizement, pride in good works, and the achievement of spiritually vacuous worldly success. "Wanting to be exalted instead of serving," says Wingren, "is an offense against vocation."[29] In modern culture, where athletes receive adulation that is tantamount to worship, this is a particular danger for those engaged in sport.

Another ploy of the devil is to try to pry the person out of his or her calling. As Wingren states, "Temptation in vocation is the devil's attempt to get man out of his vocation."[30] We see this in the temptation to quit a job, get a divorce, leave one's children, give up writing, stop making music, or quitting the team when confronted with adversity. A student-athlete acts

---

[28] As quoted in Veith, *The Spirituality of the Cross*, 99.

[29] Gustaf Wingren, *Luther on Vocation*, trans. Carl C. Rasmussen (Eugene OR: Wipf and Stock, 2004), 128.

[30] Wingren, *Luther on Vocation*, 121.

out of vocation when they put so much emphasis on their sport that they neglect the habits of the mind that serve them well as a student. They also act out of vocation when they compromise their health (not getting enough sleep, poor eating habits, excessive drinking, and the like), fail to practice and play hard, or engage in other detrimental behavior.

Yet another way in which we may bear the cross in vocation is the sense that one's vocation is worthless or futile. This happens whenever our vocation appears lowly. The kid flipping burgers, the orderly cleaning bed pans or the third-string forward on the soccer team may all be frustrated in their current situation. The sense of lowliness can be resisted out of pride, or it can become an opportunity to develop humility. Our inability to succeed via our own strength (in the worldly sense) can bring us to a deeper faith in God.[31]

To connect the dots so far, while it will ultimately be an occupation for only a very few, God has blessed many students with significant talent and ability in the area of competitive athletics and he is pleased when they use these talents and abilities to serve others in light of God's two kingdoms. Thus the vocation of *college athlete* is a significant one for a substantial percentage of undergraduate students. Sponsoring teams and competitions creates opportunities for those with this vocation to pursue it fully and accrue the benefits of spiritual formation, character development, competitive excellence, and academic achievement that are afforded.

SPORTS AND CHARACTER DEVELOPMENT

As mentioned earlier, the claim that sports builds character has been popular among educators for more than a century in America and it is one of the premises cited in the vision for athletics at my institution too. Even today's highly commercialized NCAA Division I sports programs are often justified by appeal to the idea that these programs contribute educational value to the athletes by nurturing positive character traits (a visit to the NCAA website, www.ncaa.org, or viewing one of their television commercials will confirm this). Opponents of sport in the academy take the opposite view and cite an abundance of anecdotal evidence of sport-related cheating, aggression, self-aggrandizement, disrespectful or unlawful behavior, and corruption to suggest that competitive sports bring out the worst in us and undermine positive character. So, which is it?

The answer to this question can be found by looking at what is known about sports and character. While there is much work yet to be done in this field, a few evidence-based conclusions can be drawn. The evidence points

---

[31] Veith, *The Spirituality of the Cross*, 113.

us to a middle position between proponents and opponents of the idea that sport builds character. A glance at the sports page on any given day makes it clear that the early optimism regarding the character-building attributes of sport was over-stated. Participation in sport, in and of itself, does not have any automatic beneficial effects on character. On the other hand, it is equally evident that sports are powerful social experiences that may, under the right conditions, have positive benefits. If sports are to have a positive impact on the character of the team members, the leadership and behavior of the coach is critical.[32] Before looking at the results of pertinent studies, let us take a moment to clarify the word *character*.

What Is Character, Anyway?

The word *character* has been in and out of vogue with psychologists over the past century. Early in the twentieth century, it was a popular term reflecting the notion that a person had character to the degree that they possessed personality traits like honesty, integrity, generosity, or trustworthiness. By the late 1920s, studies like that done by Hugh Hartshorne and Mark May had concluded that it was the characteristics of the environment more than the character of the individual that determined behavior in a given setting.[33]

The work of Lawrence Kohlberg on moral reasoning was important in challenging the theory that the environment determined behavior.[34] Kohlberg realized that although a person's behavior may seem inconsistent to an observer, there were underlying consistencies in motive and thought. Thus, a child might believe that helping a friend is moral and right. If loyalty to the friend requires lying in one situation but not another, the outward behavior seems inconsistent despite the consistent underlying pattern of reasoning.

Based on years of longitudinal and cross-cultural research, Kohlberg proposed a six-stage sequence of moral reasoning development. While the details of his stages have been challenged and alternative models have been suggested, Kohlberg's work made three fundamental and lasting contributions: he reaffirmed that there are "stable personal characteristics related to moral and ethical decision making," which led to a renewed appreciation of character. Second, he made clear the idea that "cognition is

---

[32] Bredemeier and Shields, "Sports and Character Development," 1.

[33] Hugh Hartshorne and Mark Arthur May, *Studies in the Nature of Character: Studies in Deceit* (New York: Macmillan, 1928).

[34] Lawrence Kohlberg, *Essays on Moral Development, Volume 2: The Psychology of Moral Development* (San Francisco: Harper and Row, 1984).

a key component of morality: how a person thinks about their ethical responsibilities is an important part of their character." Finally, he found that "character growth follows a predictable developmental progression."[35]

Today it is widely recognized that character is a complex, multifaceted concept. A person of character is a person who consistently acts in an ethical manner. Character refers to those aspects of a person that guide and enable the person faithfully to abide by their moral values, judgments, and intuitions. Deficiencies of character may reflect shallow or misguided moral desires or, alternately, failure of the will—insufficient determination, perseverance, or courage to act in accord with one's ideals.[36]

It is relatively easy and empirically sound, then, to identify important components of character. Two components that have been investigated in the context of sport, and are thus important to look at here, are moral reasoning and motivational orientation.

Intercollegiate Athletics and Moral Reasoning

For those who look simply to sport participation to stimulate advance in moral reasoning, the research has not been encouraging. A number of studies have all found lower moral judgment scores in intercollegiate team sport athletes as compared to non-athletes and individual sport athletes.[37] Overall, the results from these studies suggest that participation in some sports at the intercollegiate level, especially in team sports, may be associated with lower moral reasoning maturity. However, the results have been mixed and none of the studies controlled for academic achievement

---

[35] Bredemeier and Shields, "Sports and Character Development," 4.

[36] David L. Shields and Brenda L. Bredemeier, *Character Development and Physical Activity* (Champaign IL: Human Kinetics, 1995).

[37] Brenda L. Brememeier and David L. Shields, "Divergence in Moral Reasoning about Sport and Everyday Life," *Sociology of Sport Journal* 1, no. 4 (1984): 348–57; Brenda L. Bredemeier, Maureen R. Weiss, David L. Shields, and Richard M. Shewchuk, "Promoting Moral Growth in a Summer Sport Camp: The Implementation of Theoretically Grounded Instructional Strategies," *Journal of Moral Education* 15, no. 3 (1986): 212–20; Elizabeth R. Hall, "Moral Development Levels of Athletes in Sport-Specific and General Social Situations," in *Psychology and Sociology of Sport: Current Selected Research*, vol. 1, eds. L. Vander Velden and J. H. Humphrey (New York: AMS Press, 1986), 191–204; Mark J. Stevenson, *Measuring the Cognitive Moral Reasoning of Collegiate Student-Athletes: The Development of the Stevenson-Stoll Social Responsibility Questionnaire* (Ph.D. Diss., University of Idaho, 1998); R. F. Preist, J. V. Krause, and J. Beach, "Four-year Changes in College Athletes' Ethical Value Choices in Sports Situations." *Research Quarterly for Exercise and Sport* 70, no. 2 (1999): 170–78.

and other potentially confounding variables. Most importantly however, these all were measuring the impact of intercollegiate sport participation on moral reasoning; there was no active promotion of moral reasoning as part of the program.

There is some evidence that coaches who actively seek to promote moral reasoning development can do so.[38] The most important educational tool available is dialogue. Moral reasoning cannot be expected to advance if the athlete is simply a passive recipient of a coach's exhortations, however well-crafted they may be. Student-athletes need to talk about their values; they need to discuss their views of right and wrong with their peers and respectful adults who model Christian character. Coaches need to take time in team meetings to discuss "moral issues relevant to sports in general and to the life of the team in particular."[39] Student-athletes are subject to the same moral and ethical dilemmas as their peers when it comes to college life: cheating on tests, "borrowing" someone's work, not doing their fair share on a group project, or breaking dorm hours would be just a few examples. Athletes also face pressure to perform that makes them vulnerable to eating disorders, the lure of performance enhancing drugs, and other temptations. Finally, whether it was Charles Barkley (former NBA player turned ESPN announcer) famously saying, "I ain't no role model" or Johnny Manziel of Texas A&M, freshman winner of the Heisman Trophy in 2013, starting fights at fraternity parties and then "tweeting" about it to thousands of followers, coming to grips with the heightened visibility and responsibility that comes with the vocation of being a student-athlete is an ongoing challenge.

The value of dialogue will be amplified if it is combined with meaningful responsibility. Athletes who cooperatively share in important dimensions of team decision making are likely to benefit substantially. To maximize the moral and social growth of a team, a democratic leadership style is beneficial. Coaches who involve team members in developing team norms, goals, and expectations help them develop a sense of ownership and responsibility.

---

[38] Bredemeier, Weiss, Shields, and Shewchuk, "Promoting Moral Growth in a Summer Sport Camp" and Thomas J. Romance, Maureen R. Weiss, and Jerry Bockoven, "A Program to Promote Moral Development through Elementary School Physical Education," *Journal of Teaching in Physical Education* 5, no. 2 (1986): 126–36.

[39] Bredemeier and Shields, "Sports and Character Development," 4–5.

Intercollegiate Athletics and Motivation

As noted earlier, Kohlberg suggested that to understand morality and behavior truly we have to investigate motivation. This has been a hot topic in sport psychology research for decades. John Nicholls proposed that the task- and ego-motivational orientations are likely to be associated with moral perspectives.[40] This was put to the test in a 1991 study by Duda, Olson, and Templin that examined the relationship between motivational orientation, approval of aggression, and attitudes toward sportsmanship.[41] Low task-orientation and high ego-orientation correlated with a higher endorsement of unsportsmanlike play. In addition, ego-orientation was positively related to acceptance of aggressive acts. Other researchers have reported similar findings.[42]

To illustrate task- and ego-orientation, Bredemeier and Shields used two fictional athletes:

> When Roger plays basketball, he is motivated by the desire to improve his skills. He is good, but he knows he can get better with continued practice. He is eager to play because competing with other talented athletes enables him to improve.

> When Tameco plays basketball, she is motivated by the desire to showcase her talents. She knows she was born with innate ability and she is eager to compete so that she can demonstrate her superior skills by defeating others.[43]

While the task- and ego-orientation of athletes like Roger and Tameco are relatively stable personal characteristics, they are malleable. The environment can help shape the orientation. The term motivational climate is used to refer to aspects of the environment that promote one orientation over the

---

[40] John G. Nicholls, "Conceptions of Ability and Achievement Motivation: A Theory and Its Implications for Education," in *Learning and Motivation in the Classroom*, eds. Scott G. Paris, Gary M. Olson, and Harold W. Stevenson (Hillsdale NJ: Lawrence Erlbaum Associates, 1983), 211–37.

[41] J. L. Duda, L. K. Olson, and T. J.Templin, "The Relationship of Task and Ego Orientation to Sportsmanship Attitudes and the Perceived Legitimacy of Injurious Acts," *Research Quarterly for Exercise and Sport* 62, no 1 (1991): 79–87.

[42] See the list of research in Bredemeier and Shields, "Sports and Character Development," 5.

[43] Bredemeier and Shields, "Sports and Character Development," 5.

other.[44] When environments emphasize task and process over ego and out-comes, they are termed mastery climates. By contrast, climates that empha-size winning over process promote an ego-based motivation. The difference between mastery and performance based climates is profound. This is can be illustrated by comparing John Wooden's famous Pyramid of Success where he notably defines success as, "The peace of mind which is a direct result of self-satisfaction in knowing you made the effort to become the best of which you are capable," with the slogan that Al Davis used to build the Oakland Raiders: "Just win, baby."

The pattern in the literature is clear: mastery oriented climates tend to support positive sport-related values, behaviors, and character traits, while the reverse is generally found for performance climates.[45] While a perfor-mance climate is appropriate for a professional sports franchise, it will likely work against the objectives of a Christian university. That is not to say we do not want to win. As Paul, the apostle, famously says using a race analogy for evangelism in 1 Cor 9:24, "Do you not know that in a race all the run-ners run, but only one receives the prize? So run that you may obtain it." But a national championship ring does a student-athlete little good five years down the road, and we failed them, if they did not also become a wise, honorable, and cultivated citizen and earn their degree.

So, if the aim is to use sport as a vehicle for character development, the literature tell us that effort needs to be intentional. This effort needs to have a democratic, participatory flavor and coaches and administrators need to focus on task-orientation and its attendant mastery climate. Coaches shape the climate of their team. By emphasizing effort and mastery over ability and outcome a coach does this. Teaching athletes to focus on what lies within their control (effort and attitude), instead of what lies outside their control (opponent, officials, genetics), is also part of this. Not surprisingly, when looking at moral behavior in light of God's left-hand kingdom of Law, the degree to which character development happens in an athletic team depends in large measure on the leadership of the coach. However, it is also important to remember that only God working through the Gospel of Christ can truly change people's hearts forever (Jer 31:33–34; Ezek 11:19–20; Eph 2:8–10). Finally, coaches can help athletes appreciate the valuable role of mistakes in the learning process. They can point out the conse-quences that come with moral failure. As Christians, they can also point to

---

[44] Carole Ames, "Acheivement Goals, Motivational Climate and Motivational Processes," in *Motivation in Sport and Exercise*, ed. Glyn C. Roberts (Champaign, IL: Human Kinetics, 1992), 161–76.

[45] Bredemeier and Shields, "Sports and Character Development," 5.

full forgiveness in the cross of Christ, developing the student-athlete's spiritual character at the same time. We only lose if we fail to learn. Keeping the climate positive and constructive, while taking advantage of the teachable moments sport provides, makes character—and spiritual—development possible.

The key is not just to pay lip service to this idea. For instance, at my institution, the Masters in Coaching and Athletic Administration (MCAA) Program boldly carries out our vision to impact the culture of sport positively by training coaches and athletic administrators. The program (which numbers about 800 students currently) encourages coaches and athletic administrators to grow professionally with a practical curriculum and approach. The program strives to help these graduate students strengthen their teaching, coaching, and administrative abilities in a nationally acclaimed program. We help them to define and refine their philosophy of coaching, athletics, and leadership. Special emphasis is given across the curriculum in training coaches to enhance character development and ethical leadership from a Christian perspective wherever they are employed in an appropriate and effective manner.

ACADEMIC ACHIEVEMENT
AND INTERCOLLEGIATE ATHLETICS

A frequent justification for the inclusion of athletics programs in higher education, and one of the four core objectives of Concordia's athletic mission, is that involvement can contribute to a participant's academic success.[46] Such a rationale may seem surprising in light of arguments to the contrary throughout the years made by faculty and administrators that athletics distract students from their academic work. Indeed, in 1929 Savage saw that the "grades of athletes seem to average slightly lower than those of non-athletes" even though, as measured by one intelligence test, "athletes ... possess about the same or slightly better intellectual capacity than non-athletes." The reason for the discrepancy, Savage theorizes, is "that some factor related to intercollegiate competition, —such, for example, as time spent upon practice or games, the fatigue of contests or preparation, injuries, attitude, point of view, or something, —in general holds back the athletes from intellectual performance up to the limits of their capacities." The solution, then, is that administrators must "protect the skilful athlete from the results of excessive zeal on his own part or too many demands

---

[46] Donald Chu, *The Character of American Higher Education and Intercollegiate Sport* (Albany, NY: State University of New York Press, 1989).

upon his time and energy resulting from over-participation in intercollegiate athletics."[47]

The NCAA has attempted to limit inordinate athletic time commitments by limiting practice time to four hours a day and twenty hours a week. But considerable "wiggle room" still exists. For example, all competition and any athletically related activities on the day of competition counts as three hours regardless of the actual duration of activities. Travel to and from practices and competitions are also not included in the tally. Furthermore, individualized conditioning sessions that are not "required" or supervised by athletic staff are not counted.[48] The National Association of Intercollegiate Athletics (NAIA) has no established limits as it relies on local athletic administrators to police athletic time commitments.

A variety of studies have shown time commitments for intercollegiate athletic teams based on actual clock hours for all activities, including travel, frequently surpass thirty hours per week. If a student-athlete is taking fifteen units of class, and studying the average of two hours outside of class for every hour in session (the much debated Carnegie Unit definition currently in use) this means seventy-five hours (or more) per week, or roughly the equivalent of two full-time jobs (perhaps an apt analogy).[49]

In light of this daunting time commitment, how are student-athletes faring academically? The answer depends on the measuring stick chosen. The federal government has, rightly or wrongly, focused on cohort graduation rates over a six-year period. Student-athletes at the Division III level graduate at rates consistently higher than their non-athlete peers. Data from the Division III's voluntary academic reporting program released in April, 2014 once again demonstrate that student-athletes in general graduate at higher rates than their general student body peers. As the NCAA reports,

> Division III student-athletes continue to graduate at higher rates than their peers in the student-body, according to the most recent NCAA Academic Success Rate data.
>
> Based on a representative sample of 139 schools participating in the voluntary reporting program in the 2012–13 academic year, the

---

[47] Savage, *American College Athletics*, 124, 126–27.

[48] *2013–14 NCAA Division I Manual* (Indianapolis: The National Collegiate Athletic Association, 2013), 17.02.1, 17.02.13, 17.1.6.1, and 17.1.6.3.2.

[49] Donald Siegel, "Athletics and Education: The Union of Athletics with Educational Institutions," accessed September 19, 2014, http://www.science.smith.edu/exer_sci/ESS200/Ed/Athletic.htm.

Division III national four-year average ASR held steady at 87 percent. ... Even when utilizing the less-inclusive federal rate, Division III student-athletes again perform better than the general student body. The federal rate for student-athletes was 68 percent and the federal rate for the overall student body was 61 percent, a difference of seven percentage points.[50]

The Division II graduation rate for all freshmen student-athletes from the 2003–06 entering cohorts was 71 percent.[51] The Division I graduation rate for all freshmen student-athletes from the same cohorts was 81 percent.[52] Both graduation rates were higher than their non-athlete peers.

So, in spite of the very real time pressures associated with being a student-athlete, they are successful on the "bottom-line" measure of success at a rate higher than non-athletes. This is likely attributable to multiple factors: involvement in athletics is associated with a desire on the part of high school students to continue participating in college. This is partly a function of wanting to continue an athletic career, and partly a function of embracing values of peers, coaches, and teachers who steer athletes toward higher education. To participate fully in collegiate athletics as an incoming student, athletes must first satisfy high school requirements, grade point average (GPA) prerequisites, and standardized test criteria, which provides motivation to achieve academically. Once in college, to maintain eligibility, athletes must also sustain a minimal academic standard (2.0 cumulative GPA) and make satisfactory progress toward a degree (pass at least twelve units per term). Resources and encouragement also are typically provided to ensure that athletes maintain their eligibility and advance through their academic programs. At Concordia those resources include the academic advising staff, the Disability and Learning Resource Center, the eligibility coordinator in the Athletic Department, the faculty, tutors, and mandatory study hall for athletes with a GPA below 3.0 to name a few.

The "athletic dividend" from such treatment is that athletes complete degrees at a higher rate than non-athletic cohorts. On balance, a reasonable

---

[50] "Division III Student-Athletes Continue Academic Success," NCAA, accessed September 19, 2014, http://www.ncaa.org/about/resources/media-center/press-releases/division-iii-student-athletes-continue-academic-success.

[51] "Trends in Academic Success Rates and Federal Graduation Rates at NCAA Division II Institutions," NCAA, accessed September 19, 2104, http://www.ncaa.org/sites/default/files/2013_D2_GradRate-ASR_trends.pdf.

[52] "Trends in Graduation Success Rates and Federal Graduation Rates at NCAA Division I Institutions," NCAA, accessed September 19, 2104, http://www.ncaa.org/sites/default/files/GSR%2Band%2BFed%2BTrends%2B2013_Final.pdf

conclusion would be that although athletic involvement may present barriers to excelling academically, it does also open up opportunities for gaining access to higher education and completing a degree.

Following that thought to its conclusion, if one wishes to make the case that sport involvement enhances academic achievement, another compelling argument would be that many talented high school athletes wish to continue to compete in organized sport after graduation, and unless they are talented enough to jump to the pros, their most likely option is playing in college. Consequently, the argument may be made that involvement in formal athletic programs provides motivation and a path to higher levels of education. Not only may athletes be motivated to play out their careers through the educational hierarchy, but colleges are more than willing to accept talented athletes who meet their academic criteria. Consequently, exposure to at least some college is more than likely for those who wish to play their sport for as long as possible. Ultimately, this has the serendipitous benefit of at least exposing such individuals to higher levels of education. In so doing (and taking us back to our earlier, main point), this brings them into a "laboratory" for spiritual formation, character development, and education—ideally a collaborative effort by faculty and coaches.

CONCLUSION

All this leads me to an observation, conclusion, and suggested direction. Throughout I have suggested that one could view intercollegiate athletics as a laboratory for the development of character, spiritual formation, competitive excellence, and motivation for academic achievement. Extending this metaphor, my observation is this: the labs that are most effective are those that are closely tied to the lecture and its content. In fact, when designing a lab course, one would ideally look at the content and desired outcomes of the lecture to build upon, support, reinforce, apply, and extend them in the lab. Furthermore, if different faculty were working on the lecture and the lab, they would frequently compare notes to make sure they were on the same page and that the lecture and lab were reinforcing each other as planned. Finally, there would be an assessment plan in place with specific measurements or assignments used to give feedback on how well the lecture and lab are working together to achieve the specified goals.

My conclusion is that we have a lecture/lab disconnect on many college campuses. We may have learning outcomes for courses connected to a vision of Lutheran liberal arts education without ever having given serious attention to articulating how those outcomes are reinforced, extended, developed, or supported by a student-athlete's intercollegiate athletic experience. We quite likely have experienced as a coach, player, or fan how the absence of a key player due to injury or illness changes completely the strategy (and prospects of success) for a game or season without fully appreciating how missing six or twelve classes for games does the same thing to an entire course. These absences not only negatively impact the student's academic performance, they also take away from the learning environment and enrichment of the student's classmates. I further conclude that the questions asked at the outset cannot be answered across the board, but only locally. Intercollegiate athletics will support, complement, and accomplish the educational mission of the institution *to the extent that* we reconnect the lecture and the lab, so to speak, at each of our particular institutions.

And that leads me to a suggested direction. It is in the best interests of *all* of our constituents (faculty, staff, students, administration, governing board, alumni . . .) to be crystal clear on what specific learning outcomes we propose to accomplish via the curriculum and exactly how these will be reinforced via the student-athlete experience. An assessment plan should be developed and implemented, not to find fault, but to celebrate success and continually refine and improve our efforts.

Just three short years ago my institution began to implement an ambitious core curriculum. One of the chief obstacles to this implementation was the need for faculty to work together with their colleagues within their department and across disciplines. Three years later, in my role as dean, many of my colleagues report that one of the most rewarding aspects of teaching in the core is the deep and meaningful interaction with their colleagues that they experience regularly that is a source of support, encouragement, and enrichment to them.

It is my hope that a similar effort to connect curricular and co-curricular intentionally via agreed upon outcomes and measurement strategies will pay rich dividends. This will not happen simply because we have a plan and some learning outcomes. It will only happen when we create a regular, meaningful, on-going dialogue between faculty, coaches, administrators, and, yes, student-athletes as a means of honestly assessing our efforts to connect the lecture and the lab in meaningful ways.

QUESTIONS

1. Do you think that athletics provide a supportive "laboratory" for the educational mission of your university? Why or why not?

2. Pick an institutional learning outcome. Brainstorm some ways that it could be reinforced via participation in athletics or other co-curricular activities.

3. What is the vision behind athletics at your university? How is it connected to the educational philosophy and theological foundations of your institution?

4. How might the theological teaching of vocation alter or augment the vision and operation of athletics on your campus?

Scripture Index

SUBJECT INDEX

CPSIA information can be obtained at www.ICGtesting.com
Printed in the USA
LVOW11s2309130515

438388LV00002B/3/P